PROGRESSIVE
CONSTITUTIONALISM

CONSTITUTIONAL CONFLICTS
A Series by the Institute of Bill of Rights Law
at the College of William and Mary
Edited by Rodney A. Smolla and Neal Devins

PROGRESSIVE
CONSTITUTIONALISM

Reconstructing the Fourteenth Amendment

Robin West

DUKE UNIVERSITY PRESS   *Durham and London 1994*

©1994 by Duke University Press
All rights reserved
Printed in the United States of America on acid-free paper∞
Typeset in Sabon by Tseng Information Systems.
Library of Congress Cataloguing-in-Publication Data appear on the last
printed page of this book.

The chapters in this book originally appeared in the following publications and
are reprinted with permission: "Toward an Abolitionist Interpretation of the
Fourteenth Amendment," 94 *West Virginia Law Review* (1991); "Equality
Theory, Marital Rape, and the Promise of the Fourteenth Amendment," 42
Florida Law Review (1990); "The Meaning of Equality and the Interpretive
Turn," 66 *Chicago-Kent Law Review* (1993) (© 1990 Chicago-Kent College of
Law, Illinois Institute of Technology); "Reconstructing Liberty," 59 *Tennessee
Law Review* (1992) (Tennessee Law Review Association, Inc.); "The Ideal of
Liberty," 139 *University of Pennsylvania Law Review* (1991); "Toward a First
Amendment Jurisprudence of Respect," 14 *Cardozo Law Review* (1993);
"Constitutional Skepticism," 72 *Boston University Law Review* (1992); "The
Authoritarian Impulse in Constitutional Law," 42 *University of Miami Law
Review* (1988); "Progressive and Conservative Constitutionalism," 88 *Michigan Law Review* (1990); "The Aspirational Constitution," 88 *Northwestern
University Law Review* (1993).

For Nicholas and Benjamin

Contents

■

Introduction

■

Amendment XIV. § 1. No state shall . . . deprive any person of life, liberty, or property without due process of law; nor deny to any person within its jurisdiction the equal protection of the laws. § 5. The Congress shall have power to enforce, by appropriate legislation, the provisions of this Article.

What does the Fourteenth Amendment require? What is the content of the "equal protection of the laws," guaranteed each citizen, and which no state can deny? What is the "life, liberty or property," which also cannot be denied, at least without "due process of law"? What rights are accorded to individual citizens by virtue of these sweeping phrases, and what obligations are imposed on governments? What restrictions are placed on states, what responsibilities are placed on Congress, and what powers are delegated to the courts by the historic mandates of the Fourteenth Amendment?

The history, the logic, and certainly the language of the Fourteenth Amendment can support more than one set of answers to these questions, and in the more than 100 years since the amendment's passage, a number of interpretations have competed for prominence. The major purpose of the essays collected in this book is to argue for one possible set of answers, an approach to the Fourteenth Amendment which I will sometimes call *progressive,* and against a quite different understanding, which I will sometimes call *conservative.* The second purpose is to suggest that for a number of reasons—some practical, some jurisprudential, and some purely legal—the appropriate forums for progressive constitutional advocacy under the Fourteenth Amendment should be Congress and the state legislatures, rather than the courts.

The particular conservative understanding that these essays target is certainly not the only possible conservative interpretation of the Fourteenth Amendment, but it is an important one: it is "robust," meaning it has a great deal of explanatory power; it is widely held; and, perhaps most significant, it rests on a moral and political vision of democratic society that is in a sense deeply familiar. Drawing heavily on conservative political and moral theory, the conservative interpretation of the Fourteenth Amendment aims us toward three "Constitutional ideals." First, it envisions a generally rational state that is precluded by the Constitution, and more specifically by the equal protection clause of the Fourteenth Amendment, from taking malicious, bigoted, or in any other way patently irrational actions. Second, it envisions a society composed of free individuals, whose liberty is protected by the due process clause of the Fourteenth Amendment, and whose private life, the scope of which is defined by the nonlegalistic traditions of the culture's past, is similarly protected against benign as well as mean-spirited state intrusion. Third, it envisions a restrained Court that permits the processes of democracy to go forward unless and until a clear showing of unconstitutional action can be made. From those three ideals—a rational state, free individuals, and a restrained Court—and the conservative conception of public virtue and the quasi-traditionalist conception of individual freedom on which they rest, is derived a particular, detailed, and remarkably sturdy understanding of Fourteenth Amendment guarantees. Again, this particular conception is certainly not the only possible conservative understanding of the Fourteenth Amendment—its understanding of the liberty prong of the due process clause, to take only one example, is marked by a traditionalism profoundly at odds with the libertarianism so pronounced in the work of other conservative constitutional commentators—but it is undoubtedly an important one: it is, among other things, the understanding of the Fourteenth Amendment that presently dominates the Supreme Court. This conservative conception, I will argue, is also deeply flawed: it is not true to the history of the amendment; it is not faithful to its logic, language, or spirit; and, even were its directives perfectly heeded, it would not "aim" us toward a more just society.

The progressive interpretation rests on a very different moral vision. The ideal constitutional state envisioned by the Fourteenth Amendment under a progressive interpretation also has three overriding characteristics: (1) the state protects each citizen and all citizens equally against not only the criminality and brutality of each other but also the ravages and dangers of the natural world; (2) individuals enjoy and states guarantee the "positive liberties" of civic participation, meaningful work, and unthreatened intimacy; and (3) government quite generally—courts as well as legislatures—acts in concert to ensure to each citizen freedom from and protection against those natural, social, or private conditions that threaten to enslave her. From this general understanding, with roots in both the abolitionist and naturalist utopian politics of the nineteenth century, and an echo and reaffirmation in the feminist, humanist, and progressive politics of the twentieth, follows a quite specific account of the meaning and promise of the provisions of the Fourteenth Amendment. The progressive interpretation of the Fourteenth Amendment for which I will argue is certainly not the only possible progressive interpretation possible; indeed, it departs in a number of ways from progressive interpretations currently advanced by a number of critical race theorists and feminist legal scholars. To take just one example, I do not read the equal protection clause as a mandate of "substantive equality" in any sense, as do a number of other progressive academic constitutional commentators. Although not the only possible progressive interpretation, the one offered here is a compelling interpretation of the Fourteenth Amendment: it is true to the history of the amendment; it is true to its language, logic, and spirit; and if its mandate were heeded, it would point us toward a more just society.

Although the progressive interpretation I put forward in these essays differs in fundamental respects from other progressive readings of the amendment, all progressive interpretations, from the time of the original drafting of the Fourteenth Amendment to the present, share one telling characteristic: in sharp contrast to conservative interpretations, progressive understandings of the Fourteenth Amendment, including the one I put forward in this book, do not presently have any supporters on the Supreme Court. One of my goals is to argue that, contrary to popular wisdom, the lack of judicial support for progressive interpretations of the Constitution is not simply a matter of contemporary politics—a function of shifting political persuasions of the Supreme Court's membership. Rather, I will argue, progressive understandings of the Fourteenth Amendment do not lend themselves to judicial enforcement, and, accordingly, they have not enjoyed much success even during more "liberal" periods of constitutional interpretation. Progressive understandings of the Fourteenth Amendment did not, for example, dominate during the years of the more liberal Warren Court, although they did unquestionably receive a more respectful hearing. Judicial intolerance of progressive understandings of the Constitution, I will argue, is at least as much a matter of institutional structure and jurisprudential aspiration as of partisan politics, and, as a consequence, even a liberal or left-leaning Court will be hard put to realize the progressive constitutional vision. As a consequence of this ill fit between substantive vision and institutional limitations, progressive causes and their intended beneficiaries have been badly disserved by progressive advocates who have relied heavily or exclusively on a strategy that might be called the *adjudicated Constitution*.

Finally, I also argue in these essays that we should not conclude from this ill fit that the Constitution, or the Fourteenth Amendment, is itself antipathetic to progressive causes or progressive politics. Rather, we should consider the possibility that the apparent antipathy between progressivism and constitutionalism does not lie in the Constitution, but in our habitual reliance on courts for its interpretation and enforcement. It may be that there is indeed a progressive vision in the Fourteenth Amendment that has yet to be tapped, but that those progressive ideals, imperfectly articulated, will be realized, if at all, only through the processes of democratic deliberation rather than the analogic methods of legal reasoning. It may be, in other words, that the progressive promise the Fourteenth Amendment guarantees must be delivered through congressional enactment rather than judicial enforcement.

The chapters in this book are organized as follows. Chapters 1–3 are concerned with the equal protection clause of the Fourteenth Amendment. After considering various competing definitions—including "formal" approaches advocated by conservatives (and some liberals) and "substantive" approaches advocated by leftist radicals (and, again, some liberals)—I ultimately argue for a model I call *pure protection* or *sole sovereignty:* the purpose of the clause, I argue, is to guarantee each citizen protection against whatever threatens his or her natural rights, including, importantly, "private power," and to guarantee that protection equally. The consequence of pure protection, if perfectly realized, would be the true abolition of slavery: the state and only the state would be "sovereign" over the freedom and rights of each citizen. The citizen, on this model, should ideally have but one and only one sovereign, namely, the state. A number of modern implications might follow from a pure protection, or sole sovereign, understanding of the core meaning of the clause. For example, the clause could be read as guaranteeing residents of high-crime neighborhoods an equal degree of police protection against violent criminality as is accorded residents of other neighborhoods. But institutional implications also follow. If the clause must be read as guaranteeing, at least in part, equal protection against private abusive power, then it follows that the promise of equal protection must be delivered by congressional and state legislative action, not by judicial power. The target of the equal protection clause, so to speak, understood in this way, is, in effect, private power: what the Constitution mandates is that the states and Congress must resist its illegal and unjust accumulation. Congress, not the Supreme Court must be the primary enforcer of the constitutional mandate of equal protection, and Congress, therefore, not the Court, must bear the responsibility of the clause's substantive interpretation, as well as its political enforcement.

Chapters 4–6 concern the so-called liberty prong of the due process clause of the Fourteenth Amendment. Here I argue that current understandings of the Fourteenth Amendment rest on the mistaken premise that the substantive liberties protected by the amendment (if any at all) must be "negative" in nature, rather than protective of the positive rights to a free, civic, participatory life. Such a limitation, I argue, is contrary to the overriding intent of the framers to protect against the possibility of future enslavement or, to put the point affirmatively, to assure a positively free citizenry. Understood as a guarantee of positive rather than negative liberty, the due process clause has a number of important modern implications. It would follow, for example, that a number of the contested "rights" that progressives have from time to time argued are protected by the equal protection clause, and have characterized as being in the nature of equality rights—including, for example, the right to be free from the fear of rape, the right to be free from the specter of hunger or homelessness, or the right to be free from the fear of hateful verbal assaults—might better be understood as liberty interests. It also follows, again, that the "audience" for constitutional advocacy premised on the liberty prong of the Fourteenth Amendment should be Congress, and not the Supreme Court. If the liberty protected by the Fourteenth Amendment is the positive liberty to a quality of life which only legislation can promote, then the promise of the liberty prong of the substantive due process clause can be fulfilled not through judicial oversight, but, rather, if at all, through legislative innovation.

The last four chapters take up more general questions. In Chapter 7, "Constitutional Skepticism," in effect, I address (and ultimately reject) the case for simply abandoning constitutionalism entirely as a vehicle for progressive reform. In Chapter 8, "The Authoritarian Impulse in Constitutional Law," I argue that the Constitution might be sensibly read as an aspirational text guiding our future progress, rather than as a mandate from an authoritative past. In Chapter 9, titled "Progressive and Conservative constitutionalism," I try to identify underlying premises—jurisprudential as well as political—of conservative and progressive constitutional paradigms. Finally, in Chapter 10, "The Aspirational Constitution," I argue in more detail what is alluded to earlier: the constitutional interpretations that might emerge from legislative deliberation might, for institutional and jurisprudential reasons, be more conducive to progressive ends than those that have emerged from judicial deliberation.

Thus, taken collectively, the essays in this book urge a substantive, institutional, and jurisprudential reorientation of our understanding of the Fourteenth Amendment. Substantively, I argue that the state action doctrine, the formal understanding of the equal protection clause, and a negative rather than positive understanding of the substantive due process clause are all untrue to the history and language of the Fourteenth Amendment. Institutionally, I urge that a progressive understanding of the Fourteenth Amendment is far more likely to be realized through legislative action than judicial intervention, and that, accordingly, progressive constitutional advocates should refocus their attention away from courts and toward the legislative arena. Finally, jurisprudentially, I argue that the Fourteenth Amendment should be grounded in a progressive conception of a responsible democratic state charged with the task of guaranteeing the conditions of positive freedom and guarding against the dangers of social or private enslavement. Such a conception, somewhat paradoxically, is closer to the overriding abolitionist concerns of the framers of the amendment than are the interpretations currently argued by both liberal commentators and the conservative Court. It is also, of the competing conceptions, the interpretation most likely to point us toward a more just society—a society worthy of the costs of the political and deliberative struggle undoubtedly necessary to achieve it.

PART I

Equal Protection of the Laws

I

Toward an Abolitionist Interpretation
of the Fourteenth Amendment

It is by now an open secret that current interpretations of the meaning of the equal protection clause of the Fourteenth Amendment, and of its relevance and mandate for contemporary problems of racial, gender, and economic justice, are deeply and, in a sense, hopelessly conflicted. The conflict, simply stated, is this: to the current Supreme Court,[1] and to a sizeable and influential number of constitutional theorists,[2] the "equal protection of the laws" assured by the Constitution is essentially a guarantee that the categories delineated by legal rules will be "rational" and rationally related to legitimate state ends. To this group of jurists, the relevance of the equal protection clause to issues of racial justice rests on the important complementary minor premise to this guarantee of rationality: the claim, both descriptive and normative, that legislative distinctions based on race can simply never be rational because there are no differences between the races that can in any way be relevant to state purposes, and, consequently, racial differentiation in any context cannot be a legitimate state goal.

On this view, the equal protection clause is historically rooted in a constitutional and federal response to the pernicious slave laws, black codes, Jim Crow laws, and segregation mandates of southern states, all of which rested on a specious and false theory of racial difference and hence on presumably "natural" distinctions between the slave and the freeman, the black man and the white man, to justify the different legal treatment and protections accorded them. From the historic repudiation of this false theory of racial difference and white superiority culminating in passage of the Fourteenth Amendment—and from the further constitutional premise that categories must be rational—follows the important ethical and constitutional mandate that the central meaning of the equal protection clause, and indeed of the Fourteenth Amendment in its entirety, is that the law must be color-blind.

For a second group of jurists,[3] and a sizeable number of constitutional theorists in law schools,[4] the equal protection clause of the Fourteenth Amendment requires "substantive justice" rather than rationality in legislation. For this group, the guarantee of equal protection is a constitutional imperative for the states and Congress to take substantive steps toward eradicating the unjust subordination of one group of citizens by another, including African-Americans and other peoples of color by whites, women by men, and gays and lesbians by heterosexuals. On this view, the equal protection mandate and the Fourteenth Amendment are historically grounded not in the pernicious idea of racial difference but in the pernicious practice of racial subordination: the willful and continuing attempt of white people, with the willing acquiescence of state governments, to subordinate, deny, oppress, and use black people for their own ends. That subordination began with the enslavement of blacks by whites and their oppression through black codes and Jim Crow laws. The subordination continues in our time through the use of purportedly "neutral" but in fact unjustified and exclusionary criteria that precludes entry of not only blacks but also other people of color, along with all women, into the higher echelons of political, professional, educational, and economic life. The equal protection mandate for these theorists is a guarantee that either the states or, in the breach, Congress will act to reverse these patterns of subordination.

On this view, it most assuredly does not follow that the law must be "color-blind." Rather, the law must be sensitive and responsive to the very real and relevant differences that exist between both blacks and whites, women and men: differences in power; differences in status; and differing positions on the economic, social, and political hierarchies that comprise our public and private lives. The mandate of equal protection is minimally not to exacerbate those inequalities but, understood generously, the Fourteenth Amendment in general and equal protection in particular are mandates to eradicate them.

One purpose of this chapter is to argue against both of these understandings of equal protection and to introduce a quite different interpretation— a view grounded in human nature and governmental obligation held by the abolitionists of the early and mid-nineteenth century. These abolitionists, at least according to a number of historians,[5] propagated and popularized the phrase "equal protection of the law" in the decades immediately preceding the Civil War and the reconstruction amendments. I will ultimately argue that this abolitionist understanding of equal protection, and of the Fourteenth Amendment, is truer to both the plain language and the history of the Amendment than either the formal color-blind view or the substantive antisubordination view briefly outlined here. Before doing so, however, I want to discuss in a little more detail the nature of the conflict between the two conceptions that dominate current case law and scholarship and why I think that conflict is quite distinctive in our constitutional jurisprudence, then suggest why it seems to me to be imperative that we somehow find a way to break the deadlock. In the first section that follows, I will therefore discuss the schism in our current understanding and then introduce, by way of metaphor, the rather different abolitionist understanding of the phrase "equal protection." In the next two sections, I will discuss modern applications of the abolitionist understanding and the structural and intellectual barriers to its modern implementation.

Modern Equal Protection Jurisprudence

The two interpretations of equal protection that dominate current law, which we might call *formalist* and *antisubordinationist,* have in one form or another been present in judicial interpretations of the phrase from its genesis. However, it has only recently become clear how deeply incompatible these interpretations are and how thoroughly contradictory their implications. We can identify three modern phases in the evolution of the appearance of this contradiction.

The first phase dates from *Brown v. Board of Education*[6] up through the mid-1970s or so, roughly the period that saw the dismantling of Jim Crow laws and the integration of those southern public schools that had been intentionally segregated by state law. During this period, the contradiction between these two interpretations was almost entirely invisible, for the straightforward reason that both views were compatible with the integrationist ideal expressed and, to some degree, mandated in *Brown.* Under the formal, color-blind approach, *Brown* is correct and integration is required because the race consciousness that is the central evil at which equal protection is aimed had manifested itself in segregation laws, of which segregated schooling was a part. To these jurists and thinkers, "separate but equal" was and is a cruel anomaly because the "separate" part of the formula rested on, and was intended to communicate, a false claim of racial inferiority[7] and, hence, inequality; almost by definition, then, "separate but equal" could never yield equality. Thus, *Plessy v. Ferguson*[8] is wrong, *Brown* right, and integration required. Under the antisubordination approach as well, then, *Brown* is correct and integration required, but not because segregation rested on a false view of racial difference; but because the subordination of blacks by whites with state acquiescence and support—for this group, the quite different evil targeted by the equal protection clause—had manifested itself in profoundly unequal schooling of black and white children, which had, in turn, furthered the subordination of black adults by whites, thus completing the circle.[9] Integrating the schools is one way, certainly not the only way, and perhaps, in retrospect, not the best way to redress the inequality of an unequal and segregated school system. Again, *Plessy* is wrong, *Brown* right, and integration required, not as a way to obliterate the root of a false racial theory of black inferiority but as a remedy of substantive inequality, which happened to be manifested in segregated facilities.

By the end of the *Brown* era, it was clear that these two interpretations of both equal protection and of *Brown* itself were in fact different; they would yield divergent results in post-*Brown* cases regarding the extent of actual integration required by *Brown* of the states, rather than the mere cessation of state-ordered segregation.[10] Nevertheless, these differences could be relegated to the margins. At the time of *Brown,* and for the most part during the post-*Brown* dismantling of Jim Crow laws, the two interpretations appeared to be in harmony. They both were consistent, although for different reasons, with the distinctive and specific mandate of *Brown* to integrate the schools, and, more loosely, with the integrationist vision of Martin Luther King, Jr., Ralph Abernathy, and the other civil rights leaders of the 1950s and 1960s for whom *Brown* was (and is) the institutional secular triumph of an often religious vision of racial harmony, integration, and brotherhood.

The second phase of the evolution of this contradiction begins with *Washington v. Davis* in 1976.[11] In *Davis,* the Court held that neutral criteria employed by states (or the District of Columbia) for the distribution of governmental benefits, and which disproportionately and unjustifiably exclude blacks, are not unconstitutional unless it can be shown that those employing the neutral criteria intended to discriminate against the injured group.[12] In *Davis,* it became clear that the two interpretations of equal protection, in uneasy alliance through the dismantling of intentional discrimination accomplished during the post-*Brown* era, were in fact incompatible. For it is easy to see that under the formal understanding of equal protection, *Davis* is surely right: the evil at which equal protection is addressed—differential treatment by the state of blacks and whites, premised on a false claim of racial difference and black inferiority—is not present.[13] The state is not treating the two groups differently; they are being treated the same, in a perfectly color-blind fashion. It is also easy to see, however, that under a substantive understanding of equal protection, *Davis* is profoundly, even tragically, wrong.[14] The evil at which the equal protection clause is aimed—the unjustified subordination of blacks by whites by whatever means—was present in *Davis,* as well as in the wide range of state actions within its holding. Whites subordinate blacks (and men subordinate women) by the use of "neutral" criteria that, whether intentionally or not, reflect white (or male) interests, histories, preferences, and aspirations, no less than by laws that explicitly treat the two groups differently on a theory of racial difference. If subordination, rather than a false claim of racial superiority, is the evil targeted by equal protection of the law, then *Davis* is simply wrong. A statute, regulation, or criterion that unjustifiably injures African-Americans is no less subordinating than a statute that intentionally and differentially classifies.

The irreducible conflict between these two interpretations during the *Washington v. Davis* era was clouded, however, for a reason that echoes the invisibility of the conflict during the *Brown* era. Just as both models proved compatible with the integrationist ideal expressed and mandated in *Brown,* although for very different reasons, similarly, both models proved compatible with the tort-like conception of constitutional responsibility assumed and furthered by *Davis.* In *Davis,* constitutional responsibility for implementing the mandate of equal protection took on the contours of a garden-variety tort: equal protection, under the model that came to the fore in *Davis,* simply means that the state is liable for harm that it causes to groups injured or burdened through its legislative classifications; liability accrues, however, only if the requisite tortious mental state is present, just as individuals are liable in tort for harms caused to groups injured or burdened through their actions only if the requisite tortious mental state is present. When filtered through this quasi-constitutional tort approach to equal protection, the difference between the formal and substantive understanding of equal protection is narrowed to an almost technical difference over what requisite mental state is sufficient to trigger tort liability, rather than a fundamental difference in vision. For the formalist majority, something akin to specific intent to harm is clearly required;[15] for the substantive, antisubordination minority, something much less is sufficient: general intent, recklessness, or perhaps negligence alone. Again, the difference is real and visible, but when viewed through the filter of the quasi-tort principles adopted or assumed in *Davis,* it appears to be a difference of degree. Both approaches seem to accept the overall picture of the equal protection clause as laying out duties for states not to harm their citizens in the same way that tort law spells out duties for citizens not to harm each other. The two models appear to differ only over the reach of the constitutional tort or, putting it differently, over the extent to which the conduct of states should be interfered with or regulated by the inhibiting force of constitutional duty.

The third phase in the evolution of the conflict between these two competing interpretations dates from the Supreme Court's decision in *City of Richmond v. J. A. Croson Co.*[16] The *Croson* decision struck down, as violative of the equal protection clause, an affirmative-action plan undertaken by the city of Richmond to rectify the subordinating effect of decades of systematic, institutional, and private discrimination against African-Americans.[17] In *Croson* and its aftermath (continuing to the present), the full and explosive scope of the conflict between a formalist and an antisubordinationist account of equal protection became fully apparent, as well as its origin in fundamentally different and incompatible conceptions of equality. To the formalist, including a majority of the current Supreme Court, race-conscious affirmative action is clearly unconstitutional; it rests for its justification of the differential treatment of the races on a theory of racial difference (albeit socially, rather than biologically engendered) and therefore violates the Fourteenth Amendment for the same reason as the Jim Crow laws of the late-nineteenth to mid-twentieth centuries violated the Fourteenth Amendment.[18] For the substantive antisubordinationist, such a plan is not only clearly permitted, but, as at least a number of such theorists have argued, may well be required: the plans reverse the utterly predictable effects of private, racial subordination which is precisely the target of the equal protection clause itself.[19]

The scope and significance of this contrast should not be understated. Again, the difference is not simply that one group sees a constitutional violation where the other sees none, or that one group reads the Constitution as prohibiting X where the other sees the Constitution as silent on X, which is the standard form of constitutional disagreement. Instead, on this issue, while one group sees the Constitution as prohibiting X, the other sees the Constitution as not simply silent on X but as actually requiring it: the formalists see as prohibited by equal protection what the antisubordinationists see as required by it.

Thus, the two groups are reading the constitutional phrase not just as having differing scopes of reach but as mandating absolutely opposite obligations. It is not, to use an analogy, simply that one group reads the Constitution as requiring that we close the door while the second reads it as silent on the question; rather, it is that one group reads the phrase as requiring that we close the door, while the second reads the phrase as requiring that we open it. For this reason, both groups can, with internal plausibility and coherence, accuse the other of Orwellian doublespeak: of claiming that war is peace. Professor Charles Fried, a fervent and eloquent advocate of a formalist view, thus accuses the modern antisubordinationist approach (which he labels "collectivist") of using the equal protection clause, which was intended to combat racism, to promote it;[20] he analogizes the modern antisubordinationist position to that embraced by one of the most racist cases in our constitutional history: *Plessy v. Ferguson*.[21] Similarly a number of antisubordinationists,[22] myself included,[23] have lamented the formalist insistence, now made law by the Supreme Court, that the equal protection clause, intended to promote the eradication of the subordinating effects of racism, is now the weapon of those who would fight efforts to do precisely that. Again, from the antisubordinationist perspective, the clause, while intended as a tool to dismantle racism and inequality, is being used by formalists instead to promote such evils.

Thus, what has only now become clear is that the formalist interpretation of equal protection embraced by the current Supreme Court and the antisubordinationist interpretation endorsed by the Court's dissenters and academic critics are not simply different and equally plausible interpretations of a concededly vague constitutional phrase—a phrase inevitably, and perhaps intentionally, open to multiple claims of meanings. The problem is not simply that one view is somewhat broader or narrower than the other, such that what is constitutional under the first interpretation is unconstitutional under the second, or vice versa; nor is the problem that under the first view the constitution forbids what under the second view it permits. Rather, the contrast between these two understandings of equal protection is more fundamental than that: under the first view, the Constitution forbids what under the second it seems to require, not simply permit: race-conscious, state, city, or congressionally initiated affirmative action designed to undo the effects of widescale private and quasi-private subordination of African-American citizens. The affirmative action problem has thus fully exposed the fundamental contradiction between these two interpretations of the nature of the equality mandated by the equal protection clause. The color blindness required by the phrase, according to the formalists, is profoundly incompatible with the affirmative actions necessary to eradicate subordination, the nub of the same phrase, according to the antisubordinationists.

Furthermore, the protestations of theorists from both camps notwithstanding, neither position can be decisively refuted by reference to either the language or history of the phrase, nor by reference to fundamental, unassailable principles of political morality. It is surely possible to understand "equal protection of the laws" as requiring of the state a "blindness" to the race of its citizens. How better to rectify a historical unwillingness to protect citizens of a particular color than by insisting that state legislators be blind to such factors? In effect, this requires that legislators don John Rawls's veil of ignorance[24] with respect to all racial characteristics, whatever the circumstance, whatever the motive. It is impossible not to concede (or insist) that the formalists' insistence on color blindness is not out of line with the language and history of the phrase. Nor, for that matter, is it out of line with at least one dominant theme of Western liberal thought, at least since the American Civil War—to wit, our status as human beings renders us worthy and entitled to protection by the state, and we do not lose that entitlement by virtue of racial, ethnic, gender, age, or sexual orientation characteristics.

It also seems incontrovertible, however, that the framers of the amendment intended to rectify and reverse the subordination of African-Americans effectuated by over a century of slavery and that "equal protection of the law" can be read as requiring affirmative efforts to do precisely that. Similarly, it is not at all implausible to argue that principles of compensatory and distributive justice require any decent liberal society to undertake action that ameliorates rather than exacerbates the substantive inequalities still endured by those living with the legacy of that past. Thus, the same constitutional phrase, no matter what the interpretive methodology used, can seemingly be read to require diametrically opposed obligations. If we view the Constitution as imposing mandatory obligations, as we surely should, we have a huge problem: it seems to require of us a massive contradiction, a classic case of impossibility. If the Constitution were a contract, we would void the phrase.

Although, as I will argue in a moment, it may be a mistake, it is surely neither cynical, nihilist, or even overly skeptical to infer from this example of the confusion caused by the equal protection clause that which has been urged in the last twenty years by large numbers of critical legal scholars: that the Constitution has no pregiven, "already present" meaning awaiting discovery by fair-minded readers of the document.[25] The presence of flagrantly contradictory mandates emanating from the same constitutional phrase seems to perfectly insubstantiate the central "indeterminacy claim" of the deconstructionist wing of the Critical Legal Studies movement: that the law in general, and certainly the phrases of the Fourteenth Amendment in particular, are so radically indeterminant that they should be viewed as nothing more than repositories of the pre-formed and arbitrarily embraced political commitments of our utterly chaotic selves—"selves" and "political commitments" that are formed essentially randomly. Those selves and commitments cannot be formed or even influenced by the meanings of the given texts of our culture for the simple reason that there are no meanings or any given texts to have such an influence.[26] When formalists and substantive antisubordinationists see in the equal protection clause diametrically opposed mandates, they are simply reading into that phrase their own political commitments: again, an essentially arbitrarily-chosen-from, one-or-another conception of equality as the best means of organizing social life. From this realization it is just a short step to the conclusion that the constitutional phrase itself (as well as its history) is serving as, at most, an anachronistic pleading requirement, and that we would all be better off if we simply dispensed with the requirement and proceeded, so to speak, directly "to the merits" of the underlying debate: whether we should or should not rectify the subordination of African-Americans through affirmative action; whether we should or should not insist on a color-blind state as a matter of political morality. To be blunt, the Constitution, its supposed plain meaning, and its uncontested history (to say nothing of its contested history) have nothing to teach us. The Constitution is at best a vehicle, and a clumsy vehicle at that, for political argument; it neither constrains the substance nor adds anything of value to what we would say in its absence.

Make no mistake about it, there is something undeniably liberating, even intoxicating, in freeing oneself and political debate from the constraints of constitutional text and the political history that the text tenuously records and celebrates. The political history of the United States that culminated and is reflected in the constitutional text is in large measure a history of almost unthinkable brutality toward slaves, genocidal hatred of Native Americans, racist devaluation of nonwhites and nonwhite cultures, sexist devaluation of women, and a less than admirable attitude of submissiveness to the authority of unworthy leaders in all spheres of government and public life. Why should we bind or constrain our political argument, to say nothing of our political choices, by the texts produced by this history of ruthlessness; of brutality; and of mindless, infantile, and at times psychotic, numbing wrath? Surely a part of the motive, if not the sole motive, behind affirmation of the indeterminacy thesis among critical legal theorists (unlike, it is worth noting, among critical literary theorists) is a desire to expand the scope of our current political and constitutional imagination beyond not so much the false constraints as the pernicious constraints of a less than admirable past.

There are, however, serious problems with the critical scholars' aspiration of atextuality and ahistoricity, this urge to shed an ignoble history. First, of course, it may simply not be possible—or at least it has been the burden of a great deal of recent neopragmatist and literary-legal scholarship to so claim.[27] Our "selves" and our political dispositions are far from being the chaotic, randomly chosen bundles of inclinations insisted upon by at least some advocates of the indeterminacy thesis; in fact, our selves and political dispositions may be exhaustively constituted by precisely the history, with all its horrors, ambiguities, and contradictions that we aim, through claims of indeterminacy, to shed.

The second problem (and to my mind the more telling) with the atextual and ahistoric aspirations of the indeterminacy thesis is that the history and text being shed, although no doubt in large part a succession of waves of brutality and oppression, may also contain moments of real nobility and courage, and the text that is the culmination of those moments may embody and express part of a profoundly moral social vision. If we turn our backs on history and text, in short, we may be turning our backs on imaginings more worthy than our own. The Fourteenth Amendment, in fact, may be just such a text; its passage may have been just such a moment, and its normative implications just such a vision. If we abandon the history and text of the Fourteenth Amendment as possible guides to at least its possible meanings, whether or not those meanings exhaust the possibilities and whether or not we should regard them as "authoritative," we may be abandoning a source of moral insight and a vision of the just society that is superior to those visions our current ahistoric and parochial "selves" have managed to envision.

Let me just put the point autobiographically: my reason for embarking on this project is that the vision of a just society expressed by the equal protection clause, and advocated by some of its proponents, may be superior to both the formalist and antisubordinationist understandings of the phrase that dominate current debate and case law. Even if we assume, or insist, that the intended meaning should not be regarded as the only possible meaning—that there may have been several and conflicting intended meanings, and that the historical meaning carries no modern legal mandate—the possibility that the originally intended meaning is normatively superior to modern interpretations is surely a sufficient reason to reacquaint oneself with the text and origins of the constitutional text. The indeterminacy theorists' usually implicit and sometimes explicit suggestion might at least on occasion be false: although the appearance of contradiction counsels the abandonment of text and history, that need not be viewed as troubling in the case of legal and constitutional texts because the text being abandoned is for the most part the record of a violent and oppressive history, which not only cannot, but also should not, constrain modern moral and political imagination. In the case of the Fourteenth Amendment, this argument seems to me to be false: the vision expressed in the amendment, and advocated by some of its proponents, is stronger than both the formalist and antisubordinationist positions that dominate modern debate, or at least I will so argue.

There is one other purely pragmatic and explicitly political reason for seeking a new paradigm of meaning for the equal protection clause. The affirmative action debate in this culture, I think, has come to a dead end. Like the debate over abortion, the affirmative action debate has reached the point where further persuasion is not possible. That fact alone is unfortunate enough, but it is doubly tragic if, as a consequence of that impasse, the evolution of our understanding of the equal protection clause, to say nothing of the application of the clause, ceases: if, because of the impasse over affirmative action, the equal protection clause ceases to become, in effect, a part of the living Constitution. That may well happen, if it has not happened already. The formalist objection to affirmative action may be an unanswerable objection to an antisubordinationist view of the Fourteenth Amendment. Further, the antisubordination objection to viewing the Fourteenth Amendment as a limit to affirmative action may be an unanswerable objection to the formal, color-blind interpretation of its mandate. If these are correct, then neither side can move past affirmative action: it is the end of the debate, the end of reasoned discussion, the end of constitutional

progress. It may be time to start over, to go back to the beginning, and to construct a new paradigm. It may be time, in other words, to change the subject.

Reconstructing the Abolitionists' Understanding of the Fourteenth Amendment

In a remarkable essay entitled "The Rule of Law as a Law of Rules,"[28] Justice Antonin Scalia describes the basic idea behind the formalist interpretation of the equal protection clause by use of an analogy to family life. As patriarchically offensive as the idea of such an analogy may initially appear to be, a contrasting familial analogy may be the best way to describe the basic idea behind the abolitionist interpretation as well. Children, Scalia opines, can endure all sorts of rules that limit their freedom; in fact, although he does not say as much, children need and thrive on such rules. What they absolutely cannot and will not endure are rules that are unequally applied. A curfew for a 15-year-old is tolerable, but it is not tolerable that a younger sibling must abide by a curfew even though an older sibling, at the same age and therefore similarly situated, did not.[29] Restriction to one's room or house is a tolerable punishment, but only if all who did the crime must do the time. A parent who breaks this sacred covenant (and, let's face it, it happens frequently) will find himself faced with the fury of a child who feels herself to be, and who in fact is, suffering a fundamental, incomprehensible, unspeakable injustice. A similar scenario can be seen with regard to the equal protection clause. Citizens will not tolerate breaches of formal equality any more than will children. Rules must be evenhandedly applied to all; departures from this norm must be grounded in well-reasoned distinctions.

Scalia's metaphor has no doubt accurately captured the nub of a requirement of formal, equal justice. Formal, equal justice requires that rules be applied evenhandedly to all similarly situated persons within the scope of the rule. But as noble or central as the ideal of formal justice may be, the Fourteenth Amendment does not speak of equal justice; it speaks of equal protection. Perhaps, then, a better familial analogy for understanding the mandate of equal protection might be this: imagine not the Partridge family, with generally well-behaved children who occasionally must be punished and with generally well-intentioned parents who occasionally lapse from the norm of equal justice. Instead, imagine an island with children who are more along the lines of those portrayed by William

Golding in his horrific dystopia, *Lord of the Flies*.[30] On this island, the children have three basic instincts: to survive, to attain personal glory, and to dominate. They generally achieve the first two ends by cooperatively converting the island's natural bounty into food and shelter through their labor, and then engaging in the competitive acquisition, alienation, barter, trade, and ownership of various goods. In their spare time, and because they are nasty and aggressive creatures, they engage in fistfights, inflicting as much damage as possible on each other, all toward the end of establishing not just comparative glory, but actual physical dominance over each other.

Further imagine, however, that on this island, unlike on Golding's, there are parents present, and that these parents are a central authority whom the children generally obey on fear of sanctions if they do not. The parents on this Goldingesque island, though, are peculiar. They usually intervene in their children's economic lives to ensure that promises are kept, so that all the children can withstand natural threats to survival and have equal opportunities in the quest for glory. In addition, the parents intervene in their children's physical battles to protect each child against the violence and dominance of the others. They accomplish this latter goal by laying down a mandate prohibiting all intrafamilial violence and then punishing offenders. But for some perverse reason, they bestow this protection of parental authority on every child but one. Whether through neglect, sadism, or complicity, the parents consistently deny the protection to one of the siblings that they grant to the others.

The consequence of the denial of parental protection against private sibling violence and betrayal to one child but not the others—this denial of equal protection—is not simply the sufferance of unequal justice, although it is assuredly in part that. It is more pervasive, more disabling, and more insidious. The child denied equal protection of the parental authority, no less than the citizen denied equal protection of the state authority against private violence and violation, lives a very different life than her siblings. The child, who alone must endure the violence of the others and isolation from the economic life of the community, all with no recourse or remedy, in effect becomes the slave, subject, or subordinate of the other children against whom she has no rights. Put differently, because she has no rights against them, because she lacks parental protection, she becomes the object of the other children's wills. The potential unchecked violence and material deprivation which she will endure if she disobeys their commands will instill in her, if there is no escape, a pattern of obedience, submission, and subordination. One way to express the difference between her life and the lives of the other children is that the other children live with only one familial authority: the parents whose will must be obeyed, against whom they have no rights and against whose violence there is no recourse. By contrast, the child denied equal protection lives under the thumb of two sovereigns: the parents and the violent siblings who become, no less than the parents, an authority who must be obeyed: the source of commands that must be followed. She becomes not just a victim of injustice. She becomes a slave.

This scenario, the family that denies equal protection rather than simply equal justice, is harder to imagine than the first because, while loving parents may occasionally (even often) lapse from the ideal of equal justice, loving parents (and most parents are loving) do not even on occasion deny equal protection. The instinct to protect and to parent are too inextricably intertwined to expect these sorts of lapses in judgment or fairness, although it does sometimes happen; think of the younger sibling who suffers, and who is allowed by the parents to suffer, from sexual violation and abuse inflicted by a family relative. But generally, parents do not deny to any of their children their protection against the violence of their siblings or, to the extent possible, of their peers. States, however—the intuitive appeal of Scalia's patriarchal metaphor notwithstanding—are not families, and governments are not loving parents. States do from time to time withhold protection against private violence and private violation from a citizen or group of citizens. What then is the consequence when they do?

If the denial is complete, sweeping, and universal in scope, if the state utterly refuses to protect one group against the organized violence and violations of trust of a second, such that the violence is real and the threat of violation and betrayal is always credible, a not unexpected outcome is the institution of slavery itself. Indeed, the master-slave relationship can be defined, and often has been defined,[31] as a private relationship in which the violent assault by the master of the slave is not a criminal offense (but not vice versa), so that the assaulted slave has no recourse against the assaultive master because he has no rights that were violated. Extending this to a market economy, it is clear that the withdrawal of the state's assurance that private trusts will not be violated leaves the slave unprotected against natural threats to survival, just as the withdrawal of the state's protection against private violence leaves the slave unprotected against physical threats. The slave is able to avoid the violence of the master or the threat of starvation attendant to his betrayal and violations of trust only by obeying the master's command and accommodating to his will. This denial of protection against the violence and violation of a master is what defines, to say nothing of legitimizes, the master-slave relationship.

Once that relationship is established, one way to express the difference between the slave and the citizen is this: the citizen lives under the rule of only one sovereign—the state—while the slave lives under the rule of at least two sovereigns—the state and the master—the commands of both to be endured under the threat of unchecked violence. The citizen must abide by the commands of the state if he wishes to avoid its violent sanctions, but must not abide the commands of any other. He is protected by the state and more specifically by its criminal law against all nonstate violence; this protection is certainly a part of what it means to have rights. The slave, in marked contrast, must abide by the commands of two sovereigns, the state and the master, if he wishes to avoid violence or deprivation; this is what it is to be denied the protection of the state's law. Where one citizen, but not others, is denied protection, then protection is obviously unequal. The inequality of protection, unlike the unequal application of general laws decried by Scalia, gives rise not only to the evil of formal injustice but to the much more concrete, pervasive, and pernicious evil of slavery.

The message that I suggest we should take from the island metaphor is that the plainest possible meaning of the Fourteenth Amendment mandate that no state shall deny to any citizen "equal protection of the law" is that no state may deny to any citizen the protection of its criminal and civil law against private violence and private violation. Put differently, no state may, through denials of protection, permit any citizen to live in a state of "dual sovereignty." On this reading, the equal protection clause is at root a guarantee not of equal justice or of substantive equality, but of sole sovereignty: the state, and only the state, shall be sovereign over each and every citizen. Only the state shall have access to the use of unchecked and uncheckable violence to effectuate its will (and then, of course, only with due process). No citizen shall be subject to uncheckable violence by anyone other than the state; no citizen shall be under the will and command of anyone other than the state. Inversely, no entity, no individual, no group, no race, no gender, and no class other than the state shall have recourse to uncheckable violence as a means of effectuating his, her, or its will. No one other than the state shall have the power, backed by the credible threat of violence, to command and dominate the will of others. The equal protection clause is thus a guarantee of sole state sovereignty. Any relationship of sovereignty between a subject and master, other than that between state and citizen, that exists through state acquiescence—a refusal of the state to deter the credible threat of violence on which sovereignty depends—is evidence that the state has violated this guarantee of protection.

Although the master-slave relationship is the most logical outcome of a massive, universal, blanket denial of the protection of the law to one group of persons, the traditional relationship of slavery, with its economic meaning and consequences, is not the only possible outcome, for at least two reasons. First, it may be that the privileged, sovereign citizen in a state characterized by the denial of equal protection to others does not want the subject's labor, but, rather, wants something else. Perhaps he only wants from the subject class a general pattern of obedience, acquiescence, and subservience. Perhaps, rather than labor, he wants something very different from the unprotected subject, such as her sexuality,[32] a theme to which I will return.

But the economic relationship of master and slave may not be the outcome of a massive denial of equal protection for a rather different reason, which brings us directly to the history of the Fourteenth Amendment. Enslavement may not be the result of a denial of equal protection if slavery itself, but not the unequal protection of the law that facilitates and defines it, has been outlawed. If only slavery is outlawed, but not the denial of equal protection of the laws which is its logical underpinning, then it would not be surprising if the result of the prohibition of slavery was the subservience, acquiescence, and obedience of the subject, even if not formally enslaved, class. Indeed, in the post-Thirteenth Amendment and pre-Fourteenth Amendment world, the pattern of subservience, acquiescence, and obedience of the freed slaves to the commands, will, desires, or values of whites, all grounded in a fully justified fear of unchecked violence and unchecked violations of trust, was the clearest evidence one could possibly require that the states had denied to one class of its citizens the equal protection of the law.

In his powerful and justly influential book *The Antislavery Origins of the Fourteenth Amendment*,[33] first published in the early 1950s and re-released in the mid-1960s, Professor Jacobus tenBroek of the University of California argued that precisely this understanding of the phrase "equal protection of the law" was the same as that held by many of the amendment's framers: the state must guarantee its sole sovereignty to each citizen and must accordingly protect each citizen against the threat of both private violence and private violation. Simply put, tenBroek's history suggests that this was the understanding the abolitionists and their supporters, from the 1830s through passage of the Fourteenth Amendment, embraced, pleaded, propagandized, and advocated—the claim that every state must guarantee to every citizen the "equal protection of the laws."[34] The abolitionists, above all else, understood that it was precisely a denial of the protection of the state against private violence and private violation of trust that facilitated and even defined the status of the slave. After the passage of the Thirteenth Amendment, it became apparent to the abolitionists, their advocates, and fellow travelers in Congress that although a denial of equal protection is a necessary condition of slavery, eradication of slavery is not tantamount to a guarantee of equal protection. The wave of Ku Klux Klan violence of whites against blacks and abolitionists; the refusal of the southern states (and in many instances the northern states) to punish, check, or deter that violence; and the states' refusal to extend to freed slaves the legal forms of contract and property that were essential to their participation in the community's economic life, which was in turn the only genuine protection against natural threats to survival—all these engendered precisely the relationship of sovereign and subject, dominance and subservience, command and obedience that the unchecked violence and violation of one group against another can predictably ensure.[35] One could not have more vivid proof that the formal abolition of slavery will not necessarily guarantee the sole sovereignty of the state, and hence the true "citizen's equality," promised by the phrase "equal protection of the law."

Thus, the need for yet another amendment: one outlawing not just the symptom of slavery but the disease itself: the denial of the protection of the state against private violence and violation, of which slavery is one, but only one, possible manifestation. The equal protection clause of the Fourteenth Amendment was thus intended by the abolitionists, and at least some of its proponents, to abolish not only slavery per se,[36] but also the dual sovereignty that facilitates it; such dual sovereignty, in turn, is engendered by a state's refusal to grant to one group of its citizens protection of the law against private violence, economic isolation, and violation, and leaves its citizens profoundly and thoroughly unequal.

As far as I can tell, this particular history is not controversial; indeed, this can fairly be called the uncontested meaning of the Fourteenth Amendment. Given the degree of discord among legal theorists regarding the meaning of the equal protection clause, it is, at first blush, somewhat remarkable that there is such widespread consensus among historians, including those same legal theorists when wearing their "historian" hats, that this abolitionist meaning, or something closely akin to it, is the meaning of the equal protection clause embraced by those who most actively campaigned for its inclusion in the Constitution, from the 1830s all the way through the passage of the amendment itself. Indeed, that this abolitionist understanding was precisely the meaning intended by the Fourteenth Amendment's most influential framers is often given as an argument by both intentionalists—against modern, supposedly broader, interpretations of the clause, such as that embraced by the Warren Court in *Brown*[37]— and anti-intentionalists—as a definitive reductio ad absurdum argument against intentionalist modes of constitutional interpretation: if that is what the phrase meant historically, then history just cannot matter all that much, because whatever it means today, it means something much broader than that. For example, Richard Posner has argued against Robert Bork's intentionalism that no one, including Bork himself, can truly be an intentionalist regarding the equal protection clause because it is clear that all the equal protection clause was intended to do was to ensure that freed slaves would no longer be denied the protection of the state against Klan violence. Given that fact, under a truly intentionalist approach to constitutional meaning, *Brown* is surely wrong. Why? Because ensuring protection against Klan violence obviously has nothing to do with school segregation or desegregation. However, *Brown,* for whatever reason, is not surely wrong; in fact, it is surely right, a conclusion with which Bork himself does not quarrel. Therefore, Posner concludes, *quod erat demonstrandum,* neither Bork nor any other *Brown* sympathizer can possibly be an intentionalist.[38]

In a moment, I want to argue that Posner's view represents a cramped understanding of the abolitionist position, as well as of intentionalism. I disagree with Posner's implied charge that under an abolitionist approach, the Fourteenth Amendment has no modern content because there simply are no modern analogues to either slavery or the unchecked Klan violence and private violation of freed slaves that triggered the passage of the Thirteenth and Fourteenth Amendments. It is actually remarkably easy to find modern examples of the states' denial to one group of citizens of the protection of criminal and civil law against private violence and violation. In fact, in the next section, I will suggest several such modern applications. First, I will contrast this "abolitionist" understanding of the core guarantee of the Fourteenth Amendment with the understanding of the history of the amendment relied on by formalists and antisubordinationists, respectively.

If the abolitionist understanding is right, then the formalist insistence on a color-blind Constitution simply understates by half the nature of the evil at which the Fourteenth Amendment is aimed. Slavery was indeed bolstered by a false and invidious theory of racial difference and racial inferiority, as was the subordination facilitated by the denials of equal protection that followed its abolition. But that theory of racial difference is surely not all that is wrong with either the enslavement or the subordination of African-Americans in the nineteenth century. Otherwise, it would be a complete response to the mandate of the Fourteenth Amendment, assuming for a moment that there had been no Thirteenth Amendment, to insist on a color-blind system of slavery, to concede, so to speak, that there is indeed a "bad" form of slavery that rests on a false theory of racial difference, but if we abandon that false theory, and just enslave "natural slaves" without regard to their race, the institution is "rational," and thus constitutional, because it no longer falsely categorizes people on the basis of irrelevant racial characteristics. Color-blind slavery, in other words, is fully constitutional under the interpretation of the equal protection clause put forward by formalists. But surely it is peculiar to think that color-blind slavery, unconstitutional under the Thirteenth Amendment, is not a violation of the Fourteenth Amendment as well. Indeed, it is not only peculiar, it is absurd. Yet it is precisely this absurdity to which the formalist interpretation leads us. A color-blind institution of slavery would still be both slavery in its purest form and a denial of equal protection to one group, the slaves, against the private violence of the other group, the masters. This would be true not only because there are no "natural slaves" such that the categories, no matter how drawn, could never be rational, but also because the thing itself, the slave, is not a category that even exists in nature: it is one half of a relationship, and it is defined by precisely that which the Fourteenth Amendment explicitly prohibits: the unequal protection of law. However the categories are drawn, whether color conscious or color-blind, slavery is a violation of the Fourteenth no less than the Thirteenth Amendment because it evidences a massive denial of the equal protection of the law. Color blindness, although perhaps a condition of formal, equal justice, is simply not the nub of equal protection. Rather, protection is.

More generally, any state of dual sovereignty, whether or not it results in economic slavery, is a violation of equal protection, regardless of whether the distinctions between superior and inferior, sovereign and subject, dominant and subordinate are drawn in a color-blind fashion or along lines that track any other so-called suspect class. We can return for a moment to the hypothetical family or the small-scale society on the Goldingesque island: even if the subservient class from whom the protection of the parent or state is denied is divined in a perfectly rational or perfectly random fashion, in a way that is utterly blind to race, gender, ethnicity, or religion; even if the subject and master classes are composed of perfectly representative cross sections of every "suspect class" imaginable (some are old, some young, some black, some white, some women, some men, some gays, some straights, and so on), the result would still be a denial of equal protection. One group, the ethnically, racially, sexually diverse subject group, is denied the protection of the law granted the other group. The result is that the subject group lives under the rule of two sovereigns, the state and the other group. This result obviously holds regardless of the composition of either class. The moral is simply that rational categorization, no less than the color-blind mandate implied by the requirement of rationality, is not the nub of equal protection. Protection is the nub of equal protection. The state must protect, and it must protect equally.

If this abolitionist understanding of equal protection is correct, then the problem with the antisubordinationist interpretation of equal protection is clear: just as the formalist approach only addresses a part of the evil, the antisubordinationist account overstates the evil. The nub of equal protection is surely not rationality or color blindness, but neither is it substantive equality. Again, the nub is protection. Just as the formalist interpretation seems to imply the constitutionality under the Fourteenth Amendment of a color-blind institution of slavery, and therefore seems underinclusive, so the antisubordinationist interpretation seems to imply the unconstitutionality of an incredibly overinclusive array of inequalities, whether or not the product of the dual sovereignty forbidden by the guarantee of equal protection. On this view, the state's failure to rectify and reverse virtually any unequal distribution of power, not just between whites and blacks or women and men but between anybody and anybody, so long as the underlying cause of the inequality is a factor that is or should be morally irrelevant, would be a denial of equal protection and therefore unconstitutional. One need not be a libertarian or a free marketeer to see that this would be an unattractive world in which to live. About thirty-five years ago, Kurt Vonnegut,[39] no regressive neoconservative he, described a fictional and dystopic world in which buzzers go off in the inner ears of persons of exceptional intelligence, talented dancers wear weights, singers have their vocal chords scarred, and tall people learn to slump so as not to be intimidating on the basketball court, all in the name of a vision of equality that is very hard to differentiate from the antisubordinationist approach. A world in which all have equal power would be a world not only free of the malign inequalities that stem from the states' failure to protect, but also free of the far broader array of benign inequalities and differences that constitute not just our own, but virtually any social world. The anti-subordinationist understanding of equal protection, when severed from the focus on the states' duty to provide protection, is fatally vague and overly general. If what is prohibited by equal protection is truly any and all "subordination" that stems from inequalities in power, which themselves are rooted in morally insignificant determinants, then it seems that what is prohibited is simply social life.[40]

Finally, from an abolitionist perspective, it is clear that both the formalist and the antisubordinationist models are partial truths. A false racial theory of black difference and black inferiority is indeed the target of the Fourteenth Amendment when that false theory is used to justify the states' withdrawal of its protection from blacks and thereby facilitate the enslavement or subordination of blacks to the will of whites. But the cure for that evil is surely not "color blindness." A false racial theory is not necessary to such subordination. And subordination of blacks by whites (or women by men) is indeed the target of the Fourteenth Amendment when that subordination is the consequence of a system of dual sovereignty occasioned by the state's withdrawal of its protection against private violence or violation from one group of citizens. But the cure for that evil is not the eradication of all inequalities of power.

For all their differences, the formalist and antisubordinationist interpretations of the equal protection clause share one feature, and it is what they share that renders them both problematic: they are both interpretations, albeit conflicting ones, of equality, rather than of equal protection. They both read the phrase in the clause as though the word *protection* were not in it: formalists read it as though the phrase demanded equal justice, and antisubordinationists read it as though it demanded substantive equality. By removing "protection" from the phrase, they leave it a general mandate of equality and thus susceptible to straightforward political debate about the meaning of that illusive promise. There is no question but that we need to debate the meaning of equality and the extent to which our commitment to equality obligates us to undertake pervasive social and economic reordering. But equality, whether formal or substantive, is not the mandate of the Constitution: equal protection is. By removing the promise of protection from the equal protection clause, our modern constitutional interpreters have taken from that phrase, and hence from the amendment to which it is pivotal, its specific, distinctive, and constitutional contribution to political debate. For it is the idea of equal protection and not equality, the idea that the state must and should promise each citizen protection against the violence of others if it is truly to be a constitutional state under the rule of law, that is the distinctive contribution of the Fourteenth Amendment to our collective moral knowledge which continues to guide, however tenuously, our modern political choices.

The Conservative Court and Congressional Responsibilities under the Fourteenth Amendment

What then might an abolitionist understanding of the equal protection clause of the Fourteenth Amendment tell us about our modern world? The abolitionist understanding, which I have elsewhere called a pure protection or a sole sovereignty model, primarily guarantees that every citizen will be subject to only one sovereign, the state. Accordingly, and minimally, at least according to the abolitionists and framers who advocated the phrase "equal protection of the law," no state shall, through the withdrawal of the protection of its criminal law, permit any other group or individual to establish a relationship of sovereignty over any other through the medium of unchecked violence. Also, no state, through the withdrawal of the protections and empowerments of its civil law, shall permit any group to establish sovereignty by isolating one group from the shared, cooperative, and competitive economic life of the whole, thereby exposing that group or individual to natural threats to survival. What, if anything, does such a vision tell us about modern life or our modern problems?

First, some comments about the question itself. As James Boyd White has argued in his book, *Justice as Translation*,[41] one generation cannot simply "apply" a legal formulation, no matter how broad, to the problems of another. Any such "application" requires something akin to an act of translation from one language to another: what we must do, when we do this sort of thing, is translate the message articulated in one culture, in this case pre– and post–Civil War America, to the problems of another, late-twentieth century life. For that reason, any sort of pure intentionalist approach to the Constitution or any other legal problem, no matter how desirable, is simply impossible; it cannot be done. But it hardly follows that the original understanding has no meaning, or relevance, or that it tells us nothing, any more than the complexities and difficulties of translation render works written in another language meaningless. What it does mean, I think, is that both the abolitionists' overall philosophical principles, as well as their particular agenda, might usefully suggest what aspects of our modern lives may be within the gambit of the sorts of concerns that the Fourteenth Amendment was intended to rectify. If we can specify, to use Ronald Dworkin's helpful distinction,[42] both their particular conception of equal protection and their general concept of the problems they were attempting to address, we may be able to specify both the minimal content and the contested margins of a modern protectionist understanding of the equal protection clause. The "minimal content" will be drawn by analogy to the abolitionists' specific conception of equal protection and the "contested margins" by analogy to their general concept.

Very baldly, at the most general or conceptual level, according to the abolitionists, the equal protection clause has both a negative and an affirmative meaning. Negatively, the clause requires the state to ensure that every individual is equally free of all conditions which could potentially subjugate his will to some sovereign power other than the state. The clause prohibits a state of dual sovereignty: the state must ensure that no citizen lives under more than one sovereign. The clause affirmatively requires the state to protect each individual's positive liberty: to guarantee to every individual the freedom to direct her own life and work. To use the language of the time, the equal protection clause requires the state to affirmatively protect each person's exercise of his or her natural or human rights.

There were, according to the abolitionists, at least two specific natural rights the state is required to protect. Those specific *natural rights,* which must be protected equally, constitute the abolitionists' particular conception of equal protection. The first specific natural right is the right to physical security: each citizen must be protected against private violence perpetrated by others. The equal protection clause guarantees that protection through the evenhanded application of the criminal law; thus, Posner is right to note that, in an important sense, the wave of Klan lynchings and private violence undeterred and unpunished by the state that characterized the post–Civil War era is the paradigmatic equal protection violation, not the Jim Crow laws or segregated schools.[43]

The citizen's second specific natural right is to have available the legal means to fashion a livelihood to ward off natural threats to survival. The equal protection clause protects against such threats by guaranteeing that the legal means of sustaining a livelihood in a market economy through ownership, acquisition, alienation, and trade of one's labor, capital, and property are available to all. It is important to remember that a primary immediate political purpose of the amendment was to ensure the constitutionality of the Civil Rights Act of 1866.[44] What the equal protection clause was minimally designed to protect against, then, was private violence and material deprivation occasioned by isolation from the cooperative economic life of the community through which individual livelihoods could be fashioned. What then does the state have a duty to protect, and to protect equally? Minimally, for the abolitionists, the state must protect that which is absolutely essential to a free life: first, physical safety; second, freedom from want—forty acres and a mule or its equivalent and access to the means of participation in the community's economic life.

Later, I will explore possible modern ramifications of the abolitionists' general concept that equal protection requires the state to protect our natural rights, or our positive liberty, equally. First, though, I want to urge that even from this minimalist, specific conception of equal protection, it is not hard to see some modern violations of the equal protection mandate as understood by the abolitionists who argued for it. Let me briefly mention four. The first two derive from the state's obligation to protect against private violence, and the second two from its obligation to protect against natural threats to survival.

First, as I will argue in chapter 2, the marital rape exemption still in force, albeit in an attenuated form, in several states constitutes as literal a modern withdrawal of the states' protection against violent assault as did the states' failure to protect against murder during the heyday of Klan violence. The consequences are also not dissimilar. A woman who can be forcibly and physically intruded upon without recourse to legal protection or remedy is not a victim of crime, with the remedies and rights pertinent thereto; rather, she is, and will most likely regard herself, as subject to the sovereign whim of he who can, without fear of state reprisal, coerce her consent through legitimate threats of force and violence. Such a woman, unlike unmarried women and unlike all men, lives under the will of two sovereigns rather than one: the state and her husband against whose violence there is no recourse. Consequently, the husband's commands must be obeyed if violence is to be avoided. The marital rape "exemption" is in a very literal sense a denial of the state's promise of protection against violent assault and, as such, given an abolitionist understanding of the phrase, is clearly and unproblematically unconstitutional.

Second, the reluctance, delay, or outright refusal of some urban police forces to enter high crime neighborhoods[45] similarly constitutes a literal withdrawal of the state's protection against violence, and hence this too is a violation of the guarantee of equal protection. Again, this withdrawal of police protection leaves large numbers of citizens subject to the authority of two sovereigns rather than just one: the state, against whose legitimate forms of violence there is no recourse, and the crime lord or drug lord, against whose illegitimate but undeterred violence there is similarly no recourse. Drastically unequal police protection quite directly implies drastically unequal protection of the laws, drastically unequal sufferance of private violence, and drastically unequal subjection or enslavement to the whims, will, desires, and manipulations of one's fellow citizens.

From these two examples and the premise on which they rest—that the state's protection against private violence is the central, minimal guarantee of the equal protection clause—it follows that a number of the Court's recent decisions, whether grounded in the Fourteenth Amendment's equal protection clause or not, are wrong, or, if not wrong in their outcome, wrong in some aspect of their reasoning. The major premise of the Court's recent decision in *DeShaney v. Winnebago County Department of Social Services,*[46] and the sizeable number of similar cases that followed and preceded it,[47] that there is no constitutional right to a police force,[48] is squarely wrong. The right to a police force, or, more specifically, the right to the state's protection against the subjugating effects of private violence, are the paradigm Fourteenth Amendment rights. It is precisely these rights that make us "equal" in the eyes of the law. Given our right to police protection against private violence, we are equally subject to the commands of only one sovereign, the rule of law; and given that right, we are equally free because we are equally free of subjection to the commands of any other. It follows that little Joshua DeShaney, brutally, repeatedly, and privately assaulted by his father, suffering massive and permanent brain damage as a result, did indeed suffer a constitutional violation. This violation was not because the state had sufficiently intervened into the family's life so as to satisfy the state action requirement as (indirectly) argued by the dissent[49] but, rather, because it did not intervene enough. Through its inaction, not its action, the state failed to provide equal protection of the law.

The background inequality that gave rise to the Court's decision seven years ago in *McCleskey v. Kemp*[50] (the statistical likelihood that the murder of a white victim will result in a greater punishment than the murder of a black victim, as well as the related and similar devaluing of black rape victims over white rape victims reflected in the prosecution and punishment of rape) also has constitutional dimensions, although not necessarily those litigated in the case itself.[51] The relative withdrawal of protection, and correlatively greater vulnerability to violence reflected in that differential, again is a literal denial of the equal protection of the criminal law against private violence. Similarly, the background conditions that gave rise to *Washington v. Davis*[52]—an insufficiently integrated police force in a nearly all-black city, where the "neutral" criteria by which black applicants were excluded from the force were unrelated to job performance— also raises at least a suspicion, if not a presumption, of a denial of equal protection of the law.[53] A too-white force in a nearly all-black town, one might hypothesize, will very likely provide a police service so far removed from the felt needs and interests of those served as to constitute a denial of the police protection against violence guaranteed by the Fourteenth Amendment.

It also follows from the abolitionists' minimalist understanding of equal protection that the so-called state action requirement, at least as presently understood by the Court, and according to some of its various definitions, is drastically misconceived. The equal protection clause, under an abolitionist interpretation, targets states' refusals to protect citizens against profoundly private action that results in insubordination or enslavement. The "state action," then, which is the object of the amendment, is the breach of an affirmative duty to protect the rights of citizens to be free, minimally, of the subordinating, enslaving violence of other citizens. The act of "discrimination" that triggers equal protection analysis is the private violence and violating act which, unremedied and untouched by state law, creates a private sovereignty, separate from state sovereignty forbidden by the equal protection clause. The state breach that constitutes the violation may take the form either of action or inaction, feasance or malfeasance: the state may simply fail to protect one group from the violence of others (as in the case of unpunished and undeterred Klan or domestic violence), or the state may do something far more visible, such as pass legislation explicitly removing one group from the reach of the state's protection against the violence of others (such as in the case of marital rape exemption laws). Whether the state's failure to protect constitutes an action or inaction, however, is not determinative. What is determinative are the consequences of the state's conduct: whether by virtue of the state's action or inaction there exists a separate state of sovereignty in which one citizen is subjected to the will of another citizen as well as to the sovereignty of the state.

Are there other private actions, beyond physical violence, that have the effect of enslaving one group of citizens to another? Put differently, are there other natural rights beyond the right to be free of private violence that the state has a duty to protect? Although the Supreme Court ultimately confused and aborted the issue in the *Slaughterhouse Cases*[54] and the *Civil*

Rights Act Cases,[55] the framers of the Fourteenth Amendment unambiguously believed there were such rights: the 1866 Civil Rights Acts largely constitutionalized by the Fourteenth Amendment, sought to ensure that the state would protect all citizens not only from private violence but also from the economic isolation, deprivation, dependence, and ultimate economic subjugation that would inevitably result from the withdrawal of the state's private law. The latter goal was no less important than protecting citizens from the direct physical subjugation resulting from the withdrawal of the protection of the state's criminal law. Arguably, we must stretch a little farther to find modern analogies to this second but equally central purpose of the Fourteenth Amendment. But here as well, I think, analogous modern situations do exist, particularly if we do not read back into the Civil Rights Act, and the amendment that was intended to constitutionalize it, modern conceptions of equal protection.

The abolitionists and at least some of the framers of the amendment argued that the states have a duty to ensure equal access to the mechanisms of private law, but the reason for that obligation was not simply a concern for the symmetries of abstract justice. Rather, the state's duty arises because it is by using those mechanisms of contract and property law that a livelihood can be maintained, and the utter dependence on others and the state of subjection to which that dependency leads can be avoided.[56] It is easier to see modern analogues if we generalize the multiple purposes and ambitions of the original Civil Rights Act in this way: the states have a duty to protect the natural rights of the citizen to engage in the economic life of the community through the purchase, sale, and ownership of property and in one's own labor, thus ensuring liberty by avoiding the dependency that results from deprivation. Let me just mention two possible modern applications of this duty, although surely the list could be longer.

First, an abolitionist understanding of the Fourteenth Amendment provides at least some support for the claim that the equal protection clause guarantees minimal welfare rights, not only to shelter, food, and clothing, but also to a liveable minimum income or job. Furthermore, an abolitionist approach clarifies what an antisubordinationist approach toward the same conclusion obfuscates: the source of the right to welfare, if there is one, is not in the amendment's avowal of equality, for there is none, but rather its promise of protection.[57] Simply put, the state has an obligation to protect citizens from abject subjection to the whims of others occasioned by extreme states of poverty, no less than to protect citizens from vulnerability to the threats of physical violence from others. Indeed, chronic, multigenerational homelessness, for example, shares in many, although certainly not all, of the features of post-slave life that not only prompted the passage of, but also framed the meaning of, the amendment: for both the nineteenth-century freed slave and the twentieth-century homeless person, the total dispossession of property that defines the condition of the latter, and which was a central feature of the condition of the former, entails a similar lack of privacy, an inability to manage one's own life, a dependency on others for material survival, the difficulty or impossibility of selling one's own labor, and ultimately the impossibility or near impossibility of ever achieving the state of self-sovereignty, rather than subjection to others, which is the underlying goal of the reconstruction amendments taken in their entirety.

This abolitionist, pure protection, or sole sovereignty understanding of the equal protection clause also provides a way of thinking about the constitutionality of the so-called traditional division of labor in the most private of private spheres: the home. As numerous feminist writers from various disciplines have pointed out,[58] the vast numbers of women who perform huge and disproportionate amounts of unpaid domestic labor, from child care to housekeeping, often preventing their acquisition or development of labor skills compensable in the "real" or paid labor market, are, like slaves, rendered subject to the whim of a separate sovereign, the check-bearing spouse on whom they depend for material survival. Whether viewed through the lens of the direct prohibition of slavery provided in the Thirteenth Amendment or through the lens of the equal protection mandate of the Fourteenth Amendment, the state has failed to protect these women against the resulting state of servitude. The state has failed to ensure that no group of citizens lives under the mastery of two sovereigns rather than only under the mastery of state sovereignty. The state has failed to provide equal protection of the law.

The abolitionist history of the passage of the equal protection clause of the Fourteenth Amendment might then leave us with this minimal formulation: we have an absolute, incontrovertible right not to be subject to any sovereignty other than the state. From this absolute right are derived subsidiary rights and obligations: we have a right to be free of those conditions which, if unchecked by the state, generate separate sovereignties, including, at least, a right to be free of private violence and extreme material deprivation. Both unchecked private violence and material deprivation engender dependency on others and subjection to their whims, desires, and commands, which is constitutive of the state of slavery. Correlatively, the state has an affirmative duty to protect our natural rights to physical security and economic participation. If the state fails to grant or extend that protection to some subgroup of the community, it has failed to grant equal protection of the laws.

Finally, and still from just this minimalist sole sovereignty interpretation of equal protection, we can generate answers to the three modern dilemmas of Fourteenth Amendment law that have so badly split the constitutional community into its formalist and antisubordinationist camps. First, the very general mandate of integration and the prohibition against state-sponsored segregation that is articulated, albeit ambiguously, in *Brown v. Board of Education*[59] is supportable under a protectionist, no less than formalist or antisubordinationist, approach although the reason is somewhat different: where either private or state-sponsored segregation subjugates one class of citizens to the sovereignty of another class, and where the state acquiesces in that subjugation, the state has violated its promise of equal protection. It could surely be argued that radically unequal state-segregated public schools had both that intent and effect. Second, where a state law, rule, or criterion adversely impacts the interests of one class of citizens, whether or not intentionally, and that adverse impact has the effect of subjugating one class of citizens to the will of another, the equal protection clause is violated. The use of neutral criteria in *Washington v. Davis*[60] to exclude blacks from the city's police force may or may not be such a violation, depending on the effects and history of nonblack police forces in nearly all-black cities. If a too-white force is incapable of providing protection to a black community, then the unprotected citizen is effectively subjected to the sovereignty of both the state and the unchecked will of the local crime or drug lord. If so, then *Davis* is a quite literal denial of equal protection of the law.

And third, under a protectionist or sole sovereignty understanding of equal protection, affirmative action of the sort ruled impermissible in *City of Richmond v. J. A. Croson Co.*[63] is clearly permitted because the color consciousness intrinsic to affirmative action is not intended to subjugate, nor does it have the effect of subjugating, whites to the command of blacks, and it is constitutionally required wherever the failure to undertake affirmative action would perpetuate the continuing subjugation of the freedom of blacks to the will of whites. From the perspective of the problems that our formalist-antisubordinationist debate has highlighted, then, a *protectionist* approach is somewhere between the two poles. A protectionist approach is more permissive of affirmative action than a formalist approach: for the formalist, any race consciousness is irrational and therefore unconstitutional, while for the protectionist, race consciousness is only unconstitutional if it is part of a pattern of subjugation that elevates one class of citizens to a state of virtual sovereignty over another. On the other hand, a protectionist approach is less demanding than an antisubordinationist approach: while the antisubordinationist reads the amendment as requiring a very broad egalitarianism, the protectionist reads it as requiring liberty; and while the antisubordinationist targets subordinating conditions as constitutional violations, the protectionist targets only those subordinating conditions that are so extreme as to confer on one group a sovereign status and on the other a correlative denial of freedom.

If this is the "minimal content of the equal protection clause," what are its outer reaches, as understood by the abolitionists? What, to return to Dworkin's fruitful formulation, is implied by the very general concept of equal protection they advocated rather than the particular conception of it they urged—that is, freedom from separate sovereignties and a right to be protected against the subordinating effects of private violence, economic isolation, and material deprivation? What should be, or what might be, our modern conception of equal protection if we are to remain true to the general concept intended by the abolitionists? At the very concrete level, and the protestations of intentionalist constitutionalists notwithstanding, history can provide little guidance, as it has been the burden of the constitutional interpretivists, pragmatists, and other anti-intentionalists to demonstrate.[62] Nevertheless, the abolitionists' very general understanding of constitutionalism and politics and, in brief, their moral philosophy, does at least suggest a way to ask the question that brings into focus modern problems and modern solutions. Their formulation of the relevant questions also reveals, however, at least three reasons why the abolitionist understanding never dominated judicial interpretation of the clause during the twentieth century: it rested on a way of thinking about natural rights that is dramatically at odds with modern modes of thought; it rested on a moral and social vision largely unamenable to judicial enactment; and, finally, it rested on and presupposed a sense of civic responsibility and obligation to others that is foreign to our modern conception of citizenship. Let me suggest what the abolitionists' general concept required and then explore the obstacles to its modern realization.

To know what the equal protection of the law requires under an abolitionist understanding of the phrase, we need to know what is meant by our very general right not to be subjugated to the commands of any non-state sovereign, or, put affirmatively, our right to be free. A right not to be subjugated to the whims of a sovereign other than the state rests on (or implies, or simply restates) a positive right to be free from bondage. The Fourteenth Amendment, then, might profitably be viewed as a sort of charter of positive liberty—a charter protecting our right to be self-governing, autonomous, and free of other rulers, masters, or superiors within the confines of the rule of law. As the abolitionists themselves realized, such a guarantee requires for its full enunciation and realization a theory of natural rights and some sort of teleological account of human nature. What does it mean to be free? What, beyond physical and material security, must be protected if we are to be truly free? What needs must be met? What wants satisfied? What is so central to our human essence that only if it is protected, nurtured, or furthered, can we be called free? The central question, then, posed by the original understanding of the equal protection guarantee, is what natural rights do we possess, and possess equally, that must be protected if we are to enjoy the equal protection of the law, and hence enjoy the liberty that is its fundamental promise?

If we could answer that question, if we could specify the natural rights we each hold in the contemporary world, we would know the current reach of the abolitionist understanding of the equal protection clause. Do we have, for example, a natural right to education, for the distinctively abolitionist reason that only with an education do we have any hope of self-sufficiency, independence, or self-sovereignty? Is participation in culture and the world of knowledge so central to our humanity that unless that potential is protected and nurtured, we are not, in some important sense, truly free, but are rather enslaved by ignorance? The compulsive insistence by whites on maintaining the illiteracy and ignorance of slaves in the pre–Civil War south is some negative evidence, of course, that education is indeed essential to self-sovereignty or positive liberty—that it is, in short, a natural right. Might not pregnant women have a right to obtain an abortion for an unwanted pregnancy for the distinctively abolitionist reason that without such a right, the woman is enslaved against her wishes to not only the pregnancy, but also, very likely, at least for a large portion of her life, to the unwanted and unpaid labor that unwanted motherhood entails? Is power over one's body and one's reproductivity, as well as choice of one's life work, so central to human identity, that without those powers and choices protected, we are in some sense unfree? Might not gay men and lesbians have a right to state laws that protect their intimate and sexual orientations equally as those of heterosexuals, for the distinctively abolitionist reason that such choices and orientations are a necessary part of a free life, and without such protection, the individual is subjugated to the whims and desires of an unchecked and heterosexist cultural mandate? Might not members of distinctive cultural subgroups, such as Native Americans, Spanish-speaking Americans, or the Amish, have a right to state laws that protect the integrity and cohesiveness of their culture, for the distinctively abolitionist reason that identification with such a group is for many an essential part of a free life, and without such protection, they are subjugated to the mandatory mores of an unchecked, hostile, and hegemonic majority culture? These are difficult questions for which I do not have answers. To answer them requires a normative account of human nature: Who are we? Who should we be? What does it mean to be human? What might it mean to be free?

On the other side of the coin, an abolitionist concept of equal protection requires a teleological and normative account of sovereignty. What natural duties does the state owe its citizens, by virtue of its, and their, allegiance to the notion of a rule of law and their shared commitment to the state's sole sovereignty? Against what evils must the state provide protection if each citizen is to be free? The abolitionist held that the state must provide protection against private violence and economic isolation, but this is clearly not the only possible response. Must it also protect, for example, against the disappearance of subcultures? Must the state protect against mandatory and unpaid childbirth? Must it protect against that institution that Adrienne Rich provocatively calls "compulsory heterosexuality"[63]— compulsory, not only because its mandates are as often as not backed by violent sanctions but also because it is falsely presented as necessary, natural, and as part of the inevitable order of things? Against what private, natural, or cultural constraints on our positive liberty, our right to be self-governing, our right to be free of nonstate sovereign entities, does the state have a duty to protect us?

These too are difficult questions which I will not here attempt to answer. I do, though, want to notice one feature shared by all of them: answers to these questions about the duties of the state to provide equal protection to its citizens in a constitutional democracy in which "the state" is in some sense us, requires not just a view of human nature, and not just an understanding of our natural rights, but also a deep appreciation of our civic obligations, our natural commitments to others, and our shared responsibility for their well-being. In this culture, to ask what "the state" must protect or whether "the state" must protect against violence, hunger, oppression, and cultural annihilation is not to ask what some other entity (a distant monarch or legislature) must do to protect the weak, but what each of us must do to protect each other, as well as to protect ourselves. If protection against subjugating conditions is the essence of the equal protection clause, and if we are serious about understanding our state and ourselves as a constitutional democracy, if we are the "sovereign," then that clause is incontrovertibly about our obligations to protect each other, not simply our right to protection from a reified state. In their political activities, the abolitionists proclaimed themselves to be, and in fact became, their brothers' keepers. In their victorious insistence on equal protection of the law for all, they constitutionalized the obligation as well as the right. Through the mandate of equal protection, the insistence that we the people protect each other against the private subordination of some by others, the Constitution became not just a charter of rights but a charter of citizen responsibilities.

If all of this is right, then it is not hard to see several reasons why the abolitionist understanding of equal protection has not flourished in this century and what we need to do if we are to take the abolitionist interpretation seriously. The first reason has to do with current mores of intellectual thought. Substantive, normative, and teleological theories of natural rights, the philosophical underpinning of the abolitionist's constitutional theory, simply do not resonate with our modern ways of thinking about political morality. The conceit in contemporary political thought, buttressed by ambitions of scientism as well as fashions of postmodernism, is that we either should or must dispense with theories of nature, human nature, and natural rights in political thought. Relatedly, most (but certainly not all) modern political and constitutional thinkers view the citizen's possession of rights, not his possession of responsibilities, as of the essence of constitutionalism. For both reasons, the abolitionists' claim that each of us collectively and individually is constitutionally obligated to protect the natural rights or the central humanity of each other to guarantee each others' freedom does not rest easily with twentieth-century political and moral theory.

Another reason that even a minimalist version of the abolitionist interpretation may not have prevailed is structural. As the Supreme Court has always been quick to point out, the federal judiciary is ill equipped to remedy the structural, institutional, and social inequalities, practices, and attitudes that result in constitutionally problematic states of affairs, such as unequal sentences for killers of white victims and black victims, or the unequal participation of blacks on the Washington, D.C., police force. The federal judiciary is similarly ill equipped to fashion the massive restructuring of our market economy that would be necessary to end the millennium-long era of unpaid domestic labor and the subsequent undervaluing of women's work in the market economy. The judiciary could, of course, do some things: it could easily declare marital rape laws unconstitutional; it could reverse itself and affirm our right to protection by a police force; and it could insist that the state compensate victims of violence such as Joshua DeShaney, who are now denied that protection. But it could do little or nothing to redirect our community resources to guarantee the funds necessary to meaningfully effectuate that promise: to actually create the programs needed to deter domestic violence, to provide additional support for police forces assigned to high-crime neighborhoods, or to ensure that the social services agencies charged with protecting Joshua DeShaney would become a reality for the community at large, rather than for the rare individual who can marshal the funds and fortitude to file a lawsuit. The conservative Court and conservative theorists are probably right to insist that the reordering of priorities and redirecting of collective resources necessary to make these programs a reality must originate with legislative, not judicial action. They are wrong, though, to imply from that structural limit the nonexistence of the background constitutional right.

The last obstacle I want to mention to modern implementation of interpretation of the equal protection clause is jurisprudential: it concerns the nature of the "law" discovered or created by courts, as contrasted with the nature of "law" created by legislative process. Here, a quick contrast with the formal equality model presently adopted by the current Supreme Court is helpful. To determine whether or not a statute violates the equal protection clause under the formal equality model, the Court must essentially decide whether the legislature is "treating like groups alike." Whatever may be the shortcomings of this model, and I think there are many, it has one unassailable strength: the formal equality model of equal protection that requires rational categorization in legislation demands of the Court what might be called *adjudicative virtues*. The work required of the courts under the formal equality model in deciding whether a rule treats like cases alike converges perfectly with the essential core of the judicial task. Deciding whether a precedent or a rule treats like cases alike is what courts do all the time, and, moreover, it is what courts should do all the time. To do this well, to decide whether rules and decisions are rational in precisely this way, is the mark of a good judge. The rationality and the conception of formal justice on which it depends, and which is the central demand of the formal equality model, is itself an "adjudicative virtue": to treat like cases alike is the ideal of good judging toward which judges aspire. It is not at all surprising that judges gravitate toward an understanding of the equal protection clause that, in turn, rests on an understanding of equality that, also in turn, requires of them the exercise of precisely this familiar virtue.

By contrast, the general concept of equal protection advanced by the abolitionists (as well as modern antisubordinationists) requires the exercise not of this adjudicative virtue but of citizen and legislative virtues. To know what the equal protection clause requires us to protect, and what it requires us to protect against, requires a view, articulated or not, widely accepted or not, debated and debatable or not, of the content of liberty, of human nature, of natural rights, and, given our commitment to democracy, of human and citizen obligation. We need to know who we are and how we should distribute our collective resources: what we owe to whom. It ultimately demands a theory of distributive, not equal or formal, justice. These distributive and redistributive questions may not be questions that judges can or should answer. They are precisely the questions we need to ask of ourselves and of our representatives, however.

If we are to make sense of the equal protection clause as understood by the abolitionists, and as understood by at least many of its framers, we need to do two things. First, we need to reacquaint ourselves with old ways of thinking about our human nature and the natural rights that follow— we need to suspend our postmodernist doubts that this is a sensible and fruitful way to think about political morality. Second, and to my mind of greater importance, if we are to take seriously the view of the equal protection clause intended by its framers and advocates, we need to quit asking what that clause requires of our courts, what it directs our judges to do or refrain from doing, and how much of its vision is compatible with judicial review—whether it does or does not accord with our tripartite common-sensible conception of individual rights, majority rule, and judicial role. We need to ask instead what the clause demands of us as legislators, as citizens, as lawmakers, and as members of a community. When we ask what we are required to do to guarantee to each of us the equal protection of the law, rather than what judges are required to do, we may see very different answers. The answers to that question urged by the abolitionists well over a century ago—to which we may have blinded ourselves through our peculiarly modern intellectual focus on equality and rights rather than equal protection and responsibility and our peculiarly historic insistence on judicial enforcement rather than the congressional enforcement called for by the amendment itself—may be more progressive, more astute, more just, and more caring than either the color-blind or egalitarian charter of equality that we currently read into the clause, and which has stalemated debate and stalled our constitutional, as well as moral, progress.

2

Equality Theory, Marital Rape, and the
Promise of the Fourteenth Amendment

■

During the 1980s a handful of state judges either held or opined in dicta what must be incontrovertible to the feminist community, as well as to most progressive legal advocates and academics: the so-called marital rape exemption, whether statutory or common law in origin, constitutes a denial of a married woman's constitutional right to equal protection under the law.[1] Indeed, a more obvious denial of equal protection is difficult to imagine: the marital rape exemption denies married women protection against violent crime solely on the basis of gender and marital status. What possibly could be less rational than a statute that criminalizes sexual assault, and punishes it severely, unless the victim and assailant are married? What could be more obvious than the plain fact, repeatedly documented, that these state laws are derived from a sorry history of discriminatory, misogynist, and hateful denials of a married woman's legal right to equal dignity and respect? Where could one possibly find a sharper example of a state law that explicitly insulates and protects a separate political system of subordination and violence against a group of citizens, and thereby denies those citizens protection of the laws given others? So why has not the Supreme Court held as much?

Indeed, that a number of feminist commentators[2] and a few state court appellate judges[3] felt it necessary to argue to a still skeptical and often hostile listening audience that marital rape exemptions constitute a denial of the Fourteenth Amendment's guarantee that no state shall deny to any group of its citizens equal protection of its law evidences the degree to which women's injuries still are trivialized and rendered invisible by a pervasively misogynist legal, political, and social culture. That the arguments of these advocates met with such limited success in abolishing the exemption reveals how short a distance women have come, and how far we have yet to travel, toward full equality and the necessary result of equality: an assurance that the state will provide a modicum of safety in our private lives against sexual assault.

A number of states did make limited progress in reforming marital rape law during the 1980s and 1990s. Some abolished the exemption entirely.[4] Many continue to permit rape or sexual assault within marriage by according it a lower level of criminality than extramarital rape or sexual assault, by criminalizing only certain kinds of marital rape, or by criminalizing only first-degree rapes.[5] Some states, ironically in the name of reform, may have worsened the problem of marital rape by extending the exemption to include women who rape their husbands in order to make the exemptions appear "gender neutral."[6] This extension provides a false neutrality to an institution that almost invariably endangers only women's lives.[7] Other states have limited the exemption to exclude, among other exclusions, married partners who live apart.[8] These restrictions on the exemption, however, are a mixed blessing. While the restrictions undoubtedly limit application of the exemption, they further entrench its core rationale: protection of the privacy and integrity of the true marital relationship against legal intervention justifies whatever burden forced sex imposes on a married woman's safety and privacy. Furthermore, movements in other states to extend the marital rape exemption offset these limits. For example, some states have extended the marital rape exemption to include cohabitants and formerly married persons.[9]

This progression of one-step-forward, two-steps-backward on the criminalization of marital rape illustrates the general pattern of thinking in the 1980s regarding marital rape. While virtually every progressive commentator, judge, or legislator (feminist and otherwise) who seriously has considered the issue has readily concluded that these laws violate equal protection,[10] and while explicit vocal support from conservatives for the exemption almost entirely has disappeared from scholarly literature,[11] no major upheaval of the law reflects or foreshadows such progressive unanimity. No congressional action, or any Supreme Court analogue to *Brown v. Board of Education*,[12] has enshrined in the country's fundamental law the political judgment that "equal protection of the laws" minimally guarantees an equal protection from the states' criminal codes and enforcement agencies against violent sexual assault, regardless of marital status. In other words, no fundamental legal reform exists to bring these laws into line with what is perceived by commentators to be a constitutional mandate. Thus, the change in social consciousness that often follows constitutionally mandated legal reform has not come to fruition. Those who understand the exemption view it as an antiquated holdover from an earlier and discarded view of women.[13] But the educated public, and even the legal community, lacks general awareness that these laws do not merely inflict extensive damage on innumerable women's lives, but they also constitute a constitutional outrage.

Later in this chapter,[14] I will briefly summarize and endorse the conclusion of the feminist writers and progressive courts that have considered the issue: the marital rape exemption unconstitutionally denies married women Fourteenth Amendment equal protection rights.[15] That argument, however, is not the central concern of this chapter. For the most part, I will assume, rather than argue, that a state's refusal to protect married women against violent sexual assault is unconstitutional. Instead, I want to use the marital rape laws and the movements directed toward their reform to raise two related issues about equal protection ideology and equality theory. The first issue is theoretical; the second is strategic.

The theoretical issue is the following: Why is it that this overwhelmingly obvious constitutional flaw in our criminal law has not, in the last ten years, attracted more attention, generated more outrage, and simply collapsed of its own unconstitutional weight? Why, after several decades of case law and academic commentary on the meaning, original intent, and political vision embodied in the equal protection guarantee of the Fourteenth Amendment, do we still have marital rape exemptions, the express purpose of which is to deprive married women of the state's protection against rape? My argument will be that the endurance of marital rape exemptions, despite their apparent unconstitutionality,[16] partly results from the dominant understanding of the meaning of equality and constitutionally guaranteed equal protection. This understanding, particularly as elaborated by the present Supreme Court, obfuscates the unconstitutionality of marital rape exemptions. No matter how unequal the laws are, given the current state of equal protection doctrine, no obvious, compelling argument sustains the conclusion that they are unconstitutional. Consequently, although an emerging consensus indicates that these laws surely must be unconstitutional, no widely agreed on argument sustains that conclusion. The difficulty in presenting a case that demonstrates the blatant unconstitutionality of these laws, however, does not suggest that they are constitutional. Rather, it illustrates the inadequacies and ambiguities in the equality theory within which equal protection arguments must be framed. In other words, the endurance of marital rape exemptions is partly a function of the inadequacy of the dominant or mainstream political theory of equality, which informs dominant legal understandings of the constitutional mandate of equal protection.[17]

This much of the argument should not be surprising or unfamiliar to a feminist audience; feminist and progressive discontent with traditional equality theory and equal protection law reached an all-time high in the 1980s.[18] The endurance of marital rape exemptions simply illustrates the inadequacies in modern equal protection law alleged by feminists and progressives over the last decade. More specifically, however, and perhaps more controversially, I will argue that the inadequate theories of equality and equal protection that we have inherited and that have muted the force of constitutional challenges to the marital rape exemption are not solely the product of the bad faith, sexist, racist, classist, or conservative politics of the Supreme Court justices who authored those doctrines. They are also a product of the adjudicative institutional context in which those theories have evolved. Mainstream views on the meaning of equality and equal protection respond not only to political biases but also to the institutional constraints of their judicial origins. The Supreme Court, and therefore the rest of us, including the feminist community, generally have examined, developed, and debated the meaning of the Fourteenth Amendment equal protection guarantee in the particular context of judicial challenges to state classifications. This adjudicative context, I believe, has skewed and limited our understanding of equal protection and our understanding of how we should make the promise of equal protection a reality. More specifically, our confinement to the judicial forum has truncated a wide range of potential constitutional claims, including the particular claim that marital rape exemptions violate the Fourteenth Amendment.

The strategic issue this chapter addresses concerns the institutional audience of progressive and feminist-informed constitutional arguments. Thus, the suggestion I will make is that we should direct our arguments away from a hypothetical judicial audience and toward a congressional audience. If the dominant understandings of equal protection truly are inadequate, and if judicially developed law has determined the content of those inadequate understandings, then "equal protection" might take on a very different and more helpful meaning if developed in a congressional, rather than a judicial, context. That very different meaning might highlight, rather than obfuscate, the unconstitutionality of the marital rape exemptions. Congress might respond more aggressively than the Court to the unconstitutionality of marital rape exemptions, not only because of the different political compositions of the Court and Congress, but also because equal protection as a political principle guiding Congress might carry a broader meaning than does equal protection as a legal principle binding the Court.

The second section of this chapter discusses three contrasting understandings of the meaning of equal protection: the Supreme Court's dominant rationality approach; Catharine MacKinnon's proposed dissident "antisubordination" approach; and, as discussed in Chapter 1, what I label the pure protection understanding, which may be closest to the original meaning of the clause.[19] The third section will then reexamine the constitutionality of marital rape exemptions in light of these competing views of the meaning of equal protection.[20] The chapter will posit that even if we accept the traditional, "rationality" model of equal protection, marital rape exemptions are unconstitutional. The arguments, however, are relatively weak because of the content of the rationality model itself. Alternatively, if we understand equal protection in either the antisubordinationist sense (that no state shall participate in the social subordination of one group by another) or in the historical protectionist sense (that no state shall deny to any group of citizens the protection of its police power against criminal assault), then marital rape exemptions clearly are unconstitutional. Judicial adherence to the rationality model of equal protection, consequently, obfuscates this unconstitutionality and obstructs, or at least impedes, the abolition of these harmful exemptions.

The fourth section then demonstrates that the dominant but inadequate rationality view of equality is largely a product of the adjudicative context in which that theory arose.[21] In spite of the Supreme Court's rejection of them over the last few decades, the antisubordinationist and protectionist equal protection theories, from time to time, have been understood as the primary meaning of the clause. However, their collective mandate—that no state shall perpetuate, encourage, or insulate the social subordination of one group of citizens by another by withholding from the subordinated group the protection of its law—historically has been met through congressional, rather than judicial, action.[22] Finally, the fifth section urges feminists, over the next decade, not only to continue to press the Court to rule against these laws on the basis of their irrationality but also to urge Congress to respond to the mandate of section 5 of the Fourteenth

Amendment by passing appropriate federal legislation,[23] the purpose of which would be to guarantee all women full protection of the country's laws against criminal assault.

Three Theories of Equality

THE RATIONALITY MODEL

The dominant judicial interpretation of the equal protection clause is that the clause generally seeks to ensure that legislators govern in a fair-handed and well-motivated way, rather than out of a malicious desire to hurt some groups or a biased desire to help others.[24] Of course, all legislation unavoidably burdens some groups while helping others, but the Constitution requires the legislative allocation of those burdens and benefits to be directed toward legitimate governmental ends. Accordingly, legislation must be rational, or evenhanded: legislation must not be the product of bias, malice, or differing levels of concern for some citizens over others. Rather, legislation and the classifications of legislation must be rationally related to legitimate state ends. In accord with general usage, I call this dominant view the *rationality model* of equal protection.[25]

The rationality model, as it has developed doctrinally, imposes three easily summarized constraints on legislative classifications.[26] First, as the name of the model implies, legislative classifications must be rational: "like groups must be treated alike." Thus, a legislative classification that defines groups A and B, divides them, and then treats them differently must "map on to" or "mirror" a distinction in the world between groups A and B that is relevant to some legitimate state objective. If no relevant difference between groups A and B exists, then legislation that treats them differently is irrational and unconstitutional because it denies the citizens in the burdened group equal protection of the laws. For example, if a statute prohibits minors under the age of 16 from applying for driver's licenses, some "real world" difference must exist between those under and over 16 that correlates with some legitimate state objective. In other words, some correlation must exist between maturity and propensity to drive safely. If no such correlation exists, that is evidence that an irrational desire to burden young teenagers must have motivated the legislators rather than a legitimate governmental aim. Because most of us generally accept the notion of a correlation between maturity and driving ability, the cut-off age seems to be constitutionally unassailable, at least on rationality grounds.

The rationality model imposes a second constraint on classification. The legislative classification must be relevant to a legitimate end. If the classification furthers a legitimate state objective only marginally or not at all and imposes a significant cost on the burdened class, then the legislation might be unconstitutional. Applying this requirement to the driving statute and assuming that age correlates with driving ability, the exclusion of those under 16 from the driving population must further sufficiently the legitimate goal of driving safety in order to justify the burden placed on teenagers—the lack of mobility. Again, because most people would feel fairly confident that the exclusion does improve driving safety and because we are not terribly concerned about obstacles to teenage mobility, the driving statute passes the relevance requirement just as it did the rationality requirement.

Finally, the rationality model requires that the articulated legislative end be a legitimate one. Legislators may classify and differentially assist or burden certain groups, but only if they are doing so in the public interest or toward the vindication of some public value. Moreover, the end toward which the classification is directed must be an end that legislators are permitted to pursue. Legislators may not classify for the malicious satisfaction of hurting one sector of the community while helping another. The driving statute survives this final test, for public safety surely is a legitimate legislative end. The statute, therefore, is not aimed at maliciously burdening young teenagers.

These three basic principles of rationality, relevance, and legitimacy provide the foundation for modern equal protection jurisprudence. These three constraints motivated the Court to adopt various levels of "scrutiny" for different types of legislation. The rationality, relevance, and legitimacy requirements also explain the peculiarities of Supreme Court doctrine regarding legislation that classifies on the basis of gender[27] and the "intent" requirement that facially neutral legislation that adversely impacts upon a particular group must meet.[28] A brief summary of these three doctrinal areas reveals the Court's general commitment to rationality.

First, the logic of the Court's two-tiered, or heightened versus low-level, review more or less follows directly from rationality principles. Under the rationality, relevance, and legitimacy principles just summarized, the Court has conceded that most economic or social legislation is presumptively rational, relevant to legitimate governmental ends, and, hence, constitutional.[29] After all, relevance, rationality, and legitimacy, are all relative qualities, and the Court has developed a pattern of general deference to legislative judgment in the economic and social spheres. Classifications that involve race, however, are entirely another matter. The Court generally has held that most racially explicit classifications are presumptively suspect, and, therefore, their rationality, their relevance, and their legitimacy must be strictly scrutinized.[30] Such strict scrutiny typically has resulted in the invalidation of these statutes.[31] Racial classifications presumptively fail to mirror a real distinction in the world between the classes they categorize and presumptively fail to further legitimate governmental ends. Hence, blacks and whites possess no inherent real differences, and the Court finds irrational legislative classifications that create differences between blacks and whites. Further, such classifications, whether rational or not, are relevant to no legitimate ends.[32] Thus, the Court routinely engages in a heavy presumption that racial classifications are not good-faith attempts to classify based on real world differences that are relevant to legitimate goals. Rather, the Court views these classifications as badly motivated attempts to burden already disadvantaged subordinate groups.

The Court seems to believe that gender classifications fall somewhere between economic classifications (presumptively legitimate) and racial classifications (presumptively illegitimate). According to the Court, some biological and social "real differences" between men and women do exist; consequently, some legislative classifications that distinguish men and women may be rational.[33] Further, women have not been targeted as a class in the same way as blacks have, and, therefore, the Court does not as readily presume that gendered classifications are badly motivated.[34] Unlike racial classifications, gender classifications are not necessarily irrational, and the ends toward which they aim are not necessarily illegitimate. Thus, the judicial scrutiny that the Court applies to gender classifications is higher than that which the Court applies to economic legislation, but not as strict as that which the Court applies to racial classifications. While the Court has struck down some gender-based statutes,[35] it has upheld more than a few.[36]

Finally, as the Court held in *Washington v. Davis*,[37] legislation that does not facially discriminate between men and women or whites and blacks, but nevertheless adversely affects the interests of persons in those classes, is not, for that reason alone, unconstitutional.[38] Rather, facially neutral legislation is unconstitutional only if the law-making body intended its adverse impact.[39] This "intent" requirement with respect to Fourteenth Amendment challenges to race-neutral or gender-neutral legislation also can be derived from the Court's general commitment to rationality as the goal of equal protection and irrationality as the targeted evil. Under the rationality model, a general rule applied to all equally will not be found irrational because the burden of the rule falls more heavily on one group than on another. Instead, a rule is irrational only if the rule treats similarly situated groups differently. Such rules will adversely affect some groups because of the differential situation of the burdened groups: the rule treats differently situated groups similarly rather than similarly situated groups differently. However, if irrationality means the differential treatment of similar groups, then evenhanded treatment of different groups, regardless of its impact, is neither rational nor irrational, but simply different. Furthermore, no obvious reason compels doubt of the authors' motives of such race-neutral or gender-neutral legislation or the legitimacy of the ends the offending legislation purportedly serves. Thus, the holding in *Washington v. Davis* could be restated in this way: legislation that adversely injures blacks or women, but does so in spite of its facial evenhandedness, violates neither notions of "logical rationality" (that likes be treated alike) nor norms of "ethical rationality" (that legislation be nonmalicious in its origin and general in its societal impact). Therefore, for such legislation to violate Fourteenth Amendment norms, the challenger must show a specific legislative intent to harm. Absent a showing of specific intent, the Court will uphold a facially neutral statute as constitutional.

THE ATTACK ON FORMAL EQUALITY
AND THE RATIONALITY MODEL

The central judicial presumption of the rationality model—that racial classifications always are irrational and that gender classifications usually are irrational—rests on a theory of equality grounded in a universalist vision of our shared human nature. That vision is unquestionably noble and appealing in its aspiration. Its guiding assumption is that all persons—women, men, blacks, whites, and others—are more or less the same with respect to the traits and issues that affect or should affect political decision making.[40] Women as well as men, and blacks as well as whites, wish to lead and can lead meaningful lives ennobled by participation in the shared, political life of the public sphere, enriched by fairly compensated and intrinsically rewarding work in the private sphere, and enlivened by stimulating, nurturant relationships in the intimate sphere. Blacks no less than whites, and women no less than men, benefit from the liberal arts and educational opportunities deepening intellectual adult life. Blacks and women, like whites and men, need and value opportunities to develop athletic potential. Many women, like many men, treasure and pursue the opportunity to enlist in the country's armed services and willingly devote their lives to strengthening the country's defense capabilities against outside aggression. Women, like men, and blacks, like whites, can be competent and fair jurors, estate executors, lawyers, and doctors. The list could be extended endlessly. Legislation that classifies on the basis of gender or race and that burdens women's or blacks' political, economic, athletic, or educational opportunities in any sphere in which women and men and blacks and whites are similarly situated is irrational, and hence unconstitutional. The universalist vision promotes this formal or legal ideal of equality and provides the basis for the rationality interpretation of the equal protection clause. In all areas of life in which blacks and whites and women and men are the same, the legislator must treat them as the same.

During the 1980s, feminist legal theorists registered increasing dissatisfaction with the rationalist model of equal protection, the formal or legal vision of equality toward which it aspires, and the universalist conception of human nature in which it is rooted.[41] Such feminist dissatisfaction with formal equality stems not so much from a suspicion that the Court's practice cannot live up to the promise of equal treatment, but from the nature of the promise itself. Formal equality—across-the-board equal treatment of women and men—would have only a limited effect on women's lives for two basic reasons. First, women and men are not similar, the universalist premises of the rationality model notwithstanding. To summarize a great deal of recent feminist writings: women have different perceptions and experiences of the social world,[42] different understandings or moral obligations,[43] different biological roles in reproduction,[44] different ways of assimilating knowledge,[45] different feelings toward housework and childraising,[46] different vulnerabilities toward different potential harms,[47] different life patterns,[48] and a radically different history.[49] Insistence upon the "sameness" of men and women in the face of undeniable differences between them and social subordination of women by men enshrines male attributes as the "norm" and denies the existence and value of female attributes, pursuits, and ways of life.[50] Any constitutional standard based on the theory that men and women are the same will benefit only those women least in need of the law's protection—women, such as the professional women of the 1980s, who already are most like men.[51] Formal equality will ignore or even hurt those women least like men: traditional homemakers and women trapped in low-paying and gender-segregated jobs.[52] Finally, formal equality is irrelevant to all women in those spheres of our lives in which we are most clearly unlike men: our more marked vulnerability to sexual assault, our greater involvement in childraising and housework, and our different role in the reproductive process. The rationality model fails because it rests on a false assumption of sameness and aspires toward a goal of similar treatment that will help only marginally a few already privileged women. Its consequence will be not true equality but further harm to most women.[53]

This "sameness-difference" problem with the dominant rationality model has prompted several feminists, notably Christine Littleton, to advocate a modification or reform of the rationality doctrine itself.[54] Littleton has argued that equality should mean not just treating groups the same when they are the same, but also treating them differently when they are different, and doing so in such a way as to ensure a rough equality of outcomes.[55] Under this modified view of the rationality model of equality, which Littleton calls the *equal acceptance model,* the equal protection clause requires legislators to be "equally accepting" of men and women.[56] If women are the same as men in certain aspects, they should be treated similarly. But in aspects in which women and men differ, the law should be as equally responsive to men's and women's differing characteristics, attributes, needs, values, vulnerabilities, and aspirations. The impulse behind the "acceptance" picture of equality is strikingly feminist: the acceptance model requires legislators not only to treat like groups alike, but also to refrain from inscribing the imprimatur of "normalcy" on male attributes, characteristics, preferences, and modes of life.

Other feminists, notably Catharine MacKinnon, Ruth Colker, and Mary Becker,[57] argue that the rationality model has a deeper problem that Littleton's reform, although well-meaning and welcome, failed to address. The second problem with the rationality model is not just that women are different from men in ways that formal equality ignores, but that formal equality itself, whether or not modified by Littleton's acceptance amendment, targets the wrong evil.[58] Irrationality, or treating like groups differently, should not be the target of the equal protection clause, nor should rationality, treating like groups alike, be regarded as its goal. Rather, anti-subordinationists argue that the social subordination of some groups by others (women by men and blacks by whites) is the target of the equal protection clause. Hence, only substantive equality between these groups, or the end of social subordination, is its goal.[59] The rationality model fails to target the social, economic, and political differences that account for women's subordinate status. A constitutional mandate that legislation must presume a sameness between men and women in the face of massive inequality will be simply irrelevant to the true causes and nature of women's inequality or will backfire and harm rather than help women. Becker explained the consequences of formal equality:

> Formal equality . . . can effect only limited change. It cannot, for example, ensure that jobs are structured so that female workers and male workers are equally able to combine wage work and parenthood. Nor can it ensure that social security, unemployment compensation, and other safety nets are structured so as to provide for women's financial security as well as they provide for men's. Moreover, women, especially ordinary mothers and wives, have been harmed by the changes effected to date by the movement towards formal equality. Further movement in that direction could bring additional harm. Any other satisfactory and workable general standard to be applied by judges is as yet unimagined and likely to be so for the foreseeable future.[60]

ALTERNATIVE UNDERSTANDINGS OF EQUAL PROTECTION: ANTISUBORDINATION AND PURE PROTECTION

As discussed in Chapter 1, the critiques of the rationality model just summarized have given rise to a second, and dissident, understanding of the mandate of equal protection. MacKinnon has delineated this second understanding with great force and eloquence in her writings.[61] Often called the *antisubordination model* of equal protection, this view perceives the equality that equal protection guarantees as substantive, not formal. Hence, the test of legislation under the equal protection clause is not whether the legislative classification "fits" a preexisting reality, but whether the classification furthers the subordination of women vis-à-vis men or attempts to end that subordination. MacKinnon explained the antisubordination model:

> [The] only question for litigation is whether the policy or practice in question integrally contributes to the maintenance of an underclass or a deprived position because of gender status. This disadvantage which constitutes the injury of discrimination is not the failure to be treated "without regard to" one's sex; that is the injury of arbitrary differentiation. The unfairness lies in being deprived because of being

a woman or a man, a deprivation given meaning in the social context of the dominance or preference of one sex over the other.[62]

The antisubordination model, then, aspires not to formal equality, but to substantive equality. The goal is not a world in which state legislators treat men and women "the same," but rather a world in which men and women, whether the same or different, are social equals. The antisubordination model envisions a world in which women are no more vulnerable to assault than men are, no less valued than men are, no more underpaid than men are, no less cared for than men are, no less represented than men are, and no less participatory in the public sphere than men are. In sharp contrast to the rationality model, the antisubordination model rests not on a universalist vision of our "shared" human nature, but on a political vision of our present unequal social reality.[63] For constitutional purposes, the relevant issue is decidedly not that women are "the same" as men but are treated differently or that women are different from men and are treated the same. The relevant issue is that women are subordinate to men in the public social, economic, private, and intimate spheres. Thus, the aim of the equal protection clause should be to highlight and rectify that political reality and not to highlight and mirror similarities or differences between men and women. Legislation that promotes or encourages social equality is constitutional, but that which promotes or encourages social subordination is unconstitutional.[64]

A third possible understanding of equal protection that has received relatively little attention in either feminist commentary or cases, but which may be closer to the plain meaning, intent, and history of the clause than either the rationality or the antisubordination models, is that discussed in Chapter 1, what I call the *pure protection model.* As argued in that chapter, to deny equal protection might mean that a state refuses to grant to some citizens the protection against private wrongdoing that it grants to others. For example, a state's refusal to protect black citizens from homicidal attacks by whites or a state's passivity in the face of widespread lynching and private violence would constitute a paradigmatic violation of the constitutional guarantee of equal protection of the law. Similarly, as Justice Bradley suggested in *The Civil Rights Cases,*[65] a southern state's refusal to grant a common law cause of action to black travelers to protect them against southern white innkeepers' refusals of service would constitute a violation of the equal protection clause.[66]

In this century, for northern as well as southern municipalities to provide less-than-adequate police protection against violent crime in poorer parts of a city might constitute a denial of the equal protection of the law under the pure protection model. Likewise, for a municipality to employ an all-white police force hostile to the concerns, fears, and interests of black neighborhoods might constitute an equal protection violation. Therefore, under the pure protection model, no less than under the antisubordination model, *Washington v. Davis* is clearly wrong. The pure protection model views the target of the equal protection clause as the denial of the state's protection to some of its citizens from private violence, aggression, and wrongdoing. The goal is a community in which all are equally protected by the state against private encroachment of rights.

The Constitutionality of the Marital Rape Exemption

Predictably, most of the scholarly commentary and virtually all of the judicial opinions that have addressed the constitutionality of marital rape exemptions have analyzed the constitutionality of marital rape exemptions under the rationality model of equality and equal protection.[67] The commentary and opinions illustrate not just the strength and sensibility of the rationality model, but also the problems and limits of its formal vision of equality, its universalist vision of human nature, and its doctrinal tests of "rationality." These arguments take several different forms, depending on whether the law under scrutiny is gender-specific (exempts wives from rape laws) or gender-neutral (exempts "spouses"). A summary of these arguments follows.

First, some states employ marital rape exemptions that are explicitly gendered: rape is defined as nonconsensual intercourse with a woman other than one's wife.[68] The two-step argument that these gender-specific statutes are unconstitutional is straightforward. First, such gender-specific statutes explicitly legislate on the basis of either gender alone or gender plus marital status. Either classification constitutes a suspect class giving rise to at least the mid-level scrutiny.[69] As the Supreme Court has noted on multiple occasions, women have been the objects of stereotypical and stultifying thinking that has seriously compromised their enjoyment of and participation in the public world.[70] For that reason alone, legislation that treats women different from men deserves heightened scrutiny.[71] Furthermore, although the Court never has held as much, historically, oppressive treatment renders married women a suspect class. In American and English common law heritage, the law did not acknowledge a married woman's existence.[72] Thus, a law that burdens either women or married women, and marital rape exemptions can do both, should be subject to heightened scrutiny.

Second, under a heightened scrutiny, if the gender-specific legislation is to be sustained, the state must articulate an "important governmental interest" that is "substantially related" to the statutory classification.[73] This articulation, the argument proceeds, a state cannot possibly do. Proponents of the marital rape exemption typically assert that the state's important interest in promoting marital harmony and intimacy, or, alternatively, its interest in encouraging reconciliation of warring spouses, justifies the statute.[74] Yet, the state undeniably has little or no legitimate interest in protecting the harmony or intimacy of a marriage deteriorated to the point of violent sexual abuse, and it has equally as little interest in encouraging the reconciliation of spouses whose relations no longer are consensual, much less harmonious.[75] Thus, because these statutory classifications are not "substantially related" to an important governmental interest, gender-specific marital exemption laws are unconstitutional.

On the other hand, marital exemptions that define rape as nonconsensual sex with anyone except one's spouse, rather than nonconsensual sex with anyone except one's wife, are gender-neutral. While these statutes avoid the heightened scrutiny triggered by gender-explicit classifications, they nevertheless also are unconstitutional under traditional rationality standards. A gender-neutral classification that adversely impacts on women and appears to be motivated by an intention to hurt women is as unconstitutional as is a sex-specific classification.[76] Marital rape exemptions are strikingly easy to trace to misogynist roots, from Matthew Hale's infamous argument that a married woman is presumed to consent to all marital sex and, therefore, cannot be raped,[77] to the common law's assumption that marriage results in the unification of husband and wife and that marital rape thus constitutes rape of oneself, a legal impossibility.[78] Whether cleansed through the filter of sex-neutral language or not, the marital rape exemption clearly is rooted in an intention to deprive the married woman of the protection of the state and to subject her to the will, sovereignty, and unchecked violence of her spouse. Because this intention serves no "important governmental interest," gender-neutral marital rape exemptions are unconstitutional as well.

Furthermore, whether gender-specific or gender-neutral, marital rape exemptions create a host of irrational distinctions that underscore their unconstitutionality: between married couples and unmarried couples who cohabitate; between married, but estranged partners still living together and married partners living apart (who often are not included in the scope of the exemption); between partners who have filed for divorce and those who have not; and between partners who have indicated their intentions to end the marital union and those who have not.[79] Apart from the effects of the marital rape exemption on women, and even granting the importance of the state's interest in protecting marital harmony, these distinctions are irrational. What rational, legitimate state goal could possibly justify the lines drawn between these groups?

Paradoxically, perhaps the strongest traditional, rationality-based argument against marital rape exemptions has not appeared in case law. This argument asserts that these statutes create an irrational distinction between married women and all other persons and that this distinction is not justified by real differences between those two groups. The classification and differential treatment of married women rests on the assumption that married women, unlike all other persons, have no interest in receiving protection from the state against violent and sexual assault. But, married women, exactly like men and unmarried women, clearly need physical security in their private spheres. As is true for all human beings, without the security and dignity of knowing that the state ensures their protection, women cannot lead autonomous, meaningful, and pleasurable lives. Married women need to know that sexual assault against them is criminal and punishable when committed by their husbands. For that matter, they need to know that sexual assault is as criminal when committed against them as would be any intrafamilial crime of violence. The irrational distinction of the marital rape exemption is between the protected needs and rights of the average citizen to be safe from criminal assault and the unprotected same needs and rights of married women. The creation of a class of citizens subject to legalized violence is the core effect, if not the purpose, of the marital rape exemption. Surely, the constitutional guarantee of equal protection must guard against that effect.

Marital rape exemptions, then, are arguably unconstitutional, even under the traditional rationality model of equal protection, for reasons that are at the heart of that model's utopian vision. We do indeed share a common humanity, part of which is to need protection against private violence. Women are as much in need of that protection as are men. Like men, without that protection women are rendered vulnerable to the whim, will, sovereignty, instincts, fiat, and command of those who are stronger.

And, like men, when women are rendered weak, they become incapable of living the kinds of lives the ideal liberal state is surely meant to foster: autonomous, pleasurable, productive, civic, and educated. When state passivity renders women vulnerable to private violence, women, like men, become stunted, fearful, self-alienated, childlike, and servile. Women are no more naturally suited to such servility and dominance than are their brothers, fathers, sons, and husbands.

All of these arguments, however, pose serious doctrinal problems. These problems reflect the inadequacies of the rationality model of equal protection and formal equality that have troubled feminists throughout the 1980s. Simply stated, for each argument catalogued here, a fairly obvious legal rejoinder is available, which is equally, if not better, grounded in modern equal protection doctrine. I am not using a linguistic quirk or playing a lawyer's game. My point is not the familiar indeterminacy claim that any legal argument gives rise to an equally credible rejoinder. Rather, the doctrinal and legal bases for the legal rejoinders rest on the fundamental, political reality of women's lives: the irreducible fact of women's subordination to men through unchecked sexual violence. The universalist vision and formal equality aspirations of the rationality model of equal protection simply fail to address this reality. Thus, the very existence and viability of these rejoinders evidence the limits and dangers of current understandings of the equal protection clause.

First, the argument for the unconstitutionality of gender-specific rape exemptions just summarized is anything but airtight. As noted earlier, in contrast to the impossible requirement of a compelling state interest required to sustain racially explicit legislation,[80] gender-specific legislation is constitutional if the state can articulate an "important governmental objective" substantially furthered by the gendered classification.[81] Nothing prohibits a court from determining that protection of marital privacy, insularity, and harmony is such an important state interest that protection of the husband against criminal charges of rape substantially furthers that interest.[82] The political reality that the availability of this legal rejoinder reflects is that, to the mainstream, the very sphere of private subordination that harms women and concerns feminists appears to be not just a legitimate, but an important or even compelling state interest. This political reality also reflects a deeper social reality. The obstacles to women's equal participation in public life and enjoyment of private life are so thoroughly ingrained in our societal habits, institutions, and thought patterns that they appear to be the essence of private life, rather than obstacles to equality.

Surely, protecting the allure of romance, the domain of sentiment, and the pleasures of intimacy is a compelling state interest. The bottom line is that the same reality experienced by the raped wife as a daily ritual of violence, abuse, and horror strikes the feminist as unconscionable state passivity in the face of private subordination and strikes the feminist lawyer as the denial of equal protection. But it could conceivably appear to a court as an "important" or "compelling" state interest in marital privacy, marital harmony, and spousal reconciliation.

The argument for the unconstitutionality of gender-neutral marital rape exemptions also rests on shaky ground.[83] The legal uncertainty reflects not the uncertainty or indeterminacy of legal arguments generally, but rather societal ambivalence toward women's equality. Gender-neutral marital rape exemptions undoubtedly are the product of a history of discriminatory attitudes toward women.[84] Nevertheless, a court conceivably could decide that, ancient history notwithstanding, a statute recently cleansed of gender-specific language is freed of its misogynist heritage and that its recent legislative history provides the sole source of its constitutionality. Surely one could argue that gender-neutral marital rape exemptions, similar to the one in the Model Penal Code[85] endorsed in 1989, rest not on a desire to harm women, but on a desire to protect the institution of marriage.

As evidenced by this theory, the presumption that the gender-neutral marital rape exemptions are constitutional because they respect the sameness of men and women ignores the very real differences between husbands and wives. Women and men are very differently situated within marriage. Overwhelmingly, husbands are larger, stronger, and wealthier than wives. A gender-neutral statute that treats spouses similarly by according them the same immunities from rape prosecution and hence the same vulnerability to marital rape ignores these crucial differences and perpetuates the marital subordination of women. As many feminists suggest, in light of the societal differences between women and men, the presumption of fairness and constitutionality on universalist grounds typically accorded gender-neutral statutes may be generally unwarranted.[86] In the case of marital rape exemptions, however, the presumption of sameness in the face of life-threatening differences looks not unwarranted but grotesque.

Most important, the arguable constitutionality of all marital rape exemptions, both gender-specific and gender-neutral, vividly exemplifies the antisubordinationist reservations about the rationality model of equal protection. The rationality arguments that underlie traditional equal protection analysis are doctrinally unstable, but they also overlook the terrifying injustice of these statutes—for precisely the reasons MacKinnon's, Colker's, and Becker's critiques of formal equality suggest. Indeed, the virtue of rationality and the vice of irrationality is worse than irrelevant to the real injustice of these exemptions. After all, rationality problems with these statutes can and sometimes have been cured by extending rather than eliminating the scope of the exception. If married couples and cohabitants cannot rationally be treated differently, the marital rape exemption should be extended to include cohabitants.[87] By the same perverse logic, if married women and unmarried women cannot rationally be treated differently, rape law should be eliminated altogether. At the extreme, if married women and all other persons cannot rationally be treated differently, the criminal sanction should be eliminated. Presumably, these arguments would and should fail, but a model of equal protection that implies their coherence is profoundly wrong.

The irrationality of marital rape exemptions is not their fundamental flaw. The evil flaw of these exemptions is not that they irrationally treat married couples different from cohabitants, or married women different from unmarried women, or husbands different from rapists unacquainted with their victims, or women different from men. The evil is that they legalize, and hence legitimate, a form of violence that does inestimable damage to all women, not only to those who are raped. In addition to the obvious violence, brutality, and terror marital rape exemptions facilitate, marital rape exemptions, like the rapes they legalize, sever the central connection to selfhood that links a woman's pleasure with her desires, will, and actions.[88] The will of the married woman who learns to accept routinized rape is no longer ruled by or even connected to her desires. Eventually, her desires are no longer a product of what she enjoys or what she has learned to enjoy. What the victim of routinized rape within marriage does, sexually, is a product not of what the victim wills but of what her attacker demands; as an immediate consequence, her will becomes a function not of her desires but of his desires. Eventually her desires become a function not of her pleasures, but of his pleasures: she wants literally to please him rather than herself because to please herself is too dangerous. The victim of marital rape gains survival, but she sacrifices self-sovereignty. In other words, she sacrifices the ability to control her own will and to determine her own actions, pleasures, and desires free from external influence. In short, she sacrifices selfhood.[89]

To call the damage occasioned by statutes protecting this direct sub-

ordination of self to the necessity of survival an irrationality is simply
wrong. The damage occasioned by these statutes is the subordination,
and in many cases the annihilation, of the psychic, physical, emotional,
and erotic female self. Under a rationality model, this clear fact entirely
escapes constitutional notice. The exemption is constitutional if rational
and unconstitutional if irrational. Surely, the state acts irrationally when it
complies with this profoundly personal, violent subordination. The determination of rationality depends on the court's assessment of the importance
of the state's goals. If the state wants to pursue the goal of marital privacy,
harmony, and spousal reconciliation at the cost of female self-sovereignty,
and if the court decides that the goal of marital privacy is important (which
surely it could), then the marital rape exemption is an eminently rational, hence constitutional, way to achieve this goal. But, whether the law
is rational or irrational, the state's complicity in this pervasive regime of
private domestic violence is clearly unequal. It denies married women, in
the most literal sense, the protection of its laws. The rationality model of
equal protection quite dramatically fails to target the state's complicity in
this subordinating annihilation of married women's selfhood.

In contrast, both the evil and the inequality perpetuated by marital rape
exemptions become strikingly apparent under either the dissident antisubordination or historical pure protection model of equal protection.
Under the antisubordination model, a state action violates the Fourteenth
Amendment guarantee if the state complies with the subordination of
women by men.[90] Without question, marital rape exemptions do precisely
that. The antisubordination model locates the target of the Fourteenth
Amendment equal protection guarantee, not in the irrationality of a state's
legislative scheme, but in a state's complicity in private or social subordination. When the state encourages or permits a significant increase in the
illegitimate power of one social group over another, it defies the safeguards
of the equal protection clause. The marital rape exemption is an instance
of state complicity in men's subordination of women through routinized
violent sexual assault and the threat of violent assault. Each assault spurs
self-denial, self-abnegation, and self-diminution for women and furthers
political ratification of women's psychological and psychic subservience.
Each assault constitutes a political act of subordination. Under the antisubordination model, even state complicity, not to mention explicit state
endorsement, in this private subordination is clearly unconstitutional.

Similarly, the pure protection model highlights the unconstitutionality of
these statutes rather than obscures it. This model recognizes that the Four-

teenth Amendment ensures that all citizens equally enjoy the basic terms of the social contract and that the state protects all from private assault, protects all from their own vulnerability, recognizes the equality of all citizens under law, and assures that all live under no separate sovereign authority.[91] Only with such protection may persons construct the public, productive, responsible, autonomous lives that the liberal state envisions. A marital rape exemption, regardless of its intent, its history, or its purported state purpose, creates precisely the insulated, separate sphere of sovereignty that the pure protection view of the equal protection clause forbids. With the exemption in place, a marriage becomes not a nurturant, safe haven offering shelter from the storm, but a separate political world in which the husband is sovereign and the wife subject. Moreover, her vulnerability to this organized, dehumanizing, and alienating violence is fully legitimated by the state under which she lives. Sexual force and violence within marriage is unleashed and legalized, and legalized force and violence, of course, are the precondition of political power. A marriage thus becomes a separate state of sovereignty. The marital rape exemption creates, fosters, and encourages not marital intimacy, harmony, or reconciliation, but a separate state of sovereignty ungoverned by law and insulated from state interference. Whatever other "legitimate" goals the state may thereby further, such a separate political order, under a pure protection model, precisely is what the Fourteenth Amendment forbids the states to tolerate.

Rationality, Antisubordination, and Equal Protection:
Institutional Responsibilities for Enforcement
of the Fourteenth Amendment

In summary, equal protection lends itself to three different interpretations: (1) a rationality model, which targets legislative classifications that are irrational or irrelevant to legitimate state goals; (2) an antisubordination model, which targets legislation that substantively contributes to the subordination of one group by another; and (3) a pure protection model, which targets a state's failure to grant protection of its law to all citizens equally, thus failing to ensure that all citizens are subject equally to one and only one sovereign, namely the sovereignty of the rule of law. Marital rape exemptions are unconstitutional under all of these approaches. However, the argument for that conclusion under the rationality model is weak, and it obscures, rather than highlights, the most unjust features of marital rape exemptions. The antisubordination and pure protection interpretations of the equal protection clause, by contrast, precisely highlight the most offensive features of marital rape exemptions—not the irrationality of marital rape exemptions, but their legitimation of a regime of private force and organized violence that creates and encourages the male subordination of women and the insulation of a separate and sovereign political regime through which that subordination is effectuated.

These three models, however, do not stand on equal footing. The rationality model, which has without question been a mixed blessing for women, is dominant black-letter law in the area of gender classifications, and the Supreme Court does not seem inclined to change that fact.[92] The antisubordination model of equal protection, although arguably closer to the Warren Court's understanding of the phrase, has played virtually no role in the development of equal protection doctrine over the last twenty years and only an ambiguous role during the previous twenty years. The pure protection model has not influenced equal protection doctrine for over 100 years. Its last judicial acknowledgement may have been in Justice Bradley's decision in 1883 in *The Civil Rights Cases*.[93] Consequently, both the antisubordination model and the pure protection model are only of limited utility. The antisubordination model aids in understanding the ambiguities and tensions in the discrimination law of the 1950s and 1960s, when it commanded some respect from the Warren Court.[94] The pure protection model provides some insight concerning the original intent of the framers of the equal protection clause. For modern purposes, however, these models clearly are dissident interpretive views. They represent what the Court could, but does not, read the equal protection clause to require.

Two questions arise. First, why has the modern court accepted a rationality model of equal protection and rejected the other two alternatives? Second, assuming continuing judicial recalcitrance, can the alternative interpretations of the clause prevail? The answer to the first question may be that the Supreme Court may have accepted the rationality model of equal protection because only that model creates the standard, legalistic issues that courts are well suited and accustomed to answering on a practical, jurisprudential level. If this assertion is correct—if the Court has settled on a rationality model simply because it facilitates judicial analysis—then other branches of government, notably Congress, may be open themselves to antisubordination and pure protection interpretations of their Fourteenth Amendment obligations.

In determining the Court's reason for accepting the rationality model, remember that the Court itself typically insists, in the course of rejecting antisubordinationist arguments, that its reasons for doing so are in large part pragmatic. For example, in *Washington v. Davis,* the most unequivocal rejection of the antisubordinationist model, the Court noted that adoption of such an interpretation of equal protection would invalidate a wide range of regulatory, social, and economic legislation that affects the average black more than it affects the average white.[95] And so it would. By this ruling, the Court clearly implied that, rightly or wrongly, it is unwilling to undertake such an intrusive restructuring of federal and state law. This unwillingness stems not from legal or moral principles, but from pragmatism. The Court itself insists that it simply cannot fulfill the antisubordinationist mandate, given its judicial identity.

Jurisprudential reasons as well may draw the Court to a rationality model of equal protection analysis. The rationality model requires state legislators and lawmakers to "treat like groups alike" and requires courts to see that they do so. Any legislative classification, then, must be based on a difference between the groups that is relevant to a legitimate state interest.[96] The Court's responsibility under the equal protection clause is to police against legislative infringement of this principle. Feminist and progressive antisubordinationist theorists, however, have identified a major defect in this interpretation: it does not challenge or change socially created inequalities between classes, genders, or races.[97] Despite this flaw, the model has an important virtue from a judicial perspective: it limits the Court's role to the familiar one of ensuring legal justice. To do justice, a court must treat like cases alike. For the most part, appellate courts, including the Supreme Court, simply police against lower court infractions of this principle. The rationality model simply imposes an equivalent duty on legislators. Thus, while judges must treat like cases alike, legislators, who deal with groups instead of cases, also must treat like groups alike. The Court's duty under the equal protection clause, then, is to ensure that the legislature metes out equal justice to the groups before it, just as the Court's appellate function is to ensure that lower courts mete out equal justice to the individuals who appear before them. The rationality model of equal protection may be the only model that so neatly dovetails with the most traditional, and even classical, view of judicial functions and domain.[98]

By construing the equal protection clause as a source of "law" to be applied by courts, the general legal culture may have to a considerable degree determined its meaning, not only because we have rendered it subject to the Court's own sense of the pragmatic limits of its powers, but also because of the nature of law. As long as courts interpret and enforce the equal protection clause, it should not be surprising that they interpret the clause as requiring "legal justice," or like groups must be treated alike, rather than distributive or even compensatory justice. There is no reason to think that the Supreme Court is not fully confident of its ability to oversee the quality of formal, legal justice dispensed by lower courts: that is the Court's traditional, appellate function. The rationality model of the Fourteenth Amendment extends the obligation of doing legal justice to legislators, but it makes absolutely no fundamental change in the Court's social role. In this area as in any other, the Court continues to oversee the quality of legal justice meted out by other institutional and governmental bodies. Consequently, the ultimate judicial embrace of the rationality model, including the formal understanding of the requirement of legal justice, the antidiscrimination principle, the intent requirement, the two-tiered or three-tiered levels of review, and the "real differences" rule in the gender cases, may have been inevitable, regardless of the political composition of the Court. The Court simply may be unable and unwilling to sustain, for any length of time, any reading of equal protection that would be less legalistic and more substantive.

The appropriate question to ask, then, may be not whether the Court will adopt a more aggressive stance toward equal protection, but whether nonjudicial enforcement of alternative meanings of the equal protection clause is possible. The answer we give to that question depends in large part on whether we view the Supreme Court as the exclusive, as well as the ultimate interpreter of the Constitution.[99] That is, a connection may exist between a pluralistic approach to constitutional meaning and a pluralistic approach to constitutional obligations. Let me first explain these admittedly awkward labels.

Under a pluralistic rather than unitary conception of constitutional meanings, a constitutional mandate might have several obligatory meanings. Under a pluralistic approach to constitutional meaning, the equal protection clause might require (1) that legislative classifications treat like groups alike; (2) that legislation not insulate or further the social subordination of women, blacks, or other suspect classes; and (3) that states ensure that all citizens enjoy the protection of its laws against private wrongdoing. In contrast, under a unitary approach, a constitutional phrase will have only one obligatory meaning. While equal protection might logically mean a range of things, and while its meaning might change over time, only one meaning at any particular time will be binding law. To put the question formally, then, the issue is why have we embraced a unitary approach to constitutional meaning that has rendered antisubordinationist and pure protection understandings of equality dead letters?

One reason may be that if the Court is the exclusive and ultimate interpreter of constitutional meaning, connotative pluralism is awkward, to say the least. Under a unitary approach to institutional obligation, which identifies the judiciary as the branch of government obligated to enforce it, the Constitution means that which the Court says it means and only that which the Court says it means. A unitary approach to meaning follows practically, if not logically, from a unitary approach to obligation. If, on the other hand, we expand our conception of who and what is obligated to ensure equal protection under the Fourteenth Amendment, then pluralistic conceptions of equal protection meaning begin to look plausible. The Court could continue to ensure that legislation treat like groups alike. However, Congress could ensure that state laws prohibit subordination. Lastly, the executive branch and Congress jointly could ensure that the states supply the fundamental benefits and burdens of the social contract to all citizens equally. The state would provide security against private violence and wrongdoing in exchange for abidance with the obligations of citizenry under a rule of law regime.

If we change our constitutional habits and learn to think pluralistically about the potential meanings of the Fourteenth Amendment, along with the potential obligations the amendment imparts on all three branches of government, then we might recognize a wider range of governmental actions as instances of constitutional decision making.[100] More important, though, if we think pluralistically not just about possible meanings, but also about possible sources of enforcement, an expansive understanding of the equality guaranteed under the Fourteenth Amendment might one day become a social reality.

A Justification For Congressional Action

Whether or not the United States Supreme Court or state supreme courts ever rule on the unconstitutionality of marital rape exemptions, Congress has the power, the authority, and arguably the duty, to do so, under section 5 of the Fourteenth Amendment.[101] Congress could enact a federal law guaranteeing protection to all women against violent sexual assault. Consistent with rationality requirements, this law would prohibit irrational discrimination against married women in the making and enforcement of rape laws. This federal law also would guarantee, consistent with the antisubordination mandate of the Fourteenth Amendment, that states would not perpetuate or insulate the sexualized social, private, or intimate subordination of women by men. Lastly, consistent with the "protection" mandate of the Fourteenth Amendment, it would guarantee that no state would deny to women protection of the state against private criminality. The political will may or may not be sufficient to sustain such a bill, but the constitutional authority for it surely exists.

A law of this sort at least would remove the anomaly that, while the marital rape exemptions strike most concerned lawyers and legal academicians as spectacularly unconstitutional, under present doctrine, no clearcut argument presents itself. Perhaps the main reason for this lag between consensus, argument, and action is logistic. Given a court-based system of constitutional adjudication in which courts have near exclusive responsibility for interpreting and enforcing constitutional law, cases that properly raise issues of this sort will be extremely rare. Thus, when a rape defendant raises the issue of the unconstitutionality of the marital rape exemption he is likely to be arguing that the state's refusal to extend the exemption to him, is an unconstitutional denial of his equal protection rights.[102] A court could respond to this sort of argument by striking the exemption in its entirety.[103] However, a court faced with this argument could avoid ruling on the constitutionality of the exemption by simply rejecting the contention that the failure of the state to extend the exemption constitutes a denial of equal protection. A suit for damages under the Civil Rights Act or directly under the Fourteenth Amendment, the other major vehicles for bringing a constitutional infirmity to a court's attention, also lacks logistical viability. A court could hardly find any branch or agent of state government liable for failing to arrest or prosecute when no state statute criminalizing the conduct exists. State immunity doctrines, of course, would bar an action against the legislature for failing to criminalize conduct. For logistic reasons alone, the issue seems ripe for legislative, rather than judicial, constitutional decision making.

The second reason for arguing a congressional rather than judicial response to the unconstitutionality of marital rape exemptions lies in the fact that Congress may be more willing than the judiciary to interpret seriously the Fourteenth Amendment as forbidding marital rape exemptions.

Congress is more likely to view marital rape exemptions as subordinating women and insulating a separate sovereignty of legitimized force, thereby denying women's rights to equal protection under law. Congress may be more open to these arguments not merely because of its present political composition, but for institutional and theoretical reasons as well. Unlike the Supreme Court, Congress is not obligated to ensure that legislation rationally map onto preexisting real distinctions. Furthermore, at least on occasion, Congress aggressively has sought to dismantle and restructure the social, private, and even intimate structures that collectively create and mask the hierarchies of daily life. Unlike the Court, Congress does not recoil inevitably at the prospect of undertaking significant reconstructions of social life. Indeed, this duty is clearly its business. The Fourteenth Amendment easily can be read as a constitutional norm that directs, guides, and legitimizes the political and moral direction those reconstructive efforts should take.

If we think of the Fourteenth Amendment as a moral and political guide for reconstructive legislation aimed at eradicating illegitimate social subordination and private spheres of insulated, violent sovereignty, marital rape exemptions surely are a sensible place for Congress to start to fulfill its constitutional obligations. A dismantling of the private regime of sexual violence against women could affect socially women's public and private lives as greatly as the dismantling of private regimes of segregation and institutionalized racism has affected African-Americans. As was the case with the desegregation campaign, the legal recognition of a constitutional right to protection against private sexual violence in the domestic sphere, without more, could change and expand not only women's rights, privacy, security, and safety but also women's senses of self and others' senses of women as fully participatory, represented, acknowledged, and respected members of society. Such recognition could help rehabilitate the damage to women's self-esteem, their feelings of self-possession, and their overall sense of wholeness. Just as the constitutional assault on desegregation triggered a change in societal perception of blacks, constitutionally motivated congressional action ensuring women's rights to be protected against marital rape could trigger wide-ranging changes in societal portrayals and perceptions of women's roles, rights, and public responsibilities.

Finally, the foundational and permanent recognition of women's rights to be free from forced marital sex that can come about only through constitutional decision making may be a prerequisite to further progress on a range of related issues regarding women's physical and sexual security. Date rape and acquaintance rape, for example, unlike marital rape, clearly are criminal, but they may be insulated from legal prosecution and public condemnation at least in part because of their shadow resemblance to marital rape, which is still protected in many states and underprosecuted in virtually all. The marital exemption, in brief, is simply the most brutal of all possible expressions of the social inclination to trivialize women's interest in physical and sexual security. Until women have physical and sexual security, both their public contributions and their private lives will be stunted, not just by personal fears but by social and legal inferiority fueled by a public perception of female personhood perverted by the deep knowledge of women's legal vulnerability. Women will not have that security until they have established their constitutional right to be equally protected against laws that encourage their psychic and sexual subordination and render them subject to private states of separate sovereignty. Conversely, when the law guarantees women that security, the gains will be immense. All women, married and unmarried, and all men might learn what it means to live in a truly democratic home, in a truly nurturant social world, transformed and inspired by a newly empowered, equally respected feminist community.

3

The Meaning of Equality and the Interpretive Turn

■

The turn to hermeneutics and interpretation in contemporary legal theory has contributed at least two central ideas to modern jurisprudential thought: first, that the "meaning" of a text is invariably indeterminate—what might be called the *indeterminacy claim*—and, second, that the unavoidably malleable essence of texts—their essential inessentiality—entails that interpreting a text is a necessary part of the process of creating the text's meaning.[1] These insights have generated both considerable angst and considerable excitement among traditional constitutional scholars,[2] primarily because, at least on first blush, these two claims seem to inescapably imply a third: that the interpreter of a text creates rather than discovers the text's meaning. A text's meaning cannot constrain an interpreter, for the simple reason that there is no single meaning embedded in a text to do the constraining; at best an interpreter must therefore choose from a range of possible meanings, and at worst the interpreter creates the meaning in the name of discovery or interpretation. In the constitutional context, the insistence that an uninterpreted, pure, or original legal text (like any text) cannot constrain in any way its subsequent interpretation seems to imply that the judge operates not in the realm of law but in the realm of arbitrary power.[3] This suggests that judges interpreting the Constitution are essentially creating its meaning and are therefore freed of any "textual"—and hence legal—constraints on their power. The judicial interpreter becomes the constitution maker; each case potentially occasions a rewriting. If the judge is not constrained by the singular meaning of the constitutional text, he must be free to basically do as he pleases. Constitutional adjudication thereby becomes, for better or for worse, an exercise of power rather than an exercise in law.

As widespread as this belief is, however, the reaction of constitutional scholars to the two fundamental insights of the "interpretive turn" in modern philosophy may be misguided.[4] Constitutional scholars who are alarmed by the interpretive turn in jurisprudence assume that judicial freedom from the constraints of the univocal, imperative meaning of "the" constitutional text implies judicial lawlessness. But the conclusion of lawlessness from hermeneutic insights simply does not follow. That judges may be free of the constraining influence of an illusion—the illusion that a text has a singular meaning, either original or "plain," awaiting proper discovery—by no means implies that they are therefore free; it only means that the text does not operate as a constraint, at least to the degree or in the manner traditionally thought. But it does not follow that the judge is unconstrained. He may well be constrained, even if not by the singular, original, or plain meaning of the text. Thus, even the judge who is free (and feels free) of the illusion that the text has a single, imperative meaning may nevertheless be "bound" by—and feel bound by—any number of other constraints, stemming from his professional role, his sense of ethics, his class interests, the expectations of a range of various "communities," or, as I shall discuss in greater detail in the bulk of this chapter, his jurisprudential identity, and the social and moral role in society that identity entails. That the judge is not bound by the intended or plain meaning of the Constitution, as of any legal text, implies next to nothing about the degree of freedom or constraint with which he decides cases.

In fact, as I shall discuss in more detail later in this chapter, most scholars who draw heavily on hermeneutic insights, or who accept in some fashion the basic interpretivist claims just outlined, insist quite strenuously that the judge is bound, or constrained, by some set of forces. Indeed, if anything, descriptions of the judicial process that deny the existence of an objective and singular meaning of legal texts more often vest the judge with too little discretion, not too much. The judge emerges from some of these depictions as so utterly at the mercy of forces over which he has little or no control, that the adjudication depicted by interpretivists often appears to be ultimately as "mechanical" as that portrayed by the formalists, intentionalists, and plain-meaning theorists they set out to decry.

Nevertheless, it is not difficult to see why the misperception persists that the new "interpretivism" in the context of legal and constitutional studies implies judicial freedom, and hence judicial lawlessness. There are two reasons. The first is that interpretivists have not paid as close attention as they should to the nature of the constraints on judicial interpretation—

whether they be textual or nontextual. Debate has centered instead around the claim that the intended or plain meaning of a legal text cannot control its subsequent interpretation. The result is that there has simply been inadequate attention given to the identification of nonintentionalist and non-plain-meaning constraints on the judge's decision. The impression, or misimpression, this neglect has fostered is the all-or-nothing claim that if neither authorial intention nor plain meaning controls judicial discretion, then nothing does. In this misguided dilemma, the judge is either bound by the text intended or its plain meaning or is free to do as she pleases.

The second and somewhat more complex reason for interpretivism's implying judicial lawlessness is that the constraints identified by interpretivists are not constraints that satisfy the ethical and legalistic imperatives driving traditional constitutional theorists toward intentionalist and plain-meaning theories of meaning.[5] That the judge who is unbound by a discoverable meaning of the constitutional text may nevertheless be bound by dominant class interests, culturally embedded constructs, unconscious bias, or even community morality will hardly be consolation to the theorist who sees in "law" the possibility of protecting the individual against those very forces—the ravages of class, the ignorance or idiocy of dominant culture, the meanness or viciousness of mainstream bias, and bigotry. To the degree that the traditionalist sees law as a bulwark against arbitrary, random, or whimsical judgment, the interpretivists' identification of nontextual constraints on interpretation might provide some solace. But to the degree that the traditional constitutionalist's insistence on a discoverable constitutional meaning is grounded in the faith or hope that the power of law can protect us against malevolent nonlegal forces—such as communal xenophobia or class oppression—the interpretivists' identification of precisely those forces as the relevant nonlegal constraints on judicial discretion is very likely to exacerbate rather than alleviate the traditionalist's anxiety.

The first purpose of this chapter is simply to expand discussion of nontextual constraints on judicial interpretation beyond its present contours. I will assume the interpretivists' major premise: judicial interpretation of the Constitution does not and cannot consist of ascertaining and applying either the plain meaning or the originally intended meaning of its authors. I will also urge, however, that the two forces interpretivists have unambiguously identified as major constraints on the judicial process—communal constraints on interpretive meaning and class interest—whether or not correct, are certainly not exhaustive. There is no reason to think that judges are not also constrained by other forces, and that they do not retain some residual degree of freedom to act against those influences as well.

I then want to explore the ramifications of one particular constraint on constitutional interpretation which seems both incontrovertible and politically unobjectionable, but which nevertheless (or perhaps for that reason) has been underexamined in the constitutional and interpretive literature. The meaning of the judicially discovered or interpreted Constitution, I will argue, is determined in part by the identification throughout the legal culture, and to a lesser degree by the mainstream culture of the Constitution as a legal rather than political document, and as a law for judicial, rather than legislative application. To the degree that we identify the Constitution as a source of adjudicative law, judicial interpretation of the constitutional text is constrained not only by the original or plain meaning, as is insisted by intentionalists and textualists, respectively, and not only by the ethical constructs, interpretive rules, class interests, and ideological forces identified by interpretivists, but also by jurisprudential conceptions of the nature of law. Obviously, if the Constitution is law, then it is not just a constitution we are expounding, but the law. Consequently, judicial understanding of what the Constitution means is heavily influenced by judges' conceptions of the nature of law: law is the general category of which the Constitution is an instance.

For this jurisprudential reason alone, in the hands of other nonlegal interpreters in the political arena, the Constitution could take on, and has taken on, very different meanings. Legislators and citizens, unlike courts, are not constrained by the need to interpret, apply, and enforce the Constitution as a legal document. Whatever constitutional meanings derive from constraints that owe their origin to the judicial forum to some degree lose their force when the Constitution is interpreted in other nonlegal forums. It is thus not surprising that the Constitution and its general phrases mean one thing to the Court and courts, and oftentimes something very different to other sectors of the community. The Second Amendment, to take an obvious example, clearly means something quite different to large sectors of the public than it means to the courts.[6] Likewise, the constitutional "right to privacy" has a different constitutional status outside the Supreme Court than inside.

These differences may reflect differences in degrees of expertise, but they also reflect differing institutional and jurisprudential responsibilities. Citizens and legislators have different interests in the Constitution and its phrases than do courts, and accordingly they operate under different constraints. One of those differences is surely that for the Court and the courts the Constitution is law, and it must be interpreted, enforced, and applied as such—that is, after all, what courts do. This constraint does not operate in anywhere near the same way on citizens or legislators. Consequently, citizens and legislators not bound by the duty of enforcing and applying the legal Constitution may see very different meanings in its general phrases.

In the first section in this chapter, I will quickly outline two "interpretivist" descriptions of the adjudicative process, which stem in different ways from the basic interpretive claims just sketched. The first is that of a group of interpretive scholars who I will call the *postmodernists,* by which I mean the neopragmatic and postmodern theorists most influenced by or responsible for the interpretive turn in constitutional theory. I will take Stanley Fish as representative of postmodernism. The second description comes from the Critical Legal Studies movement, and here I will take Mark Kelman's work as somewhat representative. Critical scholars no less than postmodernists are heavily influenced by the interpretive turn, but they have used it for very different purposes than those of the postmodern critics.

As different as they are, I will argue, these two groups have much in common. First, neither of them posit the bogeyman feared by the traditional critics of interpretivism: the untethered judge, unconstrained by a binding legal text, deciding cases according to whim. Although both accept the major premise that the legal text does not possess a preinterpreted, objective meaning there for the finding, both also describe the judge as heavily bound by external forces. Neither the Fishian nor the Kelmanesque judge decides cases according to "whim." I will then argue that both Fish's and Kelman's descriptions constitute only partial truths. Their descriptions are valuable, but they err in their implicit assumption that they have in some sense described the panoply of extratextual determinants of the judicial decision.

Second, I argue that, in addition to the nontextual constraints identified by Fish and Kelman, the role of the judge places peculiarly jurisprudential constraints on the interpretation of the constitutional text. Third, I apply the argument to one particular constitutional text: the Fourteenth Amendment's guarantee of equal protection.

The Interpretive Turn

Both critical legal scholars[7] and postmodern legal theorists[8] embrace the basic interpretive insights sketched here: that texts have no pure, uninterpreted meaning and that the interpreter of the text consequently endows the text with meaning, rather than discovers its meaning. Furthermore, both have offered descriptions of adjudication that depict a far more constrained process than the kind of account most often ascribed to them. The constraints on legal interpretation that they have identified are strikingly different, however.

Let me begin with the postmodern theorists. In sharp contrast to most critical legal scholars, postmodern theorists typically insist that the basic interpretivist claim—that the original text does not control its subsequent interpretation—does not imply, in the legal and especially the constitutional context, a pernicious politicization of the bench. For the postmodernist, there is indeed no discoverable, preinterpretive, original, or intended meaning to any text, notably including the constitutional text. And, it is indeed the process of interpretation that confers meaning on texts, and judges are undoubtedly in the business of interpretation. However, it does not follow that judges create constitutional meaning. Judges are quite fully constrained. They could not possibly, even if they set out to, decide cases on the basis of their own political whim. The reason for this goes to the heart of the "interpretive turn" itself.

The reason legal indeterminacy does not imply judicial activism, according to postmodernists, inheres in the nature of texts and in the nature of interpretation. Texts, to repeat a by now well-worn trope, come "always already" interpreted. A "text," according to the postmodernists, is not simply the recorded intention of its authors—here, the framers. Nor does it contain a plain—meaning preinterpreted—meaning. Rather, a "text" is by definition the embodiment of the stories, traditions, interests, desires, and aspirations of the communities that have produced and interpreted it,[9] and this is as true of the constitutional text as of any other. Even if the plain or originally intended meaning of a text does not constrain judges, then, this fully, always already interpreted text clearly does; the judge cannot help but read the text in a constrained way if he is going to read the text at all.

Thus, contrary to the fears of intentionalist and plain-meaning advocates, the postmodernists fully agree with the traditionalists that the constitutional text constrains interpretation. The nature of the constraint, however, is markedly different from that seen by traditionalists in the plain meaning or original intent of the constitutional document. The text does indeed constrain, but the "text" that does the constraining, for the post-modern theorist, is only partly (if that) a product of its plain meaning or the intention of its author. The text that constrains is the "interpreted text," not the pure text, or the plain text, or the intended text, or the text as put forward by its originators. This constitutional text is always already interpreted; as such, it is always already a product of the changing and evolving stories, constructs, narratives, interests, desires, and aspirations of the communities that receive, use, and live under it. Those stories, con-structs, narratives, interests, desires, and aspirations, therefore, are what constrain interpretation and thus control judicial discretion. The judge is decidedly free of the original or plain meaning of the constitutional text. But it by no means follows that she is free.

It bears emphasizing, however, that the postmodernists also agree with the radical wing of the Critical Legal Studies movement that neither in-tent nor plain meaning can possibly control judicial interpretation, and hence judicial meaning. But they disagree over the consequences. To some-what reverse the point made above: even assuming, along with the critical scholar, that the interpreter is not constrained by the originally intended meaning of a text—because no such thing exists—it does not follow that the interpreter is not constrained by the "text." Rather, the text that guides judgment is the "interpreted text": the text as endowed with meaning by its community of interpreters. It is only that text which can be read, or applied, or, in the case of law, enforced. In the constitutional context, this means that the judge is indeed constrained by the constitutional text, but the text is not, and could not be, the originally intended text or even the plain-meaning text. It is the interpreted constitutional text that constrains.

The postmodernists' insistence that the text is "always already" inter-preted implies a very different sort of answer than that propounded by critical scholars to the specter of unconstrained judicial activism that tra-ditionalists fear is implied by the interpretivists' major premise that texts lack a discoverable or even coherent original, intended meaning. The post-modern theorist agrees with the traditionalist that the judge is constrained by the text, but disagrees that this binds the judge to a singular and origi-nally intended meaning. On the other hand, the postmodernist agrees with the critical scholar that the originally intended text cannot operate as a constraint on the judge, but disagrees that it follows that the judge oper-ates in the realm of pure and arbitrary power rather than law. The judge, according to the postmodernists, is in a uniquely "mid-way" position: vis-à-vis the original, or intended, or "pure" constitutional text, he is free, but vis-à-vis the interpreted text, given meaning by the interpretive community in which it is located, he is quite fully bound. As he is a member of the "interpretive community," he cannot help but remain true to the "text's" meaning, where the text is thus understood. The judge is both bound by the constitutional text, where text definitionally includes the meanings ascribed it by the community of its interpreters, and freed from the illusory binding imperatives of the Constitution's plain meaning of its original drafters.

Thus, by insisting on the already interpreted text, the postmodernists remain true to the basic interpretive insights outlined here—that the identity of the interpreter affects the interpretation; that texts do not possess a singular, originally intended meaning; and that the interpretation of a text is what creates its meaning—while avoiding the apparently inescapable conclusion that the interpreter (here, the judge) no less than the original author, thereby has a hand in the creation of meaning. Interpretation does indeed bestow meaning on texts, but this has no implications for the separation of powers: the constitutional text is always already interpreted. The judge deals with, and ultimately decides under an already interpreted text. Stanley Fish explains:

> [R]eaders and texts are never in a state of independence such that they would need to be "disciplined" by some external rule. Since readers are already and always thinking within the norms, standards, criteria of evidence, purposes, and goals of a shared enterprise, the meanings available to them have been preselected by their professional training; they are thus never in the position of confronting a text that has not already been "given" a meaning by the interested perceptions they have developed. More generally, whereas Fiss thinks that readers and texts are in need of constraints, I would say that they are structures of constraint, at once components of an agent in the larger structure of a field of practices, practices that are the content of whatever "rules" one might identify as belonging to the enterprise.[10]

The result in the constitutional context is a more sophisticated understanding of the complexity of the constitutional text, but a nevertheless utterly conventional account of the judge's role in applying it: the judge applies the law. Interpretivism thus understood by no means implies that we are on the brink of judicial anarchism; quite the opposite. Fish's comments here (as is often the case) are representative:

On my analysis, the Constitution cannot be drained of meaning, because it is not a repository of meaning; rather, meaning is always being conferred on it by the very political and institutional forces Fiss sees as threats. Nor can these forces be described as "mere," because their shape and exercise are constrained by the very principles they supposedly endanger. And, since the operation of these forces is indeed principled, the fact that they determine (for a time) what will be thought of as "public values" is not something to be lamented, but simply a reflection of the even more basic fact that values derive from the political and social visions that are always competing with one another for control of the state's machinery.[11]

Critical legal scholars draw quite different implications from the basic indeterminacy claim that texts lack a single, identifiable, pure, uninterpreted, or preinterpreted meaning. Here it is helpful to distinguish two rather different critical positions. For some critical scholars, notably Duncan Kennedy, the absence of a textually generated pure meaning does imply that judges have considerable freedom to decide cases in line with their political convictions, and hence they have considerable responsibility for the moral value of the decisions they render.[12] For these critics, the interpretive turn does seem to imply that there is essentially no weighty difference between the institutional roles of judge and legislator, of lawmaker and law interpreter.[13] But this position is not particularly representative of critical scholars generally.[14]

For others, and I think for most critical scholars, judicial construal of legal texts is not determined by the original or plain meaning of texts, but it is nevertheless heavily constrained. For these critical scholars, judicial construction of texts is heavily influenced by pretextual "interpretive constructs" that shape the way we read, and what we read into, texts. The impression that we have reached the only textually permissible result in even an easy case is a result of our embrace, either conscious or unconscious, of an "interpretive construct" that narrows our interpretive options when we confront the text. Kelman's description of his own critical method in criminal law is illustrative:

By interpretive construction, I refer . . . both to the way we construe a factual situation and to the way we frame the possible rules to handle the situation. . . .

. . . These constructs are sometimes unconscious techniques of sorting out legal material and are sometimes consciously held political or philosophical beliefs, although even the consciously held beliefs function so that the users seem unaware of them . . . . [A] legal-sounding argument can be made only after a situation is characterized nonrationally, so that the advocate seems able to deduce a single result on principle. . . .

. . . Legal argument can be made only after a fact pattern is characterized by interpretive constructs. Once these constructs operate, a single legal result seems inevitable, a result seemingly deduced on general principle.[15]

Although nowhere fully explicated, Kelman's "interpretive constructs" are markedly different from the constraints imposed by Fish's "interpretive community." The constructs that predetermine interpretation for Kelman are nonprincipled, arational or irrational, grounded typically in class interest, unacknowledged, often unrecognized by those who employ them, and generally pernicious. They undercut what purports to be a rational, fair, and principled practice: application of general rules under a Rule of Law regime. Fish's interpretive community, by contrast, imposes constraints drawn from its openly acknowledged institutional and professional identity. Fish's constraints are as principled and rational as the practice itself, grounded in the practice's stated aspiration, openly acknowledged (although only when brought to mind), and generally strikingly benign in their operation. For Fish, there is "no need to worry": the interpretive turn is no threat to the values of legalism, for the simple reason that even though "law" does not control power in the sense hoped by intentionalists, the nontextual institutional, cultural, and professional forces that constrain legal interpretation emanate from our principles; indeed they are indistinguishable from our principles. For Kelman, unlike Fish, the indeterminacy claim seriously compromises the ideals and principles that define legal and judicial practice.

As different as they are, however, Fish's and Kelman's descriptions of legal reasoning have several things in common. First, neither posits a conscious, freely choosing, untethered, judge, making decisions in any way she wills. Second, and perhaps more significantly, both Kelman's and Fish's descriptions resolve what seems to be a major problem with the indeterminacy critique: Why is it that the process of adjudication is often felt to be determinate if it is true that the text from which it proceeds is inevitably indeterminate? Both accounts, in very different ways and with widely divergent political consequences, account for the perception of determinacy in the face of the reality of indeterminacy in a structurally similar way. They do so by denying not so much the ultimate determinacy of adjudication—for both, again, adjudication is determined, albeit not by law but by challenging the authenticity of the consciousness of judging: on both accounts the judge is more unaware than aware of the true determinants of her reasoning. It is thus possible for the legal text to be radically indeterminate, yet for the process of adjudication to feel quite determinate. The judge correctly perceives her decision as bound and may sincerely believe the law to be that which binds her. She is correct in her self-perception of her decision as determined. She is wrong, though, to think that it is determined by the singular, originally intended meaning of the preinterpreted text. Her decision is determined, but it is determined not by law (at least as conventionally understood) but by forces of which she is largely unaware.

The third feature these two accounts share is more troubling. For both Fish and Kelman the act of judging is so fully determined that the judge becomes oddly *de minimus*—even irrelevant. Thus, for Fish, the judge is not just "controlled by" but indeed "constituted by" interpretive constructs and communitarian texts, and although the "text" here is understood to include far more than the text's authors' original intentions, it is nevertheless the communally construed text that is paramount. Neither writer nor reader exercises much power under this view; it is the interpretive community, always already interpreting always already interpreted texts, which is the active agent in the process of creating meaning, through interpretation. On Fish's account, the judge, as reader, simply disappears:

> [I]t is interpretive communities, rather than either the text or the reader, that produce meanings. . . . Interpretive communities are made up of those who share interpretive strategies not for reading but for writing texts, for constituting their properties. . . .
>
> [S]ince the thoughts an individual can think and the mental operations he can perform have their source in some or other interpretive community, he is as much a product of that community (acting as an extension of it) as the meanings it enables him to produce.[16]

Strangely and somewhat dissatisfyingly, on Kelman's account no less than on Fish's, the judge's role is also peculiarly diminished, although for very different reasons, and with far less complacent results. While for Fish the judge-as-reader is bound by the relatively benign interpretive predispositions of the institutional, cultural, and professional interpretive commu nities that endow the text with meaning, for Kelman, the judge-as-reader is bound by relatively malign interpretive constructs that either reinforce (if not emanate from) class status or, alternatively, randomly mediate experience into some sort of articulable and disingenuously rational whole. Either way, though, the judge is at the mercy of larger forces over which he has little or no control. His purportedly objective, deductive, and rational interpretations of texts are either doing the bidding of the dominant class or reflecting nonrational filters he has no power to dispose of. He is not bound by a singular textual meaning, but he is bound by interpretive and, for the most part, irrational constructs of which he is only dimly, if that, aware:

> [P]articular interpretive construct[s] . . . [may] manifest a simple class conflict between those protecting the position that the legal system routinely allows them from sudden, incidental disruption, and those disfavored by the routine distortion of benefits that the legal system generates. Naturally, those disfavored by the ordinary legal distributions of economic power are most prone to use means generally considered criminal.
>
> Interpretive construction could play very distinct roles in this class conflict. It is possible that each construction might correspond to the political program of a social class. . . . Alternatively, each legal result could correspond to the political program of a social group, . . . Finally, it may be that maintaining the appearance of . . . legal argument is a significant political program of any dominant social class, so that making formal arguments which do not refer to the unexplainable interpretations that actually ground the arguments may sometimes be more vital than maintaining either the construction or particular results.
>
> . . . [A]lternatively], interpretive constructs . . . [may not be] politically meaningful at all, but simply inexplicably unpatterned mediators of experience, the inevitably nonrational filters we need to be able to perceive or talk at all. . . . I speak on behalf of those who no longer like to listen to people making arguments that mask a hidden structure of "nonarguments" with insistent, false rigor.[17]

There are two major problems with this radical diminution of the judge's power in both the postmodern and critical account of interpretation. The first is ethical. The judge whose understanding of the meaning of the law is determined by communal (Fish) or class (Kelman) constructs is a peculiarly unthinking and nonresponsible judge. The judge can hardly take credit, blame, or responsibility for his interpretation of the constitutional text if the text comes always already interpreted. Nor can the judge be blamed for skewing meaning in the direction of the status quo if he does so by employing constructs that are by definition unconscious.

The second, perhaps more serious, problem is that both descriptions seem belied by judicial experience. Adjudication is often felt (or, perhaps, always to some degree felt) to be determinate, and Kelman and Fish have provided explanations of why this might be so, even in the face of the radical indeterminacy of legal texts: judicial decisions are indeed determined, just not by the preinterpretive original meaning of legal texts. But their explanations may have overshot the target. The judges Kelman and Fish posit may be more "determined" than actual judges feel themselves to be; although judging is felt to be somewhat determined, it is also felt to be somewhat free. The commonsensible account of judging, in other words, may indeed be the correct one: the judge may be somewhat bound by "law" as understood by intentionalists, somewhat bound by legal texts as interpreted by interpretive communities, and somewhat bound by those texts as interpreted by dominant class interests and cultural constructs, but he may also be somewhat free and feel himself to be. The judge may at any point have the freedom, if she is sufficiently self-conscious, to break free of these constraints and render an authentic or novel reading. That judges describe themselves as at least on occasion possessed of this freedom, and aware of it, is surely some evidence that they have it. If they do, then there is something wrong with any identification of a constraint on interpretation that describes itself as exhaustive (there are no others) and global (the decision is totally, and not just somewhat, constrained).

However, both problems—that the interpretivists' descriptions do violence to both the ethics and experience of judging—are somewhat cured if we view Fish's and Kelman's descriptions as partial descriptions rather than as global accounts of adjudicatory practice. Judges may indeed be partly constrained by the dominant interpretations bestowed on texts by their community, as well as by the interests and desires of dominant classes and cultures. They may also, however, have some degree of freedom from those constraints—as well as from the constraint of "law"—to insist on deviant interpretations, to author novel interpretations, and to break out of class- or culture-based patterns of thought. Furthermore, only if they have such freedom can we fault them for failing to exercise it in an ethically responsible way.

And, read as partial rather than global descriptions, both accounts are underscored, rather than undercut, by judicial accounts of the experience, and even the appearance, of judging. Both postmodernists and critical scholars, like legal realists before them, have made it relatively easy for us to identify examples of decisions that purport to be driven by the original, pure, preinterpreted intended or plain meaning of a legal text—whether the Constitution, a statute, or a legal precedent—but which are in fact driven by other forces: dominant communal meanings or dominant societal and class interests. It is also possible, of course, to identify judicial decisions that markedly break free of dominant interpretive strategies, interests, and desires. That such decisions are rare speaks to the power of the constraining forces that postmodernists and critical scholars have identified.[18] But that they exist at all belies the claim that those forces cannot be overcome. When they are, the decision is all the more exemplary—whether of courage or lawlessness is another question. But their existence makes clear that in judging, as in a range of other deliberative practices, the genuinely free decision is always a possibility.

Finally, if we read Kelman's and Fish's descriptions as partial rather than global, we are free to further the projects that have begun: the identification and exploration of the constraints on judicial interpretation of legal documents. Interpretive pluralism, in other words, may be the most pragmatically sensible scholarly agenda, at least at this point in our exploration of the consequences of the interpretive turn in legal and constitutional studies. It may be that judges are partly constrained by the interpretive understandings of the communities of which they are a part and partly constrained by the interests and desires of dominant social and cultural classes. But even if that is true, they may also be partly constrained by other sorts of forces as well—ethical and professional expectations, for example, or, as I shall argue in the next section, jurisprudential aspirations stemming from definitional accounts of the Rule of Law. We should be wary on pragmatic grounds, no less than on experiential and ethical ones, of adopting accounts of the judicial decision that foreclose those possibilities.

Jurisprudential Constraints

In addition to the insights recited above, interpretivists in literary theory have put forward a third postulate that has not received as much attention in legal circles: that the way a text is identified will go a long way toward determining its audience, and consequently a long way toward determining its meanings.[19] Inversely, the audience a text captures will to some degree determine its identity, and hence to some degree its meaning. This is as true within genres as between them. Thus, if we think of Agatha Christie's stories as detective stories, we will tend to ascribe to them meanings consistent with their purpose: to amuse.[20] And, if the audience of Agatha Christie's novels are for the most part casual readers in search of amusement, we will tend to think of them as detective stories. On the other hand, if they attract a more "serious" philosophical treatment of death and mortality, we will find in them very different sorts of meanings. Similarly, if the audience of children's television consists of children who need or want to be entertained, we will think of a children's television cartoon as entertainment and we will accordingly inscribe one set of meanings; if the audience is children-consumers, we see the text as advertising, and we will inscribe a very different set of meanings. The point is a simple one: the audience of a text—the community of potential "interpreters" who receives the text—brings to the text a set of needs, desires, and interests; those needs, desires, and interests will determine at least to some degree how we categorize it (advertisement, cartoon, detective story, or high literature), and how we categorize it will determine its meanings.

Surely the same is true of legal texts, and surely the same is true of the constitutional text. That the Constitution is received for the most part by judges and lawyers who need to apply and enforce it in courts of law under established rules of legal procedure determines to some degree its identity as a legal text, and that identity determines to some degree its meaning. Conversely, that the Constitution is now conceived as law partly determines its professionalized legal and judicial audience. Lawyers and judges have a fairly well-developed sense of the necessary and sufficient jurisprudential conditions of legalism: what a text must be, in order to be "law." If the Constitution is identified as law, then it, too, no less than statutes and case law, must meet those minimums. Its interpretive meanings, then, will reflect those jurisprudential constraints.

Courts themselves, and particularly the Supreme Court, make frequent reference to prudential constraints imposed by legalism on their constitutional decision making. Yet, neither traditional nor interpretivist constitutionalists, nor the justices themselves, have focused on the jurisprudential constraints on constitutionalism imposed by legalism. Why the neglect? At least for traditionalists, and to some degree for interpretivists as well, this may be because inquiry has focused instead on the peculiarity of constitutional thought and reasoning within the legal genre.[21] Thus, the standard understanding of Justice Marshall's declaration that "it is a Constitution we are expounding,"[22] surely has been that we should understand the uniqueness, the peculiarity, and the differentness of the Constitution within the universe of law. That it is a Constitution, rather than a statute or some other more ordinary form of law, undoubtedly imposes constraints on constitutional reasoning that are unique: constitutional interpretation, unlike other forms of legal interpretation, must meet enhanced needs for permanence, coherence, integrity, and flexibility, simply because we are dealing with a fundamental charter not made for easy amendment. Perhaps even more important, the uniquely foundational status of the Constitution has engendered a peculiarly reverential attitude toward it that is not directed toward other legal entities. Scholarship has, perhaps appropriately, focused on these unique qualities, the unique needs they reflect within a system of constitutional governance, and the meanings the Constitution has acquired because of them.[23]

Somewhat more surprisingly, postmodern and critical theorists, no less than traditionalists, also have generally not pursued the possibility that the philosophical dictates of legalism, rather than prudential constraints, political commitments, class interest, or community understandings, may determine constitutional meaning, although for different reasons. For postmodernists, the reason may have to do with interdisciplinary politics: postmodern legal theorists, heavily influenced by critical literary theory, may view their work as an alternative to traditional jurisprudential inquiry, and for that awkward reason alone may be unlikely to see traditional jurisprudence as a constraint on interpretation. For critical theorists, the reason undoubtedly has to do with politics more simply defined: critical scholars are committed—perhaps overcommitted—to the claim that there is no meaningful difference between legal and political discourse.[24] For both reasons, critics and postmodernists will be disinclined to seek out jurisprudential constraints on constitutional interpretation.

Another reason for the neglect, though, may be that traditional, postmodern, and critical legal theorists, like the lawyers and judges about whom they theorize, are insiders to the practice of adjudication. It is far more difficult to "see" the constraints that define as well as limit one's own vision than to see constraints on practices that are external to one's identity. To take a roughly analogous case, a reader who absorbed only novels would have little reason to consider the definition of the "novel" as a significant determinant of a particular novel's meaning—although such a reader may be struck by the definitional constraints of the particularities of the "romance novel" or the "nineteenth-century novel." The constraints imposed by the novel form itself may—like background noise—simply become invisible. Likewise, the purely legalist constraints on the Constitution's meaning may have become similarly invisible, or faded in contrast to the striking peculiarity and uniqueness of constitutional legalism, to those of us accustomed to viewing the Constitution as a source of law and accustomed to (if not "constituted by") the mores and constraints of the legal universe.

But the differences between the Constitution and other forms of law should not obscure their family resemblances. The Constitution, because it is judicially applied law, shares in the general qualities and attributes of legality. Some of its meaning is accordingly a function of that identification. In the next section, I will examine in detail one example of constitutional interpretation that seems heavily determined by jurisprudential constraints. There are surely others, however, beyond the contours of this chapter, that could be fruitfully explored.

Judicially interpreted and applied law, for example, for the most part aspires toward a corrective model of justice: it identifies unjustifiable wrongs, violated rights, and sets remedies to restore or correct the status quo.[25] Courts, as interpreters of law, understand it in such a way as to make it consonant with this model: a legal norm must specify a wrong and a right, and provide a remedy accordingly. There is no reason to think that anything different occurs when the law being read is the Constitution. Surely the "state action" requirement, along with the "intent" requirement in equality law, stems in part from a jurisprudentially motivated need to homogenize the Fourteenth Amendment with our general conception of the nature of law: both the state action requirement and the intent requirement may be driven by the jurisprudential need to ensure that a "wrong" has indeed been committed. Similarly, the belabored and apparently "unprincipled" justiciability requirements—standing, case or controversy, and mootness—might all stem from jurisprudential rather than textual or political constraints: they may all be aimed toward ensuring that a right exists and has been violated. The source of that impulse might be jurisprudential rather than political: if the Constitution is law, it must be applied in such a way as to rectify violated rights and deter wrongdoing. Thus, at least the state action, intent, and case or controversy requirements might reflect jurisprudential, rather than political or communal, constraints on interpretation.

More generally, as I will argue in Chapter 7, the jurisprudential constraints on constitutional interpretation might make radically redistributive understandings of constitutional phrases difficult, and "conservative" readings—readings that restore or conserve the status quo—seem all the more imperative. To some degree, the source of this impulse may indeed be a political orientation toward political conservatism, as critical scholars suggest, or, alternatively, the dictates of dominant understandings of the relevant communities, as postmodernists urge. It might also be rooted in the Court's and courts' institutional identity as interpreters of law, however. The vast majority of legal actors understand law as jurisprudentially requiring, by definition, the identification of rights, wrongs, and remedies applied in a way that restores the pre-injury, or pre-wrong, status quo. Most areas of judicially created law fit this model, and those that clearly do not are for that reason widely regarded as problematic. Law, at least judicially created and applied law, is thus itself inherently conservative. There is no reason to think that we would abandon these understandings of the requirements of law when faced with the Constitution.

The Meaning of the Equal Protection Clause

Modern courts and commentators have identified two dramatically different meanings the equal protection clause of the Fourteenth Amendment might have: a substantive meaning (or *substantive equality*) and a formal meaning (or *formal equality*). The formal meaning of equality, or of "equal protection," is that legislators must treat like groups alike, and the laws they make must reflect this mandate by being "rational."[27] Thus, if two groups are alike in some relevant respect, a law may not prescribe different treatments of them. Put somewhat differently, to meet the formal criterion of equality, the distinctions a law creates must be rationally related not only to a legitimate end but also to preexisting differences between the affected groups. If a law fails to meet this standard, then the state has denied "equal protection of the law."

The substantive meaning of equality, or of equal protection, is that legislators must use law to ensure that no social group, such as whites or men, wrongfully subordinates another social group, such as blacks or women.[28] Thus, if one group wrongfully dominates another—whether economically, physically, socially, or sexually—then the legislature must at least attempt to use legal means to bring an end to that wrongful relation of domination and subordination. For a state to fail to do so is to "deny" the subordinated group "equal protection of the law."

As numerous commentators have now shown,[29] these two very different meanings of equal protection imply drastically divergent results in particular cases.[30] Most notably, they imply different results in the major affirmative action cases of the last few years, from *Regents of the University of California v. Bakke*[31] through *City of Richmond v. J. A. Croson Company*.[32] Under the formal definition, any state differentiation between whites and blacks is prima facie irrational: the two groups are "alike" for legal purposes and therefore should be treated alike. Race can't "make a difference." Benign distinctions between races are no more rational than malicious distinctions. Therefore, and as the Court clearly held in *Croson*, affirmative action policies will often be unconstitutional, absent a strong showing of identified past discrimination that would constitute a difference between the two groups, and hence provide a justification for differential treatment.[33] Under a substantive definition, however, affirmative action policies are surely permissible and may even be required.[34] Whites generally are dominant in this society, blacks are generally subordinate, and the equal protection clause's antisubordination mandate requires that states undertake affirmative obligations to equalize the two. Thus, what is clearly prohibited under one interpretation of the equal protection clause is clearly permitted and perhaps required under another.

As commentators have also now pointed out, the Supreme Court's interpretation of the equal protection clause over the last few decades has moved fairly consistently away from a substantive definition and toward a formal definition.[35] Thus, *Brown v. Board of Education*[36] can readily be read, perhaps must be read, as embracing a substantive account of the equal protection clause: separate and unequal educational facilities produce unequal educational opportunities, contributing directly to the subordination of blacks and dominance of whites in an already white-dominated society.[37] By *Bakke*, however, the meaning of both the equal protection clause and *Brown* had changed dramatically. At least according to Justice Powell, the equal protection clause does not require an end to subordination, but rather, requires that likes be treated alike.[38] Furthermore, blacks and whites are, for all purposes that matter, alike, and any segregatory scheme—whether "equal" or "unequal," and whatever its impact on the dominance or subordination of one race vis-à-vis the other—treats the two groups differently and is hence presumptively unconstitutional. Such a rule includes, although is not limited to, benign formative action plans, as well as maliciously segregated school systems. Thus, by *Bakke*, the substantive, antisubordinationist meaning of *Brown* had begun to erode as it came to be possible to read the clause as conveying only a formal, antidiscrimination meaning. By *Croson,* the transformation was complete. Far from requiring race-conscious dismantling of institutional and social subordination of blacks, a more united, as well as more conservative, Court held that the Fourteenth Amendment presumptively prohibits most race-conscious decision making, absent strong evidentiary showings of past discrimination. Affirmative action aimed at ending subordination is not only not required by the Fourteenth Amendment, it is prohibited by it.[39]

How did the modern *Croson* Court arrive at this interpretation not only of *Brown,* but of the Fourteenth Amendment as well? Was the Court free, either at the time of *Croson* or earlier, to simply choose between formal or substantive meanings of equality? Does the transition from the substantive interpretation at least arguably embraced by *Brown* to the rejection of substantive equality and embrace of formalism in *Croson* reflect nothing but the changing political views of the changing personnel on the Court?

There are at least four answers to those questions worth exploring. First, the later *Croson* Court might have been "bound by law" in the way meant by traditionalists: the Fourteenth Amendment's equal protection clause has some discoverable original or plain meaning which either permits, requires, or prohibits affirmative action. If this is correct, then the earlier substantive interpretation of the clause was simply "wrong," and the modern formal interpretation is "right" (or vice versa).[40] Second, the Court might have been (and might be) genuinely free to choose between them. If this is true, then the formal interpretation now governing the clause is not so much "right" or "wrong" as a "good" political choice, and the justices' decision to adopt it should be evaluated accordingly.[41] Third, as the postmodernists and critical scholars might contend, it might be that the "law"—the text, the history, and the intent of the drafters of the clause—is indeed too indeterminate to mandate either a substantive or a formal interpretation. On this account the justices moved toward a formal definition and away from a substantive account because of the constraints identified by interpretivists: the interpretive habits of the relevant communities and the interest and desires of dominant social groups. Fourth, the stance for which I will argue, the move toward formalism in the equal protection doctrine, whether or not it represents class interest or communal morality, also reflects constraints on interpretation that stem from the legal status of the Constitution itself.

As for the first choice, and as interpretivists (both new pragmatists and critical scholars) would surely insist, the "law," understood as either the plain meaning or the originally intended meaning of a legal text, at least in this context, did not determine outcome. The plain meaning of the text of the equal protection clause provided no help; either of these interpretations is a linguistically permissible understanding of the phrase "equal protection of the law." Nor does the history of the Fourteenth Amendment yield a clear choice in favor of one or the other of these two radically conflicting interpretations, for two reasons. First, both may have been within the original intent of the drafters. It may have been understood that the way to achieve substantive equality between the races was to insist on formal equality for state legislators. The two meanings may not have been perceived to be in tension, so that the possibility of their coming into conflict (or even being truly differentiated) and thus requiring a choice may never have been raised. Second, the history of the clause's application in Fourteenth Amendment doctrine provides ample precedential authority for the Court to adopt either interpretation.[42] Although the formal meaning of equality has tended to dominate, the Court from time to time has embraced the contrasting substantive understanding of the Constitution's mandate.[43]

As interpretivists would insist, then, at least with respect to Fourteenth Amendment jurisprudence, neither the text itself nor its authors' intent nor the history of its application provides any absolute constraint on judicial interpretation. The Supreme Court could embrace either a formal or substantive understanding of equality, striking or upholding affirmative action plans accordingly, and be well within the accepted boundaries of its own discretion. The "law," as conventionally understood, provides no answer. If we understand "law," as meaning constraints imposed on judicial decisions through the intended, historical, or plain meanings of legal texts, then the "law" of the Fourteenth Amendment's equal protection clause truly is indeterminate. Whatever does constrain the decision, if anything, it is not "law."

Moreover, the indeterminacy of the phrase might of course imply that the judge is free to simply choose, on the basis of "his own values," his own politics, whim, or any other variant of subjective desire, whichever interpretation he pleases. If this is so, then, as traditionalists fear, those opinions reflecting a substantive interpretation of the phrase stem from their authors' desire, for whatever reason, to promote the substantive equality of blacks and whites, and those reflecting a formal interpretation stem from their authors' desire, again for whatever reason, to promote only a formal equality, often at the expense of meaningful progress toward substantive racial justice.[44] In *Croson,* the Rehnquist Court unsurprisingly chose to promote formal equality; in *Brown,* the Warren Court chose to promote substantive equality. Evaluation and criticism of both decisions, on this account, should proceed on the basis of whether the Court in each instance chose wisely, not whether it decided correctly.

There is, though, at least one problem with this account: the degree of freedom it posits is wildly at odds with the language of the decisions themselves, and presumably with the experience of judging as well. Virtually none of the significant cases marking the transition from substantive to formal interpretations of equality reads as though it derives from unfettered choice. Whatever the outcome and whatever the judge, the decisions are written in the language of obligation and necessity, not in the language of free choice. To take just two examples, Justice Scalia, in *Croson,* first explains the ethical or political basis of his choice for formal over substantive equality. He then quickly proceeds, however, to describe his decision in obligatory terms:

> The benign purpose of compensating for social disadvantages, whether they have been acquired by reason of prior discrimination or otherwise can no more be pursued by the illegitimate means of racial discrimination than can other assertedly benign purposes we have repeatedly rejected. The difficulty of overcoming the effects of past discrimination is as nothing compared with the difficulty of eradicating from our society the source of those effects, which is the tendency— fatal to a nation such as ours—to classify and judge men and women on the basis of their country of origin or the color of their skin. A solution to the first problem that aggravates the second is no solution at all. I share the view expressed by Alexander Bickel that *"the lesson of the great decisions of the Supreme Court and the lesson of contemporary history have been the same for at least a generation:* discrimination on the basis of race is illegal, immoral, unconstitutional, inherently wrong, and destructive of democratic society."[45]

Justice O'Connor, reaching the same result, but with very different reasoning, also ultimately employs language of obligation:

> That Congress may identify and redress the effects of society-wide discrimination does not mean that, a fortiori, the States and their political subdivisions are free to decide that such remedies are appropriate. . . . To hold otherwise would be to cede control over the content of the equal protection clause to the 50 state legislatures and

their myriad political subdivisions. . . . *We believe that such a result would be contrary to the intentions of the Framers of the Fourteenth Amendment,* who desired to place clear limits on the States' use of race as a criterion for legislative action, and to have the federal courts enforce those limitations.[46]

The justices themselves, if we can take the language of the opinions seriously, understand the interpretive task as requiring a correct outcome in the equality cases as in others, and not as requiring a wise political or personal choice.

Another possibility, of course, is that although the text of the Fourteenth Amendment itself, as well as its history, is indeterminate, the modern Court is nevertheless "bound" to the formal interpretation—not bound by law, but by extratextual influences. The question, then, is what those influences might be. One possibility, presumably that of the postmodernists, is that the contemporary Court's adoption of the formal interpretation of equal protection was determined by the preexisting habits, interests, values, and desires of the most powerful forces within the "interpretive community" that imbued the text with meaning. A second possibility, presumably that of the critical scholars, is that the Court's adoption of the formal interpretation was determined by preexisting "interpretive constructs" that emanate from the Court's—and the social sectors' of which it is representative—willingness to tolerate institutional and unconscious racism.[47]

Both explanations have considerable merit. Indeed, the use in *Croson* of the Fourteenth Amendment to strike state and municipal action intended to aid minorities goes a long way toward vindicating the longstanding critical claim, first made by Alan Freeman, that the main function of "antidiscrimination law" in this culture is to legitimate through formalism the deep-seated and impenetrable substantive racism of the dominant white race.[48] In *Croson,* and more ambiguously in *Bakke* before it, the main tool of antidiscrimination law—the equal protection clause of the Fourteenth Amendment—was used quite explicitly to invalidate substantive measures taken to ameliorate the effects of racial subordination. Indeed, the Court's explicit holding—that for purposes of the Fourteenth Amendment, the eradication of the effects of racial subordination is not a compelling state goal—is virtually an explicit avowal of the subconscious or unconscious legitimating motive ascribed by Freeman to the entire body of antidiscrimination law.

Postmodernist explanations of judicial interpretation also have some appeal in this context. It seems entirely fair to say that the Court in *Croson* embraced the interpretation of the Fourteenth Amendment that currently dominates in the legal and nonlegal culture. To be sure, there are competing interpretations of equality and of equal protection currently circulating from which the Court could have drawn.[49] But if it is true, as the postmodernists claim, that the text comes always already interpreted, there's little doubt that at this point in our history of race relations, the interpretation in which it comes always already embedded is that of formal equality— a color-blind and mechanistic aspiration that if the states are rigorously neutral in their lawmaking, and we simply let the economic, political, and cultural chips fall where they may, racial fairness will be the outcome.

Even if the decision in *Croson* to definitively embrace formal equality at the cost of substantive equality was partly determined by interest and community, however, there surely may have been other constraining determinants as well. Specifically, there may have been jurisprudential constraints on the Court that made the formal interpretation of equality more palatable than the substantive. Not just the politics, but also the aspiration of the formal equality the Court mandated in *Croson* readily converges with the Court's peculiarly jurisprudential identity, in a way in which the aspiration of substantive equality does not. The Supreme Court, like all appellate courts, aspires toward formal justice in the cases that come before it. The Court, like any court exercising its appellate power, must decide whether the case facing it is sufficiently like an earlier case that the outcome should be identical, or whether it can be rationally distinguished. Appellate jurisprudence is almost entirely concerned with doing formal justice to litigants: like cases should be treated alike; like individuals should be treated alike. If the case can be closely analogized to an earlier case or line of cases, then its outcome should be subsumed under a general principle that rationalizes both. This jurisprudential and ethical goal—like treatment of like cases—defines the justice toward which appellate courts aim; thereby defines the reasoning they employ; and, finally, given the prominence of appellate cases in legal education, defines the essence of legal thinking itself.

It is not unreasonable to speculate that the centrality of the task of defining or discovering "likeness" or "difference" to the traditional judicial role has influenced the definition judicially accorded the constitutional mandate and ethical aspiration of "equal protection." To be treated equally by an appellate court means, simply, that one is treated the same as those who are relevantly similar, and different from those who are different. To a considerable degree, then, the word "equal," to use the language of the postmodernists, comes always already interpreted to the legally trained mind as meaning the like treatment of like cases and the disparate treatment of the relevantly different. The interpretive constraint derives not so much from competing cultural meanings as from jurisprudential identity: courts exist to assure "equality before the law." The equality thereby assured is rigorously formal: likes will be treated alike.

It is not surprising then that the "equality" mandated by the equal protection clause has ultimately come to be understood by the Supreme Court as requiring a formal rather than substantive interpretation. The formal meaning of equal protection embraced by the Court in *Croson* is simply the "equal justice" mandate applied to the legislative treatment of groups, rather than the judicial treatment of individuals. Legislators, under the Court's reading of equal protection, must treat like groups alike, just as courts, in their appellate function, must assure that laws are applied in such a way as to treat similarly situated individuals similarly. If two groups are substantially or relevantly the same, then they must be treated the same; any law that differentiates between them is presumptively irrational. Blacks and whites are "the same" with respect to their innate entitlement to government largesse. A law that differentiates between races is therefore as irrational as a court that draws an unjustified distinction between cases. Furthermore, given our history of malicious discrimination, such irrationality is, in turn, presumptively maliciously—rather than randomly or whimsically—motivated.

As the Court has itself from time to time acknowledged—most notably in *Washington v. Davis*[50]—a formal rather than substantive reading of the equal protection clause is in part mandated by the prudential constraints on the Court's jurisprudential role. A substantive definition of equal protection requires, the Court has argued, more judicial intervention into the private, social, and cultural spheres than is feasible. But a formal reading of the equal protection clause converges not only with the Court's sense of its own prudential limits but also with its sense of its aspirational jurisprudential function. Through their appellate work, courts assure rational application of laws. The equal protection clause, read formally rather than substantively, requires the same rationality of legislatures with respect to groups that the mandate of formal justice requires of courts with respect to individuals. A formal reading of the equal protection clause thus meets the Court's peculiarly jurisprudential, ethical, and aspirational goals, as well as its prudential interests and conservative politics.

If the Court's reading of equal protection as requiring formal rather than substantive equality stems in part from ethical constraints with their origins in jurisprudence, then it also seems reasonable to assume that other political or legal actors, not constrained in the same way, might read the clause in a very different way. History to some extent bears this out: in its sole major interpretation of the Fourteenth Amendment, the nineteenth-century Civil Rights Act,[51] Congress interpreted its provisions substantively rather than formally, reading it to prohibit acts of private subordination by whites of blacks and mandating that law be used in some fashion to end such subordination.[52] This sharp difference between the congressional interpretation and the interpretation insisted upon by the Supreme Court at the time[53] undoubtedly reflected the differing political commitments of the two bodies. But it may also have reflected, then and now, different institutional aspirations. Congress, as the originator of legal change, is not constrained by jurisprudential, compensatory, corrective, or formal norms of justice; its role is not to apply laws equally to groups or individuals before it. It is logical to assume, then, that its interpretations of the constitutional provisions that control its deliberations will not re-flect those constraints. Congressional interpretation of the Constitution is, though, constrained by distributive and substantive norms of justice; the laws it enacts should distribute resources fairly among the citizenry. Its understanding of the "equality," then, which the equal protection clause guarantees and which it is directed to ensure under section 5 of the Four-teenth Amendment, should be informed by a distributive and substantive ethical ideal, rather than a corrective and formal one.

Were Congress to once again take up its section-5 responsibilities under the Fourteenth Amendment, and enact legislation for the purpose of en-suring that the states provide equal protection of the laws, it would have to first interpret the meaning of that phrase. The interpretive turn, if it has done nothing else, has reaffirmed the legal realists' basic insight that the application or enforcement of a text necessarily first requires its interpre-tation. If the preceding analysis is correct, it would seem sensible to predict that congressional interpretation of the equal protection clause, grounded in congressional rather than judicial needs, interests, and institutional aspi-rations, would be quite different from that of the Supreme Court. It would minimally be freed of the constraint of jurisprudential ethics that at least in part dictates a formal rather than substantive reading of the equal pro-tection clause. It would instead, presumably, operate under a constraint of distributive rather than compensatory justice. In turn, such a constraint might render a substantive, rather than formal, interpretation of equality considerably more likely.

As various commentators have argued, and as I have discussed at length elsewhere,[54] such a reading would support not only federal affirmative action plans such as that sustained in *Fullilove v. Klutznick*,[55] but an array of other "equality-promoting" legislative proposals as well, including, for example, childcare funding and comparable worth legislation as protective of substantive gender equality, and greater funding for education, social services, and law enforcement in inner cities as protective of substantive race equality. Whether the Supreme Court would uphold such legislation against attacks grounded in formal interpretations of the equal protection clause is of course a separate question.[56] But congressional grounding of equality-promoting legislation in a substantive, congressional interpretation of the equal protection clause, rather than in the now standard commerce clause guise, would at least help clarify the ethical and aspirational purpose of congressional action.

Conclusion

The interpretive turn in legal philosophy has sensitized legal scholars to the malleability of texts and the consequent inevitability of interpretation. Because of insights garnered from interpretive and hermeneutic disciplines, we are more aware of the difficulty of locating constraints on legal interpretation of texts in their plain meaning or the original intent of their authors. Unfortunately, however, the political dimension of the interpretive turn in legal studies has truncated its value: because of the apparent consequences of the indeterminacy claim for our commitment of the separation of powers, debate in constitutional scholarship over the importance of the interpretive turn has centered on the basic question of whether the plain meaning or the originally intended meaning of a text can constrain later application of the legal text. The follow-up questions—what additional constraints might consist of, and what the implications might be of those constraining influences for constitutional meanings—have received relatively short shrift.

Hermeneutic scholars in other disciplines, however, have as much to say about the second question as about the first. Two such additional constraints on all interpretation is the identity of the text—what sort of text it is—and the identity of the interpreter, with what sort of interests, desires, needs, and aspirations. Although legal theorists have not given as much attention to these constraints as have literary theorists, they are of obvious relevance to legal interpretation. The Constitution is a legal text interpreted by judges; as such it acquires meanings quite different from those it might have were it understood either as a political text interpreted by legislators or as a moral and aspirational text interpreted by citizens. First, as the Supreme Court itself has from time to time noted, its meaning must be compatible with prudential constraints on adjudication: what sorts of remedies are available to judges, what sorts of cases can be heard, and so on. Second, and perhaps more important, its meaning must also resonate with the aspirational goals of adjudication, as well as with the prudential constraints of adjudicative forums. One such aspirational goal is surely the goal of legal justice. Courts seek to do formal justice—to treat like cases alike—in virtually every case that comes before them. All law—common, statutory, and constitutional—must be applied in such a way that litigants similarly situated are rationally distinguished.

Since the Constitution is also a form of law, this aspirational goal has undoubtedly influenced the Court's understanding of its substantive provisions, including the equal protection clause. A formal interpretation of the equal protection clause resonates deeply with the Court's, as with any court's, ethical commitment to legal justice: the clause requires legislators to treat like groups alike and courts to oversee, in a quasi-appellate manner, their performance in doing so. A substantive interpretation of the equal protection clause, by contrast, does not; thus it may be felt as conflicting with legal justice aspirations. It does not follow, however, that the formal interpretation of equality is right and the substantive interpretation wrong. It only follows that so long as the Court remains the exclusive, as well as ultimate, interpreter of constitutional meaning, substantive interpretations of the equality clause will continue to run against the grain.

There is no reason, however, for the Court to become, to be, or to remain the exclusive as well as final interpreter for the Fourteenth Amendment. The amendment itself directs Congress to play an active role in bringing its guarantees to fruition. If the interpretive turn has taught us anything, it has taught us that implementation of a legal text invariably requires its interpretation. The question is not, then, whether Congress should interpret as well as enforce Fourteenth Amendment guarantees; if it is to enforce, it must interpret. The only question is how it will do so. To answer that question, two facts are worth noting. First, as at least the Court often acknowledges, Congress operates under dramatically different prudential constraints than the Supreme Court. Second, it also operates under dramatically different aspirational constraints: it seeks to do distributive rather than legal justice; it prioritizes the "good" over the right; it seeks to enact laws wisely rather than apply them correctly. Those aspirations, no less than prudential and political constraints on its decisions, would undoubtedly affect the meaning of whatever constitutional provisions Congress sets out to interpret. Therefore, when and if Congress takes up again its section-5 obligations under the Fourteenth Amendment, we can expect to see a dramatically different meaning of equality emerge from its efforts.

PART 2

Due Process of Law

4

Reconstructing Liberty

■

It is commonly and rightly understood in this country that our constitutional system ensures, or seeks to ensure, that individuals are accorded the greatest degree of personal, political, social, and economic liberty possible, consistent with a like amount of liberty given to others, the duty and right of the community to establish the conditions for a moral and secure collective life, and the responsibility of the state to provide for the common defense of the community against outside aggression. Our distinctive cultural and constitutional commitment to individual liberty places very real restraints on what our elected representatives can do, even when they are acting in what all of us, or most of us, would consider our collective best interest. For example, we cannot outlaw marches by the Ku Klux Klan,[1] or the burning of flags by political extremists,[2] or the anti-Semitic, racist, or hateful speech of incendiary and potentially dangerous bigoted zealots.[3] Nor can we simply outlaw those practices of religious sects that may have deleterious effects on the members—such as the refusal of certain Amish sects in the Eastern United States to allow their children to receive a public education past the eighth grade;[4] the explicit exclusion (until recently) of African-Americans from positions of influence in the Mormon Church; or the continuing exclusion of women from positions of power, prestige, and influence in our dominant, mainstream, Protestant, Catholic, and Judaic faiths. We may believe correctly that a full civic education for every individual is not only desirable for its own sake but is an absolute prerequisite for meaningful participation in our shared political life. We may believe that racist speech is antithetical to the racial tolerance necessary to our continued existence as a pluralistic society, that flag-burning communicates no message worth hearing, and that women and blacks are entitled to the opportunity to aspire to positions of full participation and responsibility in religious life. Nevertheless, we are precluded from legislating in a way that would put the weight of the law behind these values because to do so ostensibly would do great violence to something we hold even more dear: the right and responsibility of the individual to think, speak, and act autonomously in matters of religious, political, and social life—to reach one's convictions on one's own and for oneself, unfettered by the moral dictates of the state, even where those dictates are benign and wise.

In constitutional discourse, this complex aspiration is often captured by the phrase *ordered liberty*.[5] The first thing to note about this aspiration of ordered liberty is that it is a relatively modern and distinctively liberal interpretation of our constitutional heritage. Thus, although Justice Cardozo coined the phrase "ordered liberty" in the 1930s, our modern understanding of ordered liberty protected by the Constitution came to full fruition with the liberty-expanding cases of the liberal Warren Court era. Quite possibly it received its most definitive formulation in the 1960s case *Poe v. Ullman*.[6] Dissenting in *Poe*, Justice Harlan wrote:

> [Implicit in the concept of ordered liberty are] those rights "which are . . . fundamental; which belong . . . to the citizens of all free governments" . . . for "the purposes [of securing] which men enter into society" . . . .
>
> Due process [which protects such ordered liberty] has not been reduced to any formula; its content cannot be determined by reference to any code. The best that can be said is that through the course of this Court's decisions it has represented the balance which our Nation, built upon postulates of respect for the liberty of the individual, has struck between that liberty and the demands of organized society. . . .
>
> . . . [T]he liberty guaranteed by the Due Process Clause . . . is not a series of isolated points [represented by the Bill of Rights] . . . . It is a rational continuum which, broadly speaking, includes a freedom from all substantial arbitrary impositions and purposeless restraints . . . and which also recognizes, what a reasonable and sensitive judgment must, that certain interests require particularly careful scrutiny of the state needs asserted to justify their abridgment.[7]

To paraphrase a bit, our modern understanding of ordered liberty implies that the state may not interfere with the personal or individual decisions that are most fundamental to a free life or with those liberties the protection of which is what prompts individuals—or would prompt individuals if given the explicit option—to enter civic society in the first place. The driving idea behind this notion of ordered liberty is that the protection of those liberties by the state against its own tendency to intrude in the name of some shared political end is of a higher order or of greater importance to civic life than any other conceivable and temporal state goal. Which particular liberties we view as fundamental and hence requiring this constitutional protection against even wise and benign state regulation is, of course, a subject of deep and profound disagreement. There is, however, a remarkably broad consensus in our contemporary legal culture and in our national community generally about the quite modern and quite liberal idea or aspiration of ordered liberty: there are some liberties, whatever they may be, so essential to an autonomous life that they must be kept free of state control.

In this chapter I will be largely critical of this understanding of ordered liberty, which I occasionally will call the "modern" or "liberal" interpretation of our constitutional heritage. I want to make two objections to this concept of liberty, one political and one historical. The political objection is that the modern conception of ordered liberty is a largely empty promise for women. My claim, very briefly, will be that even the ideal expressed by this conception of ordered liberty—to say nothing of the actual practices it protects—is skewed against women in a significant manner. The historical objection is that the liberal conception of liberty is also a cramped, inaccurate understanding of our constitutional history. I will conclude by arguing that we could fundamentally reconceive liberty in a more generous and explicitly feminist way without doing violence to either liberalism or to the document we have inherited.

Before I embark on the main project, however, one preliminary comment is in order. I want to emphasize at the outset what I am not doing. By embracing a critical posture toward the generally liberal concept of ordered liberty so eloquently spelled out by Justice Harlan and by advocating in its stead a quite different conception, I am not endorsing, and fervently hope not to be understood as endorsing, the conservative critique of ordered liberty presently being urged in a number of opinions by Justice Scalia.[8] Furthermore, I do not mean to embrace the very different conception of that ideal being developed in a disturbingly large and growing number of recent Supreme Court decisions.[9] My general aim is to argue that the liberal understanding of ordered liberty articulated by Justices Cardozo and Harlan and given full meaning by the liberty-expanding cases of the Warren Court era is unduly cramped and ungenerous. It does not go far enough to do what it purports to do on its own terms, which is to protect the autonomy and liberty of individuals. Specifically, it does not protect the autonomy and liberty of women.

Justice Scalia's critique is quite the opposite.[10] Justice Scalia, and to a lesser extent his fellow conservative colleagues on the Court, clearly believes that the liberal understanding of ordered liberty as tied to the fundamental needs and interests of the ideally autonomous individual is too generous toward the individual. He believes that it has unduly limited the sphere of legitimate state control of individual liberty and privacy and has granted the individual too much freedom vis-à-vis the community and state within which the individual must live and be a part. Accordingly, Justice Scalia and his conservative colleagues want to shrink the sphere of ordered liberty to guarantee less liberty and provide more order. In contrast, I would like to see us expand that sphere. Unlike Justice Scalia's attack, my critique of the liberal understanding of ordered liberty is decidedly friendly.

As the center of power on the Court shifts from the liberal bloc of the Warren-Burger years to the conservative bloc of the Rehnquist-Scalia years, it becomes less clear, of course, what role friendly critiques such as the one I intend to offer are to play in our constitutional conversations. We are at this moment occupying an ambiguous historical moment with regard to very basic constitutional norms. It is not clear whether the liberal understanding of ordered liberty briefly spelled out here will survive the conservative revolution on the Court presently under way. Should Justice Scalia's reformulation of ordered liberty—according to which the Constitution protects, in the name of liberty, the traditions of our collective past rather than the decisions of an ideally autonomous and individual life— prove successful, then so-called friendly critiques of the liberal understanding of ordered liberty may become, in a constitutional sense, simply beside the point.

On the other hand, if the liberal understanding of ordered liberty does survive, then it is imperative that we criticize it and try to improve it. What I am calling the *liberal conception* of ordered liberty does still dominate constitutional discussion, interpretation, and doctrine. It is still the ruling doctrine and is still a fundamental part of our constitutional law. It should go without saying (although in this time of hyperpatriotism it unfortunately often does not) that we best honor the Constitution and the law we create under it not by blindly revering its doctrines and certainly not by pledging our loyalty to its present form, but by interpreting it, struggling with it, criticizing it, setting its goals against itself, and forcing it and us to be true to our noblest selves. To the extent that the concept of ordered liberty elaborated by the liberal Court during the Warren Court years is still a part of the law that governs us, we should subject it to criticism to improve it, the principles it articulates, and the societal practices it governs.

Even if the conservative Court succeeds in replacing the liberal aspiration of ordered liberty honored by the Warren Court with the very different set of conservative aspirations urged by Justice Scalia, friendly critiques of the liberal concept of ordered liberty are still important to make and hear. The aspiration of ordered liberty imperfectly implemented by the great liberal decisions of the Warren Court is not merely a constitutional aspiration, important as constitutionalism may be, but is a cornerstone of modern liberal theory. As a part of the political theory and of the utopian dream we call liberalism, a dream that predates and heavily informs our constitutional ideas and practices, it behooves us to "get it right." We should strive to make our conception of ordered liberty the best it can be, even if the liberalism of which it is a part survives as only a dissident voice, rather than a living part, of our positive constitutional law.

Ordered Liberty

The liberal and relatively modern conception of ordered liberty I want to address has at least two salient features. First, the regime of ordered liberty to which we aspire is, to use Isaiah Berlin's famous formulation, a regime of negative rather than positive liberty.[11] It is liberty or freedom from, not liberty or freedom to, which the Bill of Rights protects. When we speak of ordered liberty, we speak of the individual's liberty or freedom from invasion, intrusion, intermeddling, or overregulation rather than the positive liberty or freedom to live in a particular way, attain one's full potential, actualize one's inner nature, or even govern oneself in a well-run democratic or majoritarian system.[12] We generally are not concerned, in our constitutional aspiration to ordered liberty, with the freedom that comes from being well-fed, clothed, sheltered, educated, or actively participating in the laws that govern us.[13] We are concerned instead with the freedom to be ourselves within some defined sphere: the freedom to make our own decisions, think our own thoughts, worship our own deities, and choose our own way of life within some sphere, the boundaries of which admittedly are not clearly discernible but which are absolutely inviolable once drawn. We are concerned with the right to be left alone[14] and not with the right to any particular way to be. Where those boundaries within which we have the right to be left alone are to be drawn will be and must be a function of our known human nature and, as such, will be debated endlessly. That the boundaries must be drawn somewhere, however, is the very essence of the liberal interpretation of our Constitution as well as, perhaps, the very essence of modern liberalism. Political philosopher Isaiah Berlin describes negative liberty in this way:

> [S]ome portion of human existence must remain independent of the sphere of social control. To invade that preserve, however small, would be despotism. . . . We must preserve a minimum area of personal freedom if we are not to "degrade or deny our nature" . . . . What then must the minimum be? That which a man cannot give up without offending against the essence of his human nature. What is this essence? What are the standards which it entails? This has been, and perhaps always will be, a matter of infinite debate. But whatever the principle in terms of which the area of non-interference is to be drawn, whether it is that of natural law or natural rights, or of utility or the pronouncement of a categorical imperative, or the sanctity of the social contract, . . . liberty in this sense means liberty from; absence of interference beyond the shifting, but always recognizable, frontier.[15]

With only a few exceptions, most notably the right to vote guaranteed by the Fifteenth Amendment, the ordered liberty that the Constitution protects, according to the modern conception, is our negative liberty to be left alone and not our positive liberty to food, shelter, a job or an income or to a fulfilled, prosperous, meaningful, and self-governed life. The constitutional preference for negative over positive liberty is captured by the oft-made claim that the Constitution itself is a negative one. The Constitution, it is said, protects our negative rights to be free from intrusion instead of our positive rights to a positively free, active, involved, civic, or healthy existence. The Constitution, at least according to its modern interpreters, is a shield of protection; it is not a sword of entitlement.

The second feature of the modern conception of ordered liberty has its origins not in liberal theory, but in constitutional doctrine. By ordered liberty, we aspire to a regime that respects the negative freedom of the individual, and more specifically, to a regime that respects the negative freedom of the individual from undue intermeddling or interference from one and only one source—the state. Accordingly, the Constitution, the document on which we rely to give teeth to our aspirations, overwhelmingly is concerned with the potential for oppression in the relationship between the individual and both federal and state government. It does not, then, address the potential for oppression between the individual and other forms of organized social authority, such as the corporate employer, the trade union, the family, or the church, which also may infringe on an individual's negative freedom. In other words, the constitutional dictate of ordered liberty places limits only on the state's potential for control. This second principle is what is often referred to in constitutional doctrine as the *state action requirement*.[16] The constitutional guarantee of negative liberty is not triggered unless the state has acted in some way that infringes on a protected and fundamental right. If we put these two principles together, the modern conception of ordered liberty means that the Constitution protects the negative liberty of the individual against excessive intrusion by the state, by state officials, or, at the outer extreme, by authorities acting under color of state authority.

Constitutional law is an admittedly complex subject, and the following generalities are subject to a host of exceptions. Nevertheless, from these two basic premises—that the liberty protected by our constitutional aspirations is negative rather than positive and that it is only liberty from state action and not liberty from other sources of social authority that is protected—we can generate not only much of the modern content but also, and more important for these purposes, most of the limits of our specific constitutional guarantees. From the first principle—that the Constitution protects negative rather than positive liberty—we can generate the limits the Court has imposed on the substance of the rights that the Constitution protects. We are guaranteed the freedom to speak, believe, associate or not associate with others, but we are not guaranteed an education,[17] adequate shelter, clothing, food, a job, or an income.[18] The former are negative freedoms while the latter, often called welfare rights, are examples of positive liberties and, hence, are not protected.[19] We are guaranteed the freedom to send our children to a private school of our choice, if we can afford it, free of state interference to the contrary because this is easily characterized as a negative freedom.[20] It is a part of the very general freedom to contract as one pleases without state interference—perhaps the quintessential negative liberty in a market economy—as well as the right to raise one's children according to one's own preferences without state interference.[21] We are not, however, guaranteed the right to a private school education, regardless of ability to pay, or even the right to a quality public school education.[22] The so-called right to an education is a positive freedom and, therefore, is not protected. We are still guaranteed (albeit narrowly) the right to procure contractually an abortion,[23] if we can afford one, because this is a negative freedom and part of our right to be left alone. We are not guaranteed the right to an abortion, whether or not we can pay for it, because that would be a positive freedom and would not be protected.[24] We are not even guaranteed the right to abortion counseling, for that, too, would be a positive right and, hence, not protected.[25] We are (more or less) guaranteed the right to read whatever we wish within the confines of our own home, but we are not guaranteed the right to literacy. The former is part of the negative right to be left alone, while the latter is, if anything, part of a positive concept of liberty. The general rule I am suggesting is this: the Constitution guarantees us the right to do certain things free of interference from social authority, but it does not guarantee us the absolute right to do those same things. The negative freedom that is the concern of the Constitution extends only to the right to procure goods or develop abilities free of interference from social authority. It does not positively guarantee the individual the goods themselves, or access to the goods, or access to the ability or skills necessary to procure them.

We can generate the limits of the scope of the rights the Constitution protects from the second principle—that the negative freedom which is the concern of the Constitution extends only to negative freedom against interference from the state, what is typically called the state action requirement. We are protected, for example, against the state's censorship of certain ideas or modes of expression. Were a state to criminalize the utterance of communist, atheistic, Catholic, feminist, or white supremacist beliefs, such a statute most certainly would be ruled unconstitutional. We are not protected, however, against censorship of those same ideas by private publishers.[26] Should the major publishers determine that certain ideas—communist, feminist, or pacifist—do not sell and, therefore, decide not to publish, or should the media decide that certain points of view—critical perspectives on the Persian Gulf War, for example—decrease ratings and, therefore, decide not to air them, effectively censoring from the public discourse those contributions, there has been an unquestionable censoring of ideas from the public sphere. Nevertheless, there has been no constitutional violation.[27] In fact, according to some commentators, Congress's attempts to correct for this private censorship and impose upon private media obligations of fairness may be a constitutional violation of the private media's right to uncensored expression.[28] Consequently, while we all are protected against a wide range of official state censorship, women are not protected against the censorial, silencing effect of a pornography industry run amok,[29] and African-Americans are not protected against the similarly silencing effect of racist hate speech[30]—the murder of the spirit, to use the expression coined by law professor Patricia Williams.[31] Similarly, while we are constitutionally protected against police violence and brutality, we receive no constitutional protection against violence and brutality from a fellow citizen, an abusive spouse, a lover, or a parent. Of course, the state's criminal law may or may not accord us protection from such private violence, but whether it does or not is of no constitutional moment. Even if the state does nothing to protect us against such violence, there has been no constitutional violation. So long as the violence came from a private citizen, there has been no state action. At worst, there has been only state inaction, and that, as the Supreme Court has made clear, is simply not enough. The citizen, we might say, has no constitutional right to a police force.[32]

To recapitulate, the modern concept of ordered liberty governing the great bulk of our modern constitutional law is constituted by, and limited by, two principles: (1) the philosophical and political notion that there is some sphere of individual conduct, belief, and expression that should be inviolable against the intrusion, intervention, or interference of social authority; and (2) the more purely constitutional (and distinctively American) notion that the individual's negative freedom has been infringed wrongly only if it is the state, rather than some other social authority or private force, responsible for the infringement. Before beginning my critique, it may be worth noting one general logical feature of the liberal concept of ordered liberty as I have just described it. Contrary to a widespread misunderstanding, the two principles that constitute and limit the modern understanding of ordered liberty—the preference for negative liberty and the state action requirement—are logically independent of each other. Not only is the state action requirement not required by the preference for negative over positive liberty, but in many cases, it is fundamentally at odds with it. If we are truly concerned with the negative freedom of individuals, then we should be concerned with unnecessary limitations on our interference with those freedoms whatever the source, whether it be the state or some other form of organized social authority. There surely are forms of organized social authority that are at times more intrusive, more interventionist, more controlling, and more interfering with an individual's right to be left alone than the state. Indeed, it may only be through state intervention that these private infringements of the individual's negative liberty can be addressed.

Imagine, for example, the profound interference with the negative liberty to do, think, act, believe, and say as one pleases, worked by some Mormon communities on the developing sense of self and society of 13- or 14-year-old adolescent girls, primed by their parents and their community not for participatory and autonomous adulthood, but for continuing infantilization and dependency through a too-early marriage. Imagine the similar effect on the negative liberty of the Amish child occasioned by the Amish community's refusal to allow their children a high school education. There may be reasons, even compelling reasons, for insisting that the state ought not interfere with the practices of these insular religious communities. We may value religious diversity in these subcommunities for their own sake, as Mill urged that we should.[33] Alternatively, we may fear the sort of spillover consequences of unleashing state power on such groups. I am not arguing for greater control of these religious minorities. I do insist that, whatever the argument might be for state nonintervention into the freedom of these religious groups to oppress their individual members, it cannot be based on the principle of negative liberty standing alone, for that principle often will cut the other way. Although the negative freedom of groups or subcommunities to be left alone might be furthered, the individual's negative freedom is hurt, not helped, by the state's policy of nonintervention into these private spheres of communal coercion, intimidation, and control. True devotion to the principle of negative liberty should sometimes counsel for state intervention into private relations and sometimes counsel against it. There is no necessary connection between the respect for individual autonomy, which informs our commitment to negative liberty, and the fear of excessive state control, which informs our constitutional state action doctrine. Both commitments might be justified, but they must be justified on independent grounds; neither follows from the other.

Ordered Liberty and Women's Rights

Whatever its internal logic, the modern conception of ordered liberty currently guiding constitutional law has not served women well. The reason is simple enough: the modern conception of ordered liberty does not capture and, so long as the modern interpretation dominates, the Constitution does not guarantee the liberties that women peculiarly lack in this country. As a consequence, the constraints under which women distinctively live are not those prohibited by constitutional mandate. In a formal sense, the problem is twofold. First, many of the liberties women lack are positive rather than negative and not protected for that reason. Second, whether characterized as positive or negative, the constraints that limit women's liberty typically are imposed not by the state but by private and sometimes very private, even intimate, relationships and are not prohibited for that reason. Indeed, the mismatch between the liberty protected by the Constitution and the liberty women distinctively lack is so great as to make the Constitution irrelevant at best and often a positive danger to women's lives. From the perspective of women's liberty, it is truly not clear at this point in our history whether the Constitution and the ordered liberty it protects are worthy of celebration or part of an immense societal problem that still remains to be solved.

I will give two examples of the general incompatibility of women's needs and our ruling, liberal conception of ordered liberty. If we look directly at contemporary women's lives, we can identify two constraints within which women live quite distinctively and which disproportionately limit our freedom. First, women, far more than men, live within the constraints of gender roles, assigning to women far greater responsibility for child-raising and domestic labor.[34] This is what Arlie Hochschild provocatively calls the "second shift" phenomenon: women, in effect, work two jobs in this society to a man's one. One of these jobs is often underpaid, and the second, the domestic shift, is utterly unpaid.[35] Consequently, by virtue of their unequal responsibility for domestic and childcare labor, women find it difficult or impossible to be economically self-sufficient through participation in the paid labor market or to be involved in the public sphere of political decision making. There are a limited number of hours in a day, and so long as women continue to work two jobs to a man's one, and continue to be trained to willingly accept this inequity and men trained to expect it, women will find it proportionately more difficult than men to live otherwise autonomous, politically engaged, economically self-sufficient lives. As long as there is laundry to wash, diapers to change, children to feed, houses to clean, and meals to make, and as long as women disproportionately are doing it, there is that much less time for women to vote, campaign, hold public office, sit on boards, create art and culture, and live otherwise positively free lives.[36] Just as important, so long as women are and feel responsible for these tasks, the absolutely obvious incompatibility of that work with the positive liberty praised by classical liberals[37] and modern civic republicans[38] alike—full, rounded, independent, politically participatory lives led in the public sphere—will continue to imply for and to women the inescapable message that we are unsuitable for the liberty men expect and often (but not always) receive as a matter of course. Indeed, as suggested by the 1960s term "Women's Liberation," the fact that women find political participation and economic self-sufficiency a much more illusive goal than men do might be described as the most important finding of the second wave of twentieth-century feminism that captured our collective political imagination in the 1960s and early 1970s.[39]

Second, women live within the constraints of a high risk of sexual violence and a pervasive fear of sexual violence inhibiting our actions in the public world and coloring our inner lives in the private.[40] This greater vulnerability obviously compromises women's physical security and psychological well-being in many ways. For instance, both the violence itself and the fear of sexual violence quite obviously and dramatically limit women's freedom to move about physically in our community to a much greater extent than such a fear limits men.[41] Moreover, sexual violence and fear of sexual violence also drastically limit our choices and even our perception of our choices of ways to live.[42] It makes marriage appear to be much safer, and hence more desirable, than it is. It makes nonmarital life styles—single, celibate, or lesbian—both appear to be and in fact to be quite dangerous, to say nothing of socially unacceptable. In addition, sexual violence and the fear of it limit many women's enjoyment of sexuality, and this, too, should be understood as a very real cost. Most damaging, however, fear of sexual violence, like fear generally, infantilizes women and leaves us more vulnerable, both in our own perceptions of ourselves and in others' perceptions of us. The fear, as much as the actual violence, badly cripples women's sense of ourselves and societal perceptions of us as autonomous, free, and independent agents. For women in abusive marriages and intimate relationships, this infantilization and depersonalization is most extreme. In such relationships, sexual violence and the fear of it can strip away virtually all sense of self-possession. The repeatedly abused woman becomes, in fact as well as in self-image, a means, rather than an end, to the fulfillment of another's desires. She quite literally lacks the capacity to be herself when she has been put under the sovereign will of a violent and violence-prone partner.[43] More generally, the fear of the potential for sexual violence from husbands, partners, potential partners, acquaintances, or strangers leaves all women, not just abused wives and rape victims, considerably more vulnerable, more dependent, and more constrained than our brothers, fathers, sons, and husbands.

Both the constraint of unequal parenting and the constraint of sexual violence profoundly limit women's political participation, economic self-sufficiency, physical security, and psychological well-being—or, in a word, women's autonomy. Both constraints limit some central aspect of women's liberty. What I want to show now is that in spite of the tremendous threat these constraints pose to women's liberty, neither of them, given the dominant, liberal understanding of ordered liberty, is particularly vulnerable to constitutional challenge or within the ambit of constitutional concern. Even worse, the societal conditions that facilitate and at times constitute these constraints may have constitutional protection, in the name of protecting negative liberty, against political or legal change. Let me comment on each of these constraints in a little more detail, showing why they are largely unamenable to constitutional challenge and why the social practices from which they arise may even be constitutionally protected.

I start with women's unequal parenting responsibility and the constraint it imposes on women's political and economic autonomy. Whatever else one might want to say about this particular constraint on women's lives, this much is clear: however unjust it may be and however pervasive its restrictive impact on women's potential, given the modern understanding of ordered liberty under the Constitution, the Constitution holds no promise of correcting it for two reasons. The first should be obvious enough from the way I have labeled the problem. The kind of autonomy of which women are deprived by virtue of the unequal distribution and unequal recognition of and compensation for domestic labor is almost paradigmatically positive rather than negative. It is the freedom to live a certain kind of involved, public, political, and economic life, not freedom from any particular kind of intrusion. It is the freedom to be, in the fullest sense, a citizen that is threatened in part by women's unequal responsibility for parenting the young. So long as we continue to pledge our allegiance to a Constitution that protects negative but not positive liberty, the tremendous constraints imposed on women's public lives by their unequal responsibilities for domestic labor will never rise to a constitutional magnitude. Whether or not it is unjust, it is not an injustice for which the Constitution as it is presently understood demands compensation.

Second, regardless of whether the liberty women lack by virtue of unequal and unpaid parenting is negative or positive, women's unequal parenting and domestic responsibility is still largely invulnerable to constitutional challenge because of the state action requirement. One need not be a naive adherent to a falsely innocent conception of the state to infer from the cross-cultural breadth and transgenerational depth of the problem that the assignment to women of disproportionate childraising labor and domestic chores, to say nothing of a lesser role in public life, is made not by any particular state or state official but by a complex, transsocietal, and transgenerational web of shared understandings about the nature of women and men, women's natural capacity for motherhood and their disinclination for the life of the citizen, artist, intellectual, artisan, or wage-paid laborer, and men's societal inclination for all of the above and their natural disinclination for parenting. We might, for purposes of brevity, call this complex, transsocietal, transgenerational web of shared understandings "patriarchy." My point is that patriarchy, so defined, is not (or certainly is not entirely) a product of state action, no matter how broadly we might define either concept. Patriarchy infects not only our laws, but also our private lives and relations. It springs not only from our legal system, but also from our private orderings. Although the state may have from time to time in our history exacerbated it, legitimated it, and enforced it, and in some ways continues to do so, the state did not create patriarchy. For that fundamental reason, simply ending the state's complicity with it will not cure it. Women living in a state whose law is rigorously neutral toward women and men still will find themselves burdened by the inequality and injustice of a private regime of patriarchal control. Women will still find themselves unable to live the positively free life of the citizen because of it.

Simply put, if patriarchy persists at least to some degree and in some of its manifestations without benefit of state action,[44] there simply is no constitutional violation, so long as we understand the Constitution to protect only our right to be free of state intervention. Regardless of whether the unjust distribution of labor and responsibility in the family sphere constrains women's positive liberty to full citizenship and autonomy or women's negative liberty to choose a way of life free of social authoritarian intervention, there is nothing unconstitutional in the injustice. The Constitution is silent on the many constraints, injustices, and inequalities perpetuated on women by the private forces we understand as patriarchal. In short, patriarchy is constitutional to the extent that it is autonomous from state control and creation.

The difficulty goes even deeper, however. Not only is patriarchy not unconstitutional, but, to the degree that patriarchy is woven into the fabric and pattern of our most private intimate lives, it may be even constitutionally protected. The Court has held repeatedly that our negative liberty to be free of state intervention at a minimum contains the liberty to create a private, familial life in whatever way the individual deems best and in line with her own beliefs about the meaning and content of the good life.[45] The central and liberal understanding that whatever else negative liberty protects it must protect the relations of our intimate and familial lives typically is captured in one word: privacy. Because the Constitution protects our familial privacy, it arguably protects our access to birth control,[46] along with our rights to procure an abortion,[47] to attend the private school of our choice,[48] and, in general, to make whatever decisions we deem best about the way our children are raised.[49] That privacy, however, comes with a terrible and often terrifying price to women. If, as a number of feminists now contend, private life is the home of patriarchy[50]—if patriarchal control of women's choices and patriarchal domination of women's inner and public lives occur in the very private realm of home life—then the Constitution, above all else, protects the very system of power and control that constrains us. The complex system of ties peculiarly binding women may be not just constitutional, but positively constitutionally protected. If this is true, then the Constitution is not only not a shield against injustice for women, but is itself a sword of injustice pointed very markedly at women. It is part of the problem, not part of the solution.

The constraint on women's liberty occasioned by sexual violence, like that imposed by gender roles, is also not amenable to constitutional challenge under current constitutional interpretation. Unlike the constraint of gender roles, sexual violence might be a constraint on negative rather than positive liberty. As was the case with gender roles, however, the constraint on liberty occasioned by sexual violence is not a constraint directly worked by state action. Instead, it is a constraint imposed by men. Although the state unarguably aggravates the harm by casual, lax, or nonexistent enforcement of the criminal laws against sexual violence,[51] it is the sexual violence actually perpetrated by men—strangers, acquaintances, dates, lovers, and husbands—rather than irrational or abusive states or state officials that most profoundly limits women's liberty. To put the same point affirmatively: while we have a panoply of rights protecting us against abusive and violent action by the state, we do not have a constitutional right to be free from sexual violence. Because of the so-called state action requirement, the profound infringement of women's liberty by sexual violence violates no constitutional right of sexual security, invokes no constitutional norm of ordered liberty, and triggers no constitutionally significant obligations. There is simply no real constitutional issue.

Thus (and this is the central point of my critique), because the fear of sexual violence is not a fear of abusive state action, it is of absolutely no constitutional consequence. In the extreme case, arguably no constitutional guarantee would be breached were the state to cease enforcing entirely its criminal laws dealing with sexual violence. This would be an example of state inaction, not state action, and although it would undoubtedly give rise to constitutional litigation, there would be no clear-cut argument supporting such a challenge. The bottom line is that our constitutional guarantee of ordered liberty—our constitutional right to be free of abusive, irrational, or unnecessary infringement of our individual freedom—is a largely empty promise for women. It addresses what is, at worst, a marginal problem in women's lives and leaves absolutely untouched the most glaring source of bondage.

In the case of the constraints of sexual violence no less than the constraints imposed by gender roles, the problem is not just that the constraint on freedom is not unconstitutional, or put affirmatively, that we do not have a constitutional right to be protected against sexual assault. The problem is deeper than that. If the state were to take affirmative actions to address sexual violence and the violence that women suffer within intimate relations and private homes in particular, such action may itself be unconstitutional or, at least, raise constitutional problems. In the interest of the individual's negative liberty to do, think, speak, and act as he or she pleases, the Constitution generally protects the liberty of the individual against excessive or overzealous criminalization of private life and protects a realm of privacy (typically as co-extensive with family life) within which it is extremely difficult for the state to intrude. I am not saying that it would be unconstitutional for the state or for the federal government to undertake legislative action addressing the problem of domestic abuse or sexual violence. If it should do so through criminalization, however, both the general concept and the particular conception of the Constitution as the guardian of individual liberty against the criminal arm of the state would burden and limit its efforts.

The general problem, of which gender roles and sexual violence are but two examples, is that the modern Constitution, in the name of ordered liberty, defines, insulates, and then protects a realm of individual privacy within which the state may not intrude. It is within that very realm, however, that the subordination of women through violence and the threat of violence, through the assumption of unequal parenting obligations, and through the imposition of restrictive gender roles occurs most egregiously. We are left with this uncomfortable and possibly life-threatening constitutional paradox: the Constitution protects and guarantees ordered liberty, but it does not secure women's liberty. The Constitution protects the individual against abusive and violent state conduct, but not only does it not protect women against the abuse and violence that most threatens them, it perversely protects the sphere of privacy and liberty within which the abuse and violence takes place.

The deep incongruity between our modern liberal conception of ordered liberty and women's needs does, of course, have historical parallels. Throughout history, in fact, feminists have felt ambivalent about the Bill of Rights—from Abigail Adams' futile attempt to urge her husband to include women's interests,[52] if not rights, in the early drafting of the original document to the late nineteenth-century abolitionist feminists' bitter disappointment with the Reconstruction Congress's refusal to include women's equality in the vision of social justice embodied in the Fourteenth Amendment.[53] The modern Constitution, however, informed by the distinctively modern liberal understanding of ordered liberty, does not only ignore women—although it does do that. It positively protects the sphere of privacy, negative liberty, and individual freedom within which women are most vulnerable and within which women are uniquely, individually, and definitively oppressed.[54] Thus, through its commitment to a liberal and modern conception of liberty, the contemporary Constitution not only fails to protect women's needs and aspirations, but affirmatively protects the sphere of privacy and conduct within which women's subordination occurs.

Liberty, Equality, and Autonomy

There are two possible ways of addressing this conflict between women's needs, interests, and aspirations and our presently dominant, liberal interpretation of ordered liberty. The first of these, which I will call the *egalitarian response,* has become the near-standard response of feminist constitutional lawyers. It is, I believe, deeply flawed. The second has not received as much development, but may ultimately have more promise.

The egalitarian response begins with this correct and telling observation: the tension between women's interests and the modern interpretation of ordered liberty is not unique to women but exemplifies a much larger and deeper phenomenon—that is, the tension, conflict, and contradiction between our constitutional commitment to liberty on the one hand and our political commitment to equality on the other.[55] The conflict is not, in other words, between women's liberty and ordered liberty, as I have been describing it, but between equality and liberty. Individual liberty, no matter how construed, always comes at the cost of equality. Individual liberty, so to speak, "frees up" the sphere of action within which private individuals oppress each other. As the New Deal constitutionalists and liberals saw it, "freeing up" individual liberty in the economic sphere exacerbates and exaggerates differences in wealth between owners and laborers. Achieving some more egalitarian distribution of income requires limiting the negative liberty of individual economic actors. Similarly, in our own time, "freeing up" the negative liberty of individuals to say exactly what they please, no matter how racist, hateful, incendiary, or vicious exacerbates the harms of the worst kind of virulent racism still visited upon African-Americans in our society and, consequently, widens the social inequality between the white majority and the black minority.[56] By allowing the individual a free rein in matters of speech, we subject members of racial minorities to injurious, belittling, sometimes emotionally crippling forms of racial insult—speech that we can all agree has absolutely no redeeming value. Likewise, by leaving the individual free to speak, hear, sell, or purchase whatever he or she wishes, we free up the multimillion-dollar pornography industry to endanger women's self-image, lives, and safety through violent imagery that arguably increases the risk of sexual violence in an already violent society. By freeing the individual to act absolutely as he wishes within the privacy of his own home, we endanger the well-being and often the lives of children at the whim and mercy of sometimes less than loving parents. Examples could be multiplied.

The lesson to be learned from these conflicts, according to this view, is that increases in individual liberty generally come at the cost of decreases in equality. Put somewhat differently, according to the egalitarian critique, individual liberty invariably exacerbates, rather than ameliorates, the subordination of some groups by others—of women by men, of blacks by whites, of workers by capitalists—and, accordingly, widens the gap in power, prestige, and wealth between these groups. Liberty and equality, on this view, are in an inevitable tension: we cannot increase one without jeopardizing the other. If we want to do something real about equalizing men and women or blacks and whites, we will have to limit, somewhat, individual freedom; and if we want to increase individual liberty, we will have to jeopardize, to some degree, equality. To whatever extent we are constitutionally "constituted by" commitments to both ordered liberty and the civic, political, or at least, formal equality of men and women, capitalists and laborers, and blacks and whites, we are committed inescapably to contradictory ideals.

The conflict I have been discussing between our modern understanding of ordered liberty and women's needs, on this view, simply partakes of this same general pattern. As noted here, "freeing up" speech facilitates the harms done to women through the propagation of pornography and, thus, exacerbates inequality. Protecting the privacy and freedom of individuals to do and say as we wish in our private, intimate lives frees men to oppress, abuse, exploit, or, in the extreme, rape, and thereby further weaken women. Protecting freedom of speech and expression frees a society riddled by inequities to perpetuate, in the name of freedom of ideas, notions of gender roles that continue to impoverish women.[57] Conversely, each gain in gender equality, like gains in equality generally, comes with the price of a diminution in individual freedom: a shrinking of First Amendment freedoms in the case of pornography, a piercing of family and individual privacy in the case of domestic violence and inequitable allocation of responsibility for parenting, and a diminution of individual liberty in the case of greater criminalization of sexual violence and greater enforcement of the sanctions already on the books.

If this general political and philosophical point is right, then the constitutional strategy we should embrace to address the ill fit between our constitutional commitment to ordered liberty and women's needs seems clear enough. Advocates for women's interests should urge a general constitutional right to equality and then argue that the right to equality is of greater magnitude than the countervailing right, with which it is in tension, to individual liberty. If women are guaranteed equality, if not through the failed ERA then through the equal protection clause of the Fourteenth Amendment, at least our commitment to liberty is limited by this counterbalancing commitment to equality. On this view, the Constitution gives weight to both values, which are concededly in tension and which, accordingly, must be weighed and balanced against each other by a court or interpretive body sensitive to both. The Constitution, therefore, not only protects the individual's negative liberty to speak and to privacy, but also protects women's right to equality. Hence, limits on pornography may be not only constitutional, but constitutionally required. Similarly, as I have argued in Chapter 2, the so-called marital rape exemption—which provides that nonconsensual sex within marriage is not rape and which is still in force in a number of states—may be unconstitutional in spite of the infringement on marital privacy and individual liberty that the criminalization of marital rape entails.[58] Lastly, if this view is right, when individuals arrange their private affairs so as to allocate to women a grossly disproportionate amount of the unpaid and underacknowledged labor of raising the next generation, we face a problem of constitutional, not just moral and political, magnitude.

I am in complete sympathy with the goal of women's equality and also have considerable sympathy for the particular arguments summarized here. There are, however, serious problems with the general conception of the Constitution on which these arguments rely. As a doctrinal matter, for example, it is not at all clear that the Constitution contains even a general commitment to anyone's equality, for women or for any other group. The Fourteenth Amendment does, of course, guarantee us equal protection of the laws, but it is unlikely that the framers intended the clause to mean, or the Court will ever interpret it as meaning, that the Constitution requires the sort of social, political, and economic equality women lack and that is threatened by an unbridled liberal devotion to ordered liberty. As a purely strategic or prudential matter, then, the attempt to balance the commitment to liberty with a countervailing commitment of an equal constitutional magnitude to equality seems doomed to failure. There is no constitutional commitment to equality that comes anywhere near the weight, depth, breadth, history, or sincerity of our constitutional commitment to liberty. In any constitutional standoff between liberty and equality, liberty is going to win. Liberty is an unmistakably constitutional requirement, as well as a political and moral aspiration, while equality is, at best, a political aspiration and, at various points in our history including most notably this one, not a widely shared one.

The more basic problem with this liberty versus equality view, however, is that by conceiving of the needs, interests, and aspirations of women that are threatened by ordered liberty—interests in security, needs for economic self-sufficiency, and aspirations for cultural and political participation—as being symptomatic of inequality, egalitarians may have misdiagnosed the problem. The sorts of needs and interests at stake in these conflicts seem to be interests in, needs for, and aspirations of liberty, not equality.[59] Women need to be free of sexual violence both in the home and out to be equal *and* to be free in the most basic sense in which that ideal is ever invoked—to have freedom of movement from place to place at the time of one's choosing and for one's own chosen ends. While freedom from sexual violence ultimately would serve to equalize the relative social and economic positions of women and men, it is basically women's liberty and only secondarily women's equality that is lost when women lose the freedom to move about in public spaces free from the fear of molestation.

Similarly, women need to be free of disproportionate obligations of labor in childraising to be equal *and* to be free to do other things—to be a fully participatory citizen; to work in the paid labor market; to create art, poetry, sculpture, or ceramics; to philosophize, educate, or study. Again, freedom from unequal and unpaid childraising obligations unquestionably would serve to equalize women and men in any number of ways. What each woman loses when she is tied to burdensome and unfair domestic obligations, however, is not simply some share of an abstract group interest in the equality of women and men generally, but, rather, and again in the most immediate sense imaginable, her own very individual and very personal liberty.

What I want to suggest is that instead of trying to limit liberty by urging equality as a counterweight, we should undertake a reconstruction of the modern interpretation of ordered liberty presently dominating both doctrine and understanding to include the liberties women distinctively lack. The place that reconstruction should start, I submit, is with the possibility that the modern interpretation of ordered liberty as protecting only negative liberty, and then only negative liberty infringed upon by the state rather than by other non-state authorities, is a flawed understanding of our constitutional tradition. The two limitations that define the modern conception of ordered liberty and render the Constitution's promise so empty from the perspective of women's lives and needs are flatly unjustified, given the breadth of political vision that inspired the general phrases of the Fourteenth Amendment, including its guarantee of liberty.

Let me begin with the distinction between negative and positive liberty. Whatever may be the merits of Berlin's assessment of the comparative abstract value of negative and positive liberty, it is far more consistent with the abolitionist history of the Fourteenth Amendment to understand the liberty guaranteed by that amendment's due process clause in a positive rather than negative sense.[60] What the post-Civil War reconstruction amendments were about fundamentally, after all, was securing the positive liberties of citizenship, self-governance, autonomy, and the end of bondage for the freed slaves.[61] The war was not fought to ensure the privacy of the slave or to secure his negative right to read, think, act, and speak as he pleased free from state intervention. It just would not have been enough for the southern states to grant the slaves rights of privacy and liberty to read, think, and speak as they see fit yet leave them slaves—nonvoting, dependent, uncompensated, and unfree. In short, the war was not fought nor the reconstruction amendments passed to ensure the negative liberty of the slave. The war was fought (and surely this was primary) to ensure the slave's positive rights to self-governance, independence, autonomy, and full citizenship. The right of the citizen to enjoy his liberty and the state's obligation not to deprive her of it other than by due process of law, as guaranteed by the due process clause of the Fourteenth Amendment, must be understood as including these positive rights of autonomy, economic self-sufficiency, and political self-governance.

Next, at least judging by the federal legislation passed in their immediate wake, a goodly part of what those amendments were intended to ensure was the positive liberty of the newly freed slaves, not just against pernicious state action but also against pernicious private action, which included the private relationship of master and slave itself, the private lynchings by the Ku Klux Klan, and the private refusals of service by innkeepers.[62] In the post–Civil War era, legislation and other actions taken by the southern states unquestionably endangered the freed slaves. The greatest threat to the slaves and to their very lives was not state action, however, but private action coupled with state inaction—in other words, the states' refusal to act against life-threatening and highly organized attempts by private individuals and organizations to deprive the freed slaves of their lives and liberty. It was private, not state action, that posed the most immediate threat to both the negative and positive liberties of the freed slaves.[63] Whatever else might be muddied about the intent of the framers of the Thirteenth, Fourteenth, and Fifteenth Amendments, one thing is vividly clear from the Civil Rights legislation and particularly the Ku Klux Klan Act that followed: what was sought by this profound enlargement of our constitutional charter was a guarantee from private violence and private oppression toward the freed slaves. This included private violence facilitated not only by actions taken by the states, but also by the states' inaction, whether by design or negligence, in the face of threats from private forces and individuals to the security of the former slaves' lives and freedoms.

Thus, the most immediate history of the Fourteenth Amendment, which is the necessary constitutional origin of our modern commitment to ordered liberty, is profoundly at odds with the modern liberal conception of the liberty that amendment was intended to ensure. There is no doubt that the reconstruction amendments were intended in part to protect a sphere of negative liberty. By virtue of their slavery, the slaves indeed lacked what we now call the negative liberties of familial privacy: reproductive freedom, control, and responsibility; and freedom of thought and religion. There is also no doubt, though, that the reconstruction amendments were intended to wipe out slavery itself and not just these manifestations of it. They were intended to ensure the negative rights of free choice and privacy, along with the full positive liberty to which slavery is the absolute antithesis. There is also little doubt that the framers of the reconstruction amendments intended to render unconstitutional a wide range of state actions that were meant to maintain the actual if not the nominal relation of slave and master. But, again, it is absolutely clear, not only from the record of the debate but also by virtue of the wide-ranging legislation that followed their passage, that the amendments were intended to effect far more than pernicious state action. They also were intended to ensure freedom from private violence and oppression and to accomplish this by obligating the state to take affirmative action (to use a modern phrase) to prohibit, penalize, and criminalize (and thereby protect against) private deprivations of that positive liberty. Lastly, according to the explicit command of section 5 of the Fourteenth Amendment, the amendments were intended to ensure that if the states failed to act accordingly, Congress would act in their stead.

Is there any modern lesson for contemporary life to be learned from this history? I think there is. As I have argued in this chapter, what women lack most profoundly in our culture is positive, not negative liberty. Women enjoy wide-ranging rights to privacy, speech, thought, and religion. But they lack the enjoyment of positive rights of autonomy, self-possession, economic self-sufficiency, and self-governance, to say nothing of the full rights and responsibilities of citizenship. Furthermore, women lack these liberties not because of pernicious state action but because of widespread and disabling patterns of private discrimination; societal indoctrination; and personal, intimate sexual violence, coupled with pernicious or at least negligent state inaction. These conditions appear to be invincible to constitutional challenge. Indeed, to some degree they appear to be constitutionally protected. The consequence is that many women are and feel themselves to be constitutionally disenfranchised.

What I have argued in this chapter is that we should be very cautious in identifying the cause of this disenfranchisement as our constitutional history and women's exclusion from it, rather than modern and contemporary understandings. The two limits most modern interpreters read into our conception of ordered liberty—a preference for negative liberty and an insistence on state action—are a product not of our constitutional history, but of modern habits of the heart and mind. In fact, as a matter of constitutional history, the liberal limits we impose on our conception of ordered liberty may be utterly unjustified. If our constitutional history, and hence our inherited constitutional meanings, is broader, more ambitious, and indeed nobler than we have grown to believe, then the disabling contradiction between our constitutional aspirations of individual liberty on the one hand and our political (whether or not constitutional) aspirations of political equality for women and men on the other may be more apparent than real. If this is correct, then Congress and the states may have an affirmative obligation under the due process clause of the Fourteenth Amendment to protect men and women's right to be left alone, as well as to protect women against private infringements of their right to be free from sexual violence and from onerous domestic responsibilities that deprive us of full economic and political autonomy. Finally, were Congress and the states to act on these obligations, then women, in spite of our historical exclusion from the process of constitutionalizing and amending this country's foundational beliefs, might come to have what women presently lack: some real stake in the constitutional system of rights and liberties that continues, however imperfectly, to give dignity to us all.

5

The Ideal of Liberty

■

What is the meaning and content of the "liberty" protected by the due process clause of the Fourteenth Amendment? In *Michael H. v. Gerald D.*,[1] Justices Brennan and Scalia spelled out what at first blush appear to be sharply contrasting understandings of the meaning of liberty and of the substantive limits liberty imposes on state action.[2] Justice Scalia argued that the "liberty" protected by a substantive interpretation of due process is only the liberty to engage in activities historically protected against state intervention by firmly entrenched societal traditions. I will sometimes call this the *traditionalist* interpretation of liberty. Justice Brennan, by contrast, argued for a much broader, and nominally more liberal, interpretation. The liberty protected by the Fourteenth Amendment, Brennan contended, means the liberty to enjoy those broad areas of life—such as parenthood, privacy, and sexuality—which have been identified as essential to liberty by the relevant judicial precedent of the liberal Warren and Burger Court era. I will sometimes call this the *precedential* interpretation.

In this chapter I will briefly argue that, appearances notwithstanding, Justice Brennan's precedential interpretation of liberty, no less than Justice Scalia's traditionalist one, is at its root deeply conservative. I will then argue that the best explanation for the conservatism of even this nominally "liberal" interpretation of liberty by an unquestionably liberal jurist is that it stems from the general need of all members of the Court—liberal and conservative—to interpret the Constitution in a way that vindicates the "jurisprudential virtues" of good judicial decision making. Those virtues, I will suggest, are themselves conservative, and perhaps necessarily so. It is therefore not surprising that constitutional interpretations rendered by even the liberal justices—such as Justice Brennan's interpretation of "liberty" in *Michael H.*—have conservative overtones and consequences.

Second, I will suggest that the justices' collective need to constrain interpretation by the ethical demands of the adjudicative virtues has cramped our understanding of liberty, as well as of the Constitution's other general phrases. We ought to liberate the interpretive questions—What is liberty? What constraints does it impose on state action?—from their historical associations with the ethical need to constrain judicial decision making. By doing this, we might achieve a more progressive, but also more accurate, understanding of the nature of individual liberty than that propounded by either Justice Brennan or Justice Scalia in their respective decisions in *Michael H.*

In his plurality opinion in *Michael H.*, Justice Scalia argued, partly in a footnote in which only one member of the Court joined,[3] that the "liberty" protected by substantive due process must be understood as including only the liberty to engage in activities or forms of life that have been "traditionally" protected against communal sanction, state action, or majoritarian control.[4] The requisite "tradition" in this formulation, Scalia went on to argue, must be interpreted as narrowly as is sensibly possible.[5] He then argued that the "liberty" interest which *Michael H.* sought to enforce— the liberty of an "adulterous biological father" to maintain a relationship with his biological daughter, when the child's mother is married to another man—has not been protected by any specific, narrowly tailored, societal tradition. Therefore, Scalia concluded, the California statute establishing a conclusive presumption in favor of the paternity of the mother's husband did not unconstitutionally deny the biological father his liberty.[6] Even assuming that we have traditionally protected "parenthood," Scalia argued, we have not traditionally protected the parental liberties of an adulterous father over his daughter born to a mother who is married to another man, and accordingly the statute establishing the conclusive presumption in favor of the "marital" father violates no constitutional stricture.[7]

Regardless of the merits of *Michael H.* itself, it seems fair to say, as Justice Brennan argued in dissent, that this interpretation of liberty and hence of substantive due process espoused by Justice Scalia is so narrow that if embraced by the Court it would lead to the effective end of the doctrine.[8] The claim that there exists a narrow, specific tradition protecting a liberty threatened by a challenged statute is fatally undermined by the existence of the statute itself. Obviously, it is difficult, if not impossible, to argue that Californians have a "tradition" protecting the rights of adulterous biological fathers when they have a statute granting a conclusive presumption of paternity to the husband of the child's mother. Furthermore, Scalia's position, if accepted, would undermine *Michael H.* along with virtually every major substantive due process case of the last twenty years.[9] For it is surely hard, if not impossible, to argue that we have a "tradition" protecting the rights of women to procure abortions in the face of multiple statutes criminalizing abortion. It is hard to argue that we have a "tradition" protecting the sexual autonomy or privacy of homosexuals in the face of sodomy laws. It is hard to argue that we have a "tradition" protecting the rights of patients in vegetative states to die with dignity free of technological intervention in the face of numerous state statutes heavily qualifying that freedom. Indeed, it is hard to argue, even, that we have a "tradition" protecting the rights of married persons to use contraceptives in the face of statutes criminalizing their distribution.[10] If Scalia is right to insist that the content of the "liberty" that limits the substantive scope of the police power must come from societal traditions, and right to insist that those traditions must be narrowly construed, then it seems fair to conclude that there is, in practical effect, no such limit. The police power of the states is substantively limited only by other express constitutional provisions, not by the content of the "liberty" guaranteed against invasion without "due process" in the Fourteenth Amendment.

At least at first blush, Justice Brennan's understanding of due process and the liberty it protects, spelled out in his dissenting opinion in *Michael H.*,[11] sharply contrasts with, and is considerably more expansive than, Scalia's understanding. The existence of a specific, firmly entrenched societal tradition, Brennan argued, cannot be the necessary condition for the existence of a liberty protected against state action. To have such a condition would be to render the clause a "redundancy": any liberty specifically enshrined in tradition will not be undercut by state law. The existence of a "tradition" is indeed relevant to the existence of a "liberty" protected against societal overreach, Brennan conceded, but the tradition must be understood generally, not specifically. Furthermore, and perhaps more important, the source of the tradition is not "society," but Supreme Court precedent. The liberties protected by due process are those general traditions that the Court has identified precedentially: parenthood, intimacy, reproduction, contraception, sexuality, and the like. Thus, under Brennan's approach, there is indeed a tradition protecting the sort of liberty *Michael H.* was seeking to enforce: "we," meaning the liberal Warren-Burger Court, have "traditionally" upheld the rights of unwed fathers to maintain relationships with their children. That tradition is not negatived, but violated, by a state statute that refuses to protect such rights if the child's mother is married to another man.

Similarly, under Brennan's approach, the major cases of the modern substantive due process revival were also correctly decided. Thus, "we"— meaning the remaining members of the Warren-Burger Court—have traditionally protected the liberty and freedom of persons seeking medical procedures and making decisions about when to start or expand families. Accordingly, that tradition is not negatived, but instead violated, by state statutes criminalizing abortion, and hence those statutes are unconstitutional, and *Roe v. Wade*[12] was decided correctly. Likewise, "we"— the relevant members of the Court—have "traditionally" protected the "right to be left alone," and again, that tradition is violated, not negatived, by the existence of statutes criminalizing consensual sodomy. Therefore, *Bowers v. Hardwick*[13] was decided erroneously. To take a final example, "we"—again the liberal members of the Court—have "traditionally" protected the right to bodily control and the right to decide one's own medical fate; this tradition is violated, not negatived, by the existence of statutes qualifying the "right to die" with weighty evidentiary presumptions. Therefore, the Court was right in *Cruzan v. Director, Missouri Department of Health*[14] to articulate a basic right to die,[15] and indeed the Court should have gone further than it was willing to go in giving substance to that right. Thus, the use of general rather than specific traditions, grounded not in societal custom, but in the Warren and Burger Courts' decisions that protected liberty, gives the formulation considerably more breadth than Scalia's explicitly narrow and conservative formulation.

In spite of the manifest differences between Justice Scalia's and Justice Brennan's accounts, however, and the sharply differing results to which those approaches lead, both positions—not just Scalia's—are deeply conservative understandings of the due process clause, for three reasons. First, and most obviously, both positions define the liberty protected by the due process clause by reference to some set of past historical traditions. The traditions on which they depend are different: Scalia prefers to defer to societal or communitarian tradition, whereas Brennan wants to rely on the traditions identified in the judicial precedent from a particular era. Both, nevertheless, define liberty in terms of past tradition rather than, for example, by reference to some understanding of the ideally free or autonomous individualist life.

Second, Justice Brennan, no less than Justice Scalia, understands the due process clause as a means by which we can "conserve" some aspect of the past against the encroachments of contemporaneous or future majoritarian or judicial power. Justice Scalia seeks to protect, or conserve, the traditions, and particularly the moral traditions, of the community against ill-advised, precipitous state actions. Brennan, by contrast, seeks to protect, or conserve, the traditions respected by a particular set of Supreme Court precedents, as well as, perhaps, the "tradition" of precedent itself, against future and contemporaneous Court betrayals of their underlying principles. But both view liberty, and the due process clause that protects it, as a means of protecting not so much individual liberty for its own sake, but individual liberty to participate in past traditions that are worthy of protection. To put the same point somewhat differently, both are "backward looking" understandings of liberty and of due process: they both define liberty by looking not at what liberty is, as understood by liberal philosophical exegesis, political oratory, or even linguistic analysis, but by examination of what it has meant according to the traditions or customs of the past.

Lastly, both justices' approaches, Brennan's no less than Scalia's, represent "communitarian" rather than "individualistic" understandings of the meaning of liberty. Neither justice asks what the ideally autonomous or liberated individual life demands or requires of the state; rather, both understand "liberty" as meaning essentially the liberty to conform to traditions, though traditions variously and differently understood. What is thus protected, at most, is the liberty to obey or conform to the dictates of relevant traditions, rather than the liberty to rebel against them, in the face of state or majoritarian action seeking to deny that liberty. For this reason as well, it is fair to characterize both Scalia's and Brennan's approaches as conservative. In summary, both justices seek to protect and conserve the traditions of the past against contemporaneous or future change, both are backward looking in their temporal orientation, and both are on their own terms anti-individualist. They protect not the individual's right to be different, idiosyncratic, iconoclastic, or rebellious, but the individual's right to conform to tradition and obey its dictates.

Furthermore, the conservatism of Brennan's discussion of liberty in *Michael H.* is not simply a peculiarity of that case. Rather, it reflects the general tenor and much of the language of the liberal justices' understanding of substantive due process that has evolved over the last twenty years. Indeed, virtually all of the recent substantive due process cases hailed as great liberal victories—*Roe v. Wade, Griswold v. Connecticut,*[16] *Eisen-*

stadt v. Baird,[17] and *Cruzan*[18]—are "conservative" in precisely the same sense as is Brennan's opinion in *Michael H.* All of these cases define liberty by reference to traditions that are themselves identified by reference to the past; they are all "backward looking" rather than forward looking in their orientation; and they all ultimately protect the "liberty" of the individual to conform to established historical traditions, rather than the liberty of the individual to rebel against them. Thus, the liberty protected in *Roe, Griswold,* and *Eisenstadt,* quite generally, is the "liberty" to participate in the traditionally protected familial and marital decisions regarding reproduction and is defended precisely on those grounds. Similarly, the "liberty" defended in *Cruzan* is the liberty to participate in the traditionally protected realm of decisions regarding one's own medical treatment.[19] Likewise, the dissenters in *Bowers v. Hardwick* rested their defense of sexual liberty not on the value of sexual liberty per se, but on the traditionally protected "right to be left alone." [20]

Why is this? Why is it that the interpretation of liberty offered by the liberal wing of the Court, not only in Brennan's expansive discussion of the issue in *Michael H.,* but also in the major modern substantive due process cases generally, differs only marginally from that offered by the conservative wing? The substantive due process doctrine is surely susceptible to more interpretations than the conservative interpretation it has received over the bulk of this century. More important, the ideal of liberty is surely susceptible to more and more progressive interpretations than either the traditionalist or precedential accounts given by Scalia and Brennan, respectively. Specifically, there are at least two understandings of "liberty" that differ dramatically from both Scalia's and Brennan's accounts. Both these understandings undoubtedly have played a role in our political debates, political history, and political dreams. Both could also—although to date they have not—play a role in constitutional interpretation as well.

First, as liberal philosophers from John Locke to John Rawls[21] have argued, the content and meaning of "liberty" might be properly derived not from historical tradition—whether communitarian or precedential—but from an ideal conception of an autonomous life. The content of that ideal is of course controversial, but that does not mean that it is not ascertainable. A life may not be ideally "autonomous," for example, without a guarantee of employment, minimal sustenance, and shelter, as John Dewey argued,[22] or without a just distribution of resources, as Rawls has argued.[23] Likewise, a life may lack autonomy without some sphere of privacy in which to conduct intimate affairs, without rights and freedoms retained from the state of nature, or without some amount of education. Whatever the merits of these arguments, they share one feature: they derive the content of liberty from liberal ideals rather than historical tradition. Their validity does not depend on the presence or absence of "traditions" guaranteeing welfare rights, privacy rights, education, or natural rights, but on the ascertainable conditions of a truly autonomous life.

A second possible understanding of liberty comes from radical politics and practice. "Liberty" might be understood in a "liberationist," rather than a "libertarian" sense. On this account, liberty requires liberation from any number of pernicious constraints, whether imposed by the state, private persons, or nature. This may include liberation from hunger, from slavery, from poverty, from sexual abuse, from "the patriarchy," and from racism itself. "Liberty," on this view, requires liberty from bondage, whether that bondage be the result of state oppression, state meddling, or private action.

Somewhat paradoxically, this "radical" interpretation of liberty has the virtue of being at least somewhat reflective of the history of the due process clause that protects it. The Fourteenth Amendment's due process clause might have meant originally that no one's "liberty" may be taken by anyone, such as a slaveowner, other than the state (and then only with due process). What due process requires, in other words, is that the state and only the state may be "sovereign" over the individual and her liberty. Correlatively, the due process clause imposes on the state an obligation to prohibit the "private sovereignty" effected by private relationships of domination and subordination, such as that of enslavement. By extension, then, in modern times the state may also have an obligation, on this view of both liberty and due process, to prohibit the private sovereignties created by unchecked racism, sexual violence, or homophobic violence. If the state fails to do this, it has deprived the individual of liberty, without due process.

Why, then, does "liberty" receive from even the liberal members of the Court at best a broad interpretation and a defense grounded in the conservative values of fidelity to the past, conformity to traditions, the primacy of the community over the individual, and respect for judicial precedent, rather than liberal commitments to autonomy or radical commitments to liberation? The easiest, but ultimately least satisfying explanation is that it is simply politics: it may be that appearances notwithstanding, Justice Brennan and the other liberals on the Court are in fact only marginally more liberal than Justice Scalia and his fellow conservatives. If so, the similarities between the two approaches might stem from their shared conservative roots, just as their manifest differences might stem from their obvious, but in the end superficial, political differences.[24] There are, though, serious problems with this explanation. First, appearances are dramatically to the contrary; Justice Brennan is a modern liberal jurist if anyone is. Second, and perhaps more important, neither Justice Brennan nor Justice Scalia, in *Michael H.* or elsewhere, writes as if politics alone dictated their different legal conclusions. Rather, both write as though their understanding of the "law," and their understanding of the appropriate scope of the judicial role, led them to their divergent formulations. It may be worthwhile exploring other possible explanations which would take seriously both their clear political differences as well as their clearly stated legal and jurisprudential aspirations.

One possible alternative explanation, put forward with tremendous force by Cass Sunstein, is that the clause itself is generally "backward looking" in its orientation and has been so from its inception.[25] In sharp contrast to the equal protection clause—which is at least potentially progressive and "forward looking"—the history of both the Fifth and Fourteenth Amendments' due process clauses fairly clearly directs the Court to traditional, historical sources for ascertainment of the content of the liberty they protect.[26] The equal protection clause is the source of, and tool for, idealistic, progressive challenge to the status quo. In contrast, the due process clause, like the takings and contracts clauses, historically has been the tool of the conservative impulse to preserve the liberties defined by the past and to protect against overzealous, imprudent change.

It is no coincidence, following Sunstein's logic, that the Court in *Lochner v. New York*[27] understood the liberty protected by the due process clause as consisting of the liberty to enter contracts on individually chosen terms, thereby preserving the status quo, free from the redistributive and paternalist influences of reformist workplace legislation. The broad mistake of the *Lochner* Court, then, was to embrace a view of the entire Constitution as essentially analogous to this conservative understanding of the due process clause. The narrow mistake of the Court in *Lochner* itself, however, simply for purposes of its due process jurisprudence, was not that it understood due process conservatively, but that it viewed it as yet another substantive limit on state action.[28]

How, on this view, does one account for the recent "substantive due process" decisions that appear to be liberal victories, such as *Roe* or, arguably, *Griswold*? Sunstein has addressed this question only indirectly. According to Sunstein, among others, the statutes involved in these cases, although determined to be violations of the due process clause, properly should be understood instead as violations of the equal protection clause.[29] What is at stake in *Roe,* for example, is not "privacy" or "liberty," but the subordination of women as a class through the imposition of laws that have the effect of "turning women's reproductive capacities into something for the use and control of others."[30] And, the equal protection clause easily can be understood as a constitutional mandate to the states to avoid or to correct for precisely this kind of subordination. Furthermore, that kind of subordination rests on precisely the same conservative impulse as the *Lochner* decision itself. Whereas the *Lochner* Court treated the common law as providing the baseline against which intrusions on liberty are determined, the impulse to criminalize abortions treats "nature" as providing such baselines. Therefore, the repudiation of *Lochner,* far from undercutting the outcome in *Roe,* as argued by scores of the case's critics, in fact mandates it, but for reasons utterly inconsistent with those espoused in the decision itself. The repudiation of *Lochner,* and of the substantive understanding of the due process clause on which it depends, far from implying that *Roe* is wrongly decided, implies a repudiation of the use of the very sorts of "baselines" that underlie the criminalization of abortion, and hence the subordination of women. The repudiation of Lochner and of substantive due process, then, requires a reading of equal protection—not of due process—that in turn justifies the outcome in *Roe.*

The understanding of the Fourteenth Amendment that emerges from this Sunsteinian view of due process and equal protection is both neat and neatly schizophrenic: the equal protection clause is forward looking, while the due process clause is backward looking; the equal protection clause uses ideals of equality and nonsubordination as a baseline, while the due process clause uses extant practices and distributions; the equal protection clause, in essence, is progressive, while the due process clause is conservative. The equal protection clause, then, protects against the very sorts of "subordination" that the due process clause, under a substantive interpretation, requires. With this understanding, the conservatism of interpretations of substantive due process, even by the liberals on the Court, is not so mysterious. It simply reflects the historic conservatism of the due process clause itself, and of the liberty it purports to protect.

One further and closely related explanation of the conservatism of due process adjudication has been suggested—more indirectly than directly—by other progressive scholars of the due process clause.[31] The conservatism of the interpretations of due process rendered by even liberal justices may be a function not so much of the historical conservatism of the clause itself, but of the political and moral conservatism of the ideal of liberty it is designed to protect. From this perspective, liberty, not the due process clause, accounts for the conservative tilt of the substantive due process cases; individual liberty simply is a conservative ideal, and it is therefore not surprising that even liberal interpretations of its content reflect that fact. Promotion of individualist values and individual freedom "frees up" private action that will inevitably entail the subordination of weaker parties, whether the particular "liberty" is physical, economic, sexual, or ideational.[32] To be free of state control means, in essence, to be free to subordinate others—whether through one's superior economic strength manifested in self-serving and exploitative contracts, superior physical force facilitating physical or sexual oppression, or superior intellectual clout and access facilitating cultural tyranny.

Implicit in this view is an unavoidable "trade-off" between individual liberty and egalitarian ideals; protecting freedom or liberty inevitably entails the reinforcement of hierarchy. Protecting the individual's liberty to set contract terms further entrenches economic hierarchy. Protecting the individual's liberty to utter racially defamatory slurs further entrenches racial hierarchies. Protecting the individual's liberty to do as he wishes within the "privacy" of his own home, marriage, or family perpetuates the subordination of the women and children over which, as a consequence of his protected liberty, he enjoys dominion. Individual liberty necessarily implies the liberty to engage in private acts of subordination. As we increase liberty, we threaten equality, and we can only promote meaningful equality by curtailing, to some extent, the individual liberty with which it is inevitably at war.

There is a great deal to be said for these explanations. Both Sunstein's analysis of due process and the related critique of liberty have the virtue of taking the due process liberty cases "at face value." The reason for their conservative tilt stems from the content of the law itself, not from deep unobservable psychological facts or impermissible political motivations. Both explanations respect the boundaries, so to speak, of legal discourse, and both have the virtue of explaining the major conservative due process decision of the century—*Lochner*—along with the more subtle conservatism behind the Court's "liberal" modern due process cases, from *Griswold* to *Roe*. There may also be historical support for both positions. The progressive account of liberty summarized above, for example, is echoed not just in modern libertarian dogma, but in the account of liberty espoused in *The*

Federalist.[33] And, as Sunstein has suggested, at least some of the framers of the Fifth Amendment may indeed have viewed the due process clause as an intrinsically conservative doctrine, directing the focus of inquiry backward to the demands of an established natural law tradition, rather than forward to the demands of only vaguely conceived utopian ideals.[34]

Both accounts, however, have real problems. First, the Sunsteinian claim that substantive due process is a conservative doctrine and equal protection is progressive, even if historically supportable, seems normatively and even linguistically indefensible. It is not at all obvious that the guarantee that liberty will not be taken without due process is intrinsically more conservative than the guarantee that the state will provide equal protection of the laws. Nor is it at all obvious that liberty itself, as a political ideal, is intrinsically more conservative than the ideal of equality. As shown in this chapter, the ideal of liberty as a restraint on state action can certainly be understood in a liberal or radical sense, as well as in a conservative one. Purely as a matter of political theory, to say nothing of political morality, both positions are unappealing: they read into the Fourteenth Amendment a peculiarly schizophrenic attitude toward social change.

Second, whatever may have been the original intent of the framers of the Fifth Amendment's liberty clause, the history as well as the judicial interpretation of the Fourteenth Amendment cut against Sunstein's claim that the equal protection clause and the due process clause point in opposite political directions. Although the equal protection clause is surely susceptible to progressive interpretations, with only occasional exceptions,[35] it has been interpreted by the Court for the most part narrowly and formally and with profoundly conservative consequences.[36] Just as "liberty" has received a predominantly conservative and traditionalist gloss, so equal protection has typically been interpreted as requiring a formal rather than substantive equality that has itself become an obstacle of, rather than a vehicle for, progressive movements toward racial or sexual justice. Sunstein sees, or perhaps wants to see, in the Fourteenth Amendment a "division of labor": due process and liberty as a vehicle for conserving the past against precipitous change, and equal protection as a vehicle for progressive challenges to the status quo. Whatever may have been the case at the amendment's inception, this theory has not been borne out by subsequent judicial implementation.

More to the point, from a progressive perspective, both of these arguments seem unwise. They concede far too much, and for no obvious reason. Even if it is true that the major judicial interpretations of substantive due process during the course of this century have been overwhelmingly conservative, it may not be because of the inherent conservatism of either the constitutional mandate of due process or the moral or political ideal of "liberty." If not, then progressives give away too much by conceding interpretive power over the moral and constitutional ideal embedded in the due process clause and the liberty it protects to conservative rhetoric and ideology. For surely either the liberal, autonomy-promoting understanding of liberty or the radical liberationist conception could have informed the Court's substantive due process analysis of the last twenty years. It seems fair to say, though, that neither has, at least not in any clear or sustained fashion.

To take just one example, the "liberty" protected by the reproductive "rights" enunciated in *Roe* can be understood in either of the two senses just sketched. Reproductive choice may be essential for an autonomous life, and "liberation from" the specter of unwanted pregnancy, childbirth, and motherhood may be an accurate understanding politically of what the "pro-choice" political and liberationist movement is all about. It is not necessary, in other words, to reconceive the progressive substantive due process decisions as "equal protection" cases in disguise to reach the same outcome, while avoiding libertarian or traditionalist understandings of the liberty that due process protects. The ideal of liberty is susceptible to multiple interpretations. Rather than reconceptualize progressive liberty cases as true equality cases—on the premise that either liberty, due process, or both are intrinsically conservative, and hence in a deep sense inconsistent with progressive outcomes—we might more profitably reconceptualize the ideal of liberty itself.

One alternative explanation of the conservatism inherent in the purportedly liberal interpretation of the liberty protected by the due process clause is as follows. Justice Brennan and the other liberals on the Court, no less and no more than Justice Scalia, try in their judging to be true to ideals of "good" judging. They therefore interpret the due process clause in such a way as to promote, or to be true to, a range of "adjudicative virtues." And it is those virtues—not the constitutional ideal of "liberty"—that are themselves inherently conservative. It is good judicial decision making, rather than any part of the Constitution, that is (and should be) sensitive to historical tradition, custom, and precedents; that is backward looking rather than forward looking in its aspiration to cohere with past patterns of law; and that is communitarian rather than individualist in its respect for the mandates of ordered liberty. If that is right, then it would not be surprising that even comparatively liberal interpretations of constitutional phrases, which are themselves a part of adjudicative discourse and which accordingly aim for adjudicative virtue, will not be as liberal as liberal interpretations of the same phrase found in other discursive contexts.

Indeed, if we take Justice Brennan's decisions at face value, it seems fair to say that his broad precedential approach to liberty, no less than Justice Scalia's narrowly traditionalist account, is heavily and explicitly constrained by his sense of the requirements of an ideal of good—meaning moral—judicial decision making. The difference, then, between the Brennan and Scalia approaches is a function not (only) of simple politics, but of the differences between the particular conception of the ideal judicial decision and, hence, the particular adjudicative virtue harbored by each justice. Thus, Scalia's narrow understanding of liberty and the due process that protects it is an explicit attempt to minimize the potential for arbitrary judicial decision making that runs counter to the dictates of democratic desire. Insistence on narrow rather than broad understandings of the general clauses of the Constitution, in Scalia's mind, is the surest way to protect against any arbitrary or whimsical decisions and against the judicial tyranny of judges acting as super-legislators in pursuit of their own political values rather than justice. Brennan's comparatively liberal or broader understanding of "tradition" is unquestionably driven in part by a very different political morality, but the conservatism of his approach, compared with nonjudicial liberal interpretations, may best be explained by its jurisprudential motivation. Brennan's reliance on precedentially identified traditions to fill in the content of "liberty" can perhaps best be understood as an attempt to protect the "integrity" and "consistency" of the considerably more liberal body of case law in which the Warren and Burger Courts broadly construed the clause in question. Integrity and consistency, no less than the avoidance of arbitrary, whimsical, or tyrannical decisions, are obviously adjudicative virtues. And like those virtues, they are themselves "conservative": they counsel for decisions that cohere with patterns of principles that speak to us from the past.

If this is all or even part of the story, then the conservatism of the due process clause derives at least in part from the fact that the Constitution receives its meaning almost entirely from judges acting under the intrinsically conservative duties imposed on them by virtue of their judicial role, and it is not a function of the inherent or historical association of the clause with conservative political ideals. This hypothesis—that the conservatism of even the liberal justices' liberty jurisprudence is in part a function of ethical constraints regarding the nature of moral judicial decision making—explains at least one puzzle: it is for this reason that judicial understandings of liberty authored by the liberal judges are so much more conservative than interpretations of "liberty" suggested by liberal political theorists or liberal political activists. For indeed, it seems to be only judges who are wedded to the peculiar idea that the content of liberty should be and has been derived from past communitarian or precedential traditions. As discussed here, liberal political philosophers and political activists think of liberty in any number of ways,[37] but virtually none of them harken back to tradition, either the conservative traditions of a society or the traditions identified as essential to liberty by a liberal Supreme Court. If the conservatism of due process interpretation is due to a quest for adjudicative virtues which are themselves conservative, then it is not surprising that judicial interpretations of liberty are so much more conservative than political interpretations of the same ideal in nonlegal discourses. If judges are heavily influenced by ethical imperatives of decision making that are peculiar to adjudication, then it is not surprising that they have developed a set of definitions of "liberty" that also seem peculiar to adjudication. Those definitions owe as much to the ethical demands placed on judges as they do to the text of the Constitution, its history, or the political will of its interpreters.

What this implies is simply that if we follow the suggestion of the growing number of commentators—neo-civic-republican and otherwise—arguing for an end to the monopolization by the Court of constitutional interpretation, then we should expect to see a far wider range of interpretations of the "liberty" which the state must respect, nurture, or "leave alone" than that represented by the Scalia-Brennan poles of debate in *Michael H. v. Gerald D.* Freed of the constraints of the panoply of demands imposed by the adjudicative virtues—the various needs to write narrow decisions, to respect the rights of similarly situated persons, to adhere to the patterns established by past decisions—constitutional interpreters, whether citizens, legislators, or commentators, may see any number of potential meanings in the due process clause to which the Court, by virtue of its identity as a court, is blind. It may be, for example, that liberty is impossible in the face of chronic homelessness, joblessness, or hunger and that this fact should operate as a constitutional constraint on what the state may refuse to do, as well as what the state may do. It may also be that liberty is impossible in the face of stultifying, demoralizing, constant, private oppression and that this fact as well should constrain constitutionally what the state may neglect as well as what it may do. The due process clause may grant us, in other words, both "affirmative" liberty rights and rights to be free of private oppression. Nonjudicial constitutional interpreters, freed of the constraints of judicial ethics, may find these arguments more persuasive than virtually any court would, not only as the conservative Rehnquist Court would.

The modern Court, of course, has held to the contrary: it has ruled consistently that liberty does not embrace affirmative welfare rights and that the Fourteenth Amendment does not reach private action. Whether they were right or wrong in doing this is not the argument of this chapter. All I want to suggest is that they have reached these conservative interpretations in large part because they are a court. Should other interpreters enter the debate—should Congress, for example, accept its section 5 burden of passing legislation for the purpose of enforcing the liberty guarantee of the Fourteenth Amendment—they may see very different and much broader meanings in the general phrases of the amendment than the Court has seen to date. Congress is not burdened by the ethical imperative to write decisions consistent with previous decisions. It is not burdened with the need to treat like cases alike. Nor is it charged with the task of "conserving" the societal traditions of the past. It has no reason to interpret liberty in such a way as to maintain a "seamless web" of precedent. It is charged with the task of enforcing the mandate of the Fourteenth Amendment, and it is generally charged with the work of distributing resources in a just manner. It is not asking too much, then, to expect Congress to do its distributive and redistributive work in a way that promotes rather than impedes or frustrates true individual "liberty"—understood not as societal tradition and not as judicial precedent, but as the necessary societal conditions for a genuinely free, autonomous life.

6

Toward a First Amendment Jurisprudence of Respect

■

As is now widely recognized, the emerging debate in the United States legal community over the constitutionality of city ordinances and university disciplinary sanctions designed to deter "hate speech" has generated two sharply polarized understandings of the nature of the First Amendment and the scope of the rights that amendment protects. George Fletcher's recent article helps us see that those understandings, in turn, rest on two very different conceptions of what he labels our sense of "constitutional identity." Although it is largely undefined by Fletcher, we might take his phrase "constitutional identity" to refer to that aspect of our collective and individual self-conception which we owe to our shared constitutional heritage, and which at least on occasion determines outcomes in close constitutional cases in ways that "overarching principles of political morality" do not.[1]

The two understandings of our constitutional identity that seem to bolster these conflicting accounts of the constitutional status of hate speech regulations might be called, however unimaginatively, the *liberal* and the *progressive* paradigm. The first section of this chapter briefly characterizes the two polarized positions on the constitutionality (or unconstitutionality) of hate speech ordinances, emphasizing only the aspects of each account that are central to its implicit conception of our constitutional identity. The second section offers a friendly criticism of the now somewhat standard defense of hate speech regulations proffered by progressives and suggests what may be a more promising line of analysis, largely because it rests on a truer account of our constitutional identity.

Finally, this chapter will demonstrate both the strength and limitation of Fletcher's fine article—namely, that while some explicit or implicit conception of our "constitutional identity" may be what determines decisions about constitutional questions in close cases, the mere articulation of such a conception in no way provides definitive answers to those questions. Our "constitutional identity" is surely as contestable and as contested as any particular and vague constitutional phrase or standard, the interpretation of which it may indeed partly determine.

Both the liberal and unquestionably dominant account of free speech and the correlative liberal argument against the constitutionality of hate speech regulations are deeply familiar. Both were recently affirmed by the Supreme Court,[2] and both are eloquently spelled out in Fletcher's article.[3] From a liberal perspective, speech is, for the most part, an expressive act engaged in by individuals toward the end of the individual's own self-fulfillment. Expression, as well as the thought and opinion that accompany it, is what gives our lives their individual definition and contour; it is what individuates us. Constitutional protection of free speech—including, of course, speech that "offends"—is therefore the means by which the state acknowledges our individual dignity, moral worth, moral responsibility, and autonomy. Like prayer in earlier times, expression of our innermost selves is a vital means of self-fulfillment, and hence is itself a moral act of high order. We each bare our individual, our innermost souls when we express ourselves. And, because we value individual souls, we protect and value our speech, whatever its context or side effects. Indeed, in his defense of the liberal conception, Fletcher makes explicit the connecting thread between the protection historically provided to religious belief and practice and the modern protection of expression. We protect expression today for essentially the same reason we once protected religion—namely, the constitutive role of expressive religion in earlier times, and expressive speech today, in the development of the individual's personality:

> All those who feel strongly about something, all those who experience what we loosely call a commitment of conscience should be able to express themselves freely. In the end, one has no tools for distinguishing the anti-patriotic conscience of Johnson from the anti-public school conscience of the Amish. The locus of special freedom, the rubric under which individuals are exempt from at least some general and nondiscriminatory laws, shifts from one clause of the First Amendment to another, from freedom of religion to freedom of speech.
>
> . . .
>
> One is left, then, with a view of the First Amendment that invests freedom of speech with a particularly heavy burden. The First Amend-

ment is the clause in our Constitution that bears the full weight of individual autonomy, the full burden of individuals bearing their souls and expressing their innermost nature in the face of organized demands of conformity and self-restraint. Here is the American spirit at work again, the irreverence of the ongoing American revolution. . . . [I]f the Smith decision survives, religion will no longer generate a legal sphere for appeals to high law, for submissions to conscience, and for resorts to values over which the state has no control. The values of dissent, freedom of the inner self, and the free flourishing of individuals must be born as emanations of free speech.[4]

From the small explosion of scholarly and adversarial writing in defense of the constitutionality of regulations designed to curb hate speech, one can discern, among several other differences from the liberal paradigm, a dramatically different understanding of the nature of speech and of its role in the development of individual personality. Speech, from the progressive perspective, is not essentially expressive (whether "free" or not). Rather, speech is essentially communicative. It creates a bond, a relationship, or community that was not there previously between speaker and listener or writer and reader, the creation of which is both the primary purpose and primary consequence of the speech. We may or may not be baring our individual souls when we speak, but what we are almost inevitably doing (willy-nilly or quite consciously) is creating a social soul: a different and transformed community. Therefore, the value of speech and the value of speech acts are importantly dependent on the quality, particularly the moral quality, of the relationships and communities they engender. Depending on the context, the content, the motive, and a host of other intangibles, speech might strengthen or enrich communities, but it also might not; speech can perpetuate hierarchies, can further subordinate already relatively disempowered peoples, can censure by shocking or scaring a listener into silence, or can render the responsive speech of the listener less free by injuring his or her dignity and self-esteem. For any of these reasons it may constitute, to use Patricia William's telling phrase, "spirit murder,"[5] regardless of whether or not it also, and incidentally, bares the speaker's innermost soul. When these spiritually murderous utterances are of little or no positive value, and when they cause the harm that is their primary purpose and most identifying consequence, it is not at all obvious, from this perspective, why we should protect them.[6]

Thus, the progressive who supports these ordinances and regulations

is consciously, firmly, and perhaps obsessively focused on the very consequences of the speech to which the liberal also deliberately, firmly, and
perhaps obsessively, is willfully blind. What the progressive sees as central—the possible belittling, injuring, endangering, subordinating, spirit-
murdering consequences of speech—the liberal sees as, at most, incidental
"offense." The liberal then views such offense, as may be taken by overly
sensitive souls, not as a sufficient reason for regulating hate speech, but
as a reason to heighten its protection.[7] The progressive views that offense
as a serious anticommunitarian injury which sharply undercuts the prima
facie reason for protecting speech, and at least at times as a sufficient
justification for its regulation.

The progressive conception of speech—motivated by an egalitarian
political impulse, but tremendously enriched theoretically by philosophical work on the nature and necessity of interpretation[8]—has in turn given
rise to a particular argument for the constitutionality of hate speech regulations. It is that argument which may be incomplete. That defense pits
our political commitment to equality against our commitment to liberty,
and on the constitutional level pits the Fourteenth Amendment against the
First. Speech may liberate the abstract individual, as the liberal insists, but
it also may oppress the very concrete and particular members of subordinated groups. Hence, gains in individual liberty—liberty to speak, to print,
or to record electronically—have come at the cost of equality, and both are
constitutionally protected values. When we liberate the private individual
we simultaneously subordinate already oppressed peoples. Our commitment to liberty, then, should be tempered or limited by our commitment
to equality.

Constitutionally, the progressive argument continues, the First Amendment's protection of speech must be read through the prism of the Fourteenth Amendment's more or less explicit promise of equality. We should,
therefore, read an additional exception into the First Amendment's protection of speech, an exception motivated by a political quest for equality
and sanctioned by the Fourteenth Amendment. Such an exception would
allow for regulations, if narrowly and skillfully crafted, of speech that is of
little expressive value and which does tremendous subordinating harm. We
should read the First Amendment as "balanced by" the Fourteenth, and
our commitment to liberty as limited by our commitment to equality.

There are a number of problems with this approach from a liberal perspective, but there are also problems from a progressive perspective. From
a progressive perspective, the first problem is simply strategic and goes

beyond the particular argument to the wisdom of advocating hate speech ordinances on equality or any other grounds. Particularly given the Court's recent pronouncement on the subject in *R.A.V. v. City of St. Paul, Minnesota*,[9] it seems clear that neither this argument nor any other is likely to succeed, and our failure to sustain these ordinances will have very real consequences. At the very least, the failure to sustain these ordinances will further trivialize the harms of speech and further denigrate its victims, both in their own eyes and in the eyes of others. It is belittling, even humiliating, and at least ostracizing to sustain an injury, the infliction of which is constitutionally protected, when the Constitution possesses as much power as it does in this culture to create our moral, our social, and our legal identity. To complain of an injury caused by a constitutionally protected act is not just whining over "names that can never hurt me," but is deeply anticommunitarian in ways that Fletcher's article helps illuminate: even to voice the complaint is an attack on our collective constitutional identity, as understood and articulated by liberalism.[10] Unsuccessful attempts to sustain such regulations may underscore the marginality and outsider status of victims of speech, simply by emphasizing the high constitutional status of the events that cause the injuries they suffer.

Other problems, however, inhere in the "equality versus liberty" construction of the issues surrounding hate speech regulations favored by progressives, and the conception of our constitutional identity that construction implies. Regardless of what the Court ultimately decides, that progressive construction—that "constitutional identity" and its attendant problems—will persist as a minority or dissident tradition in First Amendment jurisprudence. It is therefore imperative that we do what we can to get it right.

The first problem is rhetorical. In popular consciousness, as well as constitutional history, we never have had a political or moral commitment to equality that comes anywhere near the weight or intensity of our commitment to liberty. To use Fletcher's phrase, liberty is at the heart of our "constitutional identity" in a way that equality has never been. Think of the Pledge of Allegiance, the Star Spangled Banner, or the grade school ditty "My Country 'Tis of Thee," all of which mention liberty, and none of which mention equality. In any popular standoff between equality and liberty, liberty will triumph in the popular mind as well as in constitutional doctrine. The contemptuous tone of the charge of "political correctness" that accompanies arguments against hate speech regulations and also against diversity and multiculturalism in education, can be attributed, in part, to that simple rhetorical fact. The often apologetic tone of defenders of these ordinances and of victims of such speech is a much sadder reminder.

The second problem is descriptive. The progressive understanding of hate speech as harmful because of its adverse consequences for equality misdescribes, or at least does not fully describe, the problem. For it is not only the equality of subordinated persons (or the groups to which they belong) that is damaged by hate speech. It is also liberty: the liberty to walk the street, the campus, or the workplace undeterred by fear of harassment; the liberty to speak uncensored by the silencing effects of hate; the freedom to live in a community with others or to live in peace with oneself unshackled by the effects of speech which, perhaps uniquely, injures the listener by reducing her to her materiality by negating her noncorporeal existence and by equating her with her physical being—in short, by murdering her spirit. When we characterize the injury of hate speech as one to equality, rather than to liberty, we saddle ourselves not only with a constitutional argument that may well be unsustainable but also with a description of the injury that rests on an unnecessarily thin vision of social and political life. Equality is not the only value at stake—it is not the only characteristic of an ideal community to which we ought strive—nor is inequality the only harm or evil we should seek to eradicate. The claim that it is rests on a falsely narrow understanding of the community as constituted only by politics, by power, by domination, and by subordination. But there is much more to social life than power, and much more to individual thriving than relative equality.

Lastly, the standard equality-based defense of hate speech concedes what should be contested: namely, an understanding of our constitutional identity that pits abstract individual rights of liberty and speech against harms sustained by concrete members of particular groups. For if the progressive understanding of speech as essentially communicative, rather than expressive, is right, then liberals are wrong to characterize the problem as a standoff between individual "rights of expression" on the one hand and the interests of members of subordinated groups protecting against subordinating injuries on the other. If the progressive critique is right, then it is the liberal conception of our shared constitutional identity—a constitutional self-image of a community of individuals freely expressing their innermost souls and possessed of rights to do so and of group members injured by such expressions and possessed of interests and vulnerabilities—and not its favoring of individuals and rights over groups and interests, that is the flawed premise in the liberal argument against hate speech regulations. We need to challenge that conception and simply argue for a rebalancing of the rights and interests it posits.

We should at least supplement, if not supplant, the current Fourteenth Amendment equality defense of the hate speech regulations with a reinvigorated, reconstructed interpretation of the First Amendment that would take seriously the progressive understanding, not just of the magnitude of the harms caused by hate speech but also of the nature of speech and of our consequent "constitutional identity." That understanding would construe the "point" of the First Amendment, to use Ronald Dworkin's phrase,[11] as the protection and facilitation of communication rather than the soul-baring, expressive individual of conscience, as its inherent ideal. Understood as such, the First Amendment would protect much of what it now protects and be subject to many of the same exceptions as under its liberal interpretation. It would also nonproblematically weigh in favor of regulations of speech designed to counter the censorial effects on communication of private concentrations of power, whether those concentrations be racial, economic, or sexual. The First Amendment, understood as protecting communication rather than expression, and communities of speakers and listeners rather than soul-baring individuals, would thus protect the listener and potential speaker who sustains and is transformed by the consequences of speech, whether for better or ill, as well as the hateful utterance and its expressing speaker. Viewed as such, it would protect all participants—speakers, listeners, potential speakers—against not only ill-founded state efforts to enforce a stifling conformity but also malicious private attempts to induce a silence born not of a valued privacy, but of stultifying and strangling self-hatred.

This is not to argue that such a redirection would drastically improve the chances of sustaining these ordinances in court against a First Amendment attack. It would not obviate the danger and risk to victims of hate speech posed by unsuccessful defenses of the constitutionality of ordinances designed for their protection. It might, however, address some of the other problems that now plague progressive arguments for the constitutionality of hate speech regulations. On a rhetorical level, it would be tremendously helpful to begin to fashion an understanding of the First Amendment as being in alignment, rather than in tension, with both the Fourteenth Amendment and with progressive ends. It could only help progressive political efforts to rest on a noncontradictory "constitutional identity," rather than one characterized by paradox, contradiction, and tension.

More important, such a recharacterization of the First Amendment might be truer not only to the nature of the injuries victims of hate speech sustain, but also to the progressive constitutional identity the sufferance of those injuries offends. As Rodney King pleaded in the violent aftermath of the hate crime he suffered, we must learn to "get along" [12] with each other. In our current pluralist, multicultural, multiethnic, severely crowded times, the contrasting liberal constitutional identity behind standard First Amendment understandings—that we learn to let each other alone to nurture, express, or bare our own individual souls—is increasingly an unattainable, whether or not desirable, goal. Rodney King's plea may be expressive of a more appealing political vision—a more desirable constitutional identity—as well as a more realistic one.

PART 3

Institutional Responsibilities

7

Constitutional Skepticism

■

Interpretive constitutional debate over the last few decades has centered on two apparently linked issues: whether the Constitution can be given a determinate meaning, and whether the institution of judicial review can be justified within the basic assumptions of liberalism. Two groups of scholars have generated answers to these questions. The "constitutional faithful" argue that meaning can indeed be determinately affixed to constitutional clauses, by reference to the plain meaning of the document,[1] the original intent of the drafters,[2] evolving political and moral norms of the community,[3] or the best political or moral philosophical theory available[4] and that, because of that determinacy, judicial review can indeed be brought within the rubric of liberalism. Taking issue with the constitutional faithful is a group who might be called *constitutional skeptics*. Scholars in this group see, in every constitutional phrase or doctrine, the possibility of multiple interpretations, and in the application of every constitutional method the possibility of multiple outcomes. It follows from this indeterminacy that judicial review cannot be easily justified by reference to liberal assumptions, because the power of the interpreting judge irreparably compromises the stability and rationality of the "Rule of Law" so central to liberal ideals.[5]

As important as the debate over constitutional determinacy may be, its prominence in modern constitutional theory over the last thirty years has carried with it serious opportunity costs. Specifically, the prominence of the debate over the Constitution's meaning, whether it can be said to have one, and the implications for the coherence of liberalism that these questions of interpretation seem to raise, has pushed to the background an older and possibly more important debate about the Constitution's value. By asking relentlessly whether the Constitution's meaning can be made sufficiently determinate to serve the Rule of Law—by focusing almost exclusively on whether constitutionalism is possible within liberal theory and whether liberalism is possible, given an indeterminate Constitution—we have neglected to ask whether our Constitution is desirable. Does it further the "good life" for the individuals, communities, and subcommunities it governs?

We might pose these evaluative questions in any number of ways. Has the Constitution or the Bill of Rights well served the communities and individuals they are designed to protect? Are the visions of individualism, community, and human nature on which the Bill of Rights rests, and the balances it strikes between rights and responsibilities, or civic virtue and freedoms, noble conceptions of social life, true accounts of our being, hospitable to societal and individual attempts to live the good life? More specifically, does the First Amendment, for example, well serve its core values of free expression, individual actualization, and open political debate? Assuming that it does, are those values good values to have? Are they worth the damage to our social cohesion, our fragile sense of fraternity with others, and our attempts at community that they almost undeniably cause? Are the Fourteenth Amendment's sweeping and majestic guarantees of "liberty" and "equal protection of the laws," appearances notwithstanding, in fact unduly stingy? Do they simply, and cruelly, fail to guarantee a liberty that would meaningfully protect against the most serious constraints on peoples' liberties, or an equality that would even begin to address the grotesque material inequities at the very heart of our social and economic life? Do those guarantees perversely protect, rather than guarantee against, those constraints and inequities? Similarly, but from a quite different political orientation, are Fourth Amendment guarantees simply not worth their cost in law enforcement? Is it unwise to let 18-year-olds vote? Is the Second Amendment the height of foolishness?

These questions—about the value, wisdom, decency, or sensibility of constitutional guarantees—do of course receive some attention in contemporary legal scholarship, but nevertheless, it seems fair to say that in spite of the legal academy's supposed obsession with "normativity," normative questions about the Constitution have not been at the heart of constitutional discourse over the last thirty years. By contrast, normative questions of precisely this sort constitute the great bulk of scholarship in other areas of law. Scholars question the value of the holder in due course doctrine in commercial transactions, the negligence doctrine or strict liability in tort law, the rules governing acceptance of unilateral contracts in contract law, and insanity defenses in criminal law. But normative questions are neither the subject of constitutional "grand theory" nor, more revealingly perhaps, the subject of doctrinal constitutional scholarship. Instead, while theoretical constitutional scholarship centers on questions about the meaningfulness of the Constitution and its implications for the possibility or impossibility of liberalism, doctrinal constitutional scholarship centers on questions of the Constitution's meaning, rather than questions of its value. Thus, for example, rather than debate whether the First or the Fourteenth Amendment is a good idea, doctrinalists debate what the First Amendment or the Fourteenth Amendment means, and theorists debate whether they have any meaning and what it means to assert that they do or do not have meaning. In short, neither theoretical nor doctrinal constitutional scholarship places the value, rather than either the meaningfulness or the meaning, of the Constitution at the heart of constitutional analysis.

That we lack an explicitly normative debate about the Constitution's value might be evidenced by the visible effects of that absence in our substantive constitutional arguments. Let me cite a few examples, simply to convey the flavor of what I suggest is missing. One debate between constitutional scholars arising over the last few years, and of great interest to political progressives, concerns the constitutionality under the First Amendment of the attempts made by some cities and universities to control, through disciplinary sanctions, the intimidation and subordination of racial, ethnic, and sexual minorities by use of "hate speech." Those contributing to the small explosion of scholarly writing on this topic have generally taken one of two polar positions: one group of scholars and litigators (generally liberal) argues that hate speech regulations are simply unconstitutional under the First Amendment,[6] while a second, more or less minority (and generally progressive), position argues that they are constitutional, either by virtue of the similarity between hate speech regulations and traditionally accepted limits on the First Amendment, or because of limits we should imply into that amendment through the "penumbral" and balancing, or counterbalancing, effect of the Fourteenth Amendment's equality clause.[7] The position that seems to have no adherents is that hate speech regulations are desirable, for progressive reasons, but are nevertheless unconstitutional, but shouldn't be, and that this shows that, at least from a progressive perspective, the First Amendment is morally flawed. But again, this position seems to have no adherents. Instead, those who think hate speech regulations are a good idea generally think they are constitutional, while those who think they are not a good idea generally find them unconstitutional. No one seems to find them both desirable and unconstitutional, and hence exemplary of a problem with the First Amendment. No one, in other words, is led by a commitment to the desirability of hate speech regulations and a fair reading of the Constitution to take a progressive and morally skeptical stance toward the Constitution.

A second and structurally similar example involves the constitutionality of antipornography ordinances. Despite the wide range of conflicting feminist and libertarian positions on this issue, no one advances the apparently logical, and initially plausible, position that these ordinances are eminently desirable, but unconstitutional, revealing a serious problem with the First Amendment. Instead, those who view these ordinances as unconstitutional generally view them as objectionable,[8] while those who view the ordinances as desirable generally find them constitutional as well.[9] Again, no one is led by a commitment to the value of antipornography regulations and a fair reading of the Constitution to take a morally skeptical stance toward the Constitution, or at least toward the First Amendment.

Although this chapter focuses primarily on the absence of progressive skeptical arguments about the Constitution's value, the same point holds regarding the absence of skeptical stances toward the Constitution reflective of other political or moral commitments. Thus, one finds few people arguing that the Constitution does indeed protect a woman's right to an abortion and, therefore, overprotects privacy, because abortion rights are morally unjustifiable. Few argue that the Constitution protects the individual's choice of sexual lifestyle and, therefore, overprotects individual choice, because homosexuality is an immoral way to live. No one seems led by a conservative commitment to the value of regulating private morality and a fair reading of the Constitution as prohibiting that regulation to the conclusion that the Constitution is morally and politically flawed. On the other hand, no one seems to believe that the Constitution does indeed fail to protect reproductive or gay rights, but that these rights should be granted, and that this shows the Constitution's inadequacy. Again, those who view abortion rights as desirable generally view them as constitutionally protected, and those who view them as unprotected generally view them as undesirable. No one seems led by virtue of their political views on abortion or sexuality combined with a fair reading of the Constitution to the conclusion that the Constitution is flawed.

The absence of these arguments in the legal literature evidences the more basic privation noted above: there is no general tradition, at least in the legal literature, of normatively skeptical constitutionalism from a liberal, progressive, conservative, or any other developed political or moral perspective. Regardless of political viewpoint, constitutional scholars are peculiarly reluctant to see either the Constitution or a particular constitutional guarantee as being at odds with our political or moral ideals, goals, or commitments.[10] We tend to see the Constitution as an inappropriate object of criticism, and this may be even more true today than it was thirty, forty, or fifty years ago. Even in postcritical, postmodern, poststructuralist, postfeminist times, we lack a developed body of legal scholarship that takes a morally critical stance toward the Constitution and the rights it purports to protect.

The main purpose of this chapter is simply to draw attention to this absence and initiate movement toward reversing the trend. By elaborating both a progressive argument against constitutionalism and a responsive progressive argument for it, I hope to show, by example, that we should develop normative arguments, grounded in politics and morality, for and against constitutional fidelity.

My second aim, however, is to try to account for the absence of normative constitutional debate. Why is there no recognizable body of constitutional scholarship criticizing the Constitution, on moral or political grounds? Why do so few advocates endorse the positions noted above: that hate speech regulation or antipornography ordinances are desirable but unconstitutional; that the Constitution protects abortion rights, but shouldn't; that the Constitution does, but shouldn't, protect reproductive or gay rights; or doesn't, but should, allow the regulation of private morality?

There is, of course, a "psychoanalytic" or "socioanalytic" explanation for the absence of constitutional doubt in the literature. Theorists, like the rest of the culture, and across the political spectrum, may find it sociologically or psychologically difficult to view the Constitution as morally problematic, or indeed even morally flawed. Either because there is so little else that binds us together as a civic culture, or, perhaps, simply out of a psychic need to identify some sort of authority in our lives who will love us as well as authoritatively guide us, we all may have a hard time seeing the Constitution itself—rather than its erroneous interpretation by a pernicious, dishonest, overly conservative, or unduly activist Court—as being "the problem," the obstacle to the attainment of some desired political or moral goal. We have trouble seeing the Constitution as part of the problem rather than part of the solution, and, as a consequence, we tend, both in popular consciousness and at the level of theory, to blur constitutionality with morality: to see the Constitution as more or less in line with moral and political virtue. It may be that because we have this difficulty, we are disinclined to oppose the Constitution itself, rather than its erroneous interpretation, to some moral ideal, to some cherished utopian vision, or, more baldly, simply to some political ambition. Although this explanation may have some merit, it also sounds a bit dated, and even nostalgic: whatever may have been the case in the past, it is difficult to believe that, in the fractured, relativist, nihilist, minimally pluralist moral climate in which we presently live and argue, we are all still afflicted with an irrational and deeply emotional affection for a foundational legal document.

The explanation advanced in this chapter for our continuing constitutional fidelity is considerably less global: at least one reason for our modern reluctance to generate constitutional criticism, I will argue, might stem from the preemptive logic of the "interpretation debate" that has dominated scholarship over at least the last two decades. As mentioned at the outset, the absence of normative debate can be viewed as a simple "opportunity cost" of the prominence of interpretive debate. Thus, whatever may be the effects of our psychic or social attraction to the Constitution, the logic of the interpretation debate alone, I will endeavor to show, has made skeptical arguments regarding the Constitution's value extremely difficult to even articulate, much less debate, even among political radicals who almost assuredly bear no excessive patriotic, civic, or psychic loyalty to the United States Constitution. I will try to show that our focus on questions of constitutional interpretation and methodology has minimally diverted our attention from questions of constitutional value, but the logic of that debate has also made questions of constitutional value difficult, for various reasons, to even raise.

The first section of this chapter sketches one possible basis for a morally skeptical stance toward the Constitution. The skeptical position is grounded, again, not in the "indeterminacy thesis," but in a rejection of the morality (rather than coherence) of the liberalism that informs constitutional decision making, and in an affirmation of a progressive and egalitarian political and moral orientation. This section argues, very simply, that our Constitution is fundamentally and possibly irreversibly at odds with progressive egalitarianism and because of that, it is a seriously flawed document.

The second section examines why, with only a few exceptions—notably Derrick Bell's[11] and Alan Freeman's critical race theory,[12] Mark Tushnet's "rights critique,"[13] and Mary Becker's feminist analysis of the Bill of Rights [14]—this form of constitutional skepticism, what might be called *progressive constitutional skepticism,* has not been elaborated in constitutional scholarship, despite the large numbers of constitutional writers and advocates who unquestionably hold egalitarian and progressive moral and political commitments. My argument will be that the logic of the dominant interpretive debates precludes articulation and elaboration of skeptical evaluative argument. This section then examines the costs to progressivism, as well as to constitutional discourse and theory, of the absence of this form of constitutional skepticism.

The last section sketches one possible response to the progressive constitutional skepticism laid out in the first section. The response, however, is grounded neither in liberalism nor in a commitment to indeterminacy, but in the same progressive political orientation as that of the skeptics and in a relatively determinate view of constitutional meaning. It thus rejects both liberal values and the indeterminacy critique of liberalism's most prominent contemporary critiques. This position, which I will call *progressive constitutional faith,* seeks to rebut progressive skepticism not by exploiting the contradictions and ambiguities in liberalism (and hence in received constitutional interpretation), but by retelling the story of constitutionalism, emphasizing its convergence, rather than its divergence, with progressive politics. This position, unlike progressive skepticism, has received some doctrinal and theoretical elaboration in the literature, primarily in the emerging feminist and critical race theoretical movements. Mari Matsuda's groundbreaking characterization of "outsider jurisprudence," [15] Akhil Amar's and Ruth Colker's historical writings about the original meaning of the Bill of Rights and the Reconstruction Amendments,[16] Catharine MacKinnon's progressive interpretation of the Constitution's general equality mandate,[17] and several critical race theorists' writings on the constitutionality of ordinances, statutes, or university regulations prohibiting hate speech [18] are all seminal contributions to a progressive constitutional faith. This third section articulates a set of premises for this developing body of scholarship and discusses its relation to both progressive constitutional skepticism and liberal constitutional faith.

As will be apparent, both progressive constitutional skepticism and progressive constitutional faith do not rest merely on a rejection of the ideals of liberalism, but on a rejection of the indeterminacy thesis propounded by its critics or, to put it positively, on an affirmation of the determinacy of the Constitution's meaning. Thus, the progressive skeptical position holds that the relatively ascertainable and determinate meaning of the Constitution is radically inconsistent with progressive ideals, and the progressive faithful position holds that the meaning is in some deep historical or utopian sense consistent with nonliberal progressive politics. Both positions obviously depend on some degree of constitutional determinacy: for the Constitution to be pernicious or salutary, its meaning must be determinate.

This chapter does not defend the claim that the Constitution has a determinate meaning, whether that meaning is fatally inconsistent or deeply consistent with progressive ideals. It suggests instead that if we must first put aside doubts about whether the Constitution has an ascertainable meaning to debate, question, or affirm the Constitution's value from nonliberal political perspectives, then, in the spirit of pragmatism, we should put those doubts aside and see what may follow. Perhaps the doubts and faiths that may then come to the surface—doubts about the Constitution's worthiness rather than about its objectivity—might prove as central, innervating, and imperative as the questions of meaning and interpretation that continue to preoccupy our critical energies.

Progressive Constitutional Skepticism

Progressives have both substantive and methodological reasons to be skeptical about the Constitution's value. I define progressivism, in part, by its guiding ideal: progressives are loosely committed to a form of social life in which all individuals live meaningful, autonomous, and self-directed lives, enriched by rewarding work, education, and culture, free of the disabling fears of poverty, violence, and coercion, nurtured by life-affirming connections with intimates and co-citizens alike, and strengthened by caring communities that are both attentive to the shared human needs of its members and equally mindful of their diversity and differences. Much of this guiding ideal, however, is shared by liberals. What distinguishes progressives from liberals is that liberals tend to view the dangers of an overly oppressive state as the most serious obstacle to the attainment of such a world, whereas progressives, while agreeing that some obstacles emanate from the state, argue that, for the most part, the most serious impediments emanate from unjust concentrations of private power: the social power of whites over blacks, the intimate power of men over women, and the economic power of the materially privileged over the materially deprived. From a progressive perspective, it is those concentrations of private power, not state power, that presently riddle social life with hierarchic relationships of mastery and subjection, of sovereignty and subordination. Hence, it is those concentrations of private power that must be targeted, challenged, and reformed by progressive political action. That action, in turn, will often involve state intervention into the private spheres within which hierarchies of private power are allowed to thrive, and that simple fact will commonly pit the progressive strategy of ending private domination against the liberal goal of minimizing the danger of an oppressive state.

This difference between progressives and liberals largely accounts for the degree of conflict between their respective analyses and goals. For example, liberals and progressives generally agree, and lament, that the freedom of gays and lesbians to form and maintain nurturing intimate relationships is threatened by discriminatory state action. At the same time, progressives, far more than liberals, are sensitive to the degree to which that freedom is threatened by the continuing and seemingly unshakable hegemonic rage of an intolerant, abusive, and often violent minority of heterosexual private citizens. That hegemonic rage, not just state action, must somehow be challenged and transformed if gays and lesbians are to thrive. Similarly, liberals and progressive feminists agree, and lament, that the freedom of women to engage simultaneously in well-compensated work, in public life, and in a rewarding home and family life is threatened by discriminatory state law. Still, the dramatic and well-publicized split between liberal feminists and progressive feminists reflects the extent to which progressive feminists, unlike liberal feminists, realize that women's lives and freedom may be endangered more by private, intimate, economic, and social systems of power and control than by pernicious or discriminatory state action: by, for example, a family structure that saps women's time, energy, and self-esteem with unequal distributions of demanding and unpaid domestic labor; the social acceptability of private sexual violence and coercion in marriage and intimacy that threatens women's safety and drains women's sense of self-possession and self-will; and the prevalence of unequal compensation for work of comparable responsibility and difficulty that deprives women of material security, self-esteem, and independence. If we call these systems of private coercion, intimate violence, and economic disempowerment "patriarchy," then it seems that patriarchy exists and perpetuates itself to a considerable degree independent of "state action," discrimination or otherwise. Awareness of, and concern about, that social fact distinguishes progressive from liberal feminists.

Similarly, from a progressive perspective, African-Americans and other ethnic minorities are hindered in their search for meaningful freedom and full civic equality, not so much by discriminatory state laws or actions as by the continuing and escalating presence of a virulent white racism in virtually all spheres of private, social, and economic life. Awareness of, and concern about, that complex social fact in large part distinguishes progressive critical race theorists from their one-time liberal allies. To take one final example, the poor in this society are hurt not nearly so much by pernicious or discriminatory state actions as by concentrations of private economic power. Again, concern over the centrality of this social fact distinguishes progressive from liberal politics on issues of class. Generally, what defines a progressive political perspective is simply the awareness that the greatest obstacles to enjoyment of the good life valued by liberals and progressives alike are not actions of any sort taken by states or state officials, but concentrations of private power, whether of a patriarchal, racist, homophobic, or capitalist sort.

If that progressive insight is basically correct, then at least two problems exist with the scheme of individual rights and liberties protected by the Constitution. First, the Constitution does not prohibit the abuse of private power that interferes with the equality or freedom of subordinated peoples. The Constitution simply does not reach private power, and therefore cannot possibly prohibit its abuse. Even the most far-reaching liberal interpretations of the Reconstruction Amendments—the only amendments that seemingly reach private power—refuse or fail to find either a constitutional prohibition of private societal racism, intimate sexual violence, or economic coercion or a constitutional imperative that the states take affirmative action to eradicate it. Justice Harlan's famous liberal dissent in *Plessy v. Ferguson*,[19] for example, made painfully clear that, even on his reading of the amendment (which, of course, would have outlawed Jim Crow laws), the Fourteenth Amendment does not challenge the sensed or actual cultural and social superiority of the white race. More recently, Justices Brennan and Marshall's argument in their dissent in *City of Richmond v. J. A. Croson Co.*,[20] that the state may remedy private discrimination if failure to do so would enmesh the state in those discriminatory practices, did not suggest that the Constitution requires the state to address private discrimination. Similarly, virtually no liberal judges or commentators have read the Constitution and the Reconstruction Amendments to require that states take affirmative action to address the unconstitutional maldistribution of household labor, with its serious, well-proven, and adverse effects on women's liberty and equality. No liberal court or commentator reads the Constitution to require that states or Congress take action to protect against homophobic violence and rage, or to protect against the deadening, soul-murdering, and often life-threatening effects of homeless-ness, hunger, and poverty. The Constitution apparently leaves untouched the very conditions of subordination, oppression, and coercion that rele-gate some to "lesser lives" of drudgery, fear, and stultifying self-hatred. For that reason alone, the Constitution appears to be fundamentally at odds with progressive ideals and visions.

The incompatibility of progressivism and the Constitution goes deeper, however. Not only does the Constitution fail to prohibit subordinating abuses of private power, but, at least a good deal of the time, in the name of guaranteeing constitutional protection of individual freedom, it also ag-gressively protects the very hierarchies of wealth, status, race, sexual pref-erence, and gender that facilitate those practices of subordination. Thus, the Constitution seemingly protects the individual's freedom to produce and consume hate speech, despite its propensity to contribute to patterns of racial oppression. It also clearly protects the individual's right to practice religion, despite the demonstrable incompatibility of the religious tenets central to all three dominant mainstream religions with women's full civic and political equality. It protects the individual's freedom to create and use pornography, despite the possible connection between pornography and increases in private violence against women. It protects the privacy and cultural hegemony of the nuclear family, despite the extreme forms of in-justice that occur within that institution and the maldistribution of burdens and benefits visited by that injustice upon women and, to a lesser degree, children. Finally, it protects, as a coincidence of protecting the freedom and equal opportunities of individuals, both the system of "meritocracy" and the departures from meritocracy that dominate and constitute the market and economy, despite the resistance of those systems to full partici-pation of African-Americans and hence despite the subordinating effects of those "markets" upon them. Very generally, the Constitution, incident to protecting the ideational, economic, and familial spheres of individual life against the intrusive effects of benign and malign legislative initia-tives, protects that realm of private, intimate, social, and economic culture that creates and then perpetuates a spirit of intolerance toward, alienation from, and active hatred of subordinated persons. By so doing, the Con-stitution fails to protect against that subordination, and it fails to exhibit neutrality toward it: it nurtures precisely those patterns and practices that are most injurious to the economic opportunities, the individual freedoms, the intimacies, and the fragile communities of those persons already most deprived in the unequal and unfree social world in which we live.

Finally, this incompatibility of the Constitution with progressive ideals is neither momentary nor contingent. It is not a product of false or disingenuous interpretation by a particular court or justice hostile to progressive politics. Rather, the Constitution's incompatibility with progressive ideals stems from at least two theoretical and doctrinal sources that lie at the heart of our constitutional structure: (a) the conception of liberty to which the Constitution is committed and (b) its conception of equality.

First, as is often recognized, the Constitution protects a strong and deeply liberal conception of what Isaiah Berlin has termed the "negative liberty"[21] of the individual to speak, think, choose, and labor within a sphere of noninterference from social, community, or state authority. As is less often recognized, however, the Constitution creates and protects these spheres of noninterference not only in preference to, but also at the cost of, the more positive conceptions of freedom and autonomy necessary for progressive change. The cultural, intimate, private, and economic spheres of noninterference protected by the Constitution are the very spheres of private power, control, and coercion within which the positive liberty of subordinated persons to live lives of meaning is most threatened. Thus, the Constitution protects the rights of producers and consumers of racial hate speech and pornography to protect the negative liberty of those speakers and listeners. By doing this, it not only fails to protect but also actively threatens the positive freedom of women and African-Americans to develop lives free from fear for one's safety, the seeds of racial bitterness, the "clouds of inferiority,"[22] the interference with one's movements, and the crippling incapacities to participate fully in public life occasioned by the constitutionally protected cultures of racism and misogyny. The negative liberty of the individual heralded and celebrated by liberalism is not only inconsistent with but also hostile to the positive liberty central to progressivism, simply because protection of "negative liberty" necessarily creates the sphere of noninterference and privacy within which the abuse of private power can proceed unabated. The Constitution is firmly committed to this negative rather than positive conception of liberty, and is thus not only not the ally, but also a very real obstacle, to progressive ideals.

Second, the Fourteenth Amendment's mandate of equality, rather than being a limit to the Constitution's celebration of liberty, is also a bar to progressive progress, the heroic efforts of progressive litigators, judges, and commentators to prove the contrary notwithstanding. The "equal protection of the laws" guaranteed by the Fourteenth Amendment essentially guarantees that one's membership in a racially or sexually defined group will not adversely affect one's treatment by the state. As such, the mandate powerfully reinforces the liberal understanding that the only attributes that matter to the state are those shared universally by all members of the community: the possession of equal dignity, the power to form one's own plan of life, and the universal aspirations to autonomy and so forth. Precisely this understanding of equality, grounded in the liberal claim and promise of universality and equal treatment, however, renders the equal protection clause an obstacle to progressive progress. The need to acknowledge and compensate for the individual's membership in profoundly nonuniversal subordinate groups—whether racially, sexually, or economically defined— is what distinguishes the progressive political impulse from the liberal. It is precisely that membership in nonuniversal groups, and the centrality of the nonuniversal attributes that distinguish them, that both liberalism and the liberally defined constitutional mandate of equality are poised not simply to ignore, but to oppose. It is, then, both unsurprising and inevitable that the Fourteenth Amendment's equal protection clause is understood as not requiring, and indeed forbidding, the state and public interventions into private, intimate, and economic spheres of life needed to interrupt the patterns of domination, subordination, and inequality that continue to define the lives of those within these protected private realms.

Methodologically, the Constitution is also hostile to political and moral progressivism, simply because it elevates one set of moral values above others, relegating nonconstitutional ideals or visions to the sphere of the "merely political." The Constitution's peculiar status as a bridge between liberal morality and aspirations and positive law, although much heralded by liberal philosophers and constitutionalists, poses a triple danger to progressive ideals. First, because the Constitution is indeed law, and law in the ordinary as well as extraordinary sense, it imprints upon the liberalism on which it rests the imprimatur of positive legal authority. One set of political convictions hence receives not only the persuasive authority derived from its merits but also the political, willed authority of the extant, empowered, positive sovereign. These ideals simply are, as well as ought to be; and they are in a way that makes compliance mandatory. Second, because the Constitution is law in the extraordinary as well as ordinary sense, the positive political authority imprinted upon the liberal morality of the Constitution is of a higher, permanent, and constitutive sort. It severely constrains moralities and aspirations with which it is inconsistent in the name of the community from which it purportedly draws its sovereign authority. Thus, it is not just the "law" that is hostile to nonliberal moral aspirations, such as progressivism. It is also, more deeply and meaningfully, "we the people"—all of us, the intergenerational community of citizens—for whom the Constitution speaks and from whom it draws its authority that is hostile to the ideals with which it is inconsistent. Third, because the Constitution is also undeniably a moral as well as legal document, the authority it embodies is exercised not only coercively, telling us who we must be, but also instructively, telling us who we ought to be. It defines and confines not just our options—as does any law, higher or lower—but our aspirations as well. For all three reasons, the Constitution is not just a peculiarly authoritarian legal document, but is also authoritarian in a peculiarly parental way. Like a parent's authority over the identity of his or her children, the Constitution both persuades us to be a certain way and constitutes us in a certain way. It creates us as it defines a morality to which we will and should subscribe.

For all these reasons, the Constitution is methodologically and substantively hostile to progressive politics. The moral authoritarianism at its core is in many ways conducive to the reverence for the individual and distrust of the mass so central to liberalism, but it is inimical to the egalitarian, inclusive, and largely communitarian methods—the grass-roots politics at the local level and the participatory democracy at the national and state levels—that must form the foundation for genuine progressive change. Effective political challenges to the subordination of some groups by others must rest on a fundamental change of human orientation in both the dominated and oppressing groups: the dominated must come to see their interests as both shared with each other and opposed to the interests of the stronger; and the stronger must come to embrace empathetically the subordinated as sufficiently close to their own identities to be "of their concern." Neither progressive end—the mounting of sufficient power within the ranks of the subordinated through cross-group organizing or the challenge to the received self-identity of the strong—is attainable through the legal, coercive imposition of a particular moral paradigm that characterizes constitutional methodology. In fact, the moral and legal authoritarianism at the heart of our constitutional method will almost invariably frustrate it.

These three attributes of our Constitution—its commitment to negative liberty at the cost of positive liberty; its individualist and universalist, rather than particularist and antisubordinationist understanding of equality; and its moral authoritarian methodology—are just three possible grounds for skepticism about the Constitution's compatibility with progressive politics. If progressive politics are necessary for moral progress, then these three attributes are also grounds for skepticism about the compatibility of the Constitution with moral progress in this country.

This list is obviously not exhaustive. Other reasons grounded in progressive morality may exist for doubting the wisdom of the constitutional project. At the same time, the whole of the Constitution is certainly not adverse to progressivism, and some features of the Constitution, at least when properly viewed, may promote progressive projects. Nevertheless, it seems fair to say that at least the twin concepts of liberty and equality with which the Constitution is aligned, as well as our constitutional method, are not neutral toward progressive politics and ideals and collectively constitute a potent political, moral, and even social force against the realization of those aspirations.

The Absence of Progressive Constitutional Skepticism

Why is it that neither this progressive case against the value of the Constitution nor any of its implications for particular issues has a sizeable number of adherents in the legal profession, or has received more than occasional elaboration in constitutional scholarship? Although I have labeled the skeptical stance toward constitutionalism outlined above "progressive," it is by no means only those who think of themselves as political progressives who align themselves with some part of a progressive agenda. Political orientations generally are not monolithic, and progressivism in particular can be embraced in part by persons at virtually all points along the political spectrum. Thus, a sizeable number of liberals making up the mainstream of constitutional discourse, the vast majority of critical legal scholars, a probable majority of feminist legal theorists, most critical race theorists, and at least a few conservative legal theorists subscribe to some subset of "progressive" political commitments. The question posed above might be framed in this way: Of the scores of constitutional writers favoring progressive political commitments, why do only a handful also believe that these progressive initiatives are truly unconstitutional, revealing a serious moral failing in our constitutional scheme? Why are almost all of these more or less progressive writers, activists, and thinkers seemingly convinced that their beliefs are consistent with the Constitution? In contrast to whatever skepticism, nihilism, or simple pessimism progressives hold toward the Court, the public, Congress, and our public institutions, why are they so relentlessly optimistic about the Constitution itself? Why do so few think that, because of its deep incompatibility with progressive political and moral goals, the Constitution, although desirable at times, generally does more harm than good, and that we would be better off without it?

Perhaps the main reason is purely strategic. From a jurisprudential perspective, the absence of normative debate about the Constitution reflects a seemingly perverse refusal to apply the lessons of legal positivism to the document applied as a matter of course in other areas of the law: we find it difficult to separate the Constitution "as it actually is" from our moral ideals of "what it should be," although we have few difficulties separating the law of negligence, the holder in due course doctrine, or the consideration doctrine from our ideals of what tort, commercial, or contract law should be. We have not achieved the positivist "separation of law and morality" in the constitutional sphere that we seem to embrace almost automatically in most other areas of law. But this may not be as surprising, or inconsistent, as it first appears. The positivist insistence on the separation of "the law" on the one hand and its merit or demerit on the other— the separateness of the actual and the ideal—ensures a clear perception of the law's true nature, a logical prerequisite to meaningful criticism and hence reform. Only by first understanding what the law is, the positivist argues, can we determine what it should be, and only after we see what it should be can we reform it. But, perhaps what is distinctive about the constitutional context is that there simply is no realistic chance of "reforming" the Constitution, and hence no sensible reform-based motive for insisting on the positivist separation of the Constitution "as it is" from the Constitution "as it ought to be." Given the permanence, the higher status, and the "constitutiveness" of constitutional law, what one achieves through insistence on the moral inadequacy of the Constitution is not the clearheadedness essential to its enlightened reform stressed by the classical legal positivists, but rather one's own exclusion from the community whose audience is sought.

From a purely strategic perspective, then, there may simply be no gain and considerable cost from the positivist insistence on separating the constitutional "is" from the constitutional "ought." The Constitution is simply not amenable to the gradualist, piecemeal, liberal reform that positivism facilitates. Criticizing the Constitution may too closely resemble criticizing the earth for revolving around the sun. Although neither as natural nor as unchangeable as the law of the earth's rotation, the law of the Constitution is considerably more resistant to change than are the criminal codes or private law regimes to which Bentham and his positivist followers directed their critical and reformist attentions. The costs of asserting the incompatibility of the Constitution with one's own moral and political values are high, and obvious. Once the unconstitutionality of a favored reform is conceded, marginality is virtually assured. Given the dominance of lawyers in constitutional discourse and their continuing commitment to change the world through law, the absence of a critical perspective that fails to achieve meaningful reform and delegitimizes the very values according to which the law is found wanting may not be so surprising.

Strategy alone, however, does not tell the entire story. After all, many, if not most, constitutional theorists are not litigators, or even aspire to be litigators. No matter how many of the last generation of grand constitutional theorists were one-time law clerks, there are now many contemporary constitutional theorists who have no secret or express urge whatsoever to tie their constitutional views to a potential argument for effectuating a desirable legal change. The absence of normative skepticism from constitutional discourse must have causes other than the strategic desire to back the winning horse, coupled with the obvious truism that an argument that concedes unconstitutionality to argue the immorality of the Constitution will lose in court every time.

In this section I will argue that the absence of normative skepticism from constitutional discourse is also attributable, at least in part, to the logic of the poles of the interpretive debates concerning the Constitution's meaning, its meaningfulness, or meaninglessness that currently dominate constitutional scholarship. Both the constitutional faithful (those who insist on the determinacy of constitutional meaning and hence legitimacy of constitutional review within the framework of liberalism) and the constitutional skeptics (those who challenge the determinacy of the Constitution and hence the compatibility of judicial review with liberal theory) are, for different reasons, unlikely to pursue skeptical arguments about the Constitution's value, even if they adhere to the progressive political or moral premises on which that skepticism might be grounded. Thus, the absence of progressive skepticism about the Constitution might reflect the degree to which the now standard debate over interpretivism has captured the terms of constitutional discourse. Whatever the case concerning the wisdom of refraining from constitutional critique for strategic reasons, there is no good reason, I will argue, to allow the debate over interpretation to preempt debate over constitutional value. To the degree that the absence of a morally skeptical stance regarding the Constitution reflects a commitment to one or the other of the poles of debate over meaning, we should put aside, if we cannot resolve, the latter, so that we can again focus our attention on the former.

THE PROGRESSIVE CRITIQUE AND
LIBERAL CONSTITUTIONAL FAITH

All members of the constitutionally faithful[23] pole of the debate adhering to the determinacy of constitutional meaning and to the compatibility of the constitutional enterprise with liberal premises will be disinclined to express progressive critiques of constitutionalism. For these purposes, the constitutionally faithful should be divided into two subgroups: the *traditional liberals* and a possibly larger group with mixed political commitments who might be called *progressive liberals*.

First, of the sizeable number of the constitutionally faithful who are traditional or classical liberals, the disinclination to see whatever merit there is in the progressive case against the Constitution is fairly easy to explain. The traditional liberal, simply by virtue of his or her politics, will be relatively inattentive to the harms of subordination occasioned by the private sphere and insulated by constitutionalism. The progressive critique of the Constitution will therefore have no strong intuitive appeal. For this group, the constitutional commitment to the insularity of the private sphere converges perfectly with the political belief that the private sphere is the sphere of autonomy, growth, and self-actualization, rather than the "hellhole" of violation and subordination described by progressives. There is a perfect fit, in other words, of the coercive morality of the Constitution and the aspirational morality of traditional liberal politics. When the Constitution is correctly interpreted, it aligns with correct liberal moral commitments. There is simply no merit to the progressive critique.

This characterization of traditional liberalism, however, obviously does not fairly describe the broad political commitments of persons within the "constitutionally faithful" camp of the interpretation debates. A sizeable number of the constitutionally faithful are committed to some aspect of progressive politics. The hard question, then, is not why the traditional liberal is blind to the progressive critique of constitutionalism, but why those who are committed to constitutional determinacy and method but also sympathize with at least some progressive goals and methods, nevertheless shy away from attacking directly the morality of the Constitution. For them, the refusal to see the unconstitutionality of politically desirable progressive proposals as arguments against the Constitution must stem not from politics, but from a view of the Constitution as rooted in a higher, deeper, more "constitutive," or simply "prior" morality, and not simply a more coercive legal command. Hence, for this group, the unconstitutionality of proposals based on a politics incompatible with the constitutional mandate carries with it the moral justification of their demise. For the constitutionally faithful theorist who views some progressive proposals as politically wise, their unconstitutionality implies not the limits of the morality or justification of the Constitution, but rather the limits of the morality of the proposals themselves. It may be a politically and hence morally "good thing" to limit access to hate speech or pornography, but it must be a constitutionally and hence super-morally "better thing" to restrain our desires to do the (merely) politically right thing. For the constitutionally faithful, the Constitution provides a higher norm both positivistically and morally, and therefore the "lower" moralities with which it conflicts must simply give way. Their virtue cannot suggest fault with the Constitution itself.

The logic of constitutional faith, one might assume, eventually brings about a concrete reordering of moral and political priorities and a reordering of epistemological perceptions of the social world as well. To accommodate the moral and legal commitment to the priority of the constitutional norm in the face of an unconstitutional but desirable political proposal, the faithful constitutionalist must either elevate to new heights the stakes of departing from the constitutional norm or denigrate the evil the unconstitutional progressive proposal was designed to remedy. It is, then, not surprising that, in the hate speech and antipornography examples, the negative liberty of individual consumers of that speech achieves almost mystical status for faithful constitutionalists, while the harms caused by hate speech and pornography are trivialized. This simultaneous elevation of individual liberty and trivialization of group harm, in turn, affects the way the faithful constitutionalist sees the world. The harms occasioned by pornography, hate speech, and unequal distributions of domestic labor all become not just trivial, but even invisible. Their evil is "trumped" out of existence by the perceived evil of limiting a negative right. There is then no disabling conflict between the constitutional morality to which the faithful constitutionalist is definitionally committed and the political morality that may conflict with constitutional morality. The "moral dissonance" always present in the faithful constitutionalist's position is reduced to nothing through the altering of the perceptual landscape.

It is when this perceptual reordering becomes impossible that the faithful constitutionalist will switch sides and argue the constitutionality of progressive schemes designed to eradicate these harms. The harm may be so visible, concrete, and public that its trivialization requires just too great an act of will. Or, the presence of the evil may be as central to the theorist's world view as is the essential morality and determinacy of the Constitution. In either case, the moral dissonance between the Constitution and political morality must be reduced by some route other than trivialization of the harm or elevation of the constitutional value. The harm and the evil of purely private discrimination is one such example. The harm is simply too obvious and the evil too great to permit the "trumping" of this harm by the higher constitutional value of protecting the private sphere. For the faithful constitutionalist, however, even the undeniable harm of private discrimination cannot become an argument against the unassailable Constitution. Consequently, the faithful constitutionalist must find statutes or ordinances designed to remedy this evil compatible with the Constitution, either by carving exceptions to the private/public distinction or, more typically, by blurring the distinction between public and private. Not surprisingly, we have a huge body of liberal constitutional scholarship finding state action in almost any conceivable act of discrimination, but almost no liberal constitutional scholarship arguing that the prevalence and evil of constitutionally unassailable private discrimination shows that the state action requirement, itself firmly grounded in constitutional principle, is morally unjustified.

The constitutionally faithful theorist also harboring some commitment to progressive political methodology similarly risks moral dissonance created by the methodological incompatibility of the communitarian and collectivist methods of progressivism and the authoritarian methods of constitutionalism. As the faithful theorist reduces the risk of substantive dissonance by reorienting his perceptions of the social world to trivialize the private harms occasioned by subordination in the private sphere, he is inclined to minimize the risk of methodological dissonance by simply reorienting his perceptions of the virtues and vices of progressive methods. The vast majority of constitutionally faithful liberals harboring at least a fondness for the participatory democracy central to progressivism effect the accommodation between the Constitution's methods and the methods of progressive politics by simply attributing to participatory democracy the same majoritarian vices that constitutional methodology is perfectly poised to correct when directed against democratic excesses of a conservative or reactionary political hue. Whether the democratic wish being frustrated is the conservative desire to punish flag-burners or dispensers of contraception, or the progressive desire to punish or penalize hate speech or pornography, the constitutionally faithful liberal will argue that democracy has outreached its moral justification. In both cases she can readily conclude that constitutional methodology is perfectly designed to identify and rectify the excess. It just does not matter whether the democratic desire has come to fruition through the progressive methods of coalition building, consciousness raising, and democratic participation or through the politics of reaction and hate mongering. In either case, the peculiar dangers to the individual and to the private sphere posed by majoritarianism are present, and in either case, the Constitution and the courts are poised with methodological perfection to eliminate them.

There is one major exception to the preceding descriptive account. Perhaps one of the most significant developments in legal academic thought over the last decade is that, for at least a few constitutionally faithful liberals committed to some progressive goals and methods, this traditional accommodation of constitutional method and participatory democracy has become untenable. This relatively new experience of an unacceptable degree of dissonance between the authoritarianism central to traditionally conceived liberal constitutional methodology and the participatory democracy celebrated and relied on by progressive politics has given rise to the arguably oxymoronic academic movement known as *liberal civic republicanism*. Liberal republicans are, perhaps, best defined by their insistence that the dissonance between the authoritarianism of traditional constitutionalism and the democratic methods of progressivism must be reduced in some way that does not simply denigrate the value of participatory democracy.[24] Two solutions have been fruitfully explored in neo-civic liberal-republican literature.

First, for some liberal republicans, notably Frank Michelman[25] and Owen Fiss,[26] the tension between the methods of constitutionalism and progressivism can be lessened by reconceiving the function, role, and content of judicial review to align with progressive politics. The methodological contradiction between progressivism and constitutionalism is, therefore, reduced by rethinking constitutional methodology. Constitutional processes can then be seen as actually doing the work of progressivism, thus obviating the need for the progressive politics with which constitutional methodology has been traditionally conceived as inconsistent. The judge, according to this view, should do precisely what, from a progressive point of view, would otherwise be done by coalition building and consciousness changing: the judge should insist that law reflect public values that in turn reflect the good of the whole, rather than the elevation of private values and the private sphere, reflecting only the supremacy of a hegemonic group. The judge is not only the idealized progressive legislator, but also the speaker for the idealized outcome of a grass-roots progressive political campaign. She speaks for the mobilized subordinated and realigns and reorients the self-identity of the powerful, forging a new, more expansive community. The tension between constitutionalism and participatory, progressive democracy is lessened by casting the judge as the guardian of participatory democracy.

A second group of liberal neo-civic republicans, notably Cass Sunstein [27] and Paul Brest,[28] effects the accommodation of authoritarian constitutional methodology and participatory progressive method by identifying the representative branches of government, rather than the judiciary, as the primary locus of constitutional decision making, or more simply, by democratizing constitutional method. For this group as well, the potential methodological clash between constitutionalism and progressivism is somewhat averted. The dissonance between participatory politics and authoritarian constitutionalism is reduced not by rendering the judge the spokesperson and guardian of the value of participation, but rather by identifying the participatory branch of government as the site of constitutional decision making.

Although strengthening the strategic resources of constitutionalism, this new development reinforces the basic point that, for all liberals and progressive liberals committed to the determinacy of the Constitution and the legitimacy of the constitutional enterprise within liberal theory, the conflict between progressive political aspirations and constitutional substance and method will constitute not a challenge to the moral legitimacy of the Constitution but a constitutional, and hence moral, burden on progressivism itself. Consequently, even among the constitutionally faithful liberals sympathetic to progressive ends, progressive politics and progressive moral aspirations are to some degree delegitimized. This muting of the skeptical voice among liberal and progressive-liberal constitutionalists is unfortunate. As I will argue below, there are real costs from the muting of progressive doubts about the moral or political value of the Constitution. But it is also unfounded, and it is unfounded even within the assumptions of the very liberal tradition that presumably inspires constitutional faith.

The muting of skepticism is unfounded because there simply is no connection between the determinacy of the Constitution—the hallmark of constitutional faith—and the Constitution's morality. The notion that there is some connection, implicit in volumes of liberal writing on the Constitution and explicit in the remainder, rests on the fallacious argument that, because the Constitution's indeterminacy would imply its illegitimacy, and its illegitimacy in turn would imply its immorality, therefore, the Constitution's determinacy must imply both its legitimacy and morality. Not only is this wrong, but also it is profoundly illiberal. Conceding the necessity of determinacy to liberal legitimacy, it does not follow that the Constitution's determinacy is a sufficient condition of its ultimate political morality, for two reasons. First, determinacy may be a necessary but not a sufficient condition of legitimacy. Even a fully determinate Constitution might be illegitimate for reasons independent of its determinacy. Second, and more important, legitimacy may be a necessary but not a sufficient condition of morality. Even a fully "legitimate" constitutional enterprise—legitimate, for example, within the contours of either liberal or republican political theory—may be immoral for reasons independent of its legitimacy.

In other words, only through conflation of determinacy with legitimacy, and then legitimacy with morality, does interpretive faith in the determinacy of the Constitution become moral faith in its ultimate justification. No conceivable grounds, however, justify that double conflation. Determinacy no more exhausts political legitimacy than political legitimacy exhausts moral justification. The mistaken notion that it does reflects either the profoundly illiberal view of the state as fully justified if "legitimate"—rather than as fully justified if, and only if, truly liberatory—or the equally illiberal view that that which has traditionally been valued must continue to be valued, regardless of our changing appreciation of the burdens and harms it inflicts, or, using the Deweyan phrase for the "nerve" of liberalism, regardless of our changing "intelligence" about the effect of that object on our felt, experienced lives.

THE PROGRESSIVE CRITIQUE AND
CONSTITUTIONAL SKEPTICISM

Constitutional skeptics[29]—those who doubt the determinacy of constitutional phrases, and hence the compatibility of the Constitution with liberal political theory—are also disinclined to embrace a progressive normative critique of the Constitution, even if they subscribe to progressive political and moral goals and methods. This fact alone is surprising because constitutional skeptics for the most part are members of the Critical Legal Studies movement, a legal academic movement that itself may be defined by a commitment to progressive, left-wing, or radical politics. Thus, one may legitimately assume that most constitutional skeptics subscribe to most if not all of the progressive political commitments described in this chapter and would therefore be inclined to assert the moral and political desirability of progressive political proposals designed to remedy abuses of power within the private, intimate, or social sphere. Yet, even from the sizeable number of progressive, feminist, or critical constitutional writers committed to the indeterminacy thesis and clearly supportive of progressive causes, one finds very little scholarship critical of the Constitution. The question remains: Why?

The main reason may be strategic, but strategy alone cannot be the whole story. Although there may be others, one additional reason for the lack of criticism of the Constitution from constitutional skeptics may be that the logic of constitutional skepticism precludes moral criticism: for constitutional skeptics, neither the meaning nor the method of the Constitution is sufficiently determinate to be pernicious. If a text has potentially contradictory meanings, it can hardly be faulted for its substantive political implications, for it quite literally has none. Thus, for the skeptic, the Constitution's apparent incompatibility with progressive causes can hardly be attributed to the Constitution. Instead, the impulse to attribute these outcomes to the Constitution, the skeptic argues, rather than to its human interpreters and appliers, evidences the bad faith that the indeterminacy thesis is in part designed to uncover. The Constitution and the liberal tradition it purports to serve are sufficiently malleable to be susceptible to nonliberal, illiberal, conservative, tyrannical, or progressive interpretations. That it has received any particular interpretation or application, therefore, is a function not of its content, but of the constraining influences of the interpretive community or the political predilections of the interpreting judge. It follows that there is no reason intrinsic to the constitutional text for the Supreme Court's persistently non- and antiprogressive application and interpretation of the Constitution. Although the Court has generally read the Constitution to burden and limit the reach of affirmative action programs, for example, nothing in the document mandates that result. Consequently, the political inclinations of the judiciary, or the communities from which that group is drawn, must explain their interpretation. The Constitution itself can be read either to permit or to invalidate such plans. Similarly, the Constitution neither permits nor forbids hate speech ordinances. That it is read in such a way by liberal commentators and the Supreme Court is not attributable to the language, content, or history of the Constitution, but rather to the constraints of the politics of the judge or community responsible for the interpretation.

The progressive critique of constitutional methodology is also obscured by the indeterminacy critique at the heart of constitutional skepticism. The authoritarianism of constitutionalism so antithetical to progressive political methodology simply disappears if the Constitution has no definitive meaning: if the indeterminacy claim is sound, the Constitution cannot be authoritative. A text that can mean either A or not-A can hardly be characterized as authoritative. If the indeterminacy thesis is right, the authoritarianism of constitutionalism cannot be attributed to the Constitution itself, although it might be attributable to the institutional forms, such as judicial review, responsible for its implementation. Not surprisingly, of the constitutional skeptics drawn to progressive political methods, few find any serious basis for moral, as opposed to epistemological, skepticism.

Here again, though, the inferences seem flawed. Constitutional skepticism no more obviates the need for normative constitutional criticism than constitutional faith undercuts its credibility. First, even if the Constitution is contradictory in precisely the way claimed by the skeptics—so any legal rule that is intended to specify results by reference to its content can be manipulated to reach contradictory results—it does not follow that the constitutional tradition, as opposed to the constitutional document, fails to render determinate results—results which, if history is a guide, are profoundly hostile to progressive politics. The indeterminacy thesis shows merely that the constitutional text, coupled with liberal theory, does not entail determinate results. But it does not follow that constitutional results are indeterminate. It only follows that it is not the text—the law— that does the determining. If we understand the constitutional tradition to be that which determines outcomes, and understand that tradition to include the politics of the community, the predilections of the judge, and in short the hegemonic and choice-denying inclinations of the judge's social context, then not only are constitutional outcomes determined, they are despairingly overdetermined. They are overdetermined, furthermore, by the very social and private forces of racism, misogyny, and classism that render progressive interpretations of the same document untenable. The felt determinacy of the Constitution and its felt incompatibility with progressivism hold regardless of the indeterminacy of the document and of liberalism itself.

Furthermore, it is worth noting that, to the extent that the indeterminacy critique is motivated by a European and existentialist impulse to unmask the otherwise denied responsibility of the judge for her political choices, the consequences of that critique are deeply paradoxical and self-defeating. On the one hand, the indeterminacy thesis, if true, precludes the judge from avoiding responsibility for the political and moral consequences of her decisions by cloaking them in the garb of a disingenuous legalism. On the other hand, however, the same critique exonerates the Constitution's authors. Peculiarly, the same indeterminacy critique that highlights the human responsibility of the present interpretive community or judge simultaneously obscures the equally human responsibility of the text's authors. Texts no less than interpretations have consequences, and one would expect a movement committed to demystifying the human authorship of, and hence responsibility for, institutional facts to be sensitive to the very real consequences of chosen words, and hence the responsibility for those consequences of the text's drafters. The indeterminacy critique muddles that responsibility as it denies the meaningfulness of the written text. It accordingly confuses the authority upon which that responsibility is predicated, and hence the moral dangers implied by the subsequent deference to textual authoritarianism so central to traditional constitutional method.

Whatever the merits of these arguments, however, it seems fair to say that constitutional skeptics view indeterminacy as obviating the need for progressive normative critique, just as constitutionally faithful liberals view constitutionalism as undermining the justification of progressive critique. For one group the critique is obviated; for the other its justification is undermined. All of this happens with no examination of the merits. The logic and framework of interpretive debates over the Constitution's meaning and meaningfulness have obscured debate over the Constitution's ultimate value by making the debate either illegitimate or moot. We might, therefore, be wise to consider putting aside our doubts about constitutional determinacy to look afresh at questions of constitutional value.

PROGRESSIVE POLITICS AND
CONSTITUTIONAL DISCOURSE

The absence of a tradition morally skeptical toward the Constitution from a progressive perspective has weakened progressivism, weakened our constitutional debates, weakened constitutional interpretation, and consequently possibly weakened the Constitution itself. Progressivism is injured in at least two ways. First, there are obvious adverse political consequences if it is both true and unacknowledged that our constitutional guarantees of individual rights and liberties fail to guard against abuses of private power and affirmatively protect the spheres in which those abuses occur. The second type of damage, however, is more subtle and possibly more serious. The lack of a clear understanding of the obstacle to progressivism posed by constitutional guarantees further denigrates the "outlaw" position of the disadvantaged in this society simply because the advocacy of measures deemed both anticommunitarian and antiindividualist through their unconstitutionality is not consistently coupled with a critique of the Constitution that delegitimizes those initiatives. The tendency of all subordinated persons toward self-belittlement by trivializing the nature of their injuries is geometrically enhanced by the self-perception that their injuries do not exist because their infliction is constitutionally protected. To insist on the injustice of it is to injure, in a profound—because constitutional—sense, the entire community of which both the dominant and subordinate are a part. The understanding of the harms suffered by subordinated persons in the private realm is thereby frustrated when those injuries are perceived as having been the occasion of unconstitutional, and hence deeply immoral, legislative initiatives. The battle for passage of a progressive statute or ordinance, such as a hate speech regulation or an antipornography ordinance, destined to be found unconstitutional becomes the occasion not of greater public consciousness of the uniqueness, nature, and intensity of the suffering, but rather an occasion for obliterating difference by blurring the harm sustained by hate speech or pornography with other injuries sustained by other factions seeking ends at odds with constitutional guarantees. Greater understanding of the degree to which the Constitution frustrates progressivism would at least clarify the nature of the problem and might potentially demystify and hence dethrone and "untrump" constitutional morality.

A clearer understanding of the systemic threat to progressivism posed by constitutionalism that might be gained through a sustained debate over the value of constitutionalism might also enhance the quality of constitutional dialogue. Mainstream liberal constitutional discourse is presently characterized by an almost obsessive refusal to acknowledge or examine the nature of the costs of constitutional rights and liberties because of the logic and structure of rights themselves: the right exists to preclude precisely such cost-benefit analyses. Because there is no social cost that a right does not theoretically "trump," from a liberal perspective there is simply no reason to assess the costs of rights, and plenty of reason not to: assessment only threatens societal respect for the right in question. Nevertheless, this refusal to address the consequences of rights ultimately leaves them groundless, as well as dangerous. The right must implicitly, if not explicitly, rest on some intuition that in the long run the benefits of having a right—whether self-actualization, autonomy, intimacy, privacy, meritocratic treatment, or economic self-determination—outweigh any costs incurred by its possession. Failure to examine the wisdom of this balance in light of our expanding knowledge of the experience of persons most vulnerable to the harms occasioned by those rights, and failure to countenance the possibility that perhaps the balance ought to be re-struck, does not constitute "liberalism" in its best light; far from it. Instead, it constitutes a deeply conservative, traditionalist, and even reactionary posture toward the possibility of change and a profoundly illiberal rejection of the use of pragmatic knowledge to come to grips with an evolving social world.

The absence of a sustained tradition of normative constitutional skepticism also hurts the Constitution, in precisely the way that John Stuart Mill warned: unexamined institutions, ideas, and cultures become fossilized, nonvital, superstitiously worshiped, and then perversely discarded echoes of their original impulses.[30] This is surely as true of liberal ideals, institutions, and cultures as it is of the unexamined and uncriticized conservative traditions and religions that Mill ridiculed.

Finally, we should remember that the Constitution is merely difficult, not impossible, to change. It can be changed fundamentally through amendment, interstitially through judicial interpretation, and in fact if not form through patterns of practice occasioned through changes in consciousness. The strategic impulse to insist on the constitutionality of unconstitutional progressive initiatives, because of the sense that the Constitution itself cannot be changed, may be unduly pessimistic. Reform through critique is not utterly beyond the pale in constitutional dialogue or doctrine. Although the Constitution may be fundamental law, it is a fundamental charter of our self-understanding, as well, only if we permit it to be. Although a changed self-understanding is surely not a sufficient condition of change in a fundamental law, it is undeniably a necessary one. Failure to achieve it because of a sense of futility does nothing but render the immutability of an antiprogressive Constitution a self-fulfilling prophecy.

THE LATENT POSSIBILITY OF A
PROGRESSIVE CONSTITUTIONAL FAITH

Perhaps the greatest cost of the lack of a sustained tradition of normative constitutional skepticism on progressive grounds is that it has very
likely impeded the development of a responsive tradition, which I have
called a progressive constitutional faith. Progressive constitutional faith
might best be described in contrast to other constitutional approaches.
First, unlike constitutionally faithful liberals, constitutionally faithful progressives would aim to tie the determinate meaning of the Constitution,
ascertained through its text, history, and supporting moral philosophy,
not to liberal hopes, fears, and ideals, but instead to progressive ones. Unlike constitutional skeptics, progressive faithful constitutionalists would
assert the possibility of a progressive interpretation of the Constitution
on the grounds of the position's fundamental correctness rather than the
Constitution's meaninglessness. The claim would be that the Constitution
really means what the progressive insists, carries accordant obligations,
and consequently mandates a progressive conception of community to
which we all ought adhere. The possibility of a progressive interpretation of the Constitution, in other words, would rest not upon the real
or perceived contradictions latent or explicit in liberalism and the potential for interpretive exploitation that those contradictions entail, but upon
the Constitution itself: its progressive meaning, history, and text, and the
political and moral philosophy against which it should and must be interpreted. Thus, unlike liberal faithful constitutionalists, with whom they
share a belief in constitutional determinacy, progressive constitutionalists
would ground constitutional meaning in progressive rather than liberal
politics. And last, unlike constitutional skeptics with whom they share
their politics, constitutionally faithful progressives would emphasize not
the Constitution's indeterminacy, but, rather, those constitutional events
and textual passages that support the claim that the Constitution is at least
as concerned about the abuse of private and social power as it is patently
concerned with the abuse of public and political power, and is at least as
methodologically convergent with ideals of participatory democracy as it
is explicitly concerned with the limits of majoritarian will.

On this view, the antiprogressive content and method of the Constitution that presently seem so inextricably interwoven with its text and
history is revealed to be not just indeterminate, but wrong: a modern (as

well as postmodern), transitory, and misguided moment. The identification of public, rather than private, power as the concern of the Constitution, the preference for negative over positive liberty at the heart of both the First Amendment and the Fourteenth Amendment's liberty and due process clauses, and the insistence on a formal rather than substantive understanding of the equal protection clause is central not to the Constitution itself—whether understood as its text, its history, or the best political philosophy that might sustain it—but rather to the politics and felt contingent needs of the modern and postmodern world. Once seen as an unnecessary and false reading of the Constitution, the path is then cleared for a more accurate and progressive understanding of constitutional mandates and responsibilities.

Doctrinally, progressive constitutional faith would have to rest primarily on a rereading of the central message, meaning, and history of the Fourteenth Amendment. The modern understanding that the Fourteenth Amendment only reaches state action that operates injuriously upon subordinated groups, according to this view, is the result of a handful of erroneous opinions, beginning with the nineteenth-century civil rights cases[31] and culminating with the modern state action cases.[32] Historically, the Fourteenth Amendment, like all the Reconstruction Amendments, was intended to ensure that the states refrain from inflicting injury on subordinated groups and take affirmative action to guarantee that private power not be used to re-enslave the recently freed.[33] By principled extension, therefore, the amendments taken as a whole ought to be understood as requiring the states to guard against not only their own complicity in the domination of subordinate groups but also the domination of those groups themselves, and to act affirmatively to end it. On this reading, "equal protection of the laws" requires Congress to ensure that the states legislate in a fair and rational manner and that Congress protects against private subordination, whether that subordination occurs through the relationship of slave and master, of wife and husband, or of employee and employer when the parties possess radically unequal control of resources. The due process clause fundamentally requires the states to ensure that only the state be empowered to deprive people of their utterly positive liberty to work, live, participate in politics and culture, and sustain meaningful intimate relationships, and that the state only do so with due process of law. The amendment taken in its entirety, then, means that the states must take any necessary and possible action to guarantee that private social life will not regress to anything resembling either the relationship of enslavement of the slave era or the private exploitation and coercion that followed it.

If the Fourteenth Amendment was intended to address private relationships of subordination as well as public abuses of political power, then the constitutionality of progressive proposals designed to eliminate patterns of subordination logically follows. Indeed, they are not simply constitutional, but also constitutionally mandated.

Methodologically, progressive constitutional faith would view the Constitution as mandating a method of decision making and a style of discourse convergent with the progressive commitment to restrain majoritarian excess, bigotry, mistakes, or ill will through the progressive tools of participatory democracy, collective political action, and social responsibility, rather than with the liberal commitment to correct those evils through an intellectual ideology that combines glorification of the abstract individual with contempt of the concrete majority, and an institution that imposes that ideology through coercion rather than through persuasion. It would claim that a reformed constitutionalism—one emphasizing legislative and citizen participation, persuasion over coercion, and antisubordination— could shed itself of the authoritarianism of traditional constitutional discourse, yet retain the obligatoriness of constitutional meaning without which constitutionalism loses its value, whether to progressive or liberal self-understandings. To be constitutional as well as progressive, a progressive constitutional method would have to discover a means of ascertaining communal and communitarian self-understanding that implies the inclusion, unity, fraternity, sorority, mutual recognition, and obligation that makes constitutionalism a significant claim on our social life and individual existence. To be progressive, the constitutional method must be respectful of dissent, noncoercive, nonauthoritarian, and at least somewhat pluralist. The articulation of this constitutional method is a far greater challenge for a progressive constitutional faith, I think, than the historical, textual, and philosophical work required to justify a progressive interpretation of constitutional rights and liberties.

It remains to be seen whether a progressive constitutional faith could ultimately be sustained. It seems to me that there are enough "constitutional moments" in our political and social history to suggest that it could be, from the passage of the Reconstruction Amendments and their fundamental challenge to the most extreme forms of private subordination, to the attempt in the post-*Lochner* era cases to reject an interpretation of the Constitution prohibiting the states or Congress from addressing private subordination,[34] and to the Warren Court's decision in *Brown v. Board of Education*,[35] which at least arguably was concerned not only with state-ordered de jure segregation but also with the injurious consequences of private racism, inflicted through the protected and private spheres of speech, education, and the "culture" of racism.[36] Of course, if the Constitution, or at least the Fourteenth Amendment and the rights "incorporated" by it, is centrally concerned with private power, its abuse, and the injuries of racism, poverty, and sexism occasioned by its abuse, then the vast bulk of modern cases concerning those rights are wrong, and the legislative, adjudicative, and social work of implementing the true meaning of those amendments has not yet begun. That, however, ought not count against the plausibility of a progressive constitutional faith. It only restates two obvious and noncontentious points: first, at this point in history, any progressive constitutional faith would constitute a dissident tradition; second, the Constitution articulates an aspirational morality that we have only occasionally glimpsed and that we have not yet begun to honor.

Now, for reasons easily summarized because they directly mirror those outlined above, the dominance of debate over the status of the Constitution's meaning has stymied the development of a progressive constitutional faith. Neither constitutionally faithful liberals nor constitutional skeptics has much stake in the articulation of a progressive constitutional faith and, for that reason alone, the dominance of interpretation debates focused on the coherence of liberalism has somewhat retarded progressive understandings of constitutional meanings. For one thing, liberal constitutional faith is defined by its commitment to the proposition that the Constitution's meaning, as well as the justification for its imposition against the democratic will, must be drawn from the liberal tradition, a tradition that is generally hostile to progressive initiatives and understandings. A liberal faith then might share with a progressive faith a belief in the meaningfulness of the Constitution, but the meanings ascribed by the two movements are inevitably in near-diametrical opposition.

For another, constitutional skeptics, although sharing the politics of progressive constitutional faith, would have as little interest in the articulation of a view of the Constitution as essentially furthering progressive causes as they have in the articulation of a criticism of the Constitution as essentially hostile to those initiatives, for at least two reasons. First, if the Constitution's meaning is necessarily indeterminate, then it can no more be tied to progressivism than to liberalism. There is presumably no political commitment that does not share in the instability and the extreme contradictoriness of liberalism. Indeterminacy is, after all, a function not of particular politics, but of language and life. If the interpretive skeptic is right, therefore, progressive constitutional faith is impossible. Progressive, no less than liberal, constitutional faith is ruled out by the inevitable indeterminacy of the language with which the faith is constructed. Second, given the contradictions of liberalism, progressive initiatives can be argued to be either constitutional or unconstitutional. Therefore, progressive constitutional faith, and the determinate progressive politics on which it is predicated, is also strategically unnecessary. Indeterminacy is sufficient to facilitate progressive political goals.

Nevertheless, in spite of the preemptive nature of the interpretation battles, a small but growing number of progressive constitutional theorists subscribe in some form to a progressive constitutional faith. Much of it comes from critical race theory. Mari Matsuda's general characterization of "outsider jurisprudence,"[37] as well as her particular reconstruction of the First Amendment to support the constitutionality of hate speech regulations,[38] was seminal to this tradition, as was Charles Lawrence's interpretation of *Brown* as being centrally concerned with expressions of private racism, and hence supportive of the same conclusion.[39] Patricia Williams's[40] and Kimberle Crenshaw's[41] early defense of rights as conducive to liberalism and to progressive racial goals, previsioned much of the direction of this movement. All these essays stand in marked contrast not only to the liberal positions on the First Amendment or on the nature of rights that they are directly and doctrinally concerned to counter, but also to both the constitutional skepticism of the Critical Legal Studies movement and the progressive skepticism of such critical race theorists as Derrick Bell,[42] Alan Freeman,[43] and, perhaps, Richard Delgado.[44] Against progressive skepticism, the progressive constitutional faithful argue that, properly read, the Constitution indeed supports and perhaps requires these regulations. Furthermore, against the constitutional skepticism of the Critical Legal Studies movement, they assert that the Constitution requires precisely what they argue it requires, not because of the contradictions latent in its clauses or in the liberalism behind it, but because of the progressivism of the Constitution itself.

Feminists have also contributed to this tradition, none more so than Catharine MacKinnon.[45] Her argument that the equal protection clause is directly concerned with a wide range of abuses against women, and directly requires the states to do something about them, stands in direct opposition to both (a) liberal arguments that limit equal protection to rational categorizations of similarities and differences and (b) skeptical progressive claims that the Fourteenth Amendment's promise of equality is not merely irrelevant to women's progress, but indeed is hostile to it. Finally, it stands in striking opposition to the paradigmatic critical claim that, because of its indeterminacy, the Fourteenth Amendment has no meaning, pernicious or progressive, that can be effectively criticized or implemented.

All these arguments, the positions they imply, and the twin premises of both constitutional fidelity and progressive politics on which they explicitly or implicitly rest, are richly suggestive of the possibility of a progressive constitutional faith. As paradoxical as it may sound, it seems to me that further development of this tradition is, at one and the same time, possibly futile, deeply utopian, absolutely necessary, terribly risky, and one of the most imaginative, fecund, and important shared enterprises presently ongoing in the legal academy. It is possibly futile because the particular positions regarding progressive legislation that a progressive constitutional faith implies will most likely not prevail in the immediate or foreseeable future in any institutional form. It is deeply utopian in that it envisions a reconstructed understanding of our history and constructs an extraordinarily appealing vision of our distant, if not immediate, future. It is absolutely necessary because it may be impossible to attain progressive goals in this culture as long as the morality and the coercive power of the Constitution are understood, rightly or wrongly, as in direct opposition to those progressive goals. It is terribly risky because it may very likely be either tamed, co-opted, or, at worst, revealed to be in fact—as well as in the imaginations and arguments of modern liberals—nothing but the foundation of a new tyranny. It is imaginative, important, and fecund because it carries the possibility of a profoundly new understanding of our constitutional history and of constitutional meaning, and hence carries the possibility of a new and quite radical Constitution.

Conclusion

The implications of a progressive constitutional skepticism are fairly obvious and quite momentous. If the Constitution is irreversibly and deeply hostile to progressive political action targeted at abuse of power in private, intimate, and economic spheres of life, it is imperative that at least progressives know that fact, and highly desirable that the rest of us know it as well. It should occasion strategic rethinking by the former and a sustained reexamination by the rest of the community of the relative costs, benefits, virtues, and burdens occasioned by the rights and liberties that we all, to varying degrees, either "enjoy" or suffer.

The implications of a progressive constitutional faith are also quite momentous. As Catharine MacKinnon, echoing Bruce Ackerman, has suggested, such a faith, if it can be sustained, mandates a rethinking of the identity of "We the People" in whose behalf the Constitution is implemented, and by whose hand it was, and is, re-created. This chapter has argued definitively for neither of these opposed positions, but has offered instead the far more modest claim that both have merit, both need an elaboration that is presently more frustrated than furthered by the terms of contemporary constitutional debate, and both would contribute mightily to progressive politics and to our constitutional self-understanding.

At the risk of courting paradox, I would like to suggest that it is not at all unthinkable or even irrational for individual progressive theorists, litigators, or political actors to harbor both skeptical and faithful attitudes and beliefs regarding constitutional fidelity. Catharine MacKinnon's work stands as a stunning example of the possibility of rationally subscribing to both a constitutional faith and skepticism. She has authored some of the most devastating and insightful progressive criticisms of the liberal Constitution and some of the most convincing arguments that the Constitution can, and must, be read to require progressive initiatives intended to end patriarchy. This is not self-contradiction, but an example of pragmatic wisdom. Whether the Constitution can be interpreted to promote progressive politics or whether it is implacably hostile to such efforts is a momentous question that need not be resolved in a moment or a lifetime. It certainly is a question that matters, and it is one we ought not lose sight of, nor allow to be muffled by the seemingly endless debates over the Constitution's ultimate compatibility with a more liberal, but arguably less appealing, political vision.

8

The Authoritarian Impulse in Constitutional Law

■

Should there be greater participation by legislators and citizens in constitutional debate, theory, and decision making? An increasing number of legal theorists from otherwise divergent perspectives have recently argued against what Paul Brest calls the "principle of judicial exclusivity" in our constitutional processes.[1] These theorists contend that because issues of public morality in our culture either are, or tend to become, constitutional issues, all political actors, and most notably legislators and citizens, should consider the constitutional implications of the moral issues of the day. Because constitutional questions are essentially moral questions about how active and responsible citizens should constitute themselves, we should all engage in constitutional debate. We should stop relying on the courts to shoulder the burden of resolving the constitutional consequences of our political decisions. According to this argument, our methods of resolving moral issues in this country are "deeply flawed."[2] The flaw is that we have delegated to the courts, rather than kept for ourselves, the moral responsibility for our decisions. By protecting, cherishing, and relying on judicial review, we have essentially alienated our moral public lives to the courts.[3]

I agree with Brest that our methods of resolving issues of public morality in this culture are deeply flawed, and I also ultimately agree with his call for greater participation in constitutional decision making. Nevertheless, there are problems with his argument. The call for increased participation in constitutional thought by Brest and others rests on the assumptions that constitutional questions are moral questions and that constitutional debate is the forum in which we engage in moral decision making. From these assumptions it follows that all citizens, not just courts, should take up issues of constitutionalism. If we take very seriously the text of the opinions in a significant number of recent constitutional cases, however, it is clear that, as a descriptive matter, the assumption that constitutional questions are moral questions is flatly false. According to the Supreme Court justices themselves, constitutional issues are by definition legal issues, as opposed to moral issues.[4] Countless "neutral-principles" constitutional theorists also insist on making a distinction between constitutional issues and moral issues.[5] Thus, according to a well-respected strand of constitutional theory, as well as an increasing number of recent cases, constitutional questions are definitionally amoral, as are the answers they propose.

Two recent cases exemplify the amorality of modern constitutional decision making. In *Bowers v. Hardwick,*[6] Justice White, speaking for the Supreme Court of the United States, explicitly disclaimed the need to examine the morality of consensual sodomy, as well as either the wisdom or the morality of legislating against it.[7] In fact, Justice White claimed that the only issues for the Court to decide were whether individuals have a constitutional right to engage in sodomy (they don't) and whether legislators have the constitutional power to legislate against it (they do). The Court did not take up the morality of consensual homosexuality or the morality of homophobic communities. Indeed, Justice White's opinion does not even hint at what sodomy is, much less examine whether it has any moral value or detriment to communal or individual life. In remarkably similar language in *Roe v. Wade,*[8] Justice Blackmun also disclaimed the need to explore the morality of abortion or of statutes making it a criminal offense.[9] In both cases, the Court explicitly reformulated the underlying moral questions—the morality of abortion and laws restricting its availability and the morality of consensual homosexuality and of laws making it a crime— into amoral constitutional questions: What is the scope of the individual's "right to privacy" accorded by the Constitution? Does the legislature have the power to criminalize what it sees fit to criminalize? Does the Court have the power to overturn legislative outcomes? In both *Bowers* and *Roe,* the Court framed the issue in this way to at least give the appearance of avoiding, rather than participating in, the underlying moral debate regarding the conduct in question.

In the first part of this chapter, I suggest that "constitutional questions" are always ambiguous, and that according to one standard interpretation, constitutional questions are indeed amoral, as the neutral-principles theorists and the opinions in *Hardwick* and *Roe* insist. I also argue, however, that contrary to the celebratory tone of those who favor amoral constitutional decision making, the aggressive amorality of modern constitutional decision making by the Court is itself a flaw, even a disease, of our modern politics, rather than a virtue of our law. If this is correct, then constitutional decision making, at least as it is done at present, should not serve as a model for citizen and legislative debate of issues of public morality. This is especially true if the aim is to increase citizen participation in moral debate about how we should constitute our social lives. Rather, we should be thankful for those shrinking spheres of moral debate still uncontaminated by constitutional modes of argument. In other words, the cure for the problem presented by this low level of citizen participation in debate over issues of public morality in this culture is not to expand participation in constitutional decision making. If constitutional questions are by definition not moral questions, and if we want to improve the quality and quantity of public debate of moral issues, then we should strive to shrink, not expand, the sphere of constitutional influence. Our modern constitutional processes are part of the problem for which we need to find a cure. They are not part of the solution.

The remainder of this chapter examines, diagnoses, and suggests a cure for the amorality of modern constitutional discourse. I argue that it is not necessarily the case that constitutional questions are posed, debated, and resolved as amoral questions of legitimacy and power rather than as moral questions about how we should constitute our lives. Historically, it has not always been the case and it need not always be so in the future. It is neither logically nor legally mandated by the internal structure of constitutional law. Rather, the amorality of modern constitutional questions and answers is in part a psychologically, as opposed to legally, mandated authoritarian reaction to the diseased state of the modern political theory that underlies our constitutional framework. If we can improve the political theory upon which constitutional law rests, we might be able to reinvigorate constitutional decision making with a sense of moral purpose. Only after we reinject into constitutional thought and law a self-consciously moral dimension will it make sense to call for greater participation by the community in constitutional processes.

Constitutional Questions

The simple explanation for why constitutional questions strike only some of us as moral questions, and then only some of the time, is that constitutional questions are patently ambiguous. On the one hand, constitutional questions, like constitutional theory, doctrine, and law, sometimes address the manner in which we choose to constitute ourselves. In this sense, constitutional questions concern the manner in which we as a society choose to constitute the individual self, the community, and the government. Constitutional questions, so understood, are clearly moral questions: How should we constitute the individual, the community, and the government? These are, I believe, the kinds of questions that Brest and other participation theorists have in mind when they implore other political actors to engage in constitutional decision making. I call this, however unimaginatively, the *normative tradition* in constitutional law.

On the other hand, constitutional questions, as well as constitutional law, theory, issues, and history, often address something very different. "Constitutional questions" are the set of questions that concerns how we are authorized by a binding legal document—the historical Constitution— to constitute ourselves. When understood in this context, constitutional questions do not concern the manner in which we, as a society, should constitute ourselves. Rather, they concern the manner in which we, as a society, are authorized to constitute ourselves by a binding, authoritative document. Here, constitutional questions are not moral questions at all. They are at best historical questions. The question is at root, What does the Constitution command?, not, How should we constitute ourselves? Of course, constitutional questions understood in this way are more than simply historical questions, because we are asking them in our search for direction and guidance concerning how to live our lives. But this additional directive dimension does not make them moral questions. Rather, they are questions we ask of an authority, whether we perceive that authority to be the framers or the text. In this conception, constitutional questions ask, How have we been told to behave? or How have we been ordered to constitute ourselves?, not, How should we behave? or How should we constitute ourselves? I call this the *authoritarian tradition* in constitutional law. If this is the tradition that Brest and others have in mind when they call for increased citizen participation in constitutional decision making, then I would suggest that their quest is fundamentally misconceived.

The difference between the normative and the authoritarian traditions, with their distinctive ways of conceiving the meaning of constitutional questions, can be captured by an analogy. Imagine a group of children on a schoolyard trying to organize the recess play period to make that time as delightful, imaginative, fun, and free of conflict as is possible. They might go about this task by asking themselves how they want to "constitute" their time, themselves, their games, and their groups during the recess period. Should they insist that everyone participate in a game? Or, may a child stand off alone, either by choice, or because he or she has been shunned by others? Should they organize all of the time, or leave some free? Their answers to these and related "constitutional" questions will depend on how they value, perceive, and conceive of the individual, of groups, and of play. Do groups evidence a desirable social impulse that should be encouraged or mandated, or a chauvinistic, mean-spirited dislike of difference and idiosyncrasy? Is time spent standing idle valuable time, or does it always evidence misery? Is the "individual" actualized by solitary activity, or do individuals achieve their highest fulfillment in social inter-action? These are all moral questions. The answers the children give to these and other more concrete "constitutional questions," such as whether they will require mandatory participation in games, will involve them in moral debate about the value of individualism, the value of participation, and the value of their play. And, as Brest and the other participationists insist, it is surely true that all the children should participate in these con-stitutional dialogues rather than a select few, whether they view themselves as game leaders, game players, or loners who hate organized games and would rather idle the hour away alone.

The children, however, might go about the task of organizing the recess period on the playground in a different way, which corresponds roughly with what I'm calling the authoritarian tradition. They might settle the question by asking the teacher what they are and are not permitted to do. This might be a perfectly sensible way to go about the task, particularly if their unstructured normative dialogue about how they should govern them-selves has turned into fistfights rather than free-spirited debate. Of course, even if they structure the time period by submitting to the dictates of the authority, they still will have to ask themselves questions that are consti-tutional. The teacher will give them a directive, but they will still have to "interpret" it. The children will have to ask themselves what the teacher's instructions meant in order to apply them. For example, the teacher may have told them that they must all participate in loosely structured games, and if so then they will have to decide whether a child amusing herself with a sack of marbles is playing a game, or whether, on the other hand, participation in a loosely structured game requires the presence of two or more. This question, in turn, will involve them in standard interpreta-tion debates and will force them to confront questions that bear a striking resemblance to the questions that would have arisen had they proceeded in the nonauthoritarian normative tradition. Obviously, whether a child playing marbles by herself is playing a game depends on the value and meaning of both individual play and participation. The answers to these questions in turn depend not only on what the teacher intended, but also on how the children feel about the matter. This superficial resemblance between the constitutional questions asked in the normative and authoritarian traditions, respectively, will never become identical, however, no matter how great the convergence. In the latter context, the children are interpreting the teacher's directive because they have decided to resolve the constitutional question in the authoritarian rather than normative tradition. They have decided to organize their time by doing what the teacher tells them to do, rather than by figuring out what they should do. They have decided to obey an authority, rather than govern themselves. Their constitutional questions are aimed toward obedience, not the end of moral self-governance.

As a group, the schoolchildren will probably be more inclined to embrace the normative tradition if their relations with each other are minimally cordial, decent, and respectful. If they already trust each other, and have some sense of each other's good faith, they will probably be more likely to resolve the constitutional questions posed by the recess hour by discussion, debate, and consensus. On the other hand, they will be more inclined to embrace an authoritarian attitude toward the constitutional issues that face them on the schoolyard if they distrust each other, if they are afraid of bullies or gangs, or if they have already come to blows. The weaker members of the group may be more inclined to invoke the aid of the "higher" authority. To the extent that the children all fear being the weaker party themselves, or to the extent that they sympathize with the weak, they too may share the inclination to settle their basic constitutional differences by submitting to the will, direction, or mandate of a higher authority. The schoolyard terrorized by the bully or the gang is more likely to be governed ultimately by the teacher, rather than by participatory decisions of the group.

Another way to see the difference between these two constitutional traditions is to note the radically different roles the text plays in each tradition. The relation of the text to the normative tradition is highly problematic. The constitutional text at times facilitates but often obstructs decision making in the normative tradition, both on the schoolyard and in our own constitutional adjudication. If constitutional questions are questions about how we should constitute ourselves, then the existence of a text that authoritatively mandates some answers to these constitutional questions, and authoritatively precludes others, poses at least two problems. First, the constitutional answers it gives may be wrong; the Constitution may fail to mandate those forms in which we should constitute ourselves and may in fact mandate undesirable forms. Second, its very existence may deter us from engaging in the participatory discussions we need to answer our constitutive questions within the normative tradition. Of course, the text will at times facilitate our search. It is always a source of insight into how others answered similar questions in the past. This facilitative function, however, is both incidental and also shared by other significant texts of our past and present, including the writings of Aristotle, John Stuart Mill, John Rawls, and Roberto Unger. Alternatively, the text may be so general that, although it does not constitute a serious obstacle to self-discovery of our ideal constitution, it does not guide it, either. What is clear, though, is that the text as an authoritative text that tells us what we must do is in no sense necessary to the normative tradition in constitutional law. We can ask normative questions: How should we govern ourselves? How should we constitute the self, the community, the government, the recess period, our play? We might better ask them without resort to an authoritative text as the first step in answering them.

By contrast, the text, no matter how understood, is absolutely necessary to the authoritarian tradition in constitutional law. If, by "constitutional question," we mean, How must we constitute ourselves under the mandate of an authoritative text?, then there must be some text, either behavioral, written, or cultural, to which we can turn to ascertain the content of the authoritative order. We may regard the text as the means by which we ascertain the intent of the original authors, as a free-standing authority, or as reflective of our own best interests or instincts. However we regard it, though, it is something other than our present selves. We turn to it to tell us how to live, because we have abandoned the project of our own moral self-governance. We turn to the text because we wish to obey it. We crave obedience when we have despaired of our own moral competence, and hence self-governing moral authority.

Our constitutional history has never been either entirely normative or entirely authoritarian. Nevertheless, we can imagine what a purely normative constitutional tradition might look like. In a purely normative tradition, the Court, as well as every other political actor, would define a "constitutional question" as, How should we, as a society, constitute ourselves? In such a world, the constitutional text itself would have historical significance and persuasive authority as a "foundational text," but it would have no binding power. The constitutional text would be on par with other significant historical texts of our culture. These would include prior cases, as well as classics of both the liberal and republican traditions. We might turn to all these texts, including the constitutional text, for guidance, wisdom, accumulated knowledge, and historical information. We would not turn to any of them, including the constitutional text, for commands to be obeyed.

A purely authoritarian constitutional tradition is easier to imagine because it is closer to the constitutional practices of this decade. When the authoritarian tradition dominates, the authority of the text, however loosely defined, is absolute, regardless of the wisdom or merits of its mandates. The question is, What are we being ordered to do?, not, What should we do? Aristotle and Mill count for nothing, because they are not legal "authorities." Normative argument in its entirety counts for nothing, because it has no "legitimacy." [10] Constitutional opinions are short and to the point, as in *Bowers v. Hardwick*. The issues become, What does the Constitution permit? and Who has the power to do what, according to the structure mandated by the original authority?, rather than, How should we lead our lives or structure our community? There is neither foundation nor need for moral debate, for these are not moral questions; they are "purely political" in the most barren sense. When we ask a constitutional question in the authoritarian tradition, we seek to know what the authority permits, whether we understand the "authority" as the framers, majorities, precedents, or a disembodied text. The authoritarian tradition in constitutional decision making by definition precludes moral debate. For this reason, the modern vitality of the authoritarian tradition in constitutional decision making is a significant obstacle to both public and judicial debate over the issue of morality in this legal culture.

These two competing constitutional traditions, I believe, are always with us as potential ways to conceive of constitutional questions. At any time, a court posing a constitutional question can pose it either as a normative question about how we should constitute ourselves, or as an authoritarian question about the content of the Constitution's mandates. If we want to know how to improve both the quality and quantity of debate over issues of public morality in this culture, we might begin by trying to ascertain what prompts a court or a time period toward the authoritarian tradition in constitutional decision making, and what might prompt it away from authoritarianism and toward a more normative posture. When, and why, do courts or legislatures lean toward the authoritarian constitutional tradition and recoil in fear from the normative, and when do they lean toward the normative tradition and recoil from the authoritarian one?

In the remainder of this chapter I suggest one hypothesis. I suggested earlier that the children on the schoolyard might lean toward an authoritarian resolution of their constitutional questions when the social bonds between them have badly deteriorated. My hypothesis is that courts and commentators are presently inclined toward an authoritarian and hence amoral resolution of our constitutional questions in part because modern interpretations of our underlying political theories, liberal pluralism, and civic republicanism reflect our anxieties about ourselves, our fears about others, and our asocial and even psychopathological tendencies, rather than our social aspirations. The modern judicial impulse toward authoritarian decision making in constitutional cases might in part be a reaction to the sorry self-portrait we have cast in our modern political theory. If we are as we paint ourselves in our political theory—incapable of creative and moral constitutional self-governance—then we are in dire need of authoritarian control.

Agnostic Self Images and the Authoritarian Impulse

Our constitutional law and decision making rest on an uneasy alliance between two images that may be both complementary and contradictory: a liberal conception of the self, and a republican conception of the community. At some times in the history of our political theory, the liberal self dominates the republican community both in importance and in priority. When it does, value is believed to emanate from the desires, wishes, and preferences of individuals. At such times, this theoretical hierarchy is reflected in constitutional decision making: a "liberal" court tends to expand the rights of individuals to give them priority over the desires of groups, communities, and legislatures, unless the desires of groups can be defended on grounds acceptable to liberals. *Roe* was perhaps the last and clearest manifestation of the power of a strong liberal conception of the self in constitutional decision making.

At other times in the history of our political theory, the republican community dominates, in importance and priority, the liberal self. At these times, the community rather than the individual is regarded as the source of value, so that the desires, wishes, and preferences of the community are both more important than, and prior to, the desires, wishes, and preferences of individuals. Although the liberal conception of the self has strong and constant ties to both political and historical liberalism, the relationship of the republican conception of the community to our political traditions is more complex. Republicanism has potentially contradictory ties to both social conservatism and utopian radicalism, depending on the identity of the community being valued. Thus, conservatives value the various "communities" of power, wealth, and privilege that have established historical traditions and institutions, which in turn embody lasting cultural achievements. By contrast, radicals value the various communities, both actual and idealized, of the disempowered. Conservatives and radical republicans agree, however, on a communitarian rather than rigidly individualistic definition of value.

Although the influence of radical, utopian republicanism in constitutional law has been minimal,[11] conservative republicanism has enjoyed greater success. When conservative republicanism dominates our theory, as I believe it does today, the Supreme Court tends to protect the power of the extant, rather than ideal, community. Through their legislatures, these communities express and impose their desires, and thereby perpetuate the institutions and traditions that reflect their historical dominance. Correlatively, a conservative republican Court will denigrate its own power to intervene in order to protect individual freedoms. Therefore, just as the liberal instinctively distrusts legislative restraints on individual autonomy, so the conservative republican, and to a lesser extent all republicans, instinctively distrust judicial restraints on legislative freedom. *Bowers* is clearly such a conservative republican case. From a liberal point of view, the Court failed to protect the individual from group interference. From a republican perspective, however, the Court rightly affirmed the group's conception of value and the common good, as defined by and enforced through legislative pronouncement. *Bowers* and *Roe* thus represent two ends of a political spectrum. In *Roe,* the Court struck down both the group value of sanctity of life and a particular conception of family life because they conflicted with a liberal feminist conception of the self. In *Bowers,* the Court upheld the group value of family, and arguably the group prejudice of homophobia, while rejecting a liberal and libertarian vision of the self and of sexual freedom.

As different as they are, however, *Bowers* and *Roe* share one important feature. In both, the justice writing the opinion explicitly disclaimed moral debate. Both cases—one liberal, one republican—exemplify the authoritarian constitutional tradition and explicitly disavow the normative one. In both, the Court purported to explicate what the Constitution dictates, rather than to ask, much less answer the question, How should we constitute ourselves? This commonality, I believe, is not coincidental. Rather, it reveals a deeper commonality between one possible interpretation of the liberal self-image, upheld in *Roe,* and one possible interpretation of our republican communitarian image, upheld in *Bowers.*

Just as constitutionalism itself embraces both authoritarian and normative modes of decision making, so too do our liberal and republican traditions embrace competing conceptions of their primary substantive commitments. First, the liberal tradition moves ambiguously between what I call an *agnostic* conception and endorsement of the self, and a *pragmatic* conception and endorsement of the self. According to this agnostic conception, the individual and his preferences, desires, tastes, and conception of the good life are valued tautologically, independently of their worth, because value is defined as "that which the individual desires." According to this pragmatic conception, by contrast, the individual is valued because an individualistic life is believed to be a good life. Similarly, our republican tradition also moves ambiguously between what can be called an agnostic endorsement of the community and a pragmatic one. According to this agnostic conception, the community's preferences, wishes, and desires are valued because value is defined as that which the community has valued or would value in a utopian vision. According to this pragmatic conception, by contrast, the community is valued because a communitarian life is believed to be a good life.

It is important to note that agnostic liberalism and agnostic republicanism are more similar than dissimilar, as are pragmatic liberalism and pragmatic republicanism. Agnostic liberalism and agnostic republicanism share their agnosticism: they both value and prioritize what each regards as the primary moral unit tautologically. Pragmatic liberalism and pragmatic republicanism similarly share their pragmatism. My general claim is that the authoritarian impulse in constitutional law, exemplified in both *Roe* and *Bowers,* is a response to the dominance of what is an unhealthy agnosticism in both of our dominant political theories.

Thus, *Roe* rests on and endorses an agnostic liberal conception of the self: the value of an individually chosen life plan is assumed tautologically. For the most part, the Court does not defend the proposition that an individualistic life that includes reproductive choice is more worthy than a less individualistic life that does not. Rather, in keeping with agnostic liberalism, "value" and "worth" and the nature of the "good" are assumed to emanate from individual choice, rather than constitute a criterion against which to judge individual choice. Similarly, *Bowers* rests on and endorses an agnostic republican conception of the community: the value of the legislatively chosen prohibition of homosexuality is assumed tautologically. The Court does not defend the proposition that a community that criminalizes homosexuality is more worthy than one that does not, because value and worth and the good are assumed to emanate from communitarian choice, rather than constitute criteria against which to judge community choice.

In both cases, the Court moved from an agnostic conception of value to an authoritarian mode of constitutional decision making. In both cases, the Court asked the question What does the Constitution permit?, rather than How should we constitute ourselves? In each case, the Court had no way even to discuss, much less decide, whether the reproductive choice or the homophobic preference would contribute to a defensible conception of individualism or communitarianism, respectively. In each case, the Court decided whether to protect the challenged choice or preference by a nonreflective and ultimately arbitrary invocation of the "authority" of the binding Constitution, for the agnostic theory of value with which it began left the Court with little choice to do otherwise. Thus, the choice between agnostic and pragmatic conceptions of value, and not the conflict between liberalism and republicanism, may determine whether our courts will take an authoritarian or normative attitude toward constitutional questions.

To make this claim more plausible, let me briefly describe these four traditions: agnostic liberalism, agnostic republicanism, pragmatic liberalism, and pragmatic republicanism. The purely agnostic definition of value and, correlatively, the purely agnostic image of the self within the liberal tradition should be familiar to legal academics. The law and economics school embraces agnostic liberalism in its most absolute form. To the legal economist, the self is both atomistic and definitive of value. Fulfillment of the individual's desires produces wealth, and hence value, regardless of the content of the desire, preference, or choice at stake. Choice, notably economic choice, becomes the hallmark of justice and value to the agnostic liberal. Beyond ensuring equal access to economic choice, then, the community, the legislature, and most generally the state should be agnostic toward conflicting individual desires and conceptions of the good. Legislative pronouncements of the nature of the good are not simply distrusted, as they are in more classical liberal conceptions. They are nonsensical; visions of the good are definitionally individualistic, because it is the individual, not the group, that is the source of value. Given this agnostic image of the self, normative (hence moral) discourse within liberalism is impossible because it is conceptually incoherent. Our "norms" cannot be the subject of debate, because our norms, values, and moral commitments are disguised preferences, and our preferences are individualistic, given, and of equal weight. We value the individual's values tautologically. The individual is the source of value.

The agnostic image of the community within the republican tradition is also becoming familiar. Chief Justice Burger strikes an unfortunately common chord in *Bowers* when he argues that the Georgia legislature's homophobic statute should be upheld in part because sodomy historically has been regarded as a crime worse than rape. To agnostic republicanism, the group is as definitive of value as is the individual to agnostic liberalism. Fulfillment of the group's desires produces value, regardless of the content of those desires, and regardless of their lineage. Participation in the group, ideally political participation, becomes the hallmark of justice and value to the agnostic republican. Beyond ensuring full participation, then, the courts should be agnostic toward competing conceptions of the good generated by varying groups, whether ideal, as in utopian conceptions, or historical, as in conservative ones. Given this agnostic image of the group, normative discourse within republicanism is impossible because it is conceptually incoherent. We can perfect group processes to minimize the impact of impermissible hierarchy, but beyond that we cannot second-guess group values. The norms of the community are beyond the scope of moral debate because those norms are the genesis of the community's morality.

The images of the self and the community that underlie these agnostic traditions have much in common that is beyond the scope of this chapter. One thing they share, however, is the fact that when embraced, both of them cry out for an authoritarian response, whenever an individual or group value is challenged on constitutional grounds. There are two reasons, the first of which is simply logical. The question, How should we constitute the individual?, is meaningless in an agnostic liberal tradition, as is the question, How should we constitute the community?, in an agnostic republican tradition. There is no way even to discuss, much less decide, the value of a troubling and constitutionally challenged individual or group preference—such as the individual's preference for abortion in *Roe*, or the group's preference for criminalizing sodomy in *Bowers*. Agnosticism in both traditions identifies value with preference. It accordingly precludes a normative challenge to a preference, either individual or group. We cannot ask whether a challenged preference is a good or a bad preference, when good means preferred. If we wish to consider any challenge at all—and the Constitution clearly directs us to do so—we can only ask whether a challenged preference is permitted. When a difficult case arises, we have no choice but to ask only the bare authoritarian question: Does the authoritative Constitution permit it?

The second reason is psychosocial, and somewhat more speculative. The individual in the agnostic liberal tradition is not just the source of value; he is also antagonistic, atomistic, selfish, and psychopathic or sociopathic. He is incapable of social bonding without the added incentive of an authoritarian, Leviathan threat. Nor will he benefit from social bonding beyond that needed to minimize violent antagonism. Similarly, the group in the agnostic republican tradition is not just the source of value; it is also intensely conformist internally, and intensely chauvinistic and xenophobic externally. The group is defined by its comparative virtue to outsiders, whether the outsiders are out-of-staters, aliens, racial minorities, or homosexuals. The group is well bonded internally, but perhaps because it is so well bonded, it is incapable of accepting idiosyncrasy, differences, or minorities on its own impetus. Nor does it benefit from exposure to idiosyncrasy, difference, or minority points of view. If these self and group portraits are at all accurate, then "constitutional questions" cannot possibly facilitate normative discourse between competing liberal and republican conceptions of the good, any more than the dictates of the authoritarian teacher can facilitate normative discourse on the schoolyard populated by warring gangs. In other words, the self-portrait we have drawn in our agnostic liberal and agnostic republican traditions is that of a schoolyard populated by individual bullies and communitarian gangs. If we are as we paint ourselves as being, then we have forsaken all sense of value, worth, or well-being, other than whatever is desired or produced by the most powerful individuals and groups among us.

In such a world, the best that can be hoped for from our constitutional law and discourse is that it guarantee mutual coexistence between weak and strong individuals, and between majority and minority communities. In a relentlessly agnostic world, we cannot expect, because we cannot even conceive of, normative growth. In such a world, resort to an outside "constitutive" authority is the best means of achieving that coexistence. In such a world, resort to authority is the only way to decide the permissibility of troubling individual or communal forms of identity. In the agnostic tradition, constitutional questions are by definition questions of authority and legitimacy, and not questions of normativity.

Pragmatic Self Images and the
Normative Constitutional Tradition

Both the image of the self underlying and celebrated by liberal pluralism and the image of the community underlying and celebrated by civic republicanism, however, are susceptible to pragmatic as well as agnostic interpretations. The self and the individual celebrated by the pragmatic-liberal tradition is valued not for the tautological reason that the individual's preference are themselves the source of value, but, rather, for the pragmatic, tentative, and loosely empirical reason that an individualistic life is a good life; it is a life morally worth living. According to this tradition, the individual and the individual's values and preferences should be protected, because we believe that an individual life untrammeled by group pressure is a naturally social, moral, and productive life. The individual can contribute value to the community as well as reap benefits from association because, if nurtured, she has a natural potential for creative and moral interaction with the material and social worlds. Individualism is valuable because it is conducive to a more interesting, moral, and productive world, not because we are unable to judge between competing visions. Differences are cherished because their presence makes life more meaningful, not because we have no moral grounding from which to judge. The differing desires, preferences, and wishes of particular individuals, then, are valued because their very presence reflects our commitment to a particular conception of a shared life worth living: the exercise of individual choice helps us "constitute" ourselves. The use of intellectual and creative capacities gives joy, and the freedom to choose our associations makes our lives more loving.

Pragmatic individualism so conceived and exemplified in the liberal theories of John Stuart Mill[12] and John Dewey[13] gives us an evolving, contested, but idealistic vision for the future toward which we should strive and a conception of the role of the individual in that ideal. It is not an excuse for agnostic contentment with whatever preferences and satisfactions we presently harbor. Pragmatic liberalism gives us a substantive criterion against which to judge the kinds of individuals we have become and are becoming, rather than a denial of the power of normative judgment. It provides a way to answer the question How should we constitute the self?

Similarly, the community celebrated by civic republicanism is also susceptible to a pragmatic rather than an agnostic interpretation. The community and the group are valued by the pragmatic republican tradition not for the tautological reason that the community defines value, but for the concrete, contestable, and loosely verifiable reason that communal life is morally worthy. Living in a community with others make us more compassionate, broadens our sensitivities, enriches our discourse, and makes our lives more fulfilling. Communal living is valued not because it provides us with a common defense against outside aggressors, and a common identity against strangers and strangeness, but because it fulfills a natural need for sociability and love. According to this tradition, the group has value because it enriches, rather than just defines, the lives of the individuals whom it comprises. It enriches our lives by encouraging us to care for and about others, enlivens our tolerance by promoting different visions with which we can interact, and deepens our sense of potential by providing a community in which we can become immersed. Pragmatic communitarianism so conceived, and exemplified in the ancient writings of Aristotle,[14] and in the contemporary works of Roberto Unger[15] and Alisdair MacIntyre,[16] gives us an idealistic, evolving, and contestable vision of the future toward which we should strive, and a conception, though susceptible to change, of the role of the community within it. It does not excuse agnostic contentment with the extant groups presently conceived. Like pragmatic liberalism, pragmatic republicanism provides a criterion against which to judge the communities in which we live and which we seek to form. Pragmatic republicanism provides a way to answer the moral question, How should we constitute our community?

The pragmatic interpretations of our liberal and republican traditions also provide alternative interpretations of the constitutive liberal distrust of the state, and the republican distrust of the courts, respectively. Both pragmatic and agnostic liberals maintain that the state generally should refrain from imposing a normative vision of the good on individuals, just as pragmatic and agnostic republicans insist that the courts should not interfere with the normative visions developed by groups, including legislatures. But again, the reasons given contrast rather than compare. Pragmatic liberals agree with agnostic liberals that the state generally should not interfere in the lives of individuals, but not for the agnostic and absolutist reason that conceptions of the good are definitionally individualistic. Rather, the state should not intervene for the concrete, loosely empirical, and contestable reason that the state's power vis-à-vis the individual gives its commitments undue weight. The pragmatic liberal's distrust of state power is thus premised on an assessment and distrust of the undue effect of power, not on the definitional claim that value is exclusively a function of individual preference.[17] Similarly, pragmatic republicans agree with agnostics that the courts generally should not interfere in the visions of the good promulgated by groups, including legislatures, but not for the agnostic and absolutist reason that conceptions of the good are definitionally legislative or group produced. Rather, courts should refrain from intervening for the concrete, contingent, loosely empirical, and contestable reason that the court's elitism and insularity give its substantive commitments an undue tilt, at least when contrasted with the commitments of an ideally representative legislature. Thus, the pragmatic republican's distrust of judicial power is premised on an assessment of the effect of elitism and insularity on the value of the vision of the good promulgated by the courts, and not on the definitional claim that value is whatever a "communitarian" legislature says it is.[18]

One major difference, then, between these two interpretations of our political traditions is that the agnostic interpretations rest on definitional claims about value which permit no exception, while the pragmatic interpretations rest on contingent claims about the world which may, in any particular case, not hold. The agnostic interpretations are therefore absolute in a way that the pragmatic claims are not. The pragmatic interpretations of the liberal distrust of state intervention, and the republican distrust of judicial power over legislative determinations, provide a basis for the claim, in particular cases, that the general reason for state nonintervention or judicial passivity is not present, and that therefore state intervention or judicial activism is justified. For the pragmatic liberal, the state should generally not interfere in individuals' lives or choices—not because it is the state, and thus not a source of value, but because of its crushing and potentially oppressive power. Thus, if the state's exploitative power does not pose a danger in a particular case, or if it is outweighed by the influence of another powerful political or economic actor, then from a pragmatic liberal perspective, reasons for state nonintervention drop away, and it becomes possible that the state ought to intervene, even if this involves state interference with the private preferences of individuals. Similarly, for the pragmatic republican, the courts as a general rule should not interfere with legislative outcomes, not because they are courts, and thus not a source of value, but becaue their substantive visions are marred by their insularity and elitism. Thus, if the court's elitism and insularity do not pose a danger in a particular case or are outweighed by the influence of other elitist or insular forces, then from a pragmatic republican perspective, reasons for judicial passivity drop away, and it becomes possible that the courts ought to intervene, even if this involves judicial intervention into the legislative preferences of even legitimately constituted groups.

The images of self, community, the state, and the courts that underlie pragmatic liberalism and pragmatic republicanism have a great deal in common, as evidenced by the broad common ground shared by Mill (a pragmatic liberal) and Aristotle (a pragmatic republican). The images of self and community that underlie agnostic liberalism and agnostic republicanism are also similar, as evidenced by the law and economics theorists' dual endorsement of the sovereignty of individual choice and majoritarian power. Strikingly, the pragmatic interpretations of our two traditions jointly provide a conceptual grounding for the normative tradition in constitutional decision making, just as the agnostic interpretations provide a grounding for the authoritarian tradition. In the pragmatic liberal tradition, although there are good pragmatic reasons to distrust state intervention, there is no definitional reason for communitarian or state neutrality toward competing individualistic conceptions of the good life, and thus no definitional reason to refrain from normative decision making in difficult cases. The individual's preferences ought to be valued and protected against state interference because we have tentatively committed ourselves to a concrete but contestable conception of the value of individualism, and to a concrete, but contestable account of the danger of state power. Pragmatic liberalism accordingly entails a tentative vision of the good against which to judge particularly difficult, individual preferences for reproductive freedom, or questionable schemes of life, such as for prostitution or drug addiction. From a pragmatic liberal point of view, what we need to know, for example, in judging an individual's "preference" for contraceptives or early trimester abortion and hence whether she has a "right" to it against legislative interference, is not simply that she has the preference, but the extent to which the desired freedom from the reproductive consequences of sexuality facilitates a meaningful, strong, productive, and worthy individual life, and the extent to which legislative interference with that preference would raise the specter of state oppression. We need to ask, talk about, and assess whether this particular individual freedom for reproductive choice has made us better people. We need to ask, talk about, and assess whether legislative interference with this preference is grounded in and premised upon a felt legislative need to protect the status of the empowered, or grounded in a defensible vision of the good.

Similarly, against the pragmatic republican tradition, there are good pragmatic reasons but no definitional reason for judicial neutrality toward competing legislative pronouncements of the good and, again, no definitional bar to normative decision making in difficult cases. Communitarian values and preferences ought to be protected against judicial interference because we have tentatively committed ourselves to a concrete but contestable conception of the ideal community, and a concrete but contestable account of the dangers that an insulated judiciary pose. From a pragmatic republican point of view, then, we have a way to argue about difficult and challenged legislative preferences. What we need to know, for example, in judging the constitutionality of an antisodomy statute is whether the expressed homophobic value and the history behind it has made for a worthy community, and whether judicial interference with that vision would raise the dangers we generally associate with insulated and biased judgment. We need to ask, talk about, and assess whether homophobic bigotry, like racial bigotry, has hurt more than helped our communitarian instinct and communal life, and whether judicial intervention into that legislative vision would hinder more than promote our democratic goals.

My general claim is that against a pragmatic, substantive interpretation of our liberal and republican politics—and only against such a background—can the major "constitutional questions" of our time be answered within a normative tradition. Only if we have some inkling as to why we value individualism will we be able to ask meaningfully, and therefore answer tentatively, the constitutional question, How should we constitute the self? If we know why we value individualism, if we have in mind a vision of the ideal individualistic life, then we can meaningfully debate whether the individual should have the freedom to choose abortion, or be entitled to housing, or to say whatever she pleases. If we have no idea why we value individualism beyond our agnostic inability to express any normative commitments, then disagreement over particular individual entitlements begs for, deserves, and will receive an authoritarian answer. Similarly, only if we know why we value participation and community, will we then be able to ask the constitutional question, How should we constitute the community? If we know why we value communitarian life, then we will at least be able to discuss meaningfully the value we should give homophobic or racist group commitments. If we do not, then constitutional questions about particular communitarian commitments again beg for, and will get, no better than authoritarian answers. The group, like the individual, can do what the Constitution or some other authority permits it to do. No more and no less.

The Value of Constitutional Debate

There are many obstacles to the normative tradition in constitutional decision making, and there are as many reasons to be skeptical of the value of democratizing constitutional modes of thought and debate. Judicial review may be one such obstacle, and the presence of the historical text itself—an authoritarian response to the dangers posed by the Articles of Confederation—is surely another. Our present amnesia regarding the very existence, much less the importance, the value, and the wisdom of our pragmatic liberal and republican traditions, is a third. If we want the Constitution to be more than parental—occasionally benign as in *Brown* but more often punitive, as in *Bowers*—if we want to use constitutional processes as a way of arguing about how we should constitute ourselves, instead of a way to figure out how we are authorized to constitute ourselves, we should reacquaint ourselves with forgotten wisdom, and reimmerse ourselves in neglected work. Liberals know more, or used to know more, about the value of individualism than is presently expressed in their modern solipsistic denial of the possibility of moral knowledge. Republicans surely know more about the value of community than is presently expressed in the conservative commitment to extant communitarian and frequently chauvinistic or xenophobic institutions, or the radical commitment to the largely unargued value of political participation. Similarly, we can do more than we now do. We can do more than simply reiterate empty claims and tautological definitions. We can describe and argue over when sociability makes our lives more meaningful and when it is simply oppressive; over when individualistic effort or choice is rewarding and when it does nothing but leave us isolated.

My original analogy may serve to underscore my main point. Imagine two schoolyards, one in which the pragmatic tradition of politics prevails, and the other in which the agnostic prevails. The first yard has a collected pool of wisdom regarding the value of games, the value of participation in those games, and the value of nonparticipation. The second lacks such a tradition. Both are governed loosely by a rule requiring participation in games, and both must somehow decide whether a loner playing by himself is in violation of the rule. The first schoolyard will at least have the option of answering this constitutional question within the normative tradition. The participants will have some sense of why they value games and participation and why they disfavor isolationism. They will at least have a history of having constituted themselves by reference to that accumulated experience. The second will lack that option. In fact, the second group will lack every option, other than to glean from the authoritative text, and the authoritative teacher that wrote it, whatever direction can be gleaned. The pragmatic tradition in the first schoolyard will prompt and facilitate normative constitutional decision making. The agnosticism in the second virtually demands submission to the authority.

There are many things that we would do in some other world if our sole aim were to increase participation in and the quality of the way we decide issues of public morality, which we nevertheless cannot do in this world. We cannot, for example, simply abolish the constitutional text even if its existence frustrates more than facilitates normative debate. We cannot reverse our historical commitment to judicial review even if judicial review frustrates citizen participation, which it probably does. We can, however, reinvigorate the pragmatic interpretations of our political theory. We can do so, in part, by emphasizing the historical existence and the importance of those traditions to our legal and constitutional institutions. We can also do so by continuing to work within those interpretive strategies. We can generate pragmatic, contextual accounts of the values of our individualistic and communitarian commitments. We have all lived in racially segregated or integrated communities, and attended racially segregated or integrated schools. We have lived with legalized abortion for over a decade. We have grown up in a culture that criminalizes homosexuality. We could reinvigorate our pragmatic traditions by simply describing how those experiences have enriched or deprived our senses of self and community. We could discuss whether and how the availability of legal abortion has enriched our sense of individual self-worth. We could describe what is surely a near-universal experience in this culture, the experience of learning homophobic fears. We could flood the market with pragmatic constitutive arguments situated in our experiences of individual and social life, as those experiences relate to constitutive questions. If we do all this, the courts might be somewhat less inclined to claim that the wisdom of a majoritarian commitment or an individual contractual choice is beyond the scope of coherent debate. Constitutional debate might thereby become more normative. Only when constitutional debate becomes normative will it be a form of debate, or dialogue, in which the legal community can take pride, and which might be worth sharing.

9

Progressive and Conservative Constitutionalism

■

American constitutional law in general, and Fourteenth Amendment jurisprudence in particular, is in a state of profound transformation. The
"liberal-legalist" and purportedly politically neutral understanding of constitutional guarantees that dominated constitutional law and theory during
the 1950s, 1960s, and 1970s, is waning, both in the courts and in the
academy.[1] What is beginning to replace liberal legalism in the academy,
and what has clearly replaced it on the Supreme Court, is a very different
conception—a new paradigm—of the role of constitutionalism, constitutional adjudication, and constitutional guarantees in a democratic state.
Unlike the liberal-legal paradigm it is replacing, the new paradigm is overtly
political—and overtly conservative—in its orientation and aspiration.

Over the last few years, a substantial and growing number of Supreme
Court justices, federal judges, and some theorists, including Raoul Berger,
Robert Bork, Frank Easterbrook, Michael McConnell, Sandra Day
O'Connor, Richard Posner, and Antonin Scalia, have begun to articulate
a profoundly conservative interpretation of the constitutional tradition.[2]
There are obviously many differences between the conservative views of
each of these theorists. But there is also significant commonality: the conservatives share enough ground and sufficient themes that we can discern,
without too much difficulty, an emerging conservative paradigm of constitutional interpretation, what this chapter calls *conservative constitutionalism*. Conservative constitutionalism now dominates the Supreme Court,
may soon dominate the federal judiciary, and has already profoundly
shaped the constitutional law of the foreseeable future.

The modern transformation of constitutional law and theory, however,
goes even deeper than the influence of conservative constitutionalism. For
at the same time that conservative constitutionalism has replaced liberal

legalism on the Court, a new progressive conception of constitutional interpretation has begun to replace the critical and deconstructive scholarship
that dominated the dissenting discourse of the last two decades.[3] Over
the last decade or so, a number of progressive legal academicians, including Cass Sunstein, David Strauss, Suzanna Sherry, Catharine MacKinnon,
and Frank Michelman, among others—and joined by some critical and
liberal scholars, such as Roberto Unger and Laurence Tribe—have begun
to articulate yet another alternative, not only to the mid-century liberal-
legal understanding of constitutional interpretation but also to the view
of constitutionalism that emerged from the Critical Legal Studies movement's powerful critique of liberal legalism during those same years.[4] This
alternative constitutional paradigm, developed not in the courts, but in
the academy, is also overtly political: all of these theorists are progressive, explicitly liberatory or even liberationist in their political tilt. These
theorists as well are divided by significant internal differences, but, as
with the leaders of conservative constitutionalism, there is enough shared
ground that we can meaningfully speak of a second new jurisprudential
understanding of constitutional interpretation coming on the heels of the
demise of the liberal-legal paradigm. We might call this second postliberal
alternative *progressive constitutionalism.*

The paradigm shift, then, in its totality, is this: the liberal and critical
legal discourses that dominated constitutional law in the 1960s and 1970s
have been replaced by conservative and progressive discourses, respectively. Not just the answers but, more important, the questions posed by
our leading constitutional jurists and theorists have been radically transformed.

The first and major purpose of this chapter is to describe these two new
constitutional paradigms. The chapter's central thesis is that the understandings of the constitutional tradition most central to both paradigms
are determined by sometimes implicit, but more often explicit, political
dispositions toward various forms of social and private power, and the normative authority to which social and private power gives rise. Very broadly,
conservative constitutionalists view private or social normative authority
as the legitimate and best source of guidance for state action; accordingly,
they view both the Constitution and constitutional adjudication as means
of preserving and protecting that authority and the power that undergirds
it against either legislative or judicial encroachment. Progressive constitutionalists, in sharp contrast, view the power and normative authority of
some social groups over others as the fruits of illegitimate private hierarchy

and regard the Constitution as one important mechanism for challenging those entrenched private orders. Where the conservative is likely to see in a particular social or private institution a source of communitarian wisdom and legitimate normative authority, the progressive is likely to see the product of social or private hierarchy, and the patterns of domination, subordination, and oppression that inevitably attend such inequalities of power. The profound substantive differences between the conservative and progressive understandings of what the Fourteenth Amendment requires, and of the meaning of constitutionalism more generally, are rooted in these contrasting political attitudes toward social power. Correlatively, the debate presently ongoing between progressives and conservatives is only superficially over interpretive issues; on a more substantive level it is over the value of the visions of the good defined by the various hierarchies that make up our private and social life.

Thus, while the constitutional debate of the last two decades or so focused on the purported neutrality and the permissible scope of judicial decision making in democratic society, constitutional debate of the next decade, and into the next century, will focus instead on the merits and vices of various forms of social and private power and authority, and hence the wisdom of using state power—through either the legislative, executive, or judicial branch—to upset them. This is the sense in which the questions, and not just the answers, of constitutional discourse have been altered. Neither the modern conservatives nor the modern progressives seem overly concerned with the issues that consumed constitutionalists of the last twenty or thirty years: the antimajoritarian difficulty posed by judicial review and even constitutionalism itself; the propriety of and justifications for judicial review; the liberal requirement of judicial neutrality; the derivation of particular outcomes from neutral principles; or, on the other side, critical demonstrations that the antimajoritarian difficulty is both insoluble and necessary within the contradictory assumptions of liberal theory; that judicial review can be neither justified nor abandoned; and that derivations of favored outcomes from neutral principles are not possible.[5] These are simply not the issues that stir our most contemporary progressive and conservative constitutional scholars. Rather, both the progressives and conservatives seem increasingly willing to grant to the critics of liberal theory their main point: liberal neutrality in judging is illusory, and constitutional adjudication is consequently necessarily political. Modern constitutional scholarship is generally characterized by a desire to take up the question that such a premise quite clearly implies: If the decisions of judges, no less than of legislators, are necessarily political—and hence necessarily grounded in some normative conception of the good—what politics should judges pursue, and on the basis of what conception of the good should they act?

Conservative and progressive answers to that question are grounded in contrasting attitudes toward majoritarianism, which, in turn, directly stem from the contrasting attitudes toward social power that divide progressive and conservative political thought. Significantly, conservatives and progressives agree that untrammeled majoritarianism poses dangers, and that there is, consequently, a justification for constitutional restraints and an independent judiciary to enforce them. However, conservatives and progressives have sharply conflicting assessments of the type of danger posed by majoritarianism, and hence of the content and meaning of our constitutional guarantees. To the conservative, a governing popular "majority" carries the danger of being or becoming an irresponsible and excessively egalitarian, or "leveling," mechanism bent on the redistribution of social wealth, power, and prestige.[6] Against such democratic excess, the Constitution offers the conservative some hope of protecting, and conserving, the existing social order. To the progressive, a governing popular "majority" is dangerous for a different reason: it is always in danger of becoming excessively beholden to a staid, tradition-laden, backward, regressive political vision.[7] "Majorities" tend to guard their majority status with almost paranoid fervor, and hence overidentify with existing social orders. Against this regressive tendency the Constitution offers some disruptive inspiration.

These differing attitudes toward the danger posed by majoritarianism are, in turn, grounded in fundamentally contrasting attitudes toward the social order that the "majority" is perceived as either threatening or unduly conserving. For the conservative, social institutions depend on distributions of wealth, power, and normative authority that are worthy of respect and preservation, while for the progressive those institutions are as often as not the illegitimate fruit of damaging and hurtful patterns of oppression, domination, and subordination.

In brief, then, modern constitutional law and theory can be understood as focused on this question: Should the Constitution be read, and the courts used, as a vehicle to preserve existing social and private orderings against majoritarian political change—making it an essentially conservative document, protecting the status quo against democratic excess—or should it be read and implemented in such a way as to facilitate continuous, inventive challenges to the dominant private and social order, making it a guarantor of at least progressive inspiration, if not progressive change? This is not, in a sense, a novel claim; in fact, it is a frequently heard complaint that what constitutional theory is really—and covertly—about is the merits and demerits of private and social hierarchy. What I want to do is give content to this description of constitutional commitments and debates, enrich it, and thereby, perhaps, legitimate it.

A complete restatement, analysis, and point-by-point contrast of the conservative and progressive constitutional paradigms is obviously beyond the scope of this chapter. Instead, I focus here on three particular and topical issues of constitutional law on which conservatives and progressives have sharply divergent views, and attempt to show that at least those differences can best be understood as stemming from the divergent attitudes toward social power just described. Two of these issues are substantive and one is theoretical. First, most conservative constitutional theorists and judges vehemently reject the "privacy jurisprudence" developed by the Warren and Burger Courts during the 1960s and early 1970s, and particularly disagree with both the conclusion and reasoning of the Burger Court's most controversial decision, *Roe v. Wade*.[8] Correlatively, conservatives tend to support both the outcome reached by the Rehnquist Court in *Bowers v. Hardwick*,[9] in which the Court signaled a clear retreat from both the reasoning and outcome of the privacy cases, and the more recent *Webster v. Reproductive Health Services*,[10] in which the Court severely restricted the scope of reproductive rights by expanding the range of permissible state regulations over abortions. Progressives, in contrast both to most conservatives and to some liberal legalists[11] as well, tend to support the outcome in *Roe* and dissent from the result reached in *Bowers*.[12] In theoretical or jurisprudential terms, the difference might be cast this way: progressives tend to support an "affirmative" understanding of the liberty protected by the due process clause of the Fourteenth Amendment, in which case, reproductive and sexual freedom is at least arguably included within the sphere of due process protection, while conservatives read the clause as protecting "negative liberty" only—that is, the right to be free from certain defined interferences. This chapter ultimately argues that the difference is best explained by reference to the theorists' and justices' sharply conflicting assessments of the legitimacy and value of one important source of social authority and power: the normative authority of a community's positive morality, and the social power on which that authority is based.

Second, progressive and conservative constitutional theorists sharply divide over the constitutionality and social value of voluntarily adopted affirmative action plans that are meant to remedy the effects of past, unconscious, or institutional racism on the performance of minorities in various economic, professional, and cultural markets. Conservatives generally dispute the constitutionality of such plans, and accordingly support the Rehnquist Court's decision in *City of Richmond v. J. A. Croson Co.*,[13] which held that, except for in very narrowly drawn circumstances, affirmative action plans voluntarily adopted by state or local government entities for the purpose of rectifying the effects of past societal discrimination in economic markets are unconstitutional under the equal protection clause of the Fourteenth Amendment. Progressives, by contrast, generally support the constitutionality as well as the wisdom of affirmative action plans and tend to read the equal protection clause either as neutral toward such plans or as in fact requiring them; they are accordingly critical of the present Court's hostility toward such plans and disagree particularly with the result in *Croson*.[14]

This disagreement quite obviously rests on drastically divergent understandings of the meaning, requirements, and perhaps the history of the equal protection clause. It also rests, however, on different philosophical understandings of the meaning of the "equality" that the clause is designed to promote, encourage, or ensure. Very roughly, progressives tend to support a "substantive" understanding of the equality guaranteed by the equal protection clause, which has the effect of requiring or at least permitting affirmative action to rectify the effects of past discrimination in the private sector, while conservatives support a "formal" or "legal" interpretation, which arguably has the effect of invalidating such plans.[15] This chapter argues that the difference can best be understood as resting on contrasting assessments of the value of a second source of private authority and power: the normative authority of private markets, and the social and economic power on which that authority rests.

Finally, conservative and progressive constitutionalists differ over the nature of constitutional interpretation itself. Conservative constitutionalists tend to support two basic principles of constitutional interpretation: first, that interpreters should defer whenever possible to the originally intended meaning of the Constitution's drafters; second, that judges should defer, whenever possible, to the will of legislators. Conservatives tend to advocate originalism, judicial restraint, or both, as guiding principles of constitutional adjudication.[16] Progressives, by contrast, argue that constitutional interpretation should be in some sense "open," or what I call "possibilistic": that the constitution is always open to multiple interpretations, which at least include interpretations capable of facilitating progressive causes and policies.[17] This difference, I argue, is grounded in the contrasting attitudes toward yet a third type of social authority and power: the legitimacy, wisdom, and morality of legal authority and power.

Political attitudes toward private and social power do not, however, in any simple way, directly imply either these or any other set of particular constitutional commitments. The implication of a constitutional commitment arising from a political vision is complicated, and often masked, by two factors. First, "constitutional law" is undeniably a field of law, as well as politics, and constitutional theorists and jurists are therefore legal theorists and legal actors, as well as adherents to political points of view. Constitutional theorists accordingly combine their political outlook toward social power with some allegiance to a jurisprudential view of the nature of law, and particularly of the relation of law to social policy, to morality, and to politics itself. As a result, differences in constitutional interpretation are often believed to be and often appear to be rooted in jurisprudential differences and debates that divide conservatives and progressives along apparently apolitical lines: progressive natural lawyers debate conservative instrumentalists as though the jurisprudential difference between natural law and instrumentalism accounts for their disagreements in constitutional outlook; progressive positivists debate conservative natural lawyers on the same assumption, and so on. As I try to show, however, the deepest divisions in modern constitutional thought are a function not of jurisprudential differences, but of political orientation. Despite their casting, modern constitutional disagreements do not reflect or stem from the jurisprudential differences between natural law, legal positivism, and legal pragmatism (although they are complicated by them), but rather from the vastly divergent political assessments of the value or danger of private and social power held by conservative and progressive constitutional scholars.

The second factor complicating and sometimes masking the dependence of the conservative and progressive constitutional paradigms on their political underpinnings is that the respective political underpinnings are themselves not uniform. While there are substantial commonalities, there are also significant differences within as well as between major conservative and progressive political theories. Briefly, conservatives differ among themselves over the type of private or social authority to which the state should turn when specifying a conception of the good.[18] Progressives differ fundamentally over what types of experiences of the disempowered should be at the heart of a socially sensitive vision of the good.[19] As a result of these internal political differences, conservative and progressive constitutional commitments often—perhaps typically—command less than universal support from conservative or progressive scholars: not all conservatives support every aspect of the conservative constitutional paradigm, nor do all progressives support every aspect of the progressive paradigm. What this chapter calls the *progressive constitutional paradigm* and the *conservative constitutional paradigm,* then, are simply those core constitutional interpretations or commitments that are supported by a critical mass of progressive or conservative constitutional scholars. It is worth stressing, however, that even the theorists who agree on a particular constitutional commitment often do so for widely divergent political reasons.

The first purpose of this chapter is to describe in some detail these two constitutional paradigms and their component parts: political theory, jurisprudence, and constitutional commitments. The first section describes the conservative constitutional paradigm, beginning with a discussion of conservative political thought, then conservative jurisprudence, and finally how the three major conservative constitutional commitments can be derived from conservative political and jurisprudential theory. In a parallel fashion, the second section describes the progressive constitutional paradigm.

The second purpose of this chapter is partisan rather than descriptive and is addressed to progressives. It is not at all clear, from a progressive political point of view, that the development of a progressive constitutional paradigm—to which a conservative Court will be openly hostile— is a worthwhile project. What would be gained? It is at least arguable that progressives over the next few years should devote themselves to the development of strategies that will minimize the impact of constitutional adjudication on progressive politics, rather than to the perfection of an alternative progressive model of what the Constitution and the Fourteenth Amendment require, for adoption by a counterfactual, nonexistent, and unforeseeable progressive Court.

The concluding section of this chapter argues that even in the short term, and certainly in the long term, there are good reasons for developing an alternative, non- or postliberal, and explicitly progressive paradigm of constitutional interpretation, even if it is clear, as it seems to be, that the present conservative Supreme Court will not embrace it. It also argues, however, that for both strategic and theoretical reasons, the proper audience for the development of a progressive interpretation of the Constitution is Congress rather than the courts. The progressive Constitution should be meant for, and therefore must be aimed toward, legislative rather than adjudicative change.

The strategic reasons for this proposed reorientation of progressive constitutional discourse should be self-evident. Although the progressive Constitution is arguably consistent with some aspects of the liberal-legalist paradigm of the middle of this century, it is utterly incompatible with the conservative paradigm now dominating constitutional adjudication. It does not follow, however, that the progressive Constitution is incompatible with all constitutional decision making: both legislatures and citizens have constitutional obligations, engage in constitutional discourse, and can be moved, presumably, to bring electoral politics in line with the progressive mandates of the Constitution, as those mandates have been understood and interpreted by progressive constitutional lawyers and theorists.

I also argue, however, that for theoretical and strategic reasons, the long-range success, the sense, and even more modestly the relevance of the progressive interpretation of the Constitution depend not only on the merits of its interpretive claims but also, and perhaps more fundamentally, on a federal Congress reenlivened to its constitutional obligations. First, of course, it is Congress, not the Supreme Court, that is specifically mandated under the Fourteenth Amendment to take positive action to ensure equal protection and due process rights—the core constitutional tools for attacking illegitimate social and private power. If Congress is ever to fulfill this obligation, it will need the guidance of interpretive theories of the meaning of equal protection, due process, equality, and liberty that are aimed explicitly toward the context of legislative action and are not constrained by the possibilities and limits of adjudicative law. But more fundamentally, the progressive Constitution, I argue, will never achieve its full meaning— and worse, will remain riddled with paradox and contradiction—so long as it remains in an adjudicative forum. This is not only because of the probable political composition of the Court over the next few decades, but also because of the philosophical and political meanings of adjudicative law itself: the possibilities of adjudicative law are constrained by precisely the same profoundly conservative attitudes toward social power that underlie conservative constitutionalism. By acquiescing in a definition of the Constitution as a source of adjudicative law, progressives seriously undermine its progressive potential. Only by reconceptualizing the Constitution as a source of inspiration and guidance for legislation, rather than a superstructural constraint on adjudication, can we make good on its richly progressive promise.

Therefore, the concluding section of this chapter argues that, for structural long-term as well as strategic short-term reasons, the progressive Constitution—the cluster of meanings found or implanted in constitutional guarantees by modern progressive scholars—should be addressed to the Congress and to the citizenry rather than to the courts. The goal of progressive constitutionalists, both in the academy and at the bar, over the coming decades should be to create what Bruce Ackerman has called in other contexts a "constitutional moment"[20] and what Owen Fiss might call more dramatically an "interpretive crisis."[21] Progressives need to create a world in which it is clear that a progressive Congress has embraced one set of constitutional meanings, and the conservative Court a contrasting and incompatible set. The Supreme Court does, and always has, as Fiss reminds us, read the Constitution so as to avoid crisis.[22] The lesson to draw is surely that only when faced with such a constitutional moment will this conservative Court change paths.

The Conservative Constitutional Paradigm

CONSERVATIVE POLITICS

Modern political conservatism is grounded in and united by an aversion to the redistributive normative authority of the political state and a commitment to the preservation, or conservation, of existing social, economic, and legal entitlements and structures. Whatever else they may hold or believe, conservatives distrust both the capacity of state actors—whether judges or legislators—to generate, through dialogue or any other means, desirable novel conceptions of social life that would upset or redistribute extant entitlements; they also distrust the willingness of state actors to legislate or adjudicate in a disinterested fashion in accordance with those conceptions. Accordingly, conservatives advocate minimizing the role of the normative authority (although not the power) of the state: what the state should do is act in such a way as to preserve, not question or alter, the constituent structures of our social life. As this section attempts to show, however, even this minimal commitment is not as straightforward as it seems: conservatives differ among themselves over the contours of "the state," over what forms of normative authority do or do not come within its gambit, and over what sorts of preexisting social structures are most worthy of protection. But conservatives are more or less united in their antipathy for the specious forms of redistributive normative authority to which state power gives rise, and in their commitment to the preservation of extant social structures and entitlements.

In its distrust of the redistributive normative authority of the political state, modern conservatism can claim a share in the mantle of classical liberalism. Conservatives and classical liberals arrive at their common distrust, however, by way of different routes. Classical liberals, far more than modern conservatives, constitutively distrust centralized power of any sort, and hence centralized state power as well. Classical liberal distrust of a state's normative authority is derivative of this more fundamental distrust of power. Classical liberals accordingly require the state, wherever possible, to defer to the normative authority of the smallest unit of power—individuals—and then to promote that normative authority through noninterference. For modern conservatives, by contrast, it is the distrust of the state's redistributive normative authority, rather than distrust of either state power or power per se that is fundamental. What the state is peculiarly ill-suited to do, according to modern conservatives, is to formulate a respectable, defensible, or "legitimate" conception of the good or of the good life that departs in any significant way from the conception of the good reflected in and bolstered by extant social structures. Accordingly, what modern conservatives characteristically require of the state is not inaction, passivity, or noninterference; modern conservatives often demand quite a bit of state action and quite a bit of state interference in private lives, and from all three branches. Rather, what conservatives constitutively require of state actors is that they refrain from imposing their own conception of the good on the community, and that they instead respect, preserve, conserve, and protect the conception of the good promoted by preexisting social structures and entitlements—what I will sometimes call the community's dominant normative authority. For the conservative, the political state then has a duty to promote, protect, and encourage that form of life reflected in the community's social structures and preexisting entitlements; this duty can often be fulfilled simply through noninterference with private lives, but at least as often it requires affirmative, even aggressive, legislative, judicial, or executive intervention.

In its distrust of the redistributive normative authority of the political state, modern conservatism also claims a share in the mantle of modern liberalism, particularly modern legalistic liberalism. Many (although not all) modern legal liberals also distrust the normative authority of the state, but their distrust again rests on a very different basis from either the modern conservative's or the classical liberal's. Modern liberal legal distrust of the state's normative authority is rooted not in a particular distrust of the normative authority of the "state," but, rather, in a generally skeptical stance toward normative authority of any sort. There is no way a state actor can specify the content of the good or the good life—beyond simply recording his or her own preferences—because there is no way that anyone can do so. There is, consequently, no principled way for a legislature to second-guess the value judgments of an individual, or for a court to second-guess the value judgments of a legislature. Conservative distrust of a state's normative authority, by contrast, is rooted not in a general or philosophical value—skepticism—but in a decidedly nonskeptical preference for the value judgments enshrined in those institutions that embody social power, and in an antipathy toward the value judgments embodied in state authority that seeks to challenge that power. While the liberal legalist and the conservative share an overriding distrust of state normativity, that distrust derives from profoundly divergent political and social visions.

The difference, then, between modern conservatism and both classical and modern legal liberalism is fairly stark: while classical liberals typically urge the state simply to refrain from interfering in the private lives of individuals, and modern legal liberals urge the state to refrain from all normative judgments, conservatives, although sharing the liberal distrust of state authority, are not so tied to either the value-skepticism insisted upon by modern legal liberalism or the individualistic premises of the classical liberal. For the conservative, the state will often have a duty to exercise its power to promote, through legislation, the good life on behalf of its citizens. The conception of the good life the state is empowered to promote, however, must be derived from the normative teachings of some dominant communitarian authority, and not from the will, beliefs, preferences, or desires of state actors.

Modern conservatives differ among themselves on the type of social structures or communal authority to which the political state must defer, and those differences in turn define the major lines of distinction between popular forms of modern conservative political thought. Although the lines are fuzzy, and exceptions abound, we can nevertheless distinguish three strands of modern conservative politics, each of which has had a discernible—and distinctive—impact on the conservative constitutional paradigm.

First, some conservatives, who might be called *moralistic conservatives* or *social conservatives,* argue that the state should defer to the accumulated wisdom of a community's positive conventional morality when formulating a vision of the good as a basis for state action.[23] For these conservatives, the political state should legislate on the basis of the vision of the good promulgated by the dominant moral voices in a community's shared life, whether those voices emanate from religious or secular moral traditions.

The social conservative's deference to the vision of the good propounded by the community's conventional morality is typically motivated by an attitude of respect—sometimes justified, sometimes not—for the presumed wisdom of the dominant normative moral traditions, customs, beliefs, and values of the past. The ethical idea here is simple enough: we should decide how to live by relying heavily on the rules that have emerged from the experiences of others who have wrestled with comparable dilemmas. There is no reason, they argue, to reinvent the moral wheel. History has its lessons, normative as well as otherwise, and the moralistic conservative's embrace of traditional wisdom is simply a recognition of the proper role that humility should play toward the wisdom of the past in our attempt to make collective sense out of our lives. Michael McConnell defends the moralistic conservative's respect for communal authority in this way:

> [W]hy [do] thoughtful individuals often defer to tradition and historical experience when making moral judgments, rather than attempt a more individualistic or utopian analysis[?] Such deference is natural and inevitable, . . . but it is also sensible. An individual has only his own, necessarily limited, intelligence and experience (personal and vicarious) to draw upon. Tradition, by contrast, is composed of the cumulative thoughts and experiences of thousands of individuals over an expanse of time, each of them making incremental and experimental alterations (often unconsciously), which are then adopted or rejected (again, often unconsciously) on the basis of experience—the experience, that is, of whether they advance the good life. Much as a market is superior to central planning for efficient operation of an economy, a tradition is superior to seemingly more "rational" modes of decisionmaking for attainment of moral knowledge.[24]

It is this sense of deference to collective wisdom that drives moralistic conservatives' allegiance to communal morals.

A second group of conservatives, who might be called *legal conservatives,* argue that "the state," in the form of both legislators and adjudicators, should defer to the mandates of the community's established legal system, and its entrenched body of law, when deciding how to act. For legal conservatives, the modern political state, including both the judicial and legislative branches, should defer to the vision of the good articulated in established, historically enshrined legal traditions, including, most significantly, constitutional history and common law precedents. For these conservatives, the political "state," and its entirely specious claims to normative competence, is importantly different from the "law" and its quite legitimate claims: indeed, that there is a difference between the law and the state, such that the "law," and the rational, reasoned, normative authority it embodies and extols, operates as a welcome check on the illegitimate excesses and the irrationality and whimsy of the political "state," is becoming a central tenet of modern conservative thought.[25]

The legal conservative's deference to the authority of law on normative questions regarding the nature of the good typically does not rest on an attitude of respect toward the presumed wisdom behind dominant legal normative authority, but on one of obedience toward the power that, whether visible or not, inevitably underlies it. The motivational difference, then, between moral conservatives and legal conservatives is that whereas moral conservatives take a "respectful" deferential stance toward a community's positive morality, legal conservatives take an obedient or submissive stance toward the "legitimated" powerful voices of legal history—so long as those voices are in the sufficiently distant past to be distinguishable from the powerful voices of the contemporary political state. Legitimate legal authority, for the legal conservative, is not so much there to be respected for its wisdom as it is to be obeyed. What the modern state actor (as well as citizen) "ought" to do with his or her power, then, for the legal conservative, is to relinquish it; what the state actor ought to do with freedom is not simply to respect, but positively to obey, the dictates of lawful authority. Put differently, the way to make one's political will conform to the requirements of political morality is to constrain political willfulness, and the way to constrain willfulness is to obey the dictates of legal authority.[26]

This second strand of conservative thought, particularly the attitudinal and ethical stance toward legal authority that undergirds it—which I have discussed at length elsewhere[27]—rests on an entirely different ethical account of the realtionship between the individual and communal authority than the first strand (with which it is often confused). Unlike respectful deference to the normative authority of moral tradition, the justification for an obedient attitude to legal authority does not rest on the quasi-empirical McConnellian claim that the moral actor, without relinquishing autonomy in any meaningful sense, might nevertheless sensibly defer to lessons of the past. Rather, the morality of submissive, obedient deference to legal authority is typically defended instead on the ground that the authority of the legal other is "legitimate" (rather than wise). For the legal conservative, legal authority generates a near-absolute ethical duty of obedience so long as that authority is "legitimate." [28]

For the legal conservative, legal authority can be legitimated—and hence give rise to a duty of obedience—in one of two ways: either by the apparent or actual "consent of the governed" [29] or by the distance of time.[30] If the imperative command behind the legal norm has sufficiently receded in history, or is perceived as sufficiently "consensual"—even if the consent is the consent of the vanquished on a distant battlefield—then the law becomes "legitimate": it is law, rather than mere politics, and thus authoritative.[31] It is that which actors have a moral duty to obey. The "legitimacy" of the power of this distant military-victor-turned-legal-authority is then coupled with the claim that a state actor's own power, or autonomy, is not to be trusted; that the felt moral autonomy of individual state agents is, indeed, the core evil from which most political turmoil springs. Where distant or past legal authority is legitimate, and the state actor's own power is untrustworthy, then the moral thing for the state actor to do with freedom is to relinquish it. The central ethical claim of the legal conservative is that the moral state act is the obedient act, so long as the legal authority being obeyed is legitimate. The central psychic disposition of the legal conservative is a felt imperative to relinquish power and responsibility, and acquiesce instead in the power and authority of a totemized, triumphant, legalized Other.

Finally, for a third group, *libertarian conservatives* or *free-market conservatives,* the source of social authority to which the state should defer is the authority of actors and forces operating in private economic markets.[32] For free-market conservatives, it is the market, and the economic power to which it gives voice, that is the sole legitimate source of normative authority. The political state should accordingly defer to the normative authority of successful market processes and the economic power that underlies them. Motivationally, the free-market conservative's constitutive deferential stance toward the authority of dominant market actors rests neither on respect nor obedience, but instead on a celebratory attitude toward economic authority, and toward the success, the triumph, the power, and the strength evidenced by its ascendance. To the free-market conservative the will of the economic actor does not simply reflect value, but constitutes value, and hence constitutes the "good" that the state, basically through noninterference, has a duty to promote. Morally justifiable legislation should, then, reflect, mimic, or promote the bargained-for outcomes of economic actors rather than the political or ethical visions of legislators, and morally justifiable adjudication should uphold those legislatively encoded private and public bargains.

The ethical argument for this celebratory stance toward the will of the economically powerful is some version of "moral Darwinism." Moral Darwinism unabashedly asserts and celebrates the normative rightness of economic power: for the moral Darwinist, at least in the economic sphere, that which is, ought to be; that which endures, ought to endure; that which lasts, ought to last; and that which triumphs, rightly triumphs. Thus, celebratory, Darwinian, free-market conservatism rests explicitly on an awestruck and admiring stance toward the power that underlies economic authority: we should defer to the authority of the market, according to the moral Darwinian, because market authority necessarily reflects a triumphant conquest of strength over weakness, of power over impotence, and of that which is over that which could have been—of existence over possibility.[33]

Conservative political theory, then, is united by its antipathy to state normative authority and preference for social authority, but conservative theorists differ over the particular social authority to which the state should defer. Moralistic or social conservatives urge the state to defer to the visions of the good embedded in a community's moral institutions; legal conservatives view the legal system as the appropriate authority to which the state should turn; and free-market conservatives locate normativity in the outcomes generated by and the preferences reflected in economic markets. All, however, view these forms of authority as importantly higher or better than the normative authority of "the state." All view the visions of the good and the good life that they generate as superior to those reflected in the "mere preferences," desires, or will of state actors.

CONSERVATIVE JURISPRUDENCE

Conservative political thought grounds, but does not directly compel, the core tenets of the conservative constitutional paradigm. Conservative constitutionalists, as noted, are lawyers as well as political theorists, and as such they adhere to some sort of jurisprudential position regarding the nature of law, as well as some sort of conservative political theory regarding the legitimacy of social and state power. Constitutional theory is surely as indebted to jurisprudence as it is to politics. However, it would

be a mistake to think that those jurisprudential commitments that undoubtedly influence the conservative constitutional paradigm have in any
way "de-politicized" the constitutional paradigm itself. Rather, the jurisprudence embraced by conservative constitutional thinkers, and which in
turn helps ground the conservative constitutional paradigm, is itself profoundly political. As this section attempts to show, the three conservative
understandings, canvased above, of the proper source of communal normative authority for state action imply, in turn, distinctively conservative
interpretations of our three major jurisprudential traditions: natural law,
positivism, and legal instrumentalism.

Moral conservatism, and the respect for the community's conventional
morality on which it rests, implies a distinctively conservative interpretation of the natural law jurisprudential tradition. For all natural lawyers,
conservative and otherwise, those political edicts that deserve to be called
"law" must meet at least minimal moral criteria.[34] Now this basic jurisprudential definition of the nature of law need not be conservative. The
political consequences of the natural lawyer's definitional claim depend
entirely on the content and source of the "morality" the law must incorporate. Obviously, if the moral criteria the law must definitionally meet (in
order to be true "law") is informed by the unrealized morality or ideals of
the disenfranchised, natural law can be (and has been) profoundly revolutionary in its implication: the natural lawyer's claim then implies that
extant positive law that fails to meet the moral criteria, in some higher
sense, is not true "law" at all, and hence carries with it no claim to the
people's allegiance.

For the moral conservative, however, the natural lawyer's identification
of law with morality turns out to have profoundly conservative consequences. For the moral conservative, the content of the "morality" that
the law incorporates does not consist of the unrealized aspirations of the
disempowered, but of the community's authoritative moral commitments
and traditions. Therefore, for the moral conservative drawn to the natural law tradition, society's law is properly and explicitly, even necessarily,
informed by the community's traditional, conventional beliefs. Thus, for
the conservative natural lawyer—such as, for example, England's Lord
Devlin, or Justice Sandra Day O'Connor, or Professor Michael McConnell—a community's historical and "moral" revulsion to homosexuality,
its abhorrence of abortion or interracial marriage, its endorsement of traditional gendered roles, or its resistance to the commodification of babies,
sexuality, or reproductive services, might all properly inform legislative

governance.[35] Traditional morality—a community's dominant understandings of the content of the good life—is the form of normative authority
that properly informs and guides legislation.

Just as deference to the conventional morality of a community implies a
conservative version of the natural law tradition, so the deference toward
legal power that characterizes legal conservatism implies an archly conservative version of legal positivism. For legal positivists generally, unlike
natural lawyers, the "law" is, definitionally, that which is spelled out in
historically authoritative legal sources. For the positivist, then, there is
no definitional link between a society's law and either its conventional
or its aspirational morality. Again, as with natural law, there is nothing
necessarily conservative about this positivistic understanding of law. The
positivistic separation of law and morality is at least analytically helpful
and arguably necessary to establish the immorality of a particular law or
legal regime, and hence the moral case for change.[36] When legal positivism
is combined with the obedient stance toward legal authority characteristic
of legal conservatism, however, it becomes conservative and profoundly
so. For all positivists, "law" is the product of historical, political, and
military victories: it is the will of the strong channeled through processes
themselves determined by the will of the strong, and thereafter legitimated
by tradition. But distinctively for legal conservatives, a duty to obey the
"law" thus defined immediately follows: the political and military victor
whose will is expressed in law becomes the legitimate and hence "legal" authority. The moral actor, whether judge or citizen, when faced with a legal
mandate, behaves morally by disempowering himself through unstinting
obedience.

Hence, the combination of legal conservatism and legal positivism yields
a strand of positivism that might best be called *conservative positivism:*
for the conservative positivist, it is law itself (rather than, as for the conservative natural lawyer, a community's conventional morality) that is and
ought be the source of authority on questions regarding the nature of the
good to which state actors ought defer and which the state then has a duty
to promote. When an agent of the state, then, such as a court, seeks to
inform legal interpretation by some conception of the good, it should do
so by rearticulating a conception of the good held by some higher or earlier
"legitimate" legal authority, such as a "founding father," and then obeying
that mandate.[37] Again, the argument is not that such a conception should
be respected because its holder was wise. Rather, the conservative posi-

Table 9-1.

Source of Authority	Conservative Political Theory	Conservative Jurisprudence
Positive morality	Moral conservatism	Conservative natural law
Legal system	Legal conservatism	Conservative legal positivism
Market economy	Free-market conservatism	Conservative instrumentalism

tivist's position, more simply, is that such a conception should be obeyed because its holder was "legitimate."

Finally, the adoration, celebration, or, more simply, love of economic power characteristic of modern free-market conservatives implies an archly conservative version of legal pragmatism or instrumentalism. Obviously, as the legal-realist experiments with instrumentalism and pragmatism established, legal instrumentalism, no less than natural law or legal positivism, can be put to either radical, liberal, or conservative political ends. For all instrumentalists, law is a tool with which to achieve other independently defined purposes. When legal pragmatism is combined with the politics of free-market conservatism, however, the result is again a profoundly conservative jurisprudential doctrine: what might be called *conservative instrumentalism.* For the conservative instrumentalist, law should be organized in such a way as to promote free economic competition. Economic competition—the process by which the wishes, instincts, and desires of the strongest appropriately become the will of the community, and by which their perceptions of the world become the truth about reality—is not just a fact or practice, but a normative principle of modern life. Law, then, both adjudicative and otherwise, should be used and interpreted in such a way as to promote best the substantive values and norms of competitive life.[38] The consequence for decision making is that when law must be informed or guided by a conception of the good, it should embrace whatever decision will liberate competition.

The relationship between conservative politics and conservative jurisprudence might be schematized as in Table 9-1.

CONSERVATIVE CONSTITUTIONALISM

The conservative interpretations of the Constitution now dominating Supreme Court adjudication and conservative academic commentary may or may not be mandated by the constitutional text itself or by our constitutional history. If the last thirty years of substantive debate over the meaning of constitutional clauses, the nature of the document itself, and the possibilities the process of interpretation opens or forecloses has taught us anything at all, it should have taught us to be skeptical of any such claim. What this section shows, however, is simply that whatever may be the interpretive status of the conservative paradigm, at least three of its core tenets—(1) the characteristically conservative denial that a "right to privacy" can be found in the Constitution, and particularly in the liberty prong of the due process clause; (2) the conservative insistence on a "color-blind" interpretation of the equal protection clause and on a "formal" understanding of the equality that clause protects, such that state- or city-initiated affirmative action plans meant to eradicate the effects of societal discrimination are unconstitutional; and (3) an intentionalist view of constitutional interpretation, such that the Supreme Court is not free to "discover" fundamental rights not clearly implied by the document's text or history—follow immediately from the various conservative jurisprudential and political commitments outlined above. Whether or not the text or history of constitutional law mandates these interpretations, in other words, conservative politics and conservative jurisprudence clearly do.

Privacy Jurisprudence. Let me start with the present Supreme Court's privacy jurisprudence. Although the abortion debacle triggered by *Webster v. Reproductive Health Services*[39] presently dominates public consciousness of the Court's privacy jurisprudence, *Bowers v. Hardwick*[40] is nevertheless more representative of the conservatives' distinctive understanding of the right to privacy and the liberty it is designed to protect. *Bowers,* which predates *Webster* by three years, gives a far clearer articulation of the conservative jurisprudential premises that underlie both decisions. In upholding the antisodomy statute at issue in *Bowers,* a majority of the Supreme Court, arguably for the first time in modern constitutional history, embraced an explicitly conservative political account of the meaning of the good, an explicitly conservative jurisprudential account of the "natural" right of the community to define and enforce the good in law, an explicitly conservative political account of the normative weight of positive law, and an explicitly conservative jurisprudential account of the duty of courts and citizens faithfully to obey the law. From a jurisprudential understanding of law as definitionally incorporating morality and of the courts' and citizen's duty to obey it, and a political understanding of both the conventional nature of morality and the moral content of positive law, the Court drew its profoundly conservative constitutional inference: legislation that reflects conventional morality is entirely proper and thus must be fully constitutional, unless it conflicts with an explicit constitutional provision to the contrary.

To put the same point negatively, and more familiarly, the Court in *Bowers* emphatically rejected the classically liberal account of the relation of law to morality, the classically liberal trust of the individual and correlative suspicion of "community," and hence the paradigmatically liberal inference that any legislation incorporating the community's conventional moral belief and thereby constraining individual freedom is suspect. For classical liberals, it is the individual, not the community, who is the authority on the nature of the good, not only with respect to religious beliefs and political ideas (separately insulated from community control by the first amendment), but also with respect to ways of life. Consequently, legislation that interferes with such individual authority is strongly disfavored, and properly subject to constitutional check. The obvious importance of *Bowers* is that it was the first "privacy" case to reject definitively this classically liberal and individualist account of the good, of law, and hence of the constitutional right to privacy, and adopt in its stead a conservative communitarian conception. In his concurrence, Chief Justice Burger rejected liberal individualism unequivocally:

[T]he proscriptions against sodomy have very "ancient roots." Decisions of individuals relating to homosexual conduct have been subject to state intervention throughout the history of Western civilization. Condemnation of those practices is firmly rooted in Judeao-Christian [*sic*] moral and ethical standards. Homosexual sodomy was a capital crime under Roman law. . . . Blackstone described "the infamous crime against nature" as an offense of "deeper malignity" than rape, an heinous act "the very mention of which is a disgrace to human nature," and "a crime not fit to be named . . . ." The common law of England, including its prohibition of sodomy, became the received law of Georgia and the other Colonies. In 1816 the Georgia Legislature passed the statute at issue here, and that statute has been continuously in force in one form or another since that time. To hold that the act of homosexual sodomy is somehow protected as a fundamental right would be to cast aside millenia of moral teaching. This is essentially not a question of personal "preferences" but rather of the legislative authority of the State. I find nothing in the Constitution depriving a State of the power to enact the statute challenged here.[41]

In addition to the Court's rejection of liberal individualism, there is another reason that *Bowers* is a central part of the emerging conservative paradigm of Fourteenth Amendment and due process law. The opinion is central to modern conservatism not only because it tumbled what was on the verge of becoming a hegemonic liberal interpretation of the requirements of privacy, due process, and liberty—an interpretation that had dominated Supreme Court privacy jurisprudence for almost two decades. The significance of *Bowers* is that it was not only revolutionary but also "integrative": it uniquely and cleanly integrated two of the three competing, and potentially contradictory, strands of modern conservative political and jurisprudential theory.

First, the result in *Bowers*, and Chief Justice Burger's concurrence most dramatically, rests on an understanding of "liberty" and the due process clause that gives constitutional backing both to the moral conservative's respect for a community's authoritative accounts of the good and to the conservative natural lawyer's belief that law should embrace that positive morality. The liberty to which individuals are legally entitled, to the conservative natural lawyer, is the liberty to live the good life as determined by the traditional moral customs and norms of the community itself and as reflected in its legislation, and not, as for the classical liberal, the liberty to live the good life as determined by the individual's own rights. The individual does not have the "liberty" to determine for herself the content of the good life and then pursue it, for the simple reason that the "good life" according to the conservative natural lawyer, is what the community's normative traditions have established it to be, and law properly and constitutionally reflects that conception.[42] "Liberty" therefore not only does not include "privacy," it is antithetical to it: the liberty we enjoy is the liberty to live a moral life as defined by the community's moral convictions. The Court in *Bowers* decisively endorsed this conservative understanding. The Court respectfully deferred to the normative authority of the Georgia legislature, which had, in turn, deferred to the conventional morality of the Georgian citizenry—to say nothing of the normative authority of Roman Law, the classics, Blackstone, the common law, and the Christian religion. From a conservative natural lawyer's perspective, the "political state" of Georgia had acted entirely properly in a moral sense, as well as in a constitutional one: it enacted legislation that articulated and deferred to the wisdom of the community's normative authority.

Second, the Court's reasoning in *Bowers* is at least as rigorously positivistic as its result is moralistic, and the case is for that reason alone likely to be as appealing to conservative legalists and positivists as its result is to conservative natural lawyers. Justice White's opinion in particular makes clear that certainly conventional morality should be respected by legislators, but, furthermore, the Constitution is a law to be obeyed by Courts. Only the judgments contained in the Constitution itself have "authority." All else is nothing but the justices' own value judgments and hence lacks legitimacy. White explained:

> This case does not require a judgment on whether laws against sodomy between consenting adults in general, or between homosexuals in particular, are wise or desirable. It raises no question about the right or propriety of state legislative decisions to repeal their laws that criminalize homosexual sodomy, or of state court decisions invalidating those laws on state constitutional grounds. The issue presented is whether the Federal Constitution confers a fundamental right upon homosexuals to engage in sodomy and hence invalidates the laws of the many States that still make such conduct illegal and have done so for a very long time. The case also calls for some judgment about the limits of the Court's role in carrying out its constitutional mandate.
>
> . . .
>
> . . . [R]espondent would have us announce, as the Court of Appeals did, a fundamental right to engage in homosexual sodomy. This we are quite unwilling to do.
>
> . . .
>
> . . . The Court is most vulnerable and comes nearest to illegitimacy when it deals with judge-made constitutional law having little or no cognizable roots in the language or design of the Constitution. That this is so was painfully demonstrated by the face-off between the Executive and the Court in the 1930's, which resulted in the repudiation of much of the substantive gloss that the Court had placed on the Due Process Clauses of the Fifth and Fourteenth Amendments. There should be, therefore, great resistance to expand the substantive reach of those clauses, particularly if it requires redefining the category of rights deemed to be fundamental. Otherwise, the Judiciary necessarily

takes to itself further authority to govern the country without express constitutional authority. The claimed right pressed on us today falls far short of overcoming this resistance.[43]

Both the Georgia legislature's and the Constitution's sovereign authority are to be obeyed, then, no less than should the wisdom they incorporate be respected. *Bowers* thus satisfies not only the need to respect tradition central to conservative natural law, but the equally central search for legitimate authority critical to conservative positivism. It affirms both the centrality of communal tradition to the development of morality and the centrality of law to legitimate political authority.

Of the major strands of conservative political and jurisprudential thought, only conservative instrumentalists will dispute the *Bowers* result. Conservative instrumentalists cannot unequivocally support the Georgia legislature's attempt to cut off experimental social competition between competing lifestyles and sexual orientations. *Bowers* dampens competition between lifestyles, no less than the legislation at issue in *Lochner*[44] dampened competition in economic markets. It is worth noting, though, that on another level—perhaps a deeper level—the opinion is profoundly pro-competitive, even though, so far as I know, no conservative instrumentalist has explicitly supported the outcome on this rationale. By upholding the Georgia legislature, the Court in effect embraced a competitive, and rejected a hedonistic, understanding of the nature of human sexuality. Nonreproductive, pleasure-seeking, hedonistic sexuality only impedes reproductive competition. The outcome in *Bowers,* like the legislation it sustains, can surely be read as an endorsement of the pro-competitive, "biological market"–based understanding of reproduction propounded by conservative sociobiologists and a simultaneous rejection of a hedonistic, pleasure-based understanding of our sexual practices.

If all of this is right, then *Bowers* is destined to become as central to conservative dominance over the next few decades as *Brown v. Board of Education*[45] was to liberalism during the last few. In *Bowers,* the Court managed in just a few pages to incorporate at least two and perhaps three of the competing strands of conservative constitutionalism into a coherent whole: it respected the normative authority of the community to propound on matters of conventional private morality, obeyed the positive law of both the Georgia legislature and the overarching will of the constitutional founders, and, at the same time, at least arguably celebrated the biological competition between members of the species to which reproductive heterosexuality, in contrast to hedonistic homosexuality, is conducive. *Bowers* achieved what *Lochner* could not: a positivistic, obedient Court upheld a statute backed by what the Court perceived to be the dominant moral sense of the community. *Bowers,* then, unlike either the majority or the dissenting opinion in *Lochner,* is paradigmatically conservative. It was not only the vehicle for the triumph of conservative over liberal values on the Supreme Court; *Bowers* did something more deeply ideological than that—it synthesized and accommodated multiple strands of modern conservative constitutionalism.

A sizeable number of recent Supreme Court cases—including *Webster v. Reproductive Health Services,*[46] *DeShaney v. Winnebago County Department of Social Services,*[47] *Penry v. Lynaugh,*[48] *Stanford v. Kentucky,*[49] and *Michael H. v. Gerald D.*[50]—cleanly fit the *Bowers* "model": in each of these cases, regardless of the doctrinal right at issue, the Court interpreted the constitutional language in such a way as to underscore both the Court's positivist obligation to obey the constitutional mandate and the state's right and obligation to enact legislation embracing the normative authority of the community's conventional morality. Thus, in *Webster,* the Court held that the Constitution's protection of individual privacy and reproductive freedom does not restrict the state's power to define the "beginning of life" by reference to (its view of) the community's conventional morality.[51] In *DeShaney,* the Court further limited the scope of the liberty protected by due process, and in so doing, extended deferential respect to the normative authority of the family.[52] The Court in effect held that the due process clause does not require the state to invade the family's "separate sphere" of political authority on behalf of an individual's safety. In *Stanford* and *Penry,* the Court held that the Eighth Amendment does not restrict the right of the state to decide whether and when to execute juveniles and the mentally retarded (respectively) by reference to community standards,[53] and in *Michael H.* that a biological but nonlegal father has no constitutional right against the power of the community to decide the contours of the "nuclear family."[54] In each of these cases, the Court combined conservative-positivist methodology with conservative natural law results to reach paradigmatically conservative readings of individual rights embodied in the Fourteenth and Eighth Amendments: what the liberty due process clause of the Fourteenth Amendment guarantees, according to these cases, is only that the state may not (without providing due process) deprive the individual of the liberty to live the good life as defined by the community's moral traditions, and what the cruel and unusual punishment clause ensures is that individuals will not be subjected to cruel punishments, where cruelty is defined, roughly, as out of line with the community's "moral sense."

The Court's conservative due process jurisprudence, then, might be summarized in this way. The due process clause, according to the conservative jurists, cannot and does not, in any way, restrict, constrain, define, or guide the community's authority to dictate, by reference to whatever traditions have become dominant, the content of the life that individuals must be free to enjoy, unimpeded by illegal process. By this view, to identify and define the "good life" is definitionally the community's natural right and moral responsibility, and it is consequently the Court's positive legal and political duty to defer to that communal authority (limited by other constitutional provisions, notably the First Amendment). The due process clause grants rights to individuals and accordingly restrains communitarian will, but the right granted is only the right to pursue the community-defined good unimpeded by illegal state action, and the power restrained is only the power of the state to deprive the individual illegally of the liberty that the state, by reference to the community's authoritative conventional traditions, has deemed compatible or necessary to pursuit of the good life and the good society. The legislature, and through it the community, and through the community authoritative traditions, remain empowered to define the content of the good life (and hence the content of evil) and legislate accordingly. Constitutional restraints leave the authority of tradition and its authoritative power over our lives intact.

Equality Jurisprudence. City of Richmond v. J. A. Croson Co.,[55] decided in 1989, may well be the conservative Court's paradigm equal protection clause case, destined to become as central to the conservatives' developing understanding of equality doctrine as is *Bowers* to due process. As others have argued, and as countless others no doubt will argue in the near future, the minimalist understanding of equal protection rendered by the Court in *Croson* cannot be traced to any neutral reading of either political history or constitutional law.[56] What I want to argue here is the somewhat different point that *Croson* can readily and easily be traced to conservatism's political and jurisprudential premises.

First, and most obviously, the result in *Croson* (rather than the reasoning) is a conservative instrumentalist's triumph, no less than the result in *Bowers* was a conservative natural lawyer's victory. For the free-market conservative, race ought not be a determinant of legislative decision making that affects the success of individuals in competitive economic markets—regardless of whether the motive for such legislation is benign or malignant—because and to the degree that race is not a rational proxy for any characteristic that could conceivably be of relevance to the competitive process. For the conservative instrumentalist, the purpose of law should be to free economic competition, so that economic power can prevail unimpeded by extrinsic considerations. The equal protection clause should therefore be read in such a way as to further this purposive mandate. Discriminatory, race-conscious legislation generally inhibits rather than furthers competition, and hence trenches on competitive values. If competitive rationality is the purpose, and therefore the meaning, of equality and of equal protection, it obviously makes no difference whether the discriminatory legislation is malignant or benign: either way it inhibits competition. The result in *Croson* is substantially in accord. Thus, Justice O'Connor's summary of the Court's holding emphasizes both the value of competition and conservative instrumental themes:

> The Equal Protection Clause of the Fourteenth Amendment provides that "[N]o State shall . . . deny to any person within its jurisdiction the equal protection of the laws" . . . . As this Court has noted in the past, the "rights created by the first section of the Fourteenth Amendment are, by its terms, guaranteed to the individual. The rights established are personal rights." The Richmond Plan denies certain citizens the opportunity to compete for a fixed percentage of public contracts based solely upon their race. To whatever racial group these citizens belong, their "personal rights" to be treated with equal dignity and respect are implicated by a rigid rule erecting race as the sole criterion in an aspect of public decisionmaking.
>
> Absent searching judicial inquiry into the justification for such race-based measures, there is simply no way of determining what classifications are "benign" or "remedial" and what classifications are in fact motivated by illegitimate notions of racial inferiority or simple racial politics. . . . We thus reaffirm the view expressed by the plurality in *Wygant* that the standard of review under the Equal Protection Clause is not dependent on the race of those burdened or benefited by a particular classification.[57]

For the conservative positivist as well, the decision is a victory. As the concurring opinions of Justices Scalia and Kennedy were at pains to establish, no distanced, historical "other" has ever "legitimated," through military, political, or judicial victory, the quest for substantive racial equality in this country's history.[58] Substantive racial equality—the clear goal of affirmative action—is simply not a part of the normative authority of our positive constitutional law. Formal racial equality—the neutrality standard under which affirmative action laws are struck down—by contrast, is. Thus, the conservative positivist, like the conservative instrumentalist, will endorse a reading of equal protection that precludes benign as well as malicious uses of race in legislative decision making, but the reason will be different: for the conservative instrumentalist, such a reading furthers competition; for the conservative positivist, such a reading is commanded by the Constitution. As Justice Scalia explained:

> The benign purpose of compensating for social disadvantages, whether they have been acquired by reason of prior discrimination or otherwise, can no more be pursued by the illegitimate means of racial discrimination than can other assertedly benign purposes we have repeatedly rejected. . . . The difficulty of overcoming the effects of past discrimination is as nothing compared with the difficulty of eradicating from our society the source of those effects, which is the tendency—fatal to a nation such as ours—to classify and judge men and women on the basis of their country of origin or the color of their skin. A solution to the first problem that aggravates the second is no solution at all. I share the view expressed by Alexander Bickel that "[t]he lesson of the great decisions of the Supreme Court and the lesson of contemporary history have been the same for at least a generation: discrimination on the basis of race is illegal, immoral, unconstitutional, inherently wrong, and destructive of democratic society."[59]

The conservative natural lawyers' support of *Croson* is considerably more tentative, as is reflected in both the tone and content of Justice O'Connor's opinion. For O'Connor, as well as for other conservative natural lawyers, the moral sense of the community, as expressed through its legislature, is the proper source of authority on issues concerning the good. It would seem to follow that if the community has embraced substantive race equality as a desirable legislative goal, that commitment should be respected. The only limit to this principle (and the equal protection clause is surely a limit) for the conservative natural lawyer must come not from an abstract commitment to a particular understanding of "equality" as constitutive of the good that conflicts with communitarian conceptions, but, rather, from limits on the community's normative authority: if history has proven the community untrustworthy with respect to some aspect of its authority to define the good, then to that degree the community has lost its claim to authority. The meaning of "equal protection," then, should be derived from a moralistic understanding of the limits on the community's normative authority, not from any understanding of equality itself.

Because history has proven the local community's authority on the nature of the good untrustworthy in matters regarding race, O'Connor reasoned, benign as well as malicious racial categorizations made by local and state governments are clearly unconstitutional. The state and municipal community, otherwise authoritative, cannot be trusted with racially explicit classifications, whether they be in the service of apartheid or in the service of affirmative action:

> That Congress may identify and redress the effects of society-wide discrimination does not mean that, a fortiori the States and their political subdivisions are free to decide that such remedies are appropriate. Section 1 of the Fourteenth Amendment is an explicit constraint on state power, and the States must undertake any remedial efforts in accordance with that provision. To hold otherwise would be to cede control over the content of the Equal Protection Clause to the 50 state legislatures and their myriad political subdivisions. The mere recitation of a benign or compensatory purpose for the use of a racial classification would essentially entitle the States to exercise the full power of Congress under section 5 of the Fourteenth Amendment and insulate any racial classification from judicial scrutiny under section 1. We believe that such a result would be contrary to the intentions of the Framers of the Fourteenth Amendment, who desired to place clear limits on the States' use of race as a criterion for legislative action, and to have the federal courts enforce those limitations.[60]

Thus, to summarize, equality means "formal equality" and no more in the conservative paradigm, just as "due process" means protection against procedural illegality and procedural illegality only. For conservative theorists and jurists, the equal protection clause protects the individual's right not to be irrationally discriminated against by state officials: like individuals must be treated alike by the legislature as well as in the market, no less than like cases must be treated alike by judges. Racial classifications are irrational classifications, or should be presumed to be such, because they breach this formal justice mandate (similar individuals are treated differently) and are accordingly unconstitutional. The clause does no more than this. It does not guarantee, in any way, a right to substantive social or economic equality. It does not guarantee or even suggest that states should take action to ameliorate the substantive inequality suffered by particular historical groups during the country's history. The right granted is an individual right to be free from the effects of legislation that categorizes on the basis of irrational factors, such as race or, in some circumstances, gender. It neither recognizes nor protects group grievances, group histories, or group entitlements.

In this decade, what this conservative interpretation of equality means, most importantly, is that other than in truly extraordinary circumstances, no individual's or corporation's competitive chances in the marketplace will be compromised by societal efforts to put an end to the substantive, subordinating effects of private, social, or institutional racism through anticompetitive affirmative action programs. The clause thus construed protects not equality so much as the integrity of the competitive process, and targets not racism (to say nothing of classism, misogyny, or heterosexism), but race-conscious governmental decision making. The conservative's conception of the guarantee of equality thus has nothing to do with putting an end to racism if "racism" is understood as the white majority's hatred, contempt, and subordination of nonwhites, and little if anything to do with achieving equality. Rather, it has everything to do with protecting competitive values against progressive political attempts by the state to achieve substantive racial equality.

Constitutional Interpretation. Finally, two central and arguably inconsistent propositions about the nature and scope of constitutional interpretation are paradigmatically conservative: first, that the Constitution should be interpreted in such a way as to give effect to the meaning most likely intended by its authors ("intentionalism" or "originalism");[61] second, that in the absence of clear constitutional authority to the contrary, the Court should defer whenever possible to legislative will.[62] Most conservatives subscribe to one or the other of these two claims, and many, if not most, subscribe to both. Interpretation, for the conservative constitutionalist, is a matter of ascertaining the original meaning of the Constitution, and in cases of doubt, deferring to legislative judgment. Judicial restraint and originalism constitute the core of a conservative theory of constitutional interpretation.

At first glance, this dual endorsement of judicial restraint and originalism is hard to rationalize: it is not clear why a strict originalist would advocate judicial restraint over judicial activism; either, from time to time, might be necessary to achieve the original intent of the framers. Nor is it at all clear why an advocate of judicial restraint would insist on obedience to original intent. The conservative approach to interpretation, in other words, seems to flow from neither a commitment to majoritarian democracy nor an adherence to strict constitutionalism. When viewed as an outgrowth of the politics and jurisprudence of conservatism, however, it is less mysterious why so many conservatives try to hold both commitments.

Certainly the two imperatives within the conservative view of constitutional interpretation—that courts should interpret the Constitution narrowly so as to effectuate the will of its authors, and that the courts should whenever possible defer to legislative will—are each directly responsive to the need for obedience to legitimated authority that drives conservative positivism. Originalism compellingly satisfies the conservative positivist's quest for legitimated authority. The original Constitution, to the conservative positivist, is a legal document laid down by earlier embodied political sovereigns in positions to command, is therefore "legitimate," and should be construed accordingly.[63] Consequently, the conservative positivist will read the Constitution wherever possible as a command that does and should trigger an attitude of obedience. The Constitution is not, for the conservative positivist, a "text" requiring active, creative, and hence morally responsible interpretation by particular judges within the context of particular historical circumstances. Rather, the text is a command within a hierarchy of commands, to which the judge's only distinctively moral duty is one of unflinching obedience. The judge's moral duty, then, is exhausted by his duty to obey; judicial morality is a "morality of obedience." The judge behaves morally by obeying authority, rather than capriciously acting on his or her "own" values.

Judicial restraint similarly satisfies the psychic and ethical mandate of obedience that drives conservative positivism. Judicial restraint continues to be a central commitment of conservative positivism, not for the narrowly political reason that the judiciary's politics are substantively at odds with conservatism, for this is clearly no longer the case, but for the deeply political reason that it is the lawmaking, imperativist activity of legislation, rather than the deliberative work of adjudication, that gives rise to imperatives that invite obedience. The conservative positivist judge will tend to construe the more general and less imperative provisions of the Constitution narrowly, so as to maximize deference—and hence obedience—to the legislative will. The legislator is an embodied authority speaking in unambiguously imperative language. Where the constitutional command can be traced to equally clear and clearly imperative authority it will surely trump; but where the constitutional text does not do so—where it neither appears nor operates as an imperative command, and where the "embodiment" of its authority is unclear—the conservative judge will read it narrowly, so as to retain the form and substance of a hierarchic, legalistic structure of command.

The Court, then, as a state actor, should obey rather than act; should defer rather than interpret; should acquiesce in authority rather than question it. The Court (like all moral agents) should defer to, or submit to, the law, as established by the legislature or the constitutional founders—not because the legislature or the founders were necessarily wise, but because the power on which their authority rests is legitimate. Judge Easterbrook defends both conservative legal positivism and the legal conservative's constitutive stance of obedience in the judicial realm in this representative passage:

> [T]he proper judicial role combines honest interpretation of decisions made elsewhere with careful discharge of powers expressly granted. . . . Judges have no authority to reconstitute the values of the people or to exalt redistribution at the expense of competing objectives selected by the political branches. . . . The Constitution demands that all power be authorized. . . . Judges applying the Constitution we have, rather than the one Professor Tribe wishes we had, must take their guidance and authority from decisions made elsewhere. Otherwise they speak with the same authority they and Professor Tribe and I possess when we fill the law reviews with our speculations and desires: none. And the other branches owe no obedience to those who speak without authority.
>
> This is not to say that the judicial process is mechanical. Far from it. . . . Knowledge is ephemeral, and doubts about both the meaning of words and the effects of rules tax the greatest interpreters. But none of this changes the source of the power to decide. Judges can legitimately demand to be obeyed only when their decisions stem from fair interpretations of commands laid down in the texts.[64]

It is not surprising, then, that conservative positivists are drawn to principles of interpretation mandating both originalism and judicial restraint. The reason this is so, however, is not narrowly political in the sense often meant by critics of intentionalism. It is, however, political in a deeper sense: for positivist conservatives, a Constitution, like a statute, is there to be obeyed. The Constitution binds just as the law commands; they are both authoritative; they constitute our capacity for self-rule. That a rigid intentionalism and originalism dominates conservative constitutionalism thus has everything to do with the conservative need and desire to constrain one's freedom and hence moral responsibility by submitting to and obeying legitimated authority. The conservative positivist's insistence that the Constitution must be construed and obeyed in accordance with the intent of its Framers—that the Constitution must be "obeyed," not freely interpreted—follows inexorably from the psychic need to constrain choice, freedom, fluidity, motion, and the will to power, with prior, objective, and controlling authority.

A strand of moral conservatism as well supports the centrality of both judicial restraint and strict originalism to the interpretive model at the core of the conservative paradigm. The evident wisdom, intelligence, and vast practical and historical knowledge of the Founding Fathers ought surely to be respected. Somewhat less obviously, however, the legislature also constitutes, at least in its ideal form, a group whose substantive judgments command respect. Moralistic conservatives and conservative natural lawyers thus have independent reasons to endorse both originalism and judicial restraint, although their support for these interpretive commitments is more likely to be ambivalent than that of conservative positivists. Precedent, or the common law tradition, constitutes for the moralistic conservative an important competing body of accumulated wisdom, and the wisdom of precedent may of course diverge from the wisdom of original intent, and may counsel considerable judicial activism. This may not, however, be as great a conflict as first appears. As moral conservatives correctly note, constitutional decisions, with only rare exceptions, are in fact far less likely to deal meaningfully with underlying moral issues than is commonly supposed. Thoughtful moral conservatives are accordingly skeptical of the "precedential wisdom" of judicial decisions, and are more inclined to value the culmination of wisdom expressed in moments of legislative and constitutional enactment. As Professor McConnell explained:

[J]udicial decisionmaking contains very little serious deliberation on moral issues. In the abortion decision, for example, the Court majority thought it "need not resolve" the moral-legal status of the unborn child . . . while the dissenters devoted their entire opinion to issues of standing to sue and the power of the states. . . . *Bowers v. Hardwick,* which dealt with state power to regulate private consensual sexual conduct, presented an unedifying face-off between a majority that believed the claims of homosexuals to sexual autonomy were "at best, facetious," and dissenters who reflexively equated longstanding religious moral teaching with "religious intolerance," without pausing to reflect on its possible moral underpinnings. . . . [T]he decision of gay rights in and around the Chicago City Council had more substance than the opinions in *Bowers v. Hardwick.* The Court's treatment of other prominent moral-constitutional questions . . . has not been much better. . . .

Nor . . . has there been much more moral deliberation behind the curtains. The Justices are far too busy to spend much time thinking about the cases. . . . In contrast to the months, even years, that are devoted to major legislative deliberation, the Justices devote one hour to oral argument and somewhat less than that to discussion at conference.[65]

For obvious reasons, the dual principles of originalism and judicial restraint do not resonate nearly as strongly with conservative instrumentalism. For the conservative instrumentalist, the Constitution, like all law, should be interpreted to free economic competition, not to effectuate the will of either founders or legislators, and this will often require considerable judicial activism in the face of legislation that inhibits economic competition. Free-market libertarianism, as is increasingly well understood, requires considerable judicial activism and seems to mandate legislative rather than judicial restraint.

Nevertheless, even conservative instrumentalists can find some reason to support the principles of judicial restraint and original intent. As Justice Holmes's famous dissent in *Lochner*[66] makes clear, judicial restraint in the face of legislative will not only facilitates judicial submission to the imperatives of legislation but also frees competitive victories, albeit of a political, rather than economic, stripe. For Holmes, as for some of his present-day moral-Darwinian followers, the legislature, no less than the market, constitutes a sphere of competitive normativity. Post-Holmesian moral-Darwinian conservatives are therefore understandably split, not only over the value of judicial restraint but also over the value of Holmes's famous *Lochner* dissent: on the one hand, an activist judiciary could overturn anti-

Table 9-2.

	Interpretation (Originalist/Restraint)	Liberty (*Bowers*)	Equality (*Croson*)
Moralistic, natural law	Respect for wisdom of founders/legislators	Respect for religious teachings; community's traditions	Respect for the limits of community's wisdom
Imperativist positivism	Obedience to legitimate legislative and constitutional commands	Obedience to Georgia legislative and constitutional mandate	Obedience to constitutional imperative
Competitive Instrumentalism	Celebration of legislative and constitutional outcomes as products of normative competition	Celebration of proreproductive, competitive sexuality	Celebration of competitive processes over substantive equality

competitive legislation, thus freeing competition and competitive market outcomes, but on the other hand (as Holmes's dissent argued), legislation is itself (at least at times) the outcome of competitive processes, and when it is, an activist court that upsets those outcomes is undermining, rather than furthering, competitive values and competitive victories.[67] For the instrumental moral-Darwinian conservative—who views the public competition of interest and ideologies regarding the nature of the good that is characteristic of legislation as of greater consequence to the struggle for survival than the competition of wealth, skills, and talents in private markets—judicial restraint will be a constitutional imperative, even in the face of anticompetitive legislation. Particularly where legislation is the product of economic-styled bargaining, the legislature's will ought to remain untrammeled: legislative will ought to trump both the conflicting outcomes that competitive markets would dictate and the conflicting principles that moralistic courts might wronghandedly seek to enforce. At least a strand, then, of moral-Darwinian conservatism supports rather than contests the primacy of judicial restraint to the conservative paradigm.

Thus, conservatives converge on an originalist-judicial restraint understanding of constitutional interpretation and support the outcomes in *Bow-*

ers and *Croson,* although for different reasons. The developing conservative constitutional paradigm, and the divergent reasons for its conservative support might be schematized as in Table 9-2.

The Progressive Constitutional Paradigm

PROGRESSIVE POLITICAL THEORY

Modern progressive political theory begins with a central, even definitive, insight: conservative deference to communal authority, whatever form it takes, directly implies a parallel deference to the clusters of social power that invariably underlie it.[68] Communal "authorities" on how we ought to live—whether they be moral, legal, or economic—no less than the state authorities so distrusted by conservative theorists, are "authoritative" not because they are necessarily right (although they may be) but because they have, use, reflect, and wield social power. They may have power, in turn, because they are right (and thus have survived centuries of critical inquiry) or, as Michel Foucault's social "archeologies" have aimed to reveal, they may have power for some other reason, such as that they serve the interests of dominant social groups.[69] In any case, normative authority rests on some form of social power. The authority of the market to dictate what is and is not of value directly depends on the power of particular market actors to shape the preferences of others.[70] Similarly, the normative authority of the Rule of Law to demand obedience to lawful authority depends on the power of the legal system to coerce, where need be, its mandates.[71] Lastly, the authority of the community to dictate particular moral values depends on some part of the community achieving sufficient power so as to transform its "will" into received "wisdom."[72] In all three cases, when the conservative embraces, preserves, respects, and defers to the teachings of communal authority, he or she necessarily, whether or not intentionally, embraces the social power that underlies it. Thus, progressives conclude, political and jurisprudential conservative thought rests on attitudes of deference not merely to a community's normative authority, but also toward the social power that underlies it.

Progressivism, in part, defines itself in opposition to this conservative deference toward social power. Progressive political theory is grounded in feelings of antipathy and resistance, rather than attraction, to both social authority and social power. Progressives reject both the wisdom and often the legitimacy of the normative authority that emanates from social institutions, including the three particular institutions that presently dominate conservative political and legal thought: the community's conventional morality, its positive law, and its economic markets. According to progressives, state actors, whether legislators or adjudicators, should not defer to the normative authority that rests on those sources when deciding how to act. Instead, progressives argue, state actors should rely on the experiences, ideals, and aspirations of the relatively disempowered, rather than the established traditions or customs of the socially empowered. The progressive is thus willing to countenance state action designed to disrupt patterns of social hierarchy, just as the conservative is typically quite willing to countenance state action designed to reinforce those patterns.

The particular experiences of the disempowered to which the progressive turns, however, and their reasons for doing so, diverge, just as conservatives split on the type of community authority to which, in their view, state actors ought to defer. Again, it is useful to distinguish at least three major strands of progressive political thought—and three correlative jurisprudential movements—all of which have had an impact on progressive constitutional theorists.

First, for some progressives, the meaning of the good and hence the content of the good life that should be the goal of state action should be understood by reference to a set of ideals that derive from the experiences and aspirations of the relatively disempowered. These progressives, whom I call *idealistic progressives,* identify the content of their progressive politics—the meaning of the "good life" that citizens must have the right to pursue and that the state has an obligation to encourage—by reference to a particular utopian vision of social life which is, in turn, grounded in those experiences: a world in which each individual enjoys some degree of meaningful individual autonomy, some degree of life-fulfilling rather than life-threatening connection to others and freedom from fear of oppression, want, violence, or subordination.[73] To make such a life possible for all citizens, according to idealistic progressives, is and should be the proper aim of state action.

The "experiences" that inform this utopian vision of the good, for the idealistic progressive, are not culled from the lessons of objective tradition, as for the moralistic conservative; rather, they are derived from the experiences—which may include memories, glimpses, or dreams—of true freedom or equality that occur "in the interstices" (as it were) of a daily life constructed for the most part within conditions of hierarchy, inequality, subordination, and bondage. Let me offer two examples of progressive thought explicitly defined and informed by such interstitial moments; one more familiar, one less so. In both cases, the moral reasoning contrasts sharply with the conservative "idealistic" method outlined for "thoughtful people" by Michael McConnell.[74]

First, along with a number of radical feminists, lesbian feminist Adrienne Rich has argued eloquently and persuasively that the widespread participation of women in practices of heterosexuality, family, and motherhood is best explained as a product not of nature or biology, nor of benign culture, and certainly not of individual choice, but rather as a product of patterns of coercion, gendered hierarchy, sexual violence, and male control of women's sexual and reproductive labor—patterns that transcend culture, race, and era.[75] What is distinctive about Rich's work, what distinguishes it from other radical feminist writings on the same topic, is her explicit reliance on women's "aspirational experiences"—fleeting, occasional, generally unrecorded, and often distrusted, even by the woman herself—of a better, fuller, "woman-identified" and woman-bonded emotional, spiritual, and, at times, erotic life. It is this reliance on interstitial experiences of true liberty and equality that renders Rich's work idealistic and gives her argument its moral core. It is because women experience these fleeting, interstitial moments of freedom from male coercion, Rich suggests, that we can be confident that patriarchy and its attendant sexual violence are indeed very real obstacles to the enjoyment of the good life. Rich calls these experiences, collectively, the "lesbian continuum" and argues that virtually all women, at some point in their lives, have an experience of nondominated life that at least tangentially touches that continuum:

> I mean the term lesbian continuum to include a range—through each woman's life and throughout history—of woman identified experience, not simply the fact that a woman has had or consciously desired genital experience with another woman. If we expand it to embrace many more forms of primary intensity between and among women, including the sharing of a rich inner life, the bonding against male tyranny, the giving and receiving of practical and political support . . . we begin to grasp breadths of female history and psychology which have lain out of reach as a consequence of limited, mostly clinical, definitions of lesbianism.
>
> Lesbian existence comprises both the breaking of a taboo and the rejection of a compulsory way of life. It is also a direct or indirect attack on male right of access to women. But it is more than these, although

we may first begin to perceive it as a form of naysaying to patriarchy, an act of resistance. . . . The destruction of records and memorabilia and letters documenting the realities of lesbian existence must be taken very seriously as a means of keeping heterosexuality compulsory for women, since what has been kept from our knowledge is joy, sensuality, courage, and community, as well as guilt, self-betrayal and pain.[76]

The second, and more familiar, example comes from Martin Luther King's writing and oratory. King's thought was not just "progressive" in its opposition to racial hierarchy. It was also, like Rich's, idealistic in its method: King's conviction that a life lived in a world free of racial hierarchy would indeed be a better life was explicitly informed not only by traditions culled from religious history but also by occasional experiences, religious visions, and "dreams" of a utopian future. It was these interstitial moments and dreams, for King, that gave him confidence that a life free of the damaging effects of racism would indeed be better, for both the individual and the community:

I have a dream that one day even the state of Mississippi, a desert state sweltering with the heat of injustice and oppression, will be transformed into an oasis of freedom and justice.

I have a dream that my four little children will one day live in a nation where they will not be judged by the color of their skin but by the content of their character.

I have a dream today.

I have a dream that one day the state of Alabama, whose governor's lips are presently dripping with the words of interposition and nullification, will be transformed into a situation where little black boys and black girls will be able to join hands with little white boys and white girls and walk together as sisters and brothers.

I have a dream today.

I have a dream that one day every valley shall be exalted, every hill and mountain shall be made low, the rough places will be made plains, and the crooked places will be made straight, and the glory of the Lord shall be revealed, and all flesh shall see it together.[77]

These experiences of the ideal "in the interstices" of everyday lives of subordination and domination, occasional and fleeting as they may be, are arguably essential to any progressive movement: they are the basis of the conviction that there is another possible life, and a life that is qualitatively better than the life defined and constrained by the social hierarchy of the present. Without such idealistic experiences, the progressive insight that a present social reality is riddled with hierarchy and power imbalances runs the risk of triviality: it is hard to imagine a social reality that is not. Idealism that relies directly on interstitial experiences of true liberty and equality is thus one way (which is not to deny that there are others) by which the progressive can assert the normative superiority of a more egalitarian and less hierarchical social life, and thus one way that progressivism becomes a normative and moral vision, rather than merely a political imperative fueled by the discontent of the disempowered. Idealistic progressives, distinctively of all progressives, focus on these experiences of ideal forms of life, not only as a minimal constituent of a moral vision, but as constituting the moral vision itself. For the idealistic progressive, the content of the good, and the good life, that the state ought to use its power to ensure and create, is quite self-consciously constructed from these intensely subjective, although by no means individualistic, direct, occasional, and for the most part "un-lived" experiences of the good life.

For some progressives, the meaning of the good and the good life that the state ought to promote, should be understood by reference to the recurrent experience of freedom, and the understanding of its necessity, even within objective conditions of constraint, subordination, deprivation, and bondage. These progressives—whom I call *existential progressives*—identify the content of the good life with these concrete lived experiences of freedom. The good life, for the existential progressive, is the life that both understands and constructs itself as authentically constituted by its possibilities; appreciates the open and identified choice; and maintains a passion for free play, ambiguity, and change. For the existentialist, the "good life" is the life consciously lived in conditions of constant internal subjective growth and external flux. The core value, then, is authenticity, and the core political imperative is to maximize the social conditions that make possible an authentic life. Life is that which changes, and the good life is the self-conscious realization of that ideal. Political and social life should be organized in such a way as to make such a life realizable for all.

This existential understanding of freedom, choice, possibility, and openness has had tremendous influence on the Critical Legal Studies movement, and hence indirectly on progressive constitutionalism as well. To avoid confusion, we should identify two quite different lines of influence. First, existential progressives, like critical scholars and critical legal scholars, have generally embraced the descriptive critical claim that behind the facade of control, determinacy, or rigidity in any particular political choice—including, significantly, the judicial choice—lies an underlying reality of possibility, indeterminacy, and freedom. This idea has played a tremendously important role in the development of the "indeterminacy critique" in the Critical Legal Studies movement. In an early and seminal piece, Duncan Kennedy described the existential and phenomenological experience of judicial choice in this way:

> [T]he acknowledgement of contradiction makes it easier to understand judicial behavior that offends the ideal of the judge as a supremely rational being. The judge cannot, any more than the analyst, avoid the moment of truth in which one simply shifts modes. In place of the apparatus of rule making and rule application, with its attendant premises and attitudes, we come suddenly on a gap, a balancing test, a good faith standard, a fake or incoherent rule, or enthusiastic adoption of a train of reasoning all know will be ignored in the next case. In terms of individualism, the judge has suddenly begun to act in bad faith. In terms of altruism, she has found herself. The only thing that counts is this change in attitude, but it is hard to imagine anything more elusive of analysis.[78]

Second, existential progressives, like critical scholars, have also generally embraced the related ethical claim that the destruction of socially constructed hierarchies and the limits on freedom they impose would be a gain in freedom and hence a gain in the good life for all affected individuals. In a series of books and articles, Roberto Unger, still the foremost spokesperson for normative critical thought, insists that the destruction of social hierarchy in all its forms is a sufficiently rich normative agenda for a progressive movement.[79] Any such "disentrenchment" constitutes a gain in both freedom and empowerment. In his 1987 book, *False Necessity,* Unger puts the point this way:

> The guiding theme of the program of social reconstruction is the attempt to imagine institutional arrangements and social practices that can advance the radical project beyond the point to which contemporary forms of governmental and economic organization have carried it. By the . . . project of the modernist visionary I mean the attempt to realize the many forms of individual or collective empowerment that result from our relative success in disengaging our practical and

passionate dealings from the restrictive influence of entrenched social roles and hierarchies. . . . The program suggests how our contemporary formative contexts might be disentrenched, . . . how they might be more fully opened to challenge in the midst of our routine conflicts and therefore also how they might undermine or prevent rigid forms of social division and hierarchy. . . . The weakening of the influence of this prewritten social script is to be valued not only negatively, as an occasion for a broader range of choice, but affirmatively for the forms of empowerment it makes possible. . . .

. . .

. . . [D]ifferent institutional arrangements reflect varying degrees of advance in the denaturalization of society. Society becomes denaturalized to the extent that its formative practices and preconceptions are open to effective challenge in the midst of ordinary social activity . . . . The concept of denaturalization or emancipation from false necessity includes the idea of a weakening of rigid roles and hierarchies. It therefore also refers to the development of forms of production, exchange, and passionate attachment that are less marked by such rankings and divisions. . . . I use the term negative capability to suggest the variety of forms of empowerment that denaturalization makes possible.[80]

For existential progressives, then, as for critical legal scholars, the state should act in a way that furthers a program of disentrenchment and denaturalization. The goal is a social world in which each individual and group is as free as possible to "find herself" through discovering her multiple selves; to disentrench herself from rigid roles imposed from without; to "shift modes"; to denaturalize her roots; and to discover her essence not in her essentiality, but in her potentiality. The means by which this might happen is, in part, state action responsive to social rigidity: the state should properly be viewed as one mechanism, among others, for destabilizing social entrenchment. By so doing, and only by so doing, can it further rather than frustrate the "good life" of the citizens over whom it unquestionably holds dominion.

Lastly, for a third group of progressives—who can be called *antisubordination progressives*—the meaning of the good and the good life that the state ought to promote is understood by reference to the experiential understanding of the damage done by private and social hierarchies of authority and power. Antisubordination progressives typically concern themselves not with the nature of the good life which the state has a duty to promote, but with the nature of its absence which the state has a duty to prevent. The meaning of the good, for antisubordination progressives, is negatively inferred from varying experiences of subordination, bondage, and invasion. The sorts of experiences of inequality that inform antisubordinationist politics and legal thought are vast. They include, for example, the daily, numbing joylessness of a materially impoverished existence; the self-contempt from being regarded as essentially less than human, less than whole, less than entitled, or less than respected; the pain of being a target of hatred and abuse; the dehumanization of being an object of property, of sexuality, or of another's goals and ambitions; the general day-to-day horror of being systematically lessened or "handicapped" so that another can feel whole; of being systematically dirtied or polluted so that another can feel pure and clean; of being systematically rendered contingent, natural, bodily, of the dirt, or of the earth so that another can feel transcendental, free, spiritual, or rational; and of being systematically perverted, bent, and marginalized so that another can feel normal, straight, or central.

Subjective experiences of constraint, invasion, and bondage are also vast: they include the experience of the physical bondage of shackles, chains, whips, bits, and gags; the experience of the sexual bondage of an unwanted partner in a false intimacy; the constraints on life itself of the often unchosen and more often unwanted career of motherhood; the restrictions on livelihood, social contribution, career, and public work brought on even by wanted and celebrated mothering; and the invasiveness of mandated constructions of sexual intimacy and sexual choice. The meaning of bondage, invasion, constraint, and restriction, to the antisubordination progressive, is in large part the content of these experiences. The meaning of the good to antisubordination progressives, is informed by the content of those experiences; the good life, very simply, would mean their absence.[81] The state, then, should aim to create a world free from these experiences. The good life that the state ought to promote is the life unconstrained by the foot on one's neck and the gag in one's throat.

PROGRESSIVE JURISPRUDENCE

As is the case with conservative political theory, these three responses to social power inform three distinctive interpretations of our major jurisprudential traditions: natural law, legal positivism, and legal instrumentalism. First, like conservative moralists, progressive idealists tend to be "natural lawyers": progressive idealists, like conservative moralists, view law as definitionally aspiring toward a moral ideal. However, whereas the conservative natural lawyer gives content to the moral ideal toward which law aspires by reference to a community's conventional morality, the progressive natural lawyer gives content to the ideal by reference to the glimpses, memories, or dreams of a truly good life as experienced by the relatively disempowered: a life lived within actual conditions of liberty, equality, or freedom. Progressive idealism and the natural law tradition thus combine in a distinctively progressive version of natural law: the "legalism" of "natural law" gives foundation, permanence, and a link to the past to an otherwise unfettered idealism, while the progressive's unique blend of idealism and experientialism frees the natural law tradition from the shackles of social conventionality.

Thus, for the progressive natural lawyer, the ideal toward which government should aim is informed not by history but by possibility, not by authority but by vision, and not by the traditions that have triumphed over unlived dreams but by the dreams that have survived in the interstices of the triumphant traditions. Law should and does aspire toward unlived ideals, not toward a perfect congruence with the wisdom of historically established tradition. Martin Luther King's letter from the Birmingham jail contains what is undoubtedly this tradition's most eloquent restatement:

> There are two types of law: just and unjust. . . . One has not only a legal but a moral responsibility to obey just laws. Conversely, one has a moral responsibility to disobey unjust laws. I would agree with St. Augustine that "an unjust law is no law at all."
>
> A just law is a man-made code that squares with the moral law or the law of God. An unjust law is a code that is out of harmony with the moral law. To put it in the terms of St. Thomas Aquinas: An unjust law is a human law that is not rooted in eternal law and natural law. Any law that uplifts human personality is just. Any law that degrades human personality is unjust. All segregation statutes are unjust because segregation distorts the soul and damages the personality. It gives the segregator a false sense of superiority and the segregated a false sense of inferiority. Segregation, to use the terminology of the Jewish philosopher Martin Buber, substitutes an "I-it" relationship for an "I-thou" relationship and ends up relegating persons to the status of things. Hence segregation is not only politically, economically and sociologically unsound, it is morally wrong and sinful. . . . Is not segregation an existential expression of man's tragic separation,

his awful estrangement, his terrible sinfulness? Thus it is that I can urge men to obey the 1954 decision of the Supreme Court, for it is morally right; and I can urge them to disobey segregation ordinances, for they are morally wrong.[82]

The difference, then, for the progressive natural lawyer, between the just and the unjust law, and the difference between the laws that do and do not command obedience, is that the just law "uplifts human personality" while the unjust law degrades it. The just law promotes and encourages the good life: the life lived in conditions of true equality, liberty, and community, as those ideals are understood in our visions, our aspirations, our dreams, and, occasionally, our experiences. The unjust law, quite simply, is the law that denies or frustrates or denigrates that law. The former commands obedience—is true law; the latter does not.

As idealism implies a progressive version of natural law, existentialism lends itself to a progressive interpretation of legal positivism. Existential progressives, like legal conservatives, tend to be legal positivists: they share with legal conservatives an overriding skepticism toward the aspiration to moral knowledge inherent in both the traditionalist and idealist versions of the natural law tradition. For the existential progressive, as for the legal conservative, the "law" is not that which aspires toward a moral ideal (whether informed by the community's tradition or the disempowered's utopian vision). Rather, law (whatever it ought to be) is nothing more than a series of actual, concrete choices made by particular, identifiable powerful actors. Both progressive and conservative positivists view "law" as importantly identified not with a continuing effort to achieve congruence with a moral ideal, but as a set of contingent choices. Law is not a set of principles that "uplifts human personality." Law is a set of acts and choices taken by particular people at particular moments in history.

The pivotal psychic difference between conservative and progressive positivists is political, not jurisprudential: whereas the conservative positivist sees in the set of acts and choices that constitute the "law" opportunities for obedience to prior legal commands, the progressive positivist sees in the same set of acts and choices opportunities for authenticity, freedom, self-actualization, and judgment. The resulting jurisprudential difference is that the conservative positivist identifies the relevant history—the set of choices—that defines the content of "law" with the past, whereas the progressive positivist identifies "law" with the future possibilities and the choices necessitated by virtually any and all verbal legal formulations.

The progressive positivist views law as an open set of possibilities, and thus a vehicle for change, growth, and authenticity, rather than the static product of an unambiguous past historical process, and thus a vehicle for obedience. Suzanna Sherry wrote:

> Above all, judging is an act of controlled creativity. Like writing at its best, it both draws on and evokes memories of what has gone before, but by innovation rather than by mimicry. It simultaneously acknowledges our debt to the past and denies that the past should control the present. The task of the pragmatist decisionmaker is to reconcile a flawed tradition with an imperfect world so as to improve both and do damage to neither. We can argue about whether a particular judge does so well or badly, but we should recognize that neither her job nor ours can ever be mechanical.[83]

"Law," then, for the conservative positivist, mandates obedience, while for the progressive positivist, it mandates choice. Law creates, rather than closes, possibility and responsibility. For the progressive positivist, the judge, like the citizen, is never bound and can never be bound: the judge, like the citizen, actively chooses the law she obeys; she has no choice but freedom. Understanding one's freedom—facing the necessity of choice—is the only moral imperative. It is the path and the only path toward authenticity. It is therefore recognition of freedom or authenticity—and not, as Judge Easterbrook insists, the acquiescence in a mandate of obedience[84]— that constitutes the standard by which the outsider or critic can judge the morality of the judge. Duncan Kennedy described the phenomenology of this necessity of choice:

> If you tell me that there is always a right answer to a legal problem, I will answer with these cases in which my experience was that the law was indeterminate, or that I gave it its determinate shape as a matter of my free ethical or political choice. It is true that when we are unselfconsciously applying rules together, we have an unselfconscious experience of social objectivity. We know what is going to happen next by mentally applying the rule as others will, and then they apply the rule and it comes out the way we thought it would. But this is not in fact objectivity, and it is always vulnerable to different kinds of disruption—intentional and accidental—that suddenly disappoint our expectations of consensus and make people question their own sanity and that of others. Thus vulnerability of the field, its plasticity, its

instability, are just as essential to it as we experience it as its sporadic quality of resistance.[85]

For the progressive positivist, then, both the reality of legal decision making and the ideal toward which law ought to aspire is a recognition of one's authenticity through the conscious recognition of the necessity of freedom. The reality of the judge's decision is in a sense a microcosm of the ideal form of social life toward which law should aspire: it is a necessarily free choice, unconstrained by prior commands, that becomes a good choice if the judge is conscious of her freedom, and hence achieves some degree of self-realization, when making it.

Finally, egalitarian, antisubordination progressives, like free-market conservatives, tend toward a pragmatic, incremental, and instrumental approach toward legal progress, and hence toward an instrumental understanding of the meaning of law as well. Both antisubordination progressives and free-market conservatives tend to identify the content of law not with a moral ideal, nor with particular concrete actions, but with its overriding purpose. The pivotal differences between progressive and conservative instrumentalists, again, are attitudinal and ethical. Whereas the conservative instrumentalist's moral skepticism is grounded in a neo-Darwinian embrace of competitive outcomes, and hence competitive values, the progressive instrumentalist's moral skepticism is grounded in antipathy to the hierarchies on which "competitive" outcomes rest. The progressive instrumentalist consequently resists precisely the hierarchies—the inequalities—that produce the competitive outcomes which the conservative embraces. The progressive instrumentalist sees law not as purposively freeing or protecting "competitive" process or outcome, as the conservative instrumentalist envisions, but as ideally and purposively ameliorating, addressing, and in the long run abolishing the hierarchical systems of domination and subordination masked as competitive processes producing "competitive" outcomes. For the progressive instrumentalist, law, in its progressive essence, resists, tempers, reduces, ameliorates, and ultimately should abolish natural, pre-, or nonlegal social hierarchy.

Progressive jurisprudence, then, is variously committed to an idealistic vision of natural law as the embodiment of a particular conception of the good, an anarchic and existential conception of positive law as inherently possibilistic and open-ended—as inviting choice, movement, and necessitating freedom—or an instrumental resistance to hierarchy and a willingness to use law as a tool to that end. The relation between the ex-

Table 9-3.

Authority	Progressive Politics	Jurisprudence
Experience of ideals	Idealistic progressivism	Progressive natural law
Experience of freedom	Existential progressivism	Progressive legal positivism
Experience of social hierarchy	Antisubordination progressivism	Progressive instrumentalism

Table 9-4.

	Natural Law	Legal Positivism	Instrumentalism
Conservative (reliance on authority; attraction to social power)	Moralism/traditionalism	"Imperativist" positivism	Procompetitive instrumentalism
Progressive (reliance on experience; antipathy to social power)	Idealism	"Possibilistic" positivism	Antisubordinationist instrumentalism

periences of subordinated persons, progressive politics and jurisprudence might be schematized as in Table 9-3.

Based on sharply contrasting politics, the jurisprudence of progressive and conservative constitutionalists thus sharply contrast as well, as in Table 9-4.

PROGRESSIVE CONSTITUTIONALISM

Progressive constitutional theory begins with a critique of conservative constitutionalism, which parallels the critique of conservative political theory of the center of progressive politics. In every case in which the Court acts to restrain the normative power of "the state" and to entrench or encourage the community's normative authority, it is also, of necessity, strengthening the social or private power of whatever social institution or private group undergirds that authority. Thus, in all of the due process cases discussed above, the Supreme Court did indeed restrain, in some way, the power of "the state" to act on "its own" normative vision: in

Bowers v. Hardwick, Michael H. v. Gerald D., and *Webster v. Reproductive Health Services* it restrained the power of the judiciary to legislate on the basis of "its own" conception of the good; in *DeShaney v. Winnebago County Department of Social Services,* the power of the executive policing branch to interfere with family life; and in *Penry v. Lynaugh* and *Stanford v. Kentucky,* the power of judges to dictate the terms of the community's conscience. It is also true, however, that in each of these cases, the Court expanded, legitimated, and further entrenched the clusters of social power that undergird the various sources of communal normative authority to which the Court insisted the political state must defer. Thus, *DeShaney* limited the power of policing agencies over families, but at the same time legitimated and further entrenched the familial power of parents, stepparents, and foster parents to abuse children physically—a power that undoubtedly underscores both the father's normative authority within the family, and the family's normative authority in society. *Bowers* limited judicial power, but left intact the power of the heterosexual majority over the subordinated homosexual minority, just as *Webster* left intact the power of some men over many women's reproductive and sexual lives. In each case, the "passive" judicial response limited "state power," and hence "state hierarchy," but it exacerbated social hierarchy and the injustices to which those hierarchies give rise.

Conservative understandings of equality and of the equal protection clause are subject to a similar criticism. The Court's opinion in *City of Richmond v. J. A. Croson Co.*[86] undoubtedly restricted "state power": the Court restricted the power of the Richmond City Council to interfere in the competitive process of the construction industry, and by so doing enhanced the individual's entitlement to compete in that market free from the influence of racial factors. What the opinion also does, however, is reinforce the social power of economically privileged whites to set the terms of inclusion for economically disenfranchised blacks, just as the Court's opinion in *Washington v. Davis*[87] helped entrench the racial identity of the Washington, D.C., police force by affirming the testing standards employed by the white-dominated department. Both opinions thus read the equal protection clause in a way that simultaneously restricts the power of states and enhances the economic and social power of whites.

Lastly, conservative understandings of the nature of constitutional interpretation, while concededly restrictive of the power of judicial state actors to impose their "own" values or conceptions of the good, expand considerably the power of the dominant forces and victors of this country's militaristic and legalistic past. Progressive scholar Suzanna Sherry makes the point this way:

> This search for interpretive devices that eliminate judicial discretion is, at bottom, profoundly positivist and profoundly relativist. It treats the written Constitution as an absolute sovereign by excluding any examination of the moral dimensions of its language. Such a view is positivist in the sense that "it makes no difference . . . if the sovereign command is nothing but arbitrary will: order still requires capitulating to it." It is relativist in that it denies the availability of any higher truth than what a particular society has already chosen to embody in its written fundamental law.
>
> . . . The desire to appeal to the absolute authority of the historical Constitution is also self-replicating. To the extent that we as a society relieve ourselves of the obligation to make difficult moral decisions, we further undermine our capacity to do so. Moral sensibilities, whether of an individual or of a community, are best developed by making moral choices.
>
> . . . To tell judges that they must engage in "value-free" judging—to confine them to the unsupplemented text—diminishes the very definition of moral choice by curtailing the sources of moral authority. Moreover, once we recognize that the legislature should not always prevail, we must delegate final moral authority somewhere: should we entrust it to judges who can reason about both morality and consent, or to an ancient document simply because it reflects our erstwhile will? Federal judges, however unrepresentative, are a part of the community in a way in which dead founders and parchment under glass cannot be.[88]

Progressive constitutional theory, however, does not stop with critique. Like conservative constitutional commitments, the affirmative progressive constitutional commitments I examine here—notably a substantive understanding of the equality guaranteed by the Fourteenth Amendment, a positive account of the liberty protected by the due process clause, and what I call a possibilistic understanding of the nature of constitutional interpretation—are ultimately rooted in political and ethical attitudes toward power and authority. Each of these three commitments is supported by most of the major progressive constitutional theorists. As was also the case with the conservative paradigm, however, different progressives support each element of the progressive paradigm for often contrasting and conflicting reasons. Those internal conflicts in turn reveal the diversity and breadth of contemporary progressive constitutional thought, as well as its political and jurisprudential roots.

Equal Protection Jurisprudence. Let me begin with the progressive understanding of the meaning of equality, and hence of the import of the equal protection clause. Very generally, "equality," for the progressive constitutionalist, means substantive equality and the "equal protection clause" constitutes a commitment to rid the culture of the stultifying, oppressive, and damaging consequences of the hierarchic domination of some social groups by others. In their view, the clause is aimed not at protecting competitive rationality against the pernicious effects of race or sex-conscious irrational legislative categorization, but at correcting maldistributions of social power, wealth, and prestige. The targeted evil is not irrational state action, but state action or inaction—rational or not, and intentional or not—that perpetuates the damaging social, economic, domestic, or private domination of some groups by others. So understood, the clause is a tool for dismantling society's racist, misogynist, homophobic, patriarchic, and economic hierarchies. The goal of the equal protection clause is not rational competition, but substantive social equality.

Thus, according to various progressive arguments, the equal protection clause not only permits, but positively requires that the community take affirmative steps to achieve substantive racial justice;[89] that a state or municipality enact ordinances to rid itself of a subordinating pornographic subculture;[90] that the state protect women's reproductive choices to rid itself of the patriarchal expropriation of women's reproductive labor;[91] that its law enforcement resources be committed to ridding women's lives of private violence, both sexual and otherwise;[92] that the state take positive steps to eliminate heterosexual privilege;[93] and that the community in some way commit its economic resources to eliminating the subordinating effects of severe material impoverishment.[94] "Equal protection," for the progressive, means the eradication of social, economic, and private, as well as legal, hierarchies that damage. The contrast with conservative understanding of that phrase is nothing less than stunning: for the conservative, the clause invalidates a wide range of state-sponsored "affirmative actions" on behalf of the disempowered; for the progressive, it not only permits such actions but may well require them.

This interpretation of the equal protection clause as requiring substantive rather than formal equality, and as targeting maldistributions of social power, rather than irrational legislative classifications, is supported by all three progressive political and jurisprudential movements, but it finds its clearest support from progressive instrumentalists. For progressive instrumentalists, as for all instrumentalists, the meaning of a law is its purpose, and for progressive instrumentalists distinctively, the purpose of the equal protection clause is antisubordination: the eradication of hierarchies. Antisubordination feminist Catharine MacKinnon expressed this point in the context of women's subordination, but her logic can readily be generalized to all subordinate groups:

> There is an alternative approach, one that threads its way through existing law and expresses, I think, the reason equality law exists in the first place. . . . In this approach, an equality question is a question of the distribution of power. Gender is also a question of power, specifically of male supremacy and female subordination. The question of equality, from the standpoint of what it is going to take to get it, is at root a question of hierarchy, which—as power succeeds in constructing social perception and social reality—derivatively becomes a categorical distinction, a difference. Here, on the first day that matters, dominance was achieved probably by force. By the second day, division along the same lines had to be relatively firmly in place. On the third day, if not sooner, differences were demarcated, together with social systems to exaggerate them in perception and in fact, because the systematically differential delivery of benefits and deprivations required making no mistake about who was who. . . .
>
> I call this the dominance approach, and it is the ground I have been standing on in criticizing mainstream law. The goal of this dissident approach is not to make legal categories trace and trap the way things are. It is not to make rules that fit reality. It is critical of reality. Its task is not to formulate abstract standards that will produce determinate outcomes in particular cases. Its project is more substantive, more jurisprudential than formulaic, which is why it is difficult for the mainstream discourse to dignify it as an approach to doctrine or to imagine it as a rule of law at all.[95]

As mentioned above, an antisubordinationist reading of the equal protection clause lends not just constitutional support, but a constitutional mandate, to state-sponsored affirmative action plans. If, as MacKinnon suggests, the reason we have equality law in the first place is to eradicate the subordination of some groups by others, then states are not only permitted, but obligated to take affirmative steps to achieve social equality. Thus, progressive constitutional theorist David Strauss reasons that the equal protection clause and that clause's most important interpretive gloss, *Brown v. Board of Education*,[96] are best read not to require color-blind legislation, as numerous conservative theorists and jurists now assume, but, rather, to require legislation that will achieve a racially equal society:

> The prohibition against discrimination established by Brown is not rooted in colorblindness at all. Instead, it is, like affirmative action, deeply race-conscious; like affirmative action, the prohibition against discrimination reflects a deliberate decision to treat blacks differently from other groups, even at the expense of innocent whites. It follows that affirmative action is not at odds with the principle of nondiscrimination established by Brown but is instead logically continuous with that principle. It also follows that the interesting question is not whether the Constitution permits affirmative action but why the Constitution does not require affirmative action.
>
> . . . The prohibition against racial discrimination prohibits—and must necessarily prohibit—the use of accurate racial generalizations that disadvantage blacks. But to prohibit accurate racial generalizations is to engage in something very much like affirmative action. Specifically, a principle prohibiting accurate racial generalizations has many of the same characteristics as affirmative action; and the various possible explanations of why accurate racial generalizations are unconstitutional lead to the conclusion that failure to engage in affirmative action may also sometimes be unconstitutional.[97]

This substantive interpretation of equality as the true meaning of equal protection is also supported by progressivism's existential strand. For the progressive existentialist, the most significant barrier to enjoyment of a free, authentic, and hence good life is the existence of rigid social, private, and domestic hierarchies, and for the progressive positivist, law is both a sphere of free choice, and a means by which social life can be made more free. The equal protection clause, then, properly read, should serve as a mechanism by which social hierarchies are constantly challenged and undermined, and the power they embody redistributed. Race-conscious affirmative action plans, then, become the prototype for legislation mandated or suggested by the equal protection clause: when undertaking affirmative action, a state uses its power under the guidance of the equal protection clause to challenge and undermine social and private racial hierarchy.

More generally, the ideal and true content of the equal protection clause, for the existential progressive, is simply its negative potential for upsetting the settled distributions of power and wealth that constrain as they define private life. Unger's reinterpretation of the equal protection clause as ideally encoding a set of "destabilization rights," set forth in his classic essay "The Critical Legal Studies Movement," [98] contains the clearest restatement of this existential ideal:

> The central ideal of the system of destabilization rights is to provide a claim upon governmental power obliging government to disrupt those forms of division and hierarchy that, contrary to the spirit of the constitution, manage to achieve stability only by distancing themselves from the transformative conflicts that might disturb them. . . . Rather than just correct specific collective disadvantages within the circumscribed area of state action, it would also seek to break up entire areas of institutional life and social practice that run contrary to the scheme of the new-modeled constitution. . . .
>
> Sometimes a destabilization right might work through a direct invalidation of established law. . . . The destabilization right might also operate in another, far less extreme way. It would act not to invalidate laws directly but to disrupt power orders in particular institutions or localized areas of social practice. The power orders to be disrupted would be those that, in violation of the principles governing social and economic organization had become effectively insulated from the disturbances of democratic conflict. As a result, they would threaten to eviscerate the force of democratic processes in just the way that citadels of private power do in the existing democracies. . . . The guiding criteria for the development of this branch of the law would be found in the principles that inform social and economic organization in the empowered democracy.[99]

Finally, progressive idealists and natural lawyers also understand the equal protection clause substantively rather than formally. For the progressive idealist, it is some measure of substantive equality and some measure of freedom from the economic, material, social, and spiritual burdens of inequality, rather than freedom from state-sponsored "irrationality" that is the precondition of a good life. For the progressive idealist, the law should embody these ideals, and therefore, for the progressive natural lawyer no less than the progressive positivist and instrumentalist, substantive equality—the eradication of damaging hierarchy—is that to which the Fourteenth Amendment directs the legislative energies of the state.

The content of that guarantee, however, is somewhat different for the progressive natural lawyer than for the progressive existentialist or antisubordinationist. As noted above, the "ideal" for the progressive idealist is the good life—in King's words the "uplifted personality"—rather than either pure freedom, as for the existentialist, or pure equality, as for the antisubordinationist. Therefore, for the progressive natural lawyer, the equal protection clause ensures "substantive equality" because by doing so it ensures those minimal conditions necessary for an ideally flourishing life; the clause is less concerned, by this view, with establishing either the conditions for truly free choice or the conditions for absolute social and political equality. Abuses of social power and the racial, sexual, and class hierarchies that sustain those abuses make the "ideal life" inaccessible to the socially subordinated. Racism occasions an invasion of body, mind, and soul that Patricia Williams has tellingly called "spirit murder";[100] misogyny engenders a self-hatred and self-denial that often precludes life itself, and certainly the good life; and poverty leaves no time, much less energy, resources, or will, for activities that enrich the individual and integrate her in the community. Idealists and progressive natural lawyers are consequently more likely to target the eradication of poverty, racism, and misogyny, rather than more abstract notions of "equality" or "freedom," as the true goal of the equal protection guarantee; it is the damage wrought by those substantive conditions, after all, that frustrates and precludes a flourishing life.

Unsurprisingly, it has been idealist progressive scholars grounded in a natural law tradition, rather than either existentialist scholars rooted in critical positivism or antisubordinationists rooted in pragmatism, who have argued most strenuously that the Fourteenth Amendment requires the state to protect against the most egregious risks of massive economic inequality—or, stated affirmatively, that the state has a constitutional duty to guarantee welfare rights. Thus, it was the constitutional theorist Frank Michelman, in the 1960s and 1970s, who did more than any other to popularize the idealistic argument that "equal protection" requires the states to guarantee a minimal level of welfare.[101] Without food, shelter, and clothing, other constitutional entitlements are virtually meaningless; but, more significantly, for the idealist, without food, shelter, and clothing, life itself is a burden and a misery. In keeping both with idealist progressive politics and with naturalist jurisprudence, Michelman argued that not only should the Constitution protect minimal welfare rights, but that, properly read, it in fact already does:

> Without basic education—without the literacy, fluency and elementary understanding of politics and markets that are hard to obtain without it—what hope is there of effective participation in the last-resort political system? On just this basis, it seems, the Supreme Court itself has expressly allowed that "some identifiable quantum of education" may be a constitutional right. But if so, then, what about life itself, health and vigor, presentable attire, or shelter not only from the elements but from the physical and psychological onslaughts of social debilitation? Are not these interests the universal, rock-bottom prerequisites of effective participation in democratic representation . . . ? How can there be . . . sophisticated rights to a formally unbiased majoritarian system, but no rights to the indispensable means of effective participation in that system? How can the Supreme Court admit the possibility of a right to minimum education, but go out of its way to deny flatly any right to subsistence, shelter, or health care? [102]

In contrast to MacKinnon's antisubordinationist argument for substantive equality given above,[103] Michelman's idealistic arguments for welfare rights are premised on the assumption that it is the good life, not the equal life, that is the "point" of equality law. Thus, Michelman tended to emphasize the difference, rather than commonality, between absolute egalitarian conceptions of equal protection, and idealist conceptions. In his seminal defense of welfare rights, he was clearly more concerned with distinguishing his idealistic argument for the protection of welfare rights through equality law from egalitarian and antisubordinationist interpretations of equal protection than with distinguishing his conception from formal antidiscrimination models of the clause:

> [T]he judicial "equality" explosion of recent times has largely been ignited by reawakened sensitivity, not to equality, but to a quite different sort of value or claim which might better be called "minimum welfare." In the recent judicial handiwork which has been hailed (and reviled) as an "egalitarian revolution," a particularly striking and propitious note has been sounded through those acts whereby the Court

has directly shielded poor persons from the most elemental consequence of poverty . . . .

Of course, the Court's "egalitarian" interventions are often occasioned by problems which would not exist but for economic inequality. Yet I hope to make clear that in many instances their purposes
could be more soundly and satisfyingly understood as vindication of a
state's duty to protect against certain hazards which are endemic in an
unequal society, rather than vindication of a duty to avoid complicity
in unequal treatment.[104]

For all three branches of progressive thought, although for different
reasons, the equal protection clause is concerned not with pernicious state
action, or irrational classifications, or even badly motivated governance,
but rather, with the profound damage brought about through gross disparities of social power. Although their reasons differ, and differ profoundly,
progressives believe the state is affirmatively obligated under the Constitution to use its legal power to protect its citizens, and protect them equally,
from the damage wrought by abusive social power and the damaging hierarchies of race, gender, and class to which that power gives rise. The goal
of equal protection for the progressive quite clearly has nothing to do with
color blindness, sex blindness, or class blindness, unless those strategies
are conducive to some other end. The goal, rather, is a social life freed of
the crushing consequences of inequality; the goal is an equal society.

Liberty and Due Process Jurisprudence. For the progressive constitutionalist, the "liberty" to which we are entitled under the due process clause is
"affirmative" just as the "equality" to which we are entitled under equal
protection is "substantive": "liberty" means the affirmative liberty to live
a meaningfully free and autonomous life, rather than, as for the conservative, the liberty to live the good life as defined by community standards and
as restricted through processes defined by law. The due process clause, for
progressives, guarantees the freedom to make choices that will truly enrich
our lives, rather than the freedom to make those choices sanctioned by a
community's authoritative traditions through processes established by its
positive law. Thus, for some progressives, the clause minimally guarantees
the freedom to choose when and with whom to have and raise children.
For others, it guarantees the freedom to decide when, if, and with whom
to be sexually intimate. For others, it guarantees the material support nec-

essary to a productive and unalienated work life, to a healthy private home and community life, and to meaningful participation in the public sphere of democratic decision making. The common thread in these progressive positions is clear: the due process clause, for progressives, commits the state to ensure the conditions necessary to the enjoyment of affirmative liberty.

The contrast with the conservative's understanding of the guarantee of liberty is again dramatic. For the progressive, the affirmative liberty the due process clause guarantees not only invalidates the antisodomy statute upheld in *Bowers v. Hardwick,* but may well affirmatively require that the state take some action to eradicate the harmful effects of the homophobia to which not only state action, but religious dogma and communitarian "traditions," have given rise.

Similarly, for the progressive, the affirmative liberty the due process clause guarantees does not just invalidate antiabortion statutes of the sort upheld in *Webster v. Reproductive Health Services,* but may require the state to take action to ensure the availability of the means of reproductive freedom to all women, regardless of their economic class. Put generally, for the progressive, the clause should be used to challenge the social power that gives rise to the very normative authority that the conservative argues constitutes the source of wisdom which law should incorporate and which the due process clause must accordingly protect.

Roe v. Wade is as central to the progressive paradigm of privacy, liberty, and due process as *Bowers* is to the conservative. In sharp contrast not only to conservative constitutionalists, but also to a number of liberal legalists, progressive constitutionalists tend to support *Roe* and the positive understanding of liberty on which it is based. Again, though, their reasons for doing so diverge.

For instance, the affirmation of the "positive liberty" to choose the meaning and content of one's reproductive life at the heart of Roe's reasoning is at least exemplary, if not emblematic, of the meaning of "authenticity" that the existentialist equates with the good life. For the existentialist, the right to abortion "denaturalizes" (to use Unger's word) and consequently humanizes the pregnant woman, ensuring the choice essential for authentic selfhood and humanness, and facilitating enjoyment of a genuinely free life. The "pro-choice" label for reproductive rights activists thus resonates with existential progressive thought: for the existentialist, the choice itself is what is of value, the choice itself is what is advocated. The freedom to decide one's life's course, rather than to have it thrust upon her, is what gives a life moral meaning. This choice, then, for the existential progressive, as a constitutional matter, cannot be legally interfered with; any interference by the state constitutes a "due process" violation. The due process clause guarantees not just freedom from undue and illegal interference with one's private life, but the affirmative liberty to pursue those choices most fundamental to the fruits of affirmative liberty. The decision to carry a pregnancy to term is clearly such a choice. Although most of Suzanna Sherry's work is idealist rather than existentialist, her defense of reproductive freedom sounds these existential themes:

> Anti-abortion laws deprive women of the opportunity to choose freely among these discretionary moral choices, and hence of the opportunity to exercise and improve their capacity for moral knowledge and moral choice. Such laws coerce women's moral decisions, stifling their ability for growth through self-criticism. Anti-abortion laws thus interfere with . . . the basic aspects of human morality and human flourishing. Furthermore, to the extent that a moral choice is coerced, the actor is less likely to accept responsibility for that choice. The coercion of anti-abortion laws discourages women from developing the moral sensibilities that come from making moral choices and accepting responsibility for them. It keeps them, in short, from becoming virtuous.[105]

Progressive positivists support the outcome in *Roe* not only for moral reasons, but for a purely jurisprudential reason as well, a reason that is also rooted in existential premises. The existentially inspired progressive positivist, of all constitutional theorists, will be the least bothered by the apparent "activism" exhibited by the Court's willingness to "discover" a fundamental right to reproductive freedom in the unwritten part of the Constitution. For the existential positivist this activism is a necessary, inevitable aspect of judicial decision making, as it is of all decision making; it is certainly not peculiar to *Roe*. What is peculiar to *Roe* is the Court's willingness to acknowledge the necessity of choice with which it is inevitably faced when making constitutional decisions. Far from condemning the decision for that acknowledgment, however, the existential positivist is likely to commend it. The Court must inevitably "act" when making decisions, and what that inevitably entails is both choice and responsibility. The acknowledgment of that existential reality in *Roe,* then, is constitutional decision making at its best.

The progressive idealist and the progressive natural lawyer will also support *Roe* and the affirmative conception of liberty on which it is based, although for a different reason. For the idealist, "affirmative liberty"— "freedom to" rather than "freedom from"—requires, above all else, self-possession; in turn, self-possession requires that the individual have the authority to make decisions regarding family, reproduction, and sexual intimacy free from interference from the community's normative commitments. This degree of authority and control over family, reproduction, and intimacy is, for the idealist, essential to any meaningful ideal of self-possession, self-will, and positive liberty that the constitutional guarantee of due process could conceivably be meant to protect.

This idealistic reasoning—that the ideal life must contain the power to make these decisions independent of the community's moral beliefs—is at least arguably one connecting strand of the pre-*Bowers* privacy cases. Although, as I suggested in Chapter 8 the *Roe* Court for the most part depended on traditionalist and conservative arguments, one unifying principle of pre-*Bowers* privacy law rested on the idealist premise that limits on the community's normative authority should be drawn from idealistic conceptions of what a qualitatively good individual life requires, and from the progressive natural lawyer's assumption that "the law," in this case, constitutional law, ideally and correctly read, incorporates those ideals. Thus, in *Meyer v. Nebraska*,[106] one of the Court's earliest privacy cases, the Court merged conservative-traditionalist with progressive-idealist arguments to strike down a state mandatory education law:

> [T]he liberty . . . guaranteed . . . [by the due process clause of the Fourteenth Amendment] denotes not merely freedom from bodily restraint but also the right of the individual to contract, to engage in any of the common occupations of life, to acquire useful knowledge, to marry, establish a home and bring up children, to worship God according to the dictates of his own conscience, and generally to enjoy those privileges long recognized at common law as essential to the orderly pursuit of happiness by free men.[107]

Justice Harlan in *Poe v. Ullman*[108] and later in *Griswold v. Connecticut*[109] similarly relied on both conservative and progressive arguments:

> Due process has not been reduced to any formula; its content cannot be determined by reference to any code. . . . The balance [it strikes between individual liberty and the demands of organized society] . . . is the balance struck by this country, having regard to what history

teaches are the traditions from which it developed as well as the traditions from which it broke. That tradition is a living thing. . . .

. . .

. . . The State . . . asserts that it is acting to protect the moral welfare of its citizenry

. . .

. . . [Society] has traditionally concerned itself with the moral soundness of its people. . . .

. . .

But, as might be expected, we are not presented simply with this moral judgment to be passed on as an abstract proposition. The secular state . . . must operate in the realm of behavior, . . . and where it does so operate . . . the choice of means becomes relevant . . . .

Precisely what is involved here is this: the State is asserting the right to enforce its moral judgement by intruding upon the most intimate details of the marital relation with the full power of the criminal law. . . . [T]he Statute allows the State to enquire into, prove and punish married people for the private use of their marital intimacy.[110]

And finally, in *Roe v. Wade,* the Court made explicit that the liberty being protected was the liberty to live a good life, as defined by ideals of autonomy and freedom from want and unreasonable restraint:

This right of privacy, whether it be founded in the Fourteenth Amendment's concept of personal liberty . . . as we feel it is, or . . . in the Ninth Amendment[], . . . is broad enough to encompass a woman's decision whether or not to terminate her pregnancy. The detriment that the State would impose upon the pregnant woman by denying this choice altogether is apparent. Specific and direct harm medically diagnosable even in early pregnancy may be involved. Maternity, or additional offspring, may force upon the woman a distressful life and future. Psychological harm may be imminent. Mental and physical health may be taxed by child care. There is also the distress, for all concerned, associated with the unwanted child, and there is the problem of bringing a child into a family already unable, psychologically and otherwise, to care for it. In other cases, . . . the additional difficulties and continuing stigma of unwed motherhood may be involved.[111]

The antisubordinationist's support for a positive understanding of the meaning of liberty is considerably more tentative than that displayed by the justices of the Warren and Burger Courts. Indeed, of all progressives, only antisubordinationists tend to be critical of both the idealism-based argument and the "authenticity" claims that resonate in the Court's reasoning. For the antisubordinationist, and hence for the progressive instrumentalist, neither the authentic, self-conscious choice which concerns the existentialist, nor the privacy necessary to the ideal life for the idealist-progressive, are truly possible within conditions of societal subordination. Consequently, neither authenticity nor privacy justifies an affirmative understanding of the liberty to which individuals are entitled. Providing individuals with the freedom to make personal or private decisions in the face of the influence of the community's normative authority, within general conditions of inequality, may do nothing to further the empowerment of the subordinate, and hence nothing to further their true well-being. Indeed, freeing the individual from the constraints of the community's normative authority may prove harmful: it may simply render her more vulnerable to the degrading and subordinating pressures of a now insulated private sphere of personal and familial political hierarchy. Thus, antisubordination progressives have little to say about "positive liberty" in general, and generally do not support the outcome in *Roe* on that basis. Catharine MacKinnon's arguments against the reasoning in *Roe* (not the outcome) are representative:

> Arguments for abortions under the rubric of feminism have rested upon the right to control one's own body—gender neutral. I think that argument has been appealing for the same reasons it is inadequate: socially, women's bodies have not been ours; we have not controlled their meanings and destinies. . . .
>
> In private, consent tends to be presumed. It is true that a showing of coercion voids this presumption. But the problem is getting anything private to be perceived as coercive. Why one would allow force in private—the "why doesn't she leave" question asked of battered women—is a question given its urgency by the social meaning of the private as a sphere of choice. But for women the measure of the intimacy has been the measure of the oppression. This is why feminism has had to explode the private. This is why feminism has seen the personal as the political. The private is the public for those for whom the personal is the political. In this sense, there is no private, either normatively or empirically. Feminism confronts the fact that women have no privacy to lose or to guarantee. We are not inviolable. Our sexuality is not only violable, it is—hence, we are—seen in and as our

violation. To confront the fact that we have no privacy is to confront the intimate degradation of women as the public order.[112]

The antisubordinationist argument for the result in *Roe,* and for positive liberty in general, is very different from the reasoning that has tended to dominate the Court's privacy jurisprudence. Antisubordination progressive constitutionalists generally urge that the result in *Roe* should be grounded in equality, rather than liberty, and, accordingly, that it should be doctrinally based on the equal protection clause, rather than the due process clause or any other penumbral constitutional right.[113] For the antisubordinationist, the right to secure an abortion should be constitutionally protected, not because such a right is essential to an ideally conceived individual life, but because it is essential to the struggle of a subordinated group—women—against the disproportionate power of a dominant group—men. Whether accomplished through constitutional, adjudicative, or legislative means, securing for women control over the abortion decision is one instrumental means, among others, by which the political imbalance occasioned by male control over female sexuality and reproduction may be righted. Thus, antisubordination constitutionalists tend to argue that the goal of equality and the constitutional right to equal protection—not liberty, privacy, or due process—should be the foundation of the Court's abortion jurisprudence.

It is worth noting that the liberal justices who continue to support *Roe* are increasingly shifting their argument away from due process and privacy arguments, toward explicitly antisubordinationist equality-based arguments. Thus, in his dissenting opinion in *Webster,* in which the Court upheld substantial regulatory restrictions on access to abortion facilities and services, Justice Blackmun opined: "I fear for the future. I fear for the liberty and equality of the millions of women who have lived and come of age in the 16 years since *Roe* was decided. I fear for the integrity of, and public esteem for, this Court."[114] He later elaborated:

Thus, "not with a bang, but a whimper," the plurality discards a landmark case of the last generation, and casts into darkness the hopes and visions of every woman in this country who had come to believe that the Constitution guaranteed her the right to exercise some control over her unique ability to bear children. The plurality does so either oblivious or insensitive to the fact that millions of women, and their families, have ordered their lives around the right to reproductive choice, and that this right has become vital to the full participation of women in the economic and political walks of American life. The plurality would clear the way once again for government to force upon women the physical labor and specific and direct medical and psychological harms that may accompany carrying a fetus to term. The plurality would clear the way again for the State to conscript a woman's body and to force upon her a "distressful life and future." [115]

Progressive dissent from the *Bowers* decision reflects the same set of concerns. For existentialist and progressive positivists, the community's authoritative control over the morality and legality of sexuality that the opinion legitimates cuts off one avenue by which the individual actualizes his or her potential for self-realization, and hence authenticity, just as does the community's authoritative control over the morality of reproduction, legitimated by the anti-*Roe* regression. Sexual activity is one sphere within which the individual creates himself or herself through making choices, living with decisions, and taking responsibility for the consequences. The normative authority of the community is nothing but an obstacle to that freedom. The "liberty" prong of the due process clause minimally protects those areas of decision making most vital to the formation of selfhood, and sexuality is one such sphere. [116]

Idealist objection to *Bowers* rests on slightly different arguments. For the idealist, individual freedom with respect to sexual choice is necessary not so much because of the centrality of choice to selfhood as because of the nature of sexuality. An ideally lived life, if it includes sexuality (which it need not), must embrace a sexuality grounded in the individual's desire for intimacy, sharing, and openness, not in training instilled by the community's normative authority, the force of its positive law, or the violence of its informal mechanisms of sexual regulation. It is for this reason that the affirmative liberty protected by the liberty clause of the Fourteenth Amendment must include the liberty to decide and act upon one's sexual orientation.

The conclusion that sexuality is "private," and therefore outside the reach of state or community control, rests, for the idealist, on a conception of the good life and a view of the nature of sexuality: for sexuality to be a part of a good life it must be chosen for reasons other than community coercion. Intimacy and sharing may be part of an ideally constructed life, but self-alienation and lack of self-possession clearly are not. Whether participation in sexuality is the former or the latter depends largely on whether or not the form of sexuality in which participation is sought is prescribed or chosen. The due process clause, by this view, protects against intrusion by the community's dominant moral or social authority, manifested in the state's criminal law, into the individual's choice of sexual orientation, for the imminently contingent reason that such intrusion renders impossible the form of life the due process clause is aimed to protect or foster.[117]

The antisubordinationist's dissatisfaction with the outcome in *Bowers* is different still. For the antisubordinationist, the Court had an opportunity and an obligation in *Bowers* to attack an illegitimate social hierarchy—the domination of the homosexual minority community by the heterosexual majority—and refused to act on it. The evil of state intrusion into sexual decisions is not so much that such intrusion interferes with decisions essential to living the good life, as that it underscores and encourages the suppression of an already subordinate group. As in the reproductive context, then, the antisubordinationists' argument against the outcome in *Bowers* rests more on equality principles than on liberty principles, and doctrinally more on the equal protection clause than on the due process clause. The target of constitutional intervention in the context of sexual orientation, according to the antisubordination constitutionalist, should not be sexual privacy and liberty, but sexual hierarchy and heterosexual privilege. Where state law furthers, underscores, or encourages that illegitimate hierarchical ordering, the Court is constitutionally obligated to strike it down.[118]

Again, then, although their reasons differ, the due process clause, for progressives, is targeted at constraints on individual liberty imposed by illegitimate social power and ordering, rather than, as for conservatives, at constraints imposed by illegal state power on individual liberty as defined and legitimated by social authority. Correlatively, the goal of the clause for progressives is a positively free life—one in which choice is genuine and conducive to growth—rather than a legitimating mark of underlying coercion. The state, through the due process clause, is required to take action to facilitate, protect, and ensure those choices most essential to that freedom. The ideal of due process, then, is an individual life free from illegitimate social coercion facilitated by hierarchies of class, gender, or race. The goal is an affirmatively autonomous existence: a meaningfully flourishing, independent, enriched individual life.

Constitutional Interpretation. Finally, for most progressives, the Constitution is an essentially open text inviting interpretation, rather than mandating obedience to original intent or legislative will. All three strands of progressive thought support this interpretive claim. The reasons are familiar and can be summarized quickly.

First, for progressive positivists, the Constitution is possibilistic rather than closed for the straightforward reason that the "law" to which the courts pledge allegiance when deciding cases is definitionally open-ended. Courts can, and therefore should, use their adjudicative power whenever possible to further progressive ends (and it is almost always possible to do so). Law is a set of possibilities, some of which are progressive. Law, including constitutional law, and emphatically including Fourteenth Amendment guarantees, is and should be a vehicle for progressive social change.

Possibilistic constitutional interpretation, built on the belief that the Constitution is always open to a range of interpretive meanings, some of which are progressive, is also supported by progressive natural lawyers. For them, the Constitution is open and possibilistic because it is the embodiment of an unlived, cultural ideal: the Constitution is itself the repository of the "glimpses," "memories," and "dreams" of the culture's moral ambitions. For progressive natural lawyers, the Constitution is indeed "possibilistic," but not for the anarchic (or existential) reason that language inevitably invites and demands choice, but for the moral reason that the Constitution on its own terms permits choice. The Constitution by its nature opens the door for morally demanding adjudication: it pushes society toward an as yet unlived ideal. The Constitution is itself the "dream." The Constitution is "possibilistic" for the idealist, rather than rigidly historic, simply because we have the good fortune to live in a culture that takes its idealism seriously.

In a passage that well expresses the view of constitutional interpretation shared by scores of progressive natural lawyers, Laurence Tribe describes the idealist Constitution and its relation to fallible adjudicative institutions:

> I do not regard the rulings of the Supreme Court as synonymous with constitutional truth. . . . [T]he Courts that held slaves to be non-persons, separate to be equal, and pregnancy to be non sex-related can hardly be deemed either final or infallible. Such passing finality as judicial pronouncements possess is an essential compromise between constitutional order and chaos: the Constitution is an intentionally incomplete, often deliberately indeterminate structure for the participatory evolution of political ideals and governmental practices. This process cannot be the special province of any single entity. . . .

While conceding the courts a less exclusive role as constitutional oracles, this book cedes them a greater authority—and duty—to advance that justice overtly. Judicial neutrality inescapably involves taking sides. The judgment of the Court, though it may be to elude an issue, in effect settles the substance of the case. Judicial authority to determine when to defer to others in constitutional matters is a procedural form of substantive power; judicial restraint is but another form of judicial activism. . . . The inescapable boundaries of societal context and consciousness argue not that judges should restrain themselves still further, but that they must raise distinctive voices of principle. . . . [T]he highest mission of the Supreme Court, in my view, is not to conserve judicial credibility, but in the Constitution's own phrase, "to form a more perfect Union" between right and rights within that charter's necessarily evolutionary design.[119]

Finally, for the progressive instrumentalist, constitutional interpretation is open, rather than closed, because at least parts of the Constitution contain an antisubordination subtext that at any point can be legitimately realized. As for the idealist, the indeterminacy of the Constitution for the antisubordinationist is a contingent fact, not an existential necessity: the Constitution contains an antisubordinationist subtext not because all texts contain such subtexts, but because this one, as a matter of historical fact, does. Parts of the Constitution, notably the Fourteenth Amendment and the precedential authority interpreting it, when properly read, explicitly target illegitimate social hierarchy. Patterns of domination that stem from the social subordination of one group by another, and that cripple, maim, impoverish, and stunt lives, are therefore not simply moral abominations (and they are surely that)—they are also unconstitutional. The progressive instrumentalist supports the possibilistic paradigm of progressive interpretation through a rigorous and careful, rather than playful and anarchic, reading of the texts themselves.

To summarize, progressives converge on a possibilistic understanding of the nature of constitutional interpretation, a substantive account of the "equality" to which individuals are entitled under the equal protection clause, and an affirmative account of the "liberty" guaranteed under due process. The contrasting grounds for support might be characterized as in Table 9-5.

Finally, the contrast between the progressive and conservative paradigms can be schematized as in Table 9-6.

Table 9-5.

	Interpretation (Open)	Equality (Substantive)	Liberty (Positive)
Idealist Progressives	Constitution as a cultural ideal	Substantive equality necessary for the good life	Positive liberty necessary for the good life
Existential Progressives	Necessity of interpretive choice	Equality the precondition of authenticity	Liberty defined as authenticity
Antisubordination progressives	Constitution as imperfect embodiment of antisubordination ideal	Eradication of hierarchy the purpose of equal protection	Ambivalence in tension with antisubordination goals

Table 9-6.

	Interpretation	Equality (Equal Protection)	Liberty (Substantive Due Process)
Conservative	Imperativist; originalist; judicial restraint	Precludes benign as well as malicious race-conscious decision making	Defined by community traditions
Progressive	Possibilistic; open; necessity of choice	Requires affirmative eradication of hierarchy	Defined by ideals

Virtually all of the significant differences between conservative and progressive understandings of constitutional meanings are squarely rooted in divergent political attitudes toward social power. What the conservative sees as the institutional form or wellspring of communitarian wisdom, legal legitimacy, or market competition, the progressive sees as an oppressive domestic, social, legal, or economic hierarchy. What the conservative sees as the wisdom of the family, the progressive sees as an institution that perpetuates sexual and heterosexual hierarchy. What the conservative sees as respect for the "ties that bind" in subcommunities, the progressive is likely to see as xenophobia toward outsiders and oppressive conformism toward members. What the conservative sees as the market institutions that facilitate free individual choice, the progressive sees as the mechanism of widescale economic oppression. What the conservative sees as legitimate legal institutions that maintain order and reduce conflict, the progressive sees as instruments of ideological oppression that induce a mind-numbing homogeneity and hegemonic conformity.

Similarly, progressive and conservative constitutional meanings stem from these divergent perceptions of the value of social hierarchy. Let me begin with the Court's due process and privacy jurisprudence. The divergent understandings of due process, and the conflicting assessments of cases such as *Griswold, Roe, Webster,* and *Bowers* central to the two constitutional paradigms, are grounded in conflicting attitudes toward social power, not in divergent understandings of the precedential authority and not in contrasting jurisprudential understandings of the nature of law. Thus, the moral conservative sees the wisdom of the ages in precisely the communitarian traditions in which the antisubordination progressive sees the oppression of ancient hierarchies. The conservative natural lawyer thus sees the proper role of law as guarding and preserving communitarian wisdom, and the proper role of constitutional law as preserving that wisdom against the erratic and whimsical dictates of popular opinion. The progressive instrumentalist, by contrast, sees the Constitution as one central tool by which social hierarchy, embedded and reflected in law, can be eradicated.

The difference between these views does not, however, lie in the difference between natural law and instrumentalism: natural law is not essentially conservative, nor is instrumentalism essentially progressive. The difference is rooted in conflicting conservative and progressive attitudes toward social power. Thus, a conservative natural lawyer morally committed to the view that communitarian moral traditions are the source of our knowledge regarding the "good" will not be able to view the various religious, secular, and familial institutional structures that generate those traditions as the source of illegitimate domination, damaging subordination, and stultifying oppression. Nor will he or she see the unlived ideals or dreams of the subordinated, rather than those traditions, as the truer aspirational purpose—and hence meaning—of the liberty clause of the Fourteenth Amendment.

Similarly, the differences between conservative and progressive understandings of equal protection, and the conflicting assessments of affirmative action programs that arise from those understandings, are rooted not in divergent interpretations of the constitutional tradition, but more deeply in divergent experiences and assessments of the normative values generated by competitive economic hierarchy. The free-market conservative sees competition, and hence the creation of value, where the progressive sees illegitimate private hierarchies of class. In jurisprudential terms, the conservative instrumentalist sees law as instrumentally aimed at freeing competition, and reads the equal protection clause to facilitate that end, while the progressive instrumentalist sees law as instrumentally aimed at eradicating illegitimate private and social hierarchy, and reads the equal protection clause to facilitate that diametrically opposed end. The difference between them lies in their divergent assessments of, and perhaps experiences with, the social arrangements that constitute both the substance and the framework of private competitive hierarchy. Free-market conservatives, who view competition as the organizing principle of authoritative normativity, will clearly not view the hierarchies that facilitate "competition" as experiences of subordination and domination against which the moral weight of the equal protection clause should be pitted.

Lastly, the difference between the conservative insistence that interpretation requires obedience toward legitimated commands and the progressive view that interpretation invites choice stems from divergent responses to the imperative dimension of legal power rather than from divergent understandings of either the nature of interpretation or of constitutionalism. Because the literature is vast and familiar, I can afford to be blunt: as the grossly disproportionate conservative response to the indeterminacy claim of the Critical Legal Studies movement has made vividly clear, a positivistic conservative wedded to the virtue of obedience is likely to respond hysterically to a view that identifies law with the necessity of choice, the burden of freedom, and the openness of possibility. What the conservative positivist sees as a source of authority facilitating moral outcomes through obedience, the progressive positivist sees as texts facilitating authentic choice through interpretive freedom. The difference, then, stems from drastically divergent assessments of the morality of obedience and the morality of choice: for the conservative, obedience facilitates morality; for the progressive, choice does so.

If this is right, then our presently constituted postliberal constitutional discourse is somewhat pathological. Rather than discuss our divergent attitudes toward social and private power, modern constitutionalists who have abandoned pretensions to constitutional neutrality avoid politics and ethics by discussing instead their manifestations in conflicting jurisprudential conceptions. These debates, unsurprisingly, resolve nothing. The differences between conservative and progressive constitutional commitments can no more be understood as rooted in jurisprudence than in contrasting understandings of constitutional authority.

Thus, to take a specific example, the contrast between progressive and conservative understandings of the privacy cases cannot be explained or resolved by prior case authority, as the progressives and conservatives themselves seem increasingly inclined to grant. But nor can they be explained by, and hence resolved by, differences between natural law on the one hand and either positivism or pragmatism on the other; natural law, positivism, and instrumentalism are all open to both conservative and progressive political use. Rather, our different assessments of *Bowers* (as well as of *Webster* rest not on contrasting jurisprudential understandings of the nature of law, but on contrasting attitudes toward various forms of social authority. First, they rest on contrasting assessments of the value of the traditional family: what the conservative natural lawyer sees as social morality and legitimate legal authority the progressive natural lawyer sees (and may well have experienced) as a political mechanism of exploitation and oppression. Second, they rest on contrasting attitudes toward sexuality: what the conservative instrumentalist sees as nonreproductive, immoral sexuality the progressive instrumentalist sees as a subordinated sexual orientation. And third, they rest on contrasting attitudes toward the import of constitutional authority: what the conservative positivist reads as mandating obedience the progressive positivist reads as mandating choice. Politics, ethics, and experience—not jurisprudence and not constitutional law—determine these differing commitments. We will not resolve those differences, or, more modestly, come any closer toward a mutual understanding of their roots, by pursuing jurisprudential battles any more than by pursuing traditional constitutional arguments.

Conclusion: Conservative Dominance or Constitutional Crisis

It seems safe to predict that the progressive understanding of the Constitution now being developed by progressive theorists will not achieve much success with the explicitly conservative Court over the next few decades. But, it is important to remember, the progressive interpretation of the Constitution did not do especially well in front of the liberal Court of the last thirty years either. During the 1950s–1970s, progressive gains were only occasional, and all of them, including both *Brown* and later *Roe,* were almost immediately compromised when accommodated into the dominant liberal vision.[120]

In this conclusion I want to suggest briefly that there may be reasons to suspect some deeper tensions, not just between the progressive and conservative interpretations of the Constitution, but between the progressive paradigm and the idea of adjudicative law within which both liberal and conservative courts operate. To the degree that progressives acquiesce in an understanding of the Constitution and of constitutional guarantees as a body of adjudicative law—as something that courts enforce as law against unwilling parties—they may be committed to a definition of constitutionalism that is antithetical to the goals of progressive politics; the phrase "progressive constitutionalism" may remain an anomaly.

The idea of "adjudicative law" may be antithetical to the progressive understanding of the Constitution for at least four reasons. First, progressives understand constitutional law as possibilistic and open, as change rather than regularity, and as freedom rather than constraint. This understanding of constitutionalism may be right, and it may even be right as an account of law, but as an account of adjudicative law—of what courts in fact do—it is perverse. Adjudicative law is persistently authoritarian: demonstration of the "truth" of legal propositions (arguably unlike other truth statements) relentlessly requires shows of positive authority. Existentialism may not be an odd foundation for a theory of politics, legislation, or constitutionalism, but it is certainly an odd (to say the least) grounding for a theory of adjudication. The lesson from this tension between the possibilistic Constitution envisioned by progressives and the authoritarian structure of adjudicative law is not necessarily that the conventional account of adjudicative law as requiring demonstrations of binding authority is wrong; rather, the important point may be that the identification of constitutional process and choices with the sphere of adjudicative rather than legislative legality—with law rather than politics—is misguided.

Second, the instrumental goal toward which the progressive Constitution is aimed is the abolition of subordinating and damaging hierarchies. The justice to which it aspires is not corrective but distributive. Yet the ideal of justice to which adjudicative law aspires has historically been primarily corrective and compensatory, rather than redistributive.[121] Another way to put the point is that adjudicative law has for the most part been essentially conservative: it maintains, stabilizes, and reifies the status quo against change. It exists to protect against change. Antisubordination is accordingly a peculiar goal to establish for adjudicative law. It is not, however, a peculiar goal for legislation, nor is it an odd or outlandish understanding of the import of the Fourteenth Amendment. Perhaps, again, we should conclude from this not that it is misguided to understand adjudicative law as aimed at corrective rather than redistributive justice, but, rather, that it is misguided to conceive of a progressive and radically redistributive directive document such as the Fourteenth Amendment as a source of adjudicative law, rather than as a source of inspiration or guidance for legislative change.

Third, the "morality" that adjudicative law undoubtedly absorbs from time to time is almost invariably conventional and traditional rather than aspirational or utopian. The Court may indeed read the "Law" through the lens of morality, but the morality that comprises the lens is the morality embraced by the dominant forces in the community,[122] not an aspirational morality of unlived ideals informed by experiences of oppression.[123] Adjudicative law typically reflects a community's moral beliefs, and only rarely its aspirational ideals. Perhaps, then, we should conclude not that the conventional understanding of the relation between adjudicative law and conventional morality is wrong, but that the Constitution—because it is indeed open to an aspirational interpretation—is simply not exclusively a source of adjudicative law.

Fourth, the form and processes of "adjudication" create additional tensions for the progressive paradigm, quite apart from and no less serious than those created by the idea of adjudicative law. As anyone who has ever been unwillingly caught in the process knows, adjudication is profoundly elitist, hierarchic, and nonparticipatory. It is itself a form of domination that creates experiences of subordination. The protestations of modern civic republicans notwithstanding, it is the antithesis of participatory democratic politics. The obsessive attention given by civic republican and liberal constitutionalists alike to the "antimajoritarian difficulty" posed by aggressive judicial review has not done anything actually to solve the difficulty; it has only served to highlight the utter incompatibility of both liberals' and republicans' substantive commitment to egalitarian and participatory democracy with their simultaneous endorsement of nonparticipatory, antidemocratic, and intensely hierarchical adjudicative processes for achieving it.[124]

There are still other distorting constraints imposed by adjudication on the progressive paradigm. To name just a few: Adjudication presupposes bipolar conflicts; progressivism does not. Adjudication requires at every turn in the road recitation of and support from "authority"; progressivism is constitutively distrustful of authority. Adjudication requires a recalcitrant, guilty, state defendant, one consequence of which is a judicially constructed "nightwatchman"-like Constitution that can act only against pernicious state action, while progressivism understands the problems of inequality, subordination, and bondage in our lives to stem not from state action, but from private and social action followed by state inaction— the failure of the state to act against private oppression. Adjudication is particularistic and individualistic; progressivism is anything but. Finally, adjudication blames, condemns, and punishes; progressivism is fundamentally uninterested, on many levels and for complex reasons, with blame and innocence. These are surely good reasons to fear that a progressive Constitution is not going to fare well in any adjudicative body, not just in front of a conservative Supreme Court.

The consequence of the tension between adjudication and progressivism is that the legalization of constitutional discourse may have seriously impoverished the progressive tradition. When we read our progressive politics through the lens of the Constitution, and then read the Constitution through the lens of law, we burden progressivism with the constraints, limits, doctrines, and nature of law. Progressivism, its very content, becomes identified with that which courts might do and that which lawyers can feasibly argue. In the process, progressivism in the courts becomes weak and diluted. The consequence of this tension is not only, however, that progressivism in the Supreme Court is impoverished, although clearly it is. The consequence is also that progressive politics outside the Court is robbed of whatever rhetorical and political support it might have received from a de-legalized conception of the progressive Constitution. In a culture that routinely identifies its political aspirations with constitutionalism, it becomes extremely difficult to demand progressive change of a nature that the adjudicated Constitution cannot support. Redistributive progressive politics, for example, may be burdened by the "shadow effect" of the refusal, both on the Court and outside it, to understand poverty as a suspect basis of classification, or minimal material well-being as a fundamental right. More generally, any antisubordinationist progressive legislation is marginalized by the inability of the Court to "find" an antisubordination principle in the Constitution. Constitutionalism defines our public morality, to some extent, and the failure of the adjudicated Constitution to accommodate progressive ends accordingly impoverishes progressive morality.

Thus, progressive politics is impoverished by the adjudicated Constitution simply because it loses the force, and power, of constitutional thought. The legal profession pervasively, and the larger culture somewhat, has come to view the Constitution as the repository of public morality; as the source, genesis, and articulation of our political obligations. If our collective social morality and our moral aspirations are embedded in our Constitution, if the Constitution is a form of adjudicative "law," and if adjudicative law exists in a state of profound and perpetual (and not particularly creative) tension with progressive morality and ideals, then this conclusion is inescapable: progressive morality will never become part of our public morality, regardless of the composition of the Supreme Court. Progressive constitutionalism may be part of the problem (as the saying goes), not part of the solution. If progressive constitutionalists care as much about progressive politics as they care about the Constitution (a big "if"), then the imperative is unavoidable: the circle must be broken.

By way of conclusion, let me briefly characterize some of the gains of reorienting progressive constitutional discourse toward legislative rather than adjudicative action, and toward a congressional rather than a judicial audience. First, and perhaps most important, if we were to recharacterize our progressive understanding of the constitutional guarantees of liberty and equality as political ideals to guide legislation, rather than as legal restraints on legislation, many of these tensions within the progressive understanding of the Constitution would disappear. If we imagine Congress, rather than the Court, as the implicit audience of constitutional argument, it becomes far easier to envision arguments to the effect that the Fourteenth Amendment requires, rather than permits (as within the liberal paradigm) or precludes (as in the conservative) progressive objectives such as affirmative action programs, child care and support programs, greater police responsiveness to private and domestic violence, reform of marital rape laws, and the criminalization of homophobic, racist, and sexist assaults. Congress, after all, has the textual obligation to do something about the states' refusal to provide what the progressive means by "equal protection": to protect the citizenry against the damaging effects of rampant social and private inequality.

It is easier to envision these arguments succeeding—it is easier, in fact, even to state them—not only because the Fourteenth Amendment is explicitly directed toward Congress rather than the Court, and not only because of the present composition of the Court, but also because of the differences between constraint and aspiration, tradition and ideal, corrective and distributive justice, the history of our settled past and the politics of our future possibilities, participatory lawmaking and adjudicative law enforcement. It is easier, in short, to envision the actualization of the progressive Constitution through legislative action than through adjudicative law because of the difference between law and politics.

Second, if progressives were to reorient progressive constitutional debate toward legislative politics rather than adjudicative law, they would invigorate and enrich the terms and stakes of public debate. It is a truism that contemporary discourse in the public sphere has become nihilistic and devoid of a sense of moral purpose. A constitutionalized legislative process might reinject a sense of moral urgency, of moral purpose, and even of moral obligation into a morally bankrupt process. Again the reason for this should not be mysterious: we have become societally accustomed to understanding the Constitution as the repository of public and public-spirited morality. We have also, however, become accustomed to understanding the courts, rather than the Congress, as the forum for constitutional articulation and obligation. The Court, then, is understood as the locus of moral understanding and debate. It is hardly surprising that the consequence is a public perception, if not the reality, of a legislative branch mired in a thicket of narrow self-interest. We have, in effect, alienated the responsibility for public morality to the courts. One solution is to invigorate nonconstitutional moral public discourse. Given the pervasiveness of the perceived equation of public morality with constitutionalism, however, that may not be possible. The other solution is to expand the scope and audience of constitutional discourse.

Third, if we were to reorient progressive constitutionalism toward Congress, we would, perhaps paradoxically, strengthen the legal position of progressive legislation when it is invariably challenged in court as violative of conservatively understood constitutional guarantees. Most of the significant items on any progressive political agenda are seriously threatened by the possibility of invalidation by the present conservative Supreme Court. A conservative *Lochner*-like[125] understanding of the due process clause such as that embraced by the early New Deal Court, like a conservative understanding of the takings clause such as that propounded by Richard Epstein,[126] obviously jeopardizes congressional action aimed at social hierarchies bolstered by gross maldistributions of wealth, including legislation ranging from the progressive tax system to comparable worth and childcare proposals presently under congressional consideration. Similarly, a conservative understanding of equal protection as protecting the individual's right to participate in a color-blind market threatens, if it has not already eviscerated, affirmative action plans, as evidenced by the Court's recent decision in *Croson*. And lastly, conservative understandings of the nature and limits of constitutional interpretation threaten the adjudicative gains made by progressives through imaginative use of a possibilistic and open-ended Constitution, as evidenced by the judicial retreat from active judicial protection of privacy in both *Bowers* and *Webster*. With conservative interpretation now dominating the Court, constitutional challenges to progressive legislation are virtually inevitable, and many will prove successful. We might be able to slow the tide of those attacks, if we strengthen the rhetorical and political base of our progressive legislative proposals, by grounding them not only in politics and policy but also in arguments drawn from constitutional mandate as well.

The gains for progressive politics would be no less tangible. A constitutionalized progressive agenda would centralize progressive concerns and lend them far greater legitimacy. Progressive politics, as discussed above, are crippled in this culture in part because of their lack of constitutional legitimacy: progressivism does not seem to be mandated by the Constitution and increasingly may come to seem precluded by it. Constitutionalism, in other words, if it remains the exclusive interpretive dominion of the Court, has the effect not just of marginalizing but even of delegitimating progressive gains: everything on the modern progressive agenda—from mandatory childcare, to zoning, to comparable worth, to reproductive freedom, to affirmative action—is now, given the dominance of the conservative paradigm, an arguably unconstitutional taking, an infringement of a constitutionally protected interest in property or contractual freedom, a denial of equal protection, or a denial of a fundamental right to life. This is, of course, in part a function of the larger societal conservatism that is infecting constitutional language. All I want to suggest is that it is surely also, in part, a function of the truncation of progressive constitutional thought through the identification of the Constitution with adjudicative law.

Finally, a reorientation of progressive constitutionalism to the legislative arena would bring progressive constitutionalism into line, for the first time in this country, with progressive politics. Progressive constitutionalists constrain the progressive constitutional tradition to fit what is perceived to be possible in the adjudicative sphere. The result is a very weak vision of progressive politics. When our politics are constrained by what courts will or will not do, we lose much of what is central to the progressive cause, including, most significantly, a constitutional as well as legislative commitment to the eradication of what must surely be the most crushing and "subordinating" hierarchy of all: poverty. The reason is clear enough: with the demands of adjudication governing the interpretation of the Constitution, and with constitutionalism in turn constraining progressivism, we have come to choose our progressive political commitments to fit our lawyerly sense of what the Court might buy, instead of our political and moral sense of what people are most in need of. During the liberal era, this may have looked like an acceptable trade-off. But it clearly is not in a period of conservative domination. The constitutional rights of the homeless, the poor, the victims of institutional and social racism, the large class of under-valued and underpaid female workers, to say nothing of the uncared-for children, cannot be allowed to disappear or remain unarticulated simply because they will not be judicially heard. When we quit thinking of the Constitution and its promise within the confines of courts, plaintiffs, defendants, causes of action, actionable intent, state action, malice or the lack thereof, standing to sue, mootness, procedural safeguards, and the rest of the legal apparatus designed for the application and adjudication of law, we will see a Constitution that is at once more progressive, more political, more challenging, more just, and more aspirational than we have yet imagined.

Progressives have clearly lost the Court to conservative domination, and they stand in danger of losing—or worse, conceding—the Constitution as well to conservative interpretation. We can easily imagine a world in which the Constitution has become thoroughly identified with conservative causes; perhaps we already live in one. In such a world, political progressives would, in effect, concede both the Court and the Constitution to conservatism; seek, instead, political victories in the interstices of Congress; dodge judicial intervention; and hope against hope for unexpected judicial victories. Progressivism would remain strictly political, and legislative; conservatism would become thoroughly constitutionalized. The conservative Court then would act as a brake—but with the full force of constitutional authority and rhetoric behind it—on progressive legislative politics. This would obviously be a disaster for progressive politics in this country. It is, however, a disaster in which progressive constitutionalists seem perversely willing to acquiesce.

There is an obvious alternative to this scenario of conservative constitutional victory. Progressive constitutionalists, as well as progressive legislators, could try to create a viable progressive interpretation of the Constitution, congressionally and popularly supported, with the explicit aim of creating a modern "constitutional moment." A conservative Court will never mandate or even seriously entertain a progressive interpretation of congressional meaning. But all courts, as Owen Fiss argues, "read [the Constitution] in a way to avoid crises." [128] This will be even more true of a Court committed not only to the prevention of crisis, but to a positivistic account of law and legal legitimacy and a deferential attitude toward conventional morality. Such a Court, if faced with a legislative agenda firmly and explicitly grounded in a second (or third) Bill of Rights (welfare rights, antisubordination rights, autonomy rights, rights of intimacy, reproductive rights, employment rights), all constitutionally mandated and all popularly supported, would learn, or relearn, to read the Constitution to avoid a confrontation with an awakened populace. A responsible and conservative Court—and there is no reason to think this is not one—would not and could not long impede the work of a progressive Congress newly enlivened to its constitutional obligations.

The key, of course, is to create a progressive Congress, and behind it a progressive citizenry. We presently have neither, to put it lightly. But surely we could, and surely we should, and maybe the likelihood of having one would be enhanced by constitutionalizing progressive causes. The question is where to invest our energies, how to spend our lives. All I want to suggest is that a life spent reorienting progressive constitutionalism toward participatory and democratic forums and away from the insulated and elitist judiciary would be a life well spent. It would well serve progressive politics and causes by giving them constitutional status. It would well serve the democratic, participatory process by giving it a sense of both idealism and constitutional purpose. Finally, it would serve even the Constitution by actualizing its as yet untapped, unexplored, but rich progressive promise.

10

The Aspirational Constitution

■

What would be the consequences for modern progressive politics of the "rule of administration" proposed by James Thayer a hundred years ago in his famous essay? In "The Origin and Scope of the American Doctrine of Constitutional Law,"[1] it will be recalled, Thayer proposed that the Supreme Court should only rule an act of Congress unconstitutional if the act is unconstitutional "beyond a reasonable doubt," or, put differently, that the Court should not overrule a congressional act unless that act is clearly unconstitutional. Would such a rule help or hinder progressive causes? Would a more restrained Court, and a less vigorously enforced Constitution, be an improvement over our present constitutional institutions, from an explicitly progressive political viewpoint? Would it leave the Congress freer to envision, and then to realize, a more egalitarian social order, along with a freer individual and collective life?

The question is complicated by the fact that Thayer's simple rule of administration appears to be susceptible to at least two plausible interpretations, each of which could have quite different consequences. First, Thayer's proposal, transported into modern politics, might be understood as urging that the Court and Congress each perform the same duties they presently perform and in more or less the same way, but that, as the title of the essay suggests, the scope of judicial review be restricted. The Congress should continue to legislate as it always has, and the Court should continue to adjudicate as it always has, but the Court should intervene and rule an act of Congress unconstitutional only if the congressional act is unconstitutional beyond all reasonable doubt. Alternatively, the rule might be understood in a quite different way. Thayer's "clearly erroneous" standard might be read as suggesting not only that the Court should, so to speak, cut the Congress some slack, but also that primary responsibility for constitutional decision making should shift away from the Court and to the Congress. Under this second interpretation of Thayer's proposal, Congress, in the course of legislating, would also explicitly (instead of implicitly) determine the constitutionality of the act under consideration, and the congressional determination of constitutionality would be overturned by the Court only if it is clearly erroneous. At various points in his essay, and particularly in his final paragraph, Thayer moves back and forth between these two interpretations as though they were more or less synonymous, or at least mutually supportive. Nevertheless, on first reading, these two interpretations of Thayer's rule seem to rest on very different anxieties about constitutional morality and politics, and they seem to express very different hopes about the possibilities of change.

If Thayer was worried that excessive judicial review—the "checking and cutting down of legislative power, by numerous detailed prohibitions in the Constitution"—leaves Congress "petty and incompetent" because it has "a tendency to drive out questions of justice and right, and to fill the mind of legislators with thoughts of mere legality, of what the Constitution allows,"[2] those problems may be alleviated by the first interpretation suggested above: cut down on the scope of judicial review, and leave Congress freer to address problems of right and justice without the inhibitory effects of constitutional nicety. If the problem, in other words, is an excess of constitutional conscience—if the problem is that because of the fear of judicial review, concern for the Constitution has actually driven out questions of justice and right from the minds of legislators—then we should indeed seek to minimize the effect of the Constitution by limiting the scope of review. That problem, however, might well be exacerbated, not abated, by the second interpretation of Thayer's rule given above, at least if we assume a Congress conscientious in its constitutional labor. For under the second interpretation, the effect of Thayer's rule of administration would be to shift to Congress the primary responsibility for the constitutionality of its actions, and a Congress itself preoccupied with constitutionalism presumably will be more worried about constitutional nicety and less worried about justice and right than a Congress which leaves the constitutional issues to the Court. If the problem is that the Constitution itself has left Congress overly concerned with legalism and not sufficiently concerned with justice, that problem will obviously not be cured by imposing on Congress primary responsibility for the constitutionality of legislative proposals.

Similarly, if the aim of Thayer's rule is to "impress[] upon our people a far stronger sense than they have of the great range of possible harm and evil that our system leaves open, and must leave open, to the legislatures, . . . so that responsibility may be brought sharply home where it belongs,"[3] then we may achieve that result by insisting on the first interpretation, but surely not the second. The first interpretation clearly expands the range of legislative options: if legislation is to be overturned only if clearly unconstitutional, then there is considerably more that Congress might do without inviting judicial intervention. By contrast, under the second interpretation—according to which Congress is to be charged with determining the constitutionality of its actions, with their decisions overturned only if clearly erroneous—the "range of possible harm and evil" may shrink, not expand, as may public awareness of it, and hence public responsibility for it. If Congress were to take seriously its obligation to pass on the constitutionality of its own proposals, and if it did so in a conscientious manner, then presumably it would tend to censor its own work product accordingly.

On the other hand, if the problem with our current understandings, as Thayer also states in his final paragraph, is that with our current distribution of responsibilities, Congress is too little concerned about the Constitution—that the legislators, "in the matter of legality, . . . have felt little responsibility; if we are wrong, they say, the courts will correct it,"[4] then shifting the primary burden of constitutional decision making to Congress may indeed correct that flaw: a Congress primarily responsible for the constitutionality of its own actions will presumably spend more time considering constitutional questions than a Congress that can legitimately view those questions as the sole province of the judiciary. Correlatively, if the aim of Thayer's proposal is to encourage Congress to operate in a more constitutionally responsible fashion, then shifting primary responsibility to Congress for constitutional decisions is a sensible first step. But, here again, if the problem is that Congress does not take sufficient responsibility for the constitutionality of its actions, then the proposal understood in the first way—as simply a proposal to limit judicial review—will be inapposite. Indeed, that problem will be exacerbated, not alleviated, by an administrative rule that does nothing but limit the scope of review. A Congress already insufficiently attuned to its constitutional obligations will presumably be less, not more, sensitive to those duties under a rule of administration which weakens the sanction and lessens the consequences of unconstitutional action.

Although I will ultimately argue in this chapter that these two interpretations are not quite as contradictory as they first appear, they nevertheless are in considerable tension. One way to put the problem is that the two hopes that seem to underlie the two interpretations of the rule appear to be simply incompatible hopes, and the anxieties that give rise to them seem to be incompatible anxieties. If the problem with our present arrangements is an excess of constitutionalism—that the brooding omnipresence of the Constitution leaves Congress feeling too legalistic and too little concerned with right and justice—then we should constrain judicial review, thereby minimize the impact of constitutionalism, and leave it at that. If, on the contrary, the problem is that Congress feels too little responsibility for the constitutionality of its actions—if the problem is that there is not enough constitutional conscience—then we should enhance the felt constitutional duty of legislators. But the problem cannot be both. There quite obviously cannot be both too much and too little of a sense of congressional constitutional duty. Thus, it looks as though Thayer has blurred two very different anxieties: the fear that Congress pays too much attention to "constitutional legalism" and hence not enough attention to questions of right and justice, and the very different fear that Congress is not sufficiently attentive to constitutionalism, and relies too heavily on the Court to correct its errors. It also looks as though Thayer has blurred two very different hopes: that by limiting the scope of judicial review, Congress will be and will feel freer to consider a full range of options for good or ill, and hence be made more responsible for the morality of its actions, and that Congress might become more responsible for the constitutionality of its actions by being given primary responsibility for constitutional determinations.

Behind the confusion in the concluding paragraph of Thayer's essay is an almost palpable ambivalence not only about judicial review but also about the Constitution itself. Dissatisfaction with a "robust Constitution" is right on the surface of the first interpretation of the proposal given above: Thayer was clearly willing to tolerate a considerable decrease in constitutional enforcement—and hence a considerable amount of unconstitutional law—in order to achieve a Congress more attuned to right and justice, and more fully responsible as a result for the full range of options open to it.[5] The rather clear inference is that the Constitution itself is part of the problem—that constitutional constraints are themselves in some way incompatible with the pursuit of right and justice, and accordingly ought to be limited in scope. Dissatisfaction with judicial review is right on the surface of the second interpretation: Thayer was clearly willing to restrict the Court's purview over what have traditionally been judicial questions and reassign those questions elsewhere, in order to achieve a Congress more attuned to its constitutional obligations.[6] The clear inference of this interpretation, in contrast, is that the Constitution itself is not the problem—indeed constitutional conscience would promote, not hinder, right and justice—but rather, that the problem is insufficient congressional attention to the Constitution, fostered by the shortcomings of judicial review.

This ambivalence was not just an idiosyncrasy of Thayer and was certainly not peculiar to his time. Indeed, the problem that gives rise to these two very different anxieties is at the heart, not the periphery, of the idea of constitutionalism itself, at least if judicial review is understood to be a necessary feature of that idea. The Constitution limits responsibility for "questions of right and justice" because it mutes some of the possible answers to those questions; at the same time, judicial review limits congressional responsibility for questions of constitutionality because it delegates those questions to the judiciary. As a consequence, dissatisfaction with congressional performance within a constitutional scheme of government may typically find itself expressed in terms of dissatisfaction with the allocation of responsibilities for constitutional enforcement, and typically may even be manifested in the somewhat contradictory form in which Thayer expresses his anxieties. If we are concerned that Congress feels insufficiently attentive to questions of right and justice because it feels overly constrained by the Constitution, we will seek to limit the scope of the Constitution. If we are concerned, on the other hand, that Congress is insufficiently attentive to the Constitution, we may seek to somehow expand its scope, or at least increase congressional awareness of its principles. And if we have simply a vague sense that Congress is not legislating in the way it should, we may think that perhaps we should try to increase its sense of responsibility for both the right and justice, as well as for the constitutionality of its actions.

In contemporary politics, this Thayerian ambivalence toward the Constitution, judicial review, and congressional decision making finds an echo in the thinking of modern political progressives about the value of judicial review, the value of the United States Constitution, and the value of constitutionalism itself. On the one hand, there are a number of progressive constitutionalists who have argued over the last few years for what I have labeled above the second interpretation of Thayer's rule—that Congress should assume a greater responsibility for the constitutionality of its actions—not only for the reasons Thayer suggests toward the end of his essay, but also for the more explicitly progressive reason that by doing so it could develop more progressive understandings of constitutional mandates than those developed by the Court, and could thereby ease the passage of progressive legislation.[7] On the other hand, there are also an increasing number of progressive calls for something like the first interpretation of Thayer's proposal provided above—that the Court should limit the scope of judicial review—and again not only for the general reasons that Thayer suggests, but also for the more specifically progressive reason that due either to the conservatism of the Court or to the conservatism of the Constitution itself, aggressive judicial review of congressional acts is likely to constitute more of a hindrance than a spur to progressive change.[8] And there are at least a few (including me) who, at the risk of inconsistency, appear to embrace both positions simultaneously.[9] Thayer's ambivalence, then, no less than the rule he proposes, should resonate with modern progressives in our current political and cultural world. I would like to explore and to some degree try to resolve that ambivalence in the remainder of this chapter.

In section one I explore the consequences for modern progressive politics of Thayer's suggested rule of administration under the first of the two possible interpretations I have suggested above: a "beyond all reasonable doubt" standard for constitutional review, the consequence of which would be to limit the scope of judicial review. I will suggest that progressives have good reason to find such a rule attractive.

In section two, I look at the second interpretation of the rule: a mandate to transfer primary responsibility for constitutional decision making to the Congress, leaving the Court to review and overturn such determinations only when clearly erroneous. I will first argue that on first reading, the consequences of such a rule seem regressive, not progressive: a conscientious Congress might well censor its own progressive instincts on behalf of constitutionalism even more than would a conservative Court. I will then argue, however, that in spite of the regressive appearances of the second interpretation, there is a conception of the Constitution and of the nature of interpretation according to which it makes some sense to hope that a Congress responsible for constitutional decision making would develop a distinctively progressive understanding of constitutional guarantees. If so, then the peculiar combination of hopes and anxieties that seems to drive Thayer's article might be not as contradictory as it first appears. If we assume that the nature of the Constitution is such that Congress could legitimately ascribe to the Constitution very different, and much more progressive, meanings than those ascribed by the Court, then the apparent contradiction between wanting a Congress freed of inhibiting judicial review of constitutionality but burdened by congressional review of constitutionality disappears.

The argument, however, that Congress could legitimately read the Constitution to mean something quite different from what the Court understands it to mean must rest on more than simply the alleged vagueness of the Constitution, as argued by Thayer, or the alleged indeterminacy of the Constitution, as propounded by modern and postmodern constitutional theorists. In order for the congressionally interpreted Constitution to be at all authoritative, those interpretations must occur within a conception of the Constitution which is both legitimate and which renders those interpretations in some sense compelling. The goal of section two of this chapter is very briefly to suggest one such conception.

Limiting the Scope of Judicial Review

Returning to the first interpretation of Thayer's rule, what might be the modern political consequences of Thayer's rule of administration, understood simply as a "clearly erroneous" standard? Would such a rule help or hinder progressive political change? A fairly straightforward argument can be made to the effect that from a progressive perspective, Thayer's clearly erroneous standard would be an improvement over our present constitutional arrangements, for three reasons.

The first reason is, loosely, historical: the "adjudicated Constitution," by which I mean the Constitution that has been construed and applied by the courts, has proven to be a markedly conservative foundational document, and, for that reason alone, a rule of restraint looks desirable. More often than not, our adjudicated Constitution has served to protect existing distributions of social, economic, racial, sexual, linguistic, and cultural power against serious threat of change. It has done so by insulating the private, social, economic, and intimate spheres of life, constituted in part by gross inequities of resources and maldistributions of power, against legislative attempts at redistribution or renegotiation of the terms of private, social, or economic struggle.[10] That foundational conservatism is evidenced not only by the *Lochner*-era [11] Court's substantive due process clause, contract clause, and takings clause jurisprudence, which insulated economic hierarchies from redistributive legislative attack, but also by the modern Scalia Court's understanding of the equal protection clause, which insulates racial hierarchies from progressive state legislative attack,[12] and the same Court's interpretation of the First Amendment, which insulates cultural hierarchies from legislative renegotiation through hate speech ordinances.[13] Although the adjudicated Constitution obviously has from time to time been used to effectuate progressive gains and to solidify progressive victories, those moments have been rare, anomalous, and often fleeting: the victory has been, as often as not, soured by near instantaneous conservative reconstruction.[14] For the most part, the clauses of the adjudicated Constitution have operated in concert to conserve present distributions of social, economic, and private power against legislative and democratic attempts at redistributing those resources or renegotiating the terms of struggle. If for no other than that reason, progressives would be well advised to break their romance with the United States Constitution. If it is true, as I have suggested, that the adjudicated Constitution is doctrinally and substantively more of a bar to than a vehicle for progressive legislation, then Thayer's rule looks attractive indeed.

But what if we assume, as countless contemporary skeptics insist we should, an indeterminate Constitution, with neither conservative nor progressive content? If we assume a Constitution of indeterminate meaning, then whether Thayer's clearly erroneous standard would help or hinder progressive causes depends on what sort of Congress and what sort of Court one hypothesizes. One can easily construct two contrasting scenarios. First, one might imagine a conservative Congress passing legislation forbidding homosexuals from serving in the armed forces, passing a Fetal Life Protection Act making the procurement of an abortion or the provision of abortion services a federal crime, abolishing Aid to Families with Dependent Children, or amending the Civil Rights Acts to render state or private voluntary affirmative action plans a civil rights violation, generously providing appropriate remedies for injured individuals. And, one might imagine a progressive Court that views much of this legislation as unconstitutional as well as unwise, but nevertheless feels itself and in a very real sense is restrained by Thayer's rule of administration from ruling such acts unconstitutional violations of the Fourteenth, Thirteenth, or First Amendments, because none of these pieces of legislation, whatever its demerits, is unconstitutional beyond all reasonable doubt. Alternatively, one might just as easily imagine a progressive Congress passing legislation mandating that employers provide paid leave for child care for new parents as well as comparable pay for comparable work; making rape, marital rape, and domestic violence against women criminal civil rights violations; prohibiting and providing sanctions for hate speech targeting racial, ethnic, or sexual minorities; and requiring or encouraging private affirmative action efforts to correct for past and present racial injustice. And, one might imagine a conservative Court that views much of this legislation as unconstitutional under the takings clause, the First Amendment, the substantive due process clause, or the equal protection clause, but nevertheless feels itself, and in a real sense is, constrained by Thayer's rule of administration from finding these legislative acts unconstitutional. None of these legislative acts, one would have to admit, is unconstitutional beyond all reasonable doubt. From a progressive standpoint, under the first scenario, Thayer's rule of administration looks unfortunate, and under the second scenario, it looks desirable. If we assume an indeterminate Constitution, then the political desirability of Thayer's rule of administration, under this first interpretation, seems to depend on what sort of political configuration one imagines.

In the next section, I will briefly argue that we should not assume an indeterminate adjudicated Constitution, for the simple reason that we do not have one. Our adjudicated Constitution's meaning is relatively determinate and relatively conservative, and the delusion that it is not so is largely responsible for the incredible drain of progressive time, resources, energy, and political capital expended in this culture on progressive constitutional litigation—time that could much more profitably be expended in other ways. Nevertheless, here I want to make a much more limited point: that from a progressive viewpoint, even if we assume an indeterminate adjudicated Constitution, adoption of Thayer's rule of administration would be an improvement over our present constitutional understandings for two different reasons.

Simply as a political matter, we may be justified in assuming that the second, rather than the first, of the two scenarios just described (a relatively progressive Congress and a relatively conservative Court) is closer to present reality and will remain so for the foreseeable future. The "progressive Congress and conservative Court" formulation better describes our present reality than the opposite, and, given the dynamics of congressional politics and judicial appointments, it is likely to remain so. But, moreover, whatever may be the politics of the future Court, there is a lot of good sense in Thayer's suggestion that for these purposes we should assume a virtuous rather than a mean-spirited Congress.[15] While for Thayer, congressional virtue meant simply a Congress of informed, public-minded, rational, and intelligent citizens,[16] our modern progressive conception of congressional virtue is quite different. By congressional virtue, from a progressive perspective, we mean the absence of corruption and some minimum of intelligence, as well as real, rather than virtual, representation of various presently underrepresented groups. An ideal Congress in our time, much unlike Thayer's, and again from a progressive perspective, is one that is truly representative of the shifting groups—defined in terms of race and sex as well as class and ethnicity—that make up the voting and non-voting public.[17] This is as much a part of our ideal as the rationalist virtues Thayer suggested, not because we have suddenly and inexplicably become sticklers for representative purity but because we have good reason to believe that a Congress with a significant number of women will be more responsive to the needs of women, family, and children; hence, Congress will be better and will enact better laws.[18] Likewise, a Congress with a significant number of African-Americans will be less likely than an all-white enclave to slight the interests of racial minorities; hence Congress will be a better Congress and enact better laws.[19] A racially and sexually mixed Congress, it is not unreasonable to suppose, would more likely sponsor progressive legislation than an all-white and all-male Congress, and a racially and sexually mixed Congress—one which is more truly representative, which "looks like America"—is closer to our ideal, if not Thayer's ideal, of what a Congress should be. If we follow Thayer's advice, then, and construct our constitutional practices against a hypothesized ideal of congressional conduct, then again from a purely pragmatic and avowedly progressive political perspective, we would be far better off operating under Thayer's proposed rule of administration than under our present constitutional understandings.

There are also pragmatic virtues for Thayer's proposed rule that are compatible with progressive politics, which make that rule appealing regardless of the content given the Constitution's general clause, and regardless of the determinacy or indeterminacy of the adjudicated Constitution. Judicial interpretation of constitutional phrases has the effect of validating one of several possible interpretations of the general aspirations that the Constitution articulates and invalidating others. Given the momentous gulf between progressive aspiration and present political reality, that process of validation and invalidation itself has real drawbacks; it shrinks our legislative options. I think it is fair to say, for example, that we need a far greater degree of material equality between Anglos, Hispanics, and African-Americans than presently exists if we are going to fulfill our aspirational ambition to live as a united community. I think it is also fair to say that we do not have a very good sense of how to go about achieving that goal. Race-specific, race-conscious affirmative action plans, for example, of the sort the Court views as constitutionally suspect, may be either anathema to the overall end of racial equality or absolutely necessary. Legislators alert to the real possibility that a hostile Court will strike down race-conscious remedial legislation obviously will be less inclined to support or even consider it, and that felt constraint on permissible means ought to be understood as a very real obstacle to racial progress. From a purely pragmatic perspective, in other words, we need—at least—a wide open and no-holds-barred public conversation about how best to achieve racial justice, and that conversation, to say nothing of the legislation that ought to follow it, is hindered, not furthered, by constitutionally imposed constraints on our options.[20]

Examples could be multiplied: arguments about the wisdom of controlling pornography are hindered, not helped, by concerns about the constitutionality of such regulation; arguments about the necessity of comparable worth legislation are similarly put back, not pushed forward, by the inhibitory effect of concerns over the takings, contract, or substantive due process clauses. Those inhibitory effects, in turn, would surely be ameliorated by Thayer's rule of administration: if we felt confident that a legislative decision would not be overturned unless it is clearly unconstitutional, presumably we would be that much less inclined to be deterred from investing our energies in the exploration of its merits. Thayer's rule, in other words, would enhance democratic conversation and legislative experimentation, and it might do so in precisely those areas of life in which conversation and experimentation are most desperately needed—and which are most drastically in short supply.

Congressional Responsibility for Constitutional Decision Making

The progressive case for the first interpretation of Thayer's rule of administration, then, is fairly straightforward: progressive causes are more likely to be helped than hurt by such a rule for three reasons. First, the adjudicated Constitution itself is so overwhelmingly conservative that any constraints on its reach would be for that reason alone a good thing. Second, even if we assume an indeterminate Constitution, the meaning of which is entirely determined by the political predispositions of the Court, it is more likely that such a rule would inhibit a conservative Court from overturning progressive legislation than the other way around. Third, regardless of the political makeup of the Court and Congress, and regardless of the determinacy of the Constitution, progressive gains require a degree of legislative experimentalism that judicially imposed constitutional constraints inhibit.

If, however, what Thayer meant by his proposed rule of administration is something closer to the second interpretation I suggested above—that Congress should shoulder the primary responsibility for deciding the constitutionality of the acts it passes, and that the Court should overturn those decisions (and therefore the legislation they affect) only if they are clearly erroneous—then the matter is more complicated. It is not nearly so clear that Thayer's rule, understood in this way, would be an improvement over our current constitutional understandings. The obvious problem with Thayer's proposed rule, understood in this second way and again from a progressive perspective, is that it is not clear that Congress's relative inattentiveness to constitutional questions is bad. If, as suggested here, the Constitution is an irredeemably conservative document, then the likelihood that Congress will respond sensitively to the moral demands of distributive justice seems to be lessened, not enhanced, by Thayer's proposed rule of administration. In other words, if modern progressives are right to worry that the Constitution itself is incompatible with egalitarian political outcomes, then the most likely outcome of Thayer's rule of administration under this second interpretation might be opposite to the outcome under the first: given the conservative nature of the Constitution itself, a Congress more attuned to constitutional questions might be less likely to consider, much less pass, legislation supporting a progressive agenda seemingly antithetical to the Constitution's core commitment to the conservation of present distributions of economic and social power. Thus, the consequences of these two interpretations of Thayer's proposal, no less than the different anxieties and hopes that seem to generate them, seem to point in diametrically opposed directions.

The regressiveness of this second interpretation may not be as great as it first appears, however. As a number of commentators have recently argued,[21] congressional interpretation of the Constitution might lead to constitutional meanings quite different from, and arguably more progressive than, those meanings ascribed to the Constitution by the Court. Put negatively, and minimally, it seems fair to say that the assumption that delegation to Congress of primary responsibility for constitutional decision making would hinder progressive politics rests on a questionable understanding of constitutional meaning: that the meaning of the Constitution would be unaffected by such a shift. In other words, both the progressive undesirability of the proposal under the second interpretation and the apparent contradiction between the two interpretations disappear if Congress could give the Constitution a meaning more in line with the demands of right and justice (in Thayer's terms) or with egalitarian ideals (in progressive terms) than that given it by the Court. If the Constitution, when interpreted by Congress, means something different, and specifically something more in line with progressive aspirations, than the meaning which it has historically been given by the Court, then it is not inconsistent to advocate both greater congressional responsibility for constitutional decision making and greater congressional sensitivity to progressive egalitarian aspirations facilitated by a weakening of traditional judicial review.

Indeed, as a number of commentators have argued,[22] it is not hard to imagine that a Congress composed of constitutional interpreters who are somewhat more progressive than the conservative Court could and very likely would interpret the Constitution to permit any number of progressive legislative initiatives that the Court in recent years has tended to view as constitutionally suspect. It is not even hard to imagine such a Congress interpreting the Constitution as not just permitting but requiring progressive legislation. Although the modern Court surely would not adopt such an interpretation, one can imagine, for example, a progressive Congress reading the Fourteenth Amendment's equal protection guarantee to require Congress to pass legislation assuring greater—more equal—police protection against private violence directed toward women, poor people, African-Americans, and gays and lesbians. Such a reading, it could even be argued, is closer than our present multitiered "rationality review" to the original meaning of the equal protection clause intended by the Reconstruction Congress that passed it—a Congress also faced with the problem of unchecked private violence against one group of citizens by another.[23] The proposed Violence against Women Act[24] as well as the nascent Civil Rights Bill aimed at protecting gays and lesbians against gay bashing,[25] could without much stretching be viewed as logical outgrowths of the Ku Klux Klan Act that inspired the Fourteenth Amendment, and, accordingly, as the modern cornerstones of a progressive congressional interpretation of the equal protection clause.

Similarly, with almost no stretching, one can imagine a progressive congressional constitutional committee interpreting the Thirteenth Amendment to require some sort of federal affirmative action aimed toward the reparation of the African-American community for the continuing harms visited upon it by the aftermath of slavery and white racism. Such legislation could readily be understood as the logical outgrowth of the aspiration of "forty acres and a mule" that informed the Thirteenth Amendment, and, accordingly, as the modern cornerstone of a progressive congressional interpretation of the Thirteenth Amendment.[26] To take a final example, one can imagine a progressive congressional constitutional committee requiring the liberty prong of the substantive due process clause to require federal legislation ensuring positive liberties, rather than simply to prohibit the denial of negative liberties. Such a reading also may be closer to the clause's original meaning than that presently embraced by the Court.[27] Examples could obviously be multiplied.

Thus, freed of the conservative ideology of the present Court, and perhaps more important, freed of the institutional responsibility of the Court to interpret the Constitution only in such a fashion as not to demand remedies beyond the realistic powers of the Court, it is not unreasonable to think that Congress could interpret the open-ended phrases of the Constitution in a way far more conducive to progressive ends than has the Supreme Court, with the end result being a body of constitutional law that looks far different, both in form and content, than that which we have today. The proposed Violence against Women Act,[28] the proposed Freedom of Choice Act,[29] various affirmative action guarantees, the Americans with Disabilities Act,[30] and, potentially, a civil rights bill for gays and lesbians would become not only permitted by such a congressional reading of the Thirteenth and Fourteenth Amendments, but constitutive of their meaning. Finally, if that is right—if, by virtue of their different overall political orientations and their different institutionally determined remedial powers, Congress could interpret the Constitution's general phrases in a manner conducive to progressive ends, and if, under Thayer's rule of administration, such interpretations would not be clearly erroneous—then the distance between the two interpretations of Thayer's proposal may not be as great as first appeared, either generally or from a progressive perspective. In short, if the Constitution can fairly be read as requiring some measure of social, racial, economic, and sexual egalitarianism, then a Congress sensitive to its constitutional obligations will surely not for that reason be deterred from egalitarian considerations.

One can, then, easily imagine such a Congress and one can construct, without too much stretching of the primary materials, arguments to support their progressive outcomes. But it does not follow from the fact that these progressive interpretations are imaginable, or even that the arguments in support of them have merit, that these interpretations—so dramatically different from those reached not just by this Court, but by most Courts over the last 200 years—would have any meaningful constitutional significance: that they would be, in a word, authoritative. Would they, in other words, be truly constitutional arguments—true to the Constitution we have, true to our understanding (whatever it may be) of what the Constitution is, true to our sense of what the Constitution should be—or would they be, rather, simply political arguments with the rhetorical flourish of constitutional language? Would there be, indeed, any connection at all between these progressive interpretations of the Constitution and the authoritative Constitution that in some sense binds us? If, as I have argued above, the adjudicated Constitution has at its core irredeemably conservative content, what significance, if any, can attach to a legislated Constitution that gives rise to very different and profoundly incompatible interpretations? These questions are the questions that Thayer's proposal truly raises, particularly if his proposal is taken seriously as urging greater congressional attention and lesser judicial attention to the Constitution. Would the different, but presumptively reasonable interpretations a progressive Congress might generate, if left untouched by a conservative Court constrained by a clearly erroneous standard, be authoritative? And if not, would they be, in any recognizable and meaningful sense, constitutional interpretations? Or would they simply be disguised political arguments? If they were the last, would the ultimate consequence of Thayer's proposal be simply a diminution—perhaps to the vanishing point—of the role of the Constitution in modern life?

There are two possible arguments—one bad, one good—that the answer to these questions is yes, that even dramatically divergent (and more progressive) congressional interpretations of the Constitution would be authoritative and hence "constitutional" in some important sense, meaning minimally that they would hold some claim over what George Fletcher has recently called our "constitutional identity."[31] The first argument, although widely held, is not ultimately successful, so let me start with it. One could argue that the sort of progressive congressional interpretations I have suggested above would indeed be authoritative, or at least would be as fully authoritative as those provided by the Court, simply because, as suggested by Thayer himself in his article,[32] and as elaborated by countless modern and postmodern proponents of indeterminacy, the meaning of the Constitution is surely sufficiently indeterminate to admit of more than one plausible, or reasonable, interpretation. The argument would simply be that the Constitution's meaning is no more essentially conservative than it is essentially anything else, and it is therefore as open to Congress as it would be open to a more progressive Court to find in that document constitutional support for progressive, no less than for conservative, outcomes. If we assume an indeterminate rather than determinate Constitution, then a progressive Congress is likely to find in the Constitution progressive meanings, just as a conservative Court will find in the same document conservative meanings. And if that is true, then there is no reason to withhold the authority from the one that is granted as a matter of course to the other.

The assumption that the Constitution's meaning is truly indeterminate, in other words, goes a long way toward resolving the apparent contradiction in Thayer's proposal. Even assuming that judicial review has overdeterred Congress from considerations of right and justice, it has done so only because of a particular crabbed meaning imposed upon it by the Court, not because of the essential meaning of the Constitution itself. Accordingly, Congress could both be more attuned to right and justice and at the same time shoulder responsibility for authoritative constitutional interpretation, by simply interpreting the latter as requiring nothing but the former. In other words, constitutional integrity does not undercut the general goals of right and justice if constitutional integrity does not meaningfully restrain or restrict judgment.

The problem, however (or at any rate the incompleteness), with this essentially negative resolution of the contradictory hopes, anxieties, and consequences at the heart of the two possible interpretations of Thayer's proposal—that they dissolve under an indeterminate Constitution—should be as obvious as its virtues: the indeterminacy of the Constitution, while facilitating the development of divergent congressional interpretations, in no way mandates those interpretations. As a consequence, while the indeterminacy of the Constitution does indeed undercut the authority of any particular interpretation of it—as both the propounders and the critics of the indeterminacy thesis generally insist—and hence undercuts the authority of regressive interpretations, it also undercuts the authority of any alternatives. A congressionally generated, progressive interpretation of the Constitution, even if permissible, if only one of an infinite number of possible interpretations, has no claim whatsoever on our collective conscience, no power to constrain our collective choices, and, in short, no authority to guide our collective life. Although the indeterminacy of the Constitution in a sense resolves the appearance of contradiction in Thayer's two proposals by facilitating alternative and presumably more progressive interpretations of the Constitution, it does so at the not insignificant cost of stripping the Constitution of any authoritative, suprapolitical force. If the

Constitution's meaning simply reiterates—because it mirrors—the political convictions of its interpreters, then the Constitution is not merely *not* an authoritative source of guidance but is redundant, and even more so should the interpretation emanate from congressional rather than judicial deliberation. To be a constitutional interpretation—an interpretation of the Constitution, rather than an interpretation of an interesting historical political document—a constitutional interpretation must be authoritative: it must have some claim to our collective deliberations and our individual reasons for acting. And, for an interpretation to be authoritative, it must follow in some way from a conception of the Constitution, and not simply from the political commitments of its interpreters.

The indeterminacy claim, in short, is not going to be of much help in salvaging the coherence of Thayer's proposal. This should not be a surprise to indeterminacy's most adamant proponents. The indeterminacy thesis is and has been a tremendously potent tool for delegitimizing power: it strips the interpreter of the peculiar form of authority that comes from attributing one's own decisions to the commands of a univocal text. For precisely that reason, however, it is of no use whatsoever to those who seek to confer power where it has not previously resided, as do proponents of congressional constitutional interpretation. Such proponents do indeed seek to decentralize or at least to delimit the authority of the interpretation of the Constitution given by the Court—thus the illusory gains of indeterminacy. But they seek to do so in order to ultimately assert the authority of a different interpretation provided by Congress. If congressional interpretations of the Constitution are permissible for no better reason than that there are simply no constraints on constitutional meaning, then even if permissible, those interpretations will have no constitutionally persuasive force. There is no reason to reject them out of hand, but there is no reason to accept them either. Whatever authority, persuasive or otherwise, that might emanate from the fact that the progressive interpretation is a constitutional one—that it stems from a shared national, intergenerational community, that it transcends politics, that it is the product of consensual government, that it emanates from "We the People," or whatever—disappears in the face of indeterminacy. Whatever the political argument for putting forward the progressive legislation in question, then, it will gain nothing by being conjoined with a progressive constitutional argument regarding its constitutional status. The progressive constitutional interpretation one might provide is simply superfluous—and hence not constitutional—if it is a permissible meaning only because the Constitution is in some significant sense meaningless.

The second argument, the argument I want to endorse, also rests on a view of the nature of interpretation. Although it is often confused with the indeterminacy thesis, it is quite different and has very different consequences. According to the "reader-response" school of interpretive theory, at least as it has been developed by Stanley Fish, a text's meaning is not determined by the text or the text's authors, but rather by some set of purposes, needs, or interests of the relevant interpreting community. A text, then, does not determine its own meanings; rather, its meaning is a product of the process of interpretation. Although often confused with the indeterminacy thesis, this reader-response thesis, which for brevity I will simply call the *interpretation claim,* is quite different. The differences between them carry significant differences for our understanding of the compatibility or incompatibility of the ideas of constitutionalism and legal authority, and, therefore, ultimately, for the significance of the second interpretation of Thayer's rule of administration. Those differences, then, and the reason for the confusion between them, are worth exploring in some detail.

What is typically meant by the interpretation claim, at least by reader-response theorists, is not that a text has multiple meanings, but that the text itself does not determine its own meanings.[33] A text, then, is "indeterminate" in the sense that the text itself is not determinative of its meaning. But it does not follow that a text does not have a meaning, nor does it follow that a text has or can have multiple meanings. Rather, it follows only that to the extent that the text's meaning is determinate, something other than the text itself is doing the determining. The meaning of a text may be determined by the social milieu in which it is read, the institutional demands of the profession or discipline that has some interest in the document, or the set of expectations which the community of readers brings to documents of the general category of which the particular text is an instance. If those constraints are themselves sufficiently entrenched, then the text's meaning will be very determined indeed. On the other hand, if those constraints are not particularly entrenched, then it will not be. But it is the community, its expectations, and its needs—not the text—that is doing the determining. The point of the interpretation thesis is not so much to insist on the ultimate plasticity of texts. Indeed, the determinacy of a text, if the interpretation thesis is right, is an entirely contingent question:

whether a text is or is not determinate depends on the homogeneity of the needs, interests, and expectations of the community of interpreters who have some use of it. Rather, the point of the interpretation thesis is simply to underscore the fact that it is the community of readers, their needs, interests, and purposes which is doing the constraining, not the text itself.

Although it is by now a widely held one (at least by lawyers), the belief that it follows from the interpretivists' claim that the readership of a text determines meaning, that a text has multiple meanings, which in turn strips any particular interpretation of authority, rests on a misunderstanding of the interpretation thesis, and in particular a confusion of it with the indeterminacy thesis. It has indeed become commonplace in the legal literature to assume, and to assert, that the interpretation thesis propounded by Fish and other reader-response theorists implies that a text, including a legal and constitutional text, can have a multitude of meanings. This is the position advocated by a number of critical legal scholars and it is more or less the position attacked by Owen Fiss in his justly famous piece, "Objectivity and Interpretation."[34] It is the position behind the claim of the Critical Legal Studies movement, and the fear of its critics, that the interpretation thesis, like the indeterminacy thesis, in some important way undermines the law's claim to legitimacy. But in spite of its widespread currency in law, the notion that the interpretation claim implies that a text can have many, or even an infinite number of interpretations with an equal claim (and therefore no claim) to validity is wrong: that is not, at any rate, what the claim means to a number of its most prominent advocates.

The interpretation thesis, properly understood, frees us of the illusion not so much that a text has only one meaning, but rather that it is the text itself, rather than the community of readers, that determines its meaning. The point of the interpretation thesis, then, is not that a text's meaning is indeterminate; quite the contrary, the meaning of a text may be fully determined, but if so, it is determined by institutional, professional, or cultural attributes of the community of its interpreters, rather than by the text itself. It follows, significantly, that a text's meaning is never a function solely of the text itself, and it also follows that a text might not carry the same meaning from one institutional context to another. But it does not follow that an interpretation of a text loses its claim to authority. Within a given interpretive community, one interpretation may well be authoritative, and its claim to authority within that context will be some combination of its intellectual and political power. In the constitutional context, then, the interpretation thesis, like the indeterminacy thesis, frees up, so to speak, constitutional interpretations from inquiries into the plain meaning of the document: whatever the meaning of a text, it is not conveyed by those sources. Unlike the indeterminacy thesis, however, the interpretation thesis does not suggest that the Constitution has no meaning or has an infinity of meanings, and it does not imply that any particular interpretation of the Constitution will have no authority. What it does imply is that the authority of a proposed constitutional interpretation—the merits of a claim to constitutional meaning—will to some degree be a function of the fit between that claimed interpretation and the purposes, needs, and interests of the community of interpreters interested in the text. Whether an interpretation of the Constitution will even be recognizable as an interpretation of the document, whether it will count as a good interpretation, and whether it will be acknowledged as the best and hence most authoritative, will be largely a matter of the degree to which the interpretation feels right— follows naturally—in the light of the shared institutional identities of the Constitution's interpreter and his critics.

In the constitutional context, the difference between the interpretation thesis and the indeterminacy thesis is a difference that matters. It is not just important, but is in some sense mandatory, that an interpretation of the Constitution be authoritative, and not just plausible. Indeed, Owen Fiss is probably right to think that if an interpretation does not claim to be authoritative, it is not for that very reason an interpretation of the Constitution. The Constitution by definition simply is that document, or that set of beliefs, or whatever, that has some hold on our behavior, our beliefs, and our collective and individual identity. If whatever we are considering does not have that sort of authority, chances are good it is not a constitution. An interpretation of the Constitution that does no more, and claims to do no more, than simply reiterate the interpreter's politics, then, is not just redundant, but it is even in a sense anticonstitutional; it is the antithesis of the idea of constitutionalism. An interpretation of the Constitution must claim authority over our political identities; otherwise, whatever else it may be, it simply is not constitutional interpretation.

That the interpretation thesis and the reader-response movement are widely viewed, and feared, as having "problematized" all of this, is ironic. The most important insight of the reader-response understanding of the nature of interpretation, at least for constitutionalists, is that far from stripping the Constitution of authority, the interpretation thesis actually accounts for it. For if this understanding of the nature of interpretation is right, then the otherwise mysterious authority of the Constitution—its peculiar claim on our behavior and beliefs—is relatively easy to explain: its authority derives from its convergence with the defining purposes and interests of the various communities that from time to time have an interest in its interpretation. Correlatively, if the interpretation thesis is right, then the relative merits of a particular interpretation, and hence the authority of an interpretation, are a function of the degree to which it renders the Constitution convergent with or divergent from those defining purposes. This hardly strips the Constitution of authority; quite the contrary, it accounts for it in a way that resonates with, rather than detracts from, the participatory and democratic ideals of constitutional forms of government.

At any rate, if we assume for purposes of argument that the reader-response understanding of the nature of interpretation is right, then to return to the second interpretation of Thayer's rule of administration, the question whether a progressive congressional interpretation of the Constitution would or could ever be authoritative depends on whether there are any attributes of a hypothetical community of congressional constitutional interpreters which might in turn suggest an interpretive context within which the progressive interpretations of the constitutional phrases suggested above would seem to be—and in fact would be—authoritative, rather than simply permitted. If the answer to that question is yes, then it would make some sense to think that Congress might meaningfully and correctly interpret the Constitution in a more progressive way than has the conservative Court, and if that is right, then it also makes some sense to argue that both freeing Congress from the constraints of judicial constitutional review and subjecting it to the constraints of congressional constitutional review might encourage legislation at once both more constitutional and more progressive. Although what follows is necessarily almost entirely speculative, it seems to me that the fundamental differences between judicial and congressional purposes, and the distinguishing features of legislative as opposed to congressional lawmaking, imply at least three foundational differences between the core content of what I have been calling the "adjudicated" and the "legislated" Constitution. Those differences, in turn, might imply an authoritative rather than simply permitted progressive interpretation of our constitutional guarantees.

The first difference between the legislated and the adjudicated Constitution has to do with the generic nature of a constitution. As a number of reader-response theorists have argued, the interests, expectations, and purposes of an interpreting community can profoundly affect the identity of the interpreted text, and the identity of a text, in turn, will affect the text's meaning. To use a common example, an Agatha Christie novel, when read by casual readers expecting a detective story and seeking a particular kind of entertainment, carries with it one set of meanings, but if read by readers expecting a philosophical treatment of the nature of death might carry a very different set of meanings.[35] Within the community of readers seeking, expecting, and responding to a detective story, the text has a determinate set of meanings, and in fact, presumably, a fairly narrowly determined set of meanings. Within that community, that set of expectations, that set of shared needs and purposes, clearly some readings are clearly wrong and some better than others. On the other hand, within the community of readers looking for a treatise on death, the same text has a different, but possibly equally determined, set of meanings. Within that context, there are similarly some readings that are clearly wrong and some superior or inferior to others.

In a similar way, the different institutional purposes of Congress and the Court might suggest profoundly different understandings of what a Constitution *is*, which might in turn suggest different understandings of what the Constitution means. Perhaps because it is so widely understood, it is often forgotten, and hence worth spelling out, that the judicial system in general, and the Supreme Court in particular, exists to do legal justice—narrowly, to treat the present case "A" like the past case "B," but broadly, to guarantee some continuity between the past and the present by conserving the legal traditions of the past and using those traditions to render coherent the social predicaments of the present. Given that general institutional purpose, it makes perfect sense to think of the Constitution as the textual embodiment of those legal traditions which, in turn, represent the culmination of our most profound historical struggles. The Constitution, in the adjudicative context, and given the legal purposes of the judicial branch, represents the authoritative past's guidance for our present predicaments. Whether or not one insists on an originalist reading of constitutional meaning, within the judicial context one's theory of constitutionalism, and hence of constitutional interpretation and meaning, almost inevitably will draw on some aspect of our past. Even if not the original intent of its authors, when we ask what the Constitution dictates about some modern predicament, within the judicial context, most of us are typically seeking authoritative guidance from the past to forge a continuous identity between that past we are given and the future we create. The constitutional text, within that context, is the text we read to illuminate the authority of our history.

Congress, in contrast, does not exist to do legal justice, either narrowly or broadly conceived. Rather, it exists to do distributive justice and to give authoritative voice, not to our traditions from the past but to our present aspirations for the future. It exists, very generally, to construct a bridge, so to speak, between those present aspirations and our future, not between our present predicaments and our past. It is not unreasonable to think, then, that were the Congress to seek out constitutional guidance, it would look to the Constitution not for authoritative guidance from our traditions, or indeed from any aspect of our shared past, but authoritative guidance from our moral and political aspirations and, particularly, our aspiration for distributive justice. The congressional Constitution, then, might sensibly be understood as a "constitutional" recordation, not of our traditions but of our aspirations—not a history of where we have been, but a speculative and avowedly utopian assessment of where we might go. Within that context, were we to ask what the Constitution tells us about a predicament, we would be asking not what might be the lesson of historical traditions, but what might be the lesson of our very contemporary hopes and dreams. The Constitution of any particular moment would be our sense of how we might best constitute our collective and individual identity. An understanding of the original, historic, or traditional Constitution of our pasts would of course be relevant to the task of identifying as well as interpreting the content of that aspirational Constitution. But it would by no means be identical with it.

The Constitution, of course, identifies itself as law, and indeed as the supreme law, but this does not undercut the possibility of an aspirational Constitution—a Constitution of present aspirations rather than a Constitution of recorded historic victories. For, if the reader-response school's understanding of textual interpretation is right, then the jurisprudential nature of law, no less than the political nature of the Constitution, is contingent on the institutional purposes and needs of the community of law's interpreters. Within the judicial context, and given judicial purposes, law is that which facilitates the primary obligation of courts to do legal justice: to treat like cases alike. Law consists of those rules of decision recorded in precedent that enable a court to fashion and apply general rules to particular cases in a way that will respect not only the particularities of each case, but far more important, the similarities of each case to some relevant aspect of our shared past. Constitutional law, then, if it is to be a part of law, must take the form of precedential rules of decision enabling the similar constitutional treatment of future with past cases, through the familiar methods of analogical reasoning.

Within the congressional context, and given congressional purposes, it is not unreasonable to ascribe to the idea of law—and particularly the idea of a higher or supreme law—a quite different essential jurisprudential nature. Congress, again, does not exist to do legal justice, to treat like cases alike, or to judge in a way that respects the similarity of present circumstances with past precedent. To the contrary, Congress has as its central mission the alteration, the deviation, and the transformation—not the conservation—of the past. It exists to bring our present circumstances in line with our ambitions and aspirations of the future, not to bring our present circumstances in line with the authoritative traditions of the past. The law relevant to such an endeavor, then, including the constitutional law, would not, presumably, be a law of binding historical precedent in search of similarly situated present circumstances. It would be a law of ideal moral principles—those principles of distributive justice toward which our politics aspire. The congressional Constitution no less than the judicial Constitution would be law, but the significance of the appellation would be quite different. The law of which the congressional Constitution would be an instance would be a law of moral principle and high ideals, not, as is the case with the judicial Constitution, a law of precedent and past rule facilitating the provision of legal justice.

For these two reasons alone, congressional interpretation of the Constitution might produce authoritative meanings more conducive to progressive change than those produced by the Court. And again, the argument is not simply that the constitutional text, like any text, can have an infinite number of meanings, can therefore have progressive as well as conservative meanings, and is therefore likely to be interpreted in a progressive manner by legislators who happen to be more progressive than the present political composition of the Supreme Court. Rather, congressional interpretation of the Constitution might be freed of the conservatism of judicial interpretation because of the quite different purposes that define each branch. The purpose of adjudicating law is conservation and preservation—respect for the traditions of the past is indeed at the heart of the work of doing legal justice. Maintaining continuity with what has gone before is a way of making sense of our present lives, and it is that form of integrity— that urge to maintain our collective identities through the affirmation of our similarities with our history—that constitutes much of the work of judicial or adjudicative law.[36] Given that the Constitution is itself a part of law, it is inevitable that constitutional law, when understood as a part of judicial work, will take on a conservative hue: the idea of constitutionalism in that purposive context simply underscores the ideal of legalism. Law exists to provide a mechanism for maintaining continuity with the past, and constitutional law exists to provide a mechanism for maintaining continuity with the most definitive and ennobling moments of that past.[37] But it does not follow that either law or the constitution, when undertaken by a community of interpreters unified by a very different set of motivating and defining purposes, will think of, perceive, or use either concept in the same way; in fact, what follows is quite the contrary. If the conservatism of constitutional law, of the concept of constitutionalism, and of the concept of law is in part a product of the purposes of the judicial community of its interpreters, as suggested by the reader-response work in interpretive and hermeneutic theory, it then follows that an interpretive community defined and constituted by a different set of purposes might develop quite different understandings.

Substantively, the different defining purposes of the Congress and the Court might imply drastically different understandings of at least two of our basic constitutional values: the liberty and the equality which are each in some way guaranteed by the Fourteenth Amendment. First, as I have argued elsewhere,[38] the Court's insistence on a formal rather than a substantive interpretation of the equal protection clause, with its antiprogressive consequences for race-conscious affirmative action plans designed to eradicate substantive, not just formal, inequality, might be a function not only of the conservative leanings of the particular Justices, but also of the Supreme Court's role, shared by all courts, as a dispenser of formal justice. Formal justice requires that likes be treated alike, and the Court's regressive jurisprudence of the equality provision of the Fourteenth Amendment simply applies that standard (in an admittedly wooden way) to legislatures: legislators must treat all like groups alike, race is not a distinction that should make a difference, and consequently benign as well as malign race-conscious legislation is unconstitutional.[39] An institution such as Congress, committed and constituted, as it is, by the mission of distributive rather than formal justice, might well be led to a quite different understanding of equality and, therefore, a different conclusion regarding the constitutionality of affirmative action. A community of interpreters organized for the purpose of redistributing resources so as to create substantive equality— rather than organized for the purpose of adjudicating cases so as to respect formal equality—might see in the Fourteenth Amendment's guarantee of equal protection a quite different, and far more egalitarian, mandate.

Similarly, the Court's institutional purpose has heavily influenced, if not determined, its understanding of the content and value of individual liberty. Given our overriding political scheme, the Supreme Court exists not only to do legal justice, but also to constrain and limit the powers of the other branches of government. Given that purpose, it is not surprising that the Court has understood liberty as meaning individual liberty from pernicious state power; such an interpretation underscores the Court's role as a watchdog of excessive state power. A Congress constituted and defined by the quite different purpose of limiting, by redistributing, not state power, but private power—whatever the form that private power might take—could surely understand the guarantee of liberty at the heart of both the First and the Fourteenth Amendments as protecting not the liberty of the individual against pernicious state power, but the liberty of the individual against infringement by powerful private sources of oppression. Were it to do so, it might view the constitutional protection of that liberty as requiring, rather than prohibiting, state regulation not only of the economic market, but of the linguistic and cultural markets as well.

A Congress, itself in part defined by its goal of distributive rather than formal or legal justice, that conscientiously set out to interpret a Constitution situated within our egalitarian and redistributive aspirations rather than by our conservationist traditions, constrained by principle rather than precedent, and informed by the values of substantive equality and individual liberty from private and intimate oppression, rather than by the values of formal equality and liberty from the state, would, very likely—even naturally—read the Constitution as requiring, not simply permitting, quite different, and far more progressive, interpretations of our constitutional guarantees than those reached by the Court. For example, if we take seriously the threat to liberty posed by private power, then the silence of the battered spouse or the incest victim or the abused child is of at least as much concern as the silence of the intimidated government dissenter. Friends of the First Amendment should be as concerned to eliminate the censorial power of domestic violence as they are concerned to eliminate the censorial power of the overzealous state. An interpretive community freed of the judicial purpose of limiting state power and animated by the general purposive goal of distributive justice might, then, be more inclined to understand the Fourteenth Amendment's mandate to Congress to ensure the guarantees of the First Amendment as requiring Congress to take some action to address the wave of private, domestic, severely silencing, and largely unchecked violence still visited upon thousands of women and children yearly by the men in their intimate lives.

Similarly, if we take seriously the threat to liberty and equality posed by the intimidating power of dominant culture, then the silence of the school-bound African-American child, cowed by the insult to and neglect of her culture by her white Eurocentric education, should be of as much concern as the silence of the hypothetical political party intimidated into silence by the powers of the omnipotent state. An interpretive community such as Congress, charged with the task of achieving redistributive justice, might view the nascent attempts to address that silence through a diversification of public school curricula not as prohibited, but as in furtherance of the liberal and pluralist goals of the First Amendment. To take one last example, if we take seriously the threat to substantive equality posed by grotesque maldistributions of material resources between majority and minority communities of citizens, then the substantive inequality visited on the African-American community through the mechanisms of the labor market should be of at least as much concern as the formal inequality visited on that community by a segregative, state-sponsored Jim Crow legal regime. Attempts to address that substantive inequality through affirmative action plans designed to remedy the effects of private and societal racism might be viewed as required, not prohibited, by Fourteenth Amendment guarantees of equality by an interpretive community constituted by the goal of distributive rather than legal justice. Examples, of course, could be multiplied.

Although relevant to congressional constitutional interpretation, the original intent of the Constitution's framers, as well as the prior historical understandings of constitutional meaning reached by the Court, would not be determinative, just as modern aspirations and moral principles, although relevant to judicial constitutional interpretation, are not determinative. Rather, the historical understandings of the Constitution would be a part—albeit a peripheral part—of a larger body of doctrine which collectively would constitute the doctrine of aspirational constitutional law. Closer to the core of that body of law would be those congressional acts designed to achieve an equal society of free individuals, including, for example, not only the Civil Rights Acts, but also the Americans with Disabilities Acts, the proposed Violence against Women Act, and the potential Gay and Lesbian Civil Rights Act. Closer yet to the core would be our specific aspirations for substantive equality and freedom from private coercion. And at the core would be the true ideals of liberty and equality toward which aspirational and political goals are, or should be, aimed.

Conclusion

There is, of course, no reason to think that Thayer envisioned or would endorse a progressive and aspirational interpretation of the Constitution as the sort I have described. Nevertheless, he must have envisioned some significant difference between those interpretations of the Constitution likely to be reached by the Court and those interpretations feasibly reached by Congress, if he was serious in his contention that a Congress freed of excessive judicial constitutional intervention, but nevertheless constrained by its own reading of the Constitution, would be more likely than otherwise to legislate toward the ends of right and justice. I have tried to suggest some reasons, in the rather different context of modern politics, to think that this belief might have been justified. There are reasons, in other words, beyond the ultimately self-defeating belief in the indeterminacy of the Constitution, to think that Congress could reach authoritative understandings of the Constitution that would be quite different from those reached by the Court. There are even good reasons to think that those decisions might be principled and not merely political. Assuming they would be principled, and assuming they would not be clearly erroneous, then, following Thayer, a Court concerned with minimizing the conflict between constitutionalism and participatory democracy, should uphold them, thus respecting not only the impulse behind the second interpretation of Thayer's rule of administration but also the impulse behind the first. A conscientious Court, in other words, should restrain from declaring such interpretations unconstitutional, not just because by practicing self-restraint the unelected Court thereby negatively promotes participatory democracy by staying its own undemocratic hand, but because by respecting the different, even radically different, interpretations of the aspirational Constitution rendered by the Congress, the Court positively promotes congressional and hence popular responsibility for those democratically shared principles that constitute us. Not coincidentally, it would by doing so also further the democratization— long overdue—of the Constitution itself.

It is highly unlikely today that Congress will accept primary responsibility for active constitutional decision making. It might be easy to imagine a progressive Congress coming up with progressive constitutional arguments, but it is very hard to imagine what set of circumstances, or what political scenarios, might prompt such a drastic administrative change in congressional and judicial behavior. Nevertheless, it is important to envision alternative understandings of the Constitution, just as it is important to fashion progressive constitutional arguments, even in the absence of a realistic chance of their acceptance by the conservative Court: constitutional arguments of the traditional sort create losers and outsiders, and the simple act of envisioning alternative understandings of our collective constitutive identity might to some degree counter that existential exclusion. All I have sought to emphasize here is that in developing those alternative understandings, it would behoove us to consider not just alternatives to received meanings of constitutional phrases, but alternatives to received understandings of the idea of constitutionalism and the idea of law, which jointly create an interpretive context within which those alternative understandings might attain some true constitutional authority, and hence some real moral claim on our felt loyalties, principles, and allegiances. Those alternative understandings of the essence of the idea of constitutionalism, and the essence of the idea of law, in turn might be prompted not so much by jurisprudential speculation as by institutional imagination: the content of the idea of constitutionalism and the content of the idea of law seem to be contingent on the purposes and ideals of the institution charged with the task of law and constitution making.

A rule of administration shifting responsibility for those tasks, then, from one institution to another, as suggested by Thayer a hundred years ago, might carry in its wake changes in our understanding of the nature of law, of the nature of a constitution, and hence of the nature and content of the constitutional law being made. What those changes might be, should a (hypothetical) conservative and conscientious Court, in the interest of promoting a more participatory and aspirational Constitution, yield to the authority of an equally hypothetical progressive congressional constitutional interpretation, is an almost entirely academic question; it is hard to see its practical import in a world in which such a dramatic shift of interpretive power is unlikely to occur. But that does not make it unimportant. It is only through asking questions of the sort Thayer raised, and by giving free rein to the speculations to which they give rise, that the possibility of even perceiving, much less realizing, any Constitution close to the understandings and aspirations of the people is kept real. Thayer's rule of administration, if understood as requiring congressional responsibility for generating authoritative constitutional interpretations, is as far from modern practice as it was a hundred years ago. But notwithstanding the air of paradox, perhaps that is the source of its modern relevance.

Notes

■

1. Toward an Abolitionist Interpretation
of the Fourteenth Amendment

1. City of Richmond v. J. A. Croson Co., 488 U.S. 469 (1989). *But see* Metro Broadcasting, Inc. v. FCC, 497 U.S. 547 (1990).

2. *See, e.g.,* Charles Fried, "Comment, *Metro Broadcasting, Inc. v. FCC:* Two Concepts of Equality," 104 *Harv. L. Rev.* 107 (1990). The classic statement of this position is Paul Brest, "The Supreme Court 1975 Term Foreword: In Defense of the Antidiscrimination Principle," 90 *Harv. L. Rev.* 1 (1976).

3. *See Croson,* 488 U.S. at 535 (Marshall, J., joined by Brennan, J., and Blackmun, J., dissenting); *Metro Broadcasting,* 497 U.S. at 567–70.

4. *See, e.g.,* Catharine A. MacKinnon, *Feminism Unmodified: Discourses on Life and Law* (1987); Laurence H. Tribe, *American Constitutional Law 15* 14–21 (2d ed. 1988); Ruth Colker, "Anti-Subordination above All: Sex, Race, and Equal Protection," 61 *N.Y. U. L. Rev.* 1003 (1986); Owen M. Fiss, "Groups and the Equal Protection Clause," 5 *Phil. Pub. Aff.* 107 (1976).

5. *See* Jacobus tenBroek, *Equal under Law* (originally *The Antislavery Origins of the Fourteenth Amendment*) (1965); John P. Frank & Robert F. Munro, "The Original Understanding of "Equal Protection of the Laws'," 1972 *Wash. U. L. Q.* 421.

6. 347 U.S. 483 (1954).

7. *Id.* at 494.

8. 163 U.S. 537 (1896).

9. *See, e.g.,* David A. Strauss, "Discriminatory Intent and the Taming of Brown," 56 *U. Chi. L. Rev.* 935 (1989); David A. Strauss, "The Myth of Colorblindness," 1986 *Sup. Ct. Rev.* 99 (1986).

10. Green v. County School Board of New Kent County, 391 U.S. 430 (1968), went the farthest toward requiring actual integration, while Milliken v. Bradley, 418 U.S. 717 (1974), and Milliken v. Bradley, 433 U.S. 267 (1977), went the farthest toward requiring only an end to intentional discrimination.

11. 426 U.S. 229 (1976).

12. *Id*. at 240.

13. *Id*. at 246. *See also* Brest, *supra* note 2 (arguing that antidiscrimination is the general principle underlying equality law, not rectification of substantive inequalities).

14. *See* Tribe, *supra* note 4, at 1514–21.

15. *Washington v. Davis*, 426 U.S. at 240.

16. 488 U.S. 469 (1989).

17. *Id*. at 480.

18. *Id*. at 518 (Kennedy, J., concurring in part and in the judgment).

19. *See, e.g., id*. at 520–28 (Scalia, J., concurring in the judgment); Strauss, "The Myth of Colorblindness," *supra* note 9. *See* Fried, *supra* note 2.

20. *See* Fried, *supra* note 2, at 111.

21. 163 U.S. 537 (1896).

22. *See, e.g.,* City of Richmond v. J. A. Croson Co., 488 U.S. 469, 528 (1989) (Marshall, J., with whom Brennan, J., and Blackmun, J., join, dissenting); Kenneth Casebeer, "Running on Empty: Justice Brennan's Plea, The Empty State, the City of Richmond, and the Profession," 43 *U. Miami L. Rev.* 989 (1989); Richard Delgado, "On Taking Back Our Civil Rights Promises: When Equality Doesn't Compute," 1989 *Wis. L. Rev.* 579; Michel Rosenfeld, "Decoding Richmond: Affirmative Action and the Elusive Meaning of Constitutional Equality," 87 *Mich. L. Rev.* 1729 (1989); Strauss, "Discriminatory Intent and the Taming of Brown," *supra* note 9; Patricia J. Williams, "The Obliging Shell: An Informal Essay on Formal Equal Opportunity," 87 *Mich. L. Rev.* 2128 (1989).

23. Robin L. West, "Progressive and Conservative Constitutionalism," 88 *Mich. L. Rev.* 641, 669–72 (1990).

24. John Rawls, *A Theory of Justice* 136–42 (1971).

25. *See, e.g.,* Mark V. Tushnet, *Red, White and Blue: A Critical Analysis of Constitutional Law* (1988).

26. *See, e.g.,* Mark Kelman, "Interpretive Construction in the Substantive Criminal Law," 33 *Stan. L. Rev.* 591, 597 (1981).

27. *See, e.g.,* "Symposium on the Renaissance of Pragmatism in American Legal Thought," 63 *S. Cal. L. Rev.* 1569 (1990); Thomas C. Grey, "Hear the Other Side: Wallace Stevens and Pragmatist Legal Theory," 63 *S. Cal. L. Rev.* 1569 (1990); Thomas C. Grey, "Holmes and Legal Pragmatism," 41 *Stan. L. Rev.* 787 (1989); Catherine W. Hantzis, "Legal Innovation within the Wider Intellectual Tradition: The Pragmatism of Oliver Wendell Holmes, Jr.," 82 *NW. U. L. Rev.* 541 (1988).

28. 56 *U. Chi. L. Rev.* 1175, 1178 (1989).

29. *Id*.

30. William Golding, *Lord of the Flies* (1962).

31. *See* Robert M. Cover, *Justice Accused* 11, 77 (1975).

32. This is the general thesis of Catharine MacKinnon's work. *See, e.g., Feminism Unmodified, supra* note 4; Catharine A. MacKinnon, *Toward a Feminist Theory of the State* (1989).

33. Jacobus tenBroek, *supra* note 5, at 4 (now retitled, *Equal under Law*).

34. *Id*. at 116–134.

35. *Id*. at 201–39.

36. *Id.*

37. This argument has its origins in the Slaughter-House Cases, 83 U.S. (16 Wall.) 36 (1873), in which Justice Miller, in the course of holding that a Louisiana law granting a corporation monopoly status does not violate the Constitution, opined that the reconstruction amendments in their entirety were intended to ensure "the freedom of the slave race, the security and firm establishment of that freedom, and the protection of the newly made freeman and citizen from the oppressions of those who had formerly exercised unlimited dominion over him." *Id.* at 407. *See generally* Raoul Berger, *Government by Judiciary: The Transformation of the Fourteenth Amendment* (1977) (arguing generally against Warren Court interpretation of the Fourteenth Amendment, as outside the perimeters of its intended meaning).

38. Richard A. Posner, "Bork and Beethoven," 42 *Stan. L. Rev.* 1365 (1990).

39. Kurt Vonnegut, "Harrison Bergeron," in *Welcome to the Monkey House* (2d ed. 1988).

40. *Cf.* Robert Nozick, *Anarchy, State, and Utopia* (1974) (arguing that a Rawlsian view of justice does not adequately respect individuals' rights to the fruits of their natural endowments).

41. James B. White, *Justice as Translation* (1990).

42. Ronald Dworkin, *Taking Rights Seriously* 134–36 (1977).

43. *See* Posner, *supra* note 38, at 1374–75. Indeed, Congress immediately passed the Ku Klux Klan Act of 1871, 17 Stat. 13, for the express purpose of ensuring Fourteenth Amendment rights.

44. 14 Stat. 27. The Civil Rights Act of 1866 was later reenacted after passage of the Fourteenth Amendment as Section 18 of the Enforcement Act of 1870, 16 Stat. 140. *See generally,* tenBroek, *supra* note 5, at 202–3.

45. *See* Elizabeth Ross, "Big City Police Fall Back on Storied Concept," *Christian Science Monitor,* May 20, 1991, at 9; Nathan McCall, "School Incumbents under Siege," *Washington Post,* Oct. 25, 1990, at J1.

46. 489 U.S. 189 (1989).

47. *See, e.g.,* Martinez v. California, 444 U.S. 277 (1980).

48. *DeShaney,* 489 U.S. at 197.

49. *Id.* at 208–10.

50. 481 U.S. 279 (1987).

51. *See* Randall L. Kennedy, "*McCleskey v. Kemp:* Race, Capital Punishment, and the Supreme Court," 101 *Harv. L. Rev.* 1388 (1988).

52. 426 U.S. 229 (1976).

53. *See* Tribe, *supra* note 4, at 1520–21.

54. 83 U.S. (16 Wall.) 36 (1873).

55. 109 U.S. 3 (1883).

56. *See* tenBroek, *supra* note 5.

57. *Cf.* Frank I. Michelman, "Welfare Rights in a Constitutional Democracy," 1979 *Wash. U. L. Q.* 659, 677–78, 178 (arguing that welfare, not equality, is behind the Warren Court's equal protection cases dealing with poor people).

58. *See, e.g.,* Arlie Hochschild, *The Second Shift: Working Parents and the Revolution at Home* (1989).

59. 347 U.S. 483 (1954).

60. 426 U.S. 229 (1976).
61. 488 U.S. 469 (1989).
62. *See, e.g.*, Paul Brest, "The Misconceived Quest for the Original Understanding," 60 *B.U. L. Rev.* 204 (1980); Dworkin, *supra* note 42, at 131–50.
63. Adrienne Rich, "Compulsory Heterosexuality and the Lesbian Continuum," in *Blood, Bread and Poetry* (A. Rich, ed., 1986).

2. Equality Theory, Marital Rape, and the
Promise of the Fourteenth Amendment

1. *See, e.g.*, Merton v. State, 500 So. 2d 1301, 1305 (Ala. Crim. App. 1986); Williams v. State, 494 So. 2d 819, 830 (Ala. Crim. App. 1986); People v. Liberta, 64 N.Y.2d 152, 474 N.E.2d 567, 573–76, 485 N.Y.S.2d 207, 213–16 (1984); People v. DeStefano, 121 Misc. 2d 113, 163–64, 170, 467 N.Y.S.2d 506, 515–16 (County Ct. 1983); Shunn v. State, 742 P.2d 775, 778 (Wyo. 1987).

2. *See* Alan D. Freeman, "But If You Can't Rape Your Wife, Who(m) Can You Rape?: The Marital Rape Exemption Re-Examined," 15 *Fam. L. Q.* 1, 29 (1981); "Note, To Have and to Hold: The Marital Rape Exemption and the Fourteenth Amendment," 99 *Harv. L. Rev.* 1255 (1986) [hereinafter "Note, To Have and to Hold"]; "Note," 24 *J. Fam. L.* 87, 87–93 (1985); "Comment, For Better or for Worse: Marital Rape," 15 *N. Ky. L. Rev.* 611, 631–34 (1988).

3. *See, e.g.*, People v. Liberta, 64 N.Y.2d 152, 163–64, 170, 474 N.E.2d 567, 573–76, 485 N.Y.S.2d 207, 213–16 (1984) (opinion by Judge Wachtler advancing the most complete argument).

4. As of 1994, twenty-four states have repealed the exemption entirely. For examples of judicial abolishment of the marital rape exemption, see *supra* note 1. For examples of legislative abolishment of the exemption, see Alaska Stat. s 11.41.443 (repealed 1989); Colo. Rev. Stat. s 18-3-409 (Supp. 1989); Fla. Stat. s 794.011 (1989); Haw. Rev. Stat. s 707-73–733 (Michie Supp. 1993); Ill. Ann. Stat. ch. 38, para. 12–13 (Michie 1993); Ind. Code Ann. s 35-42-4-1 (Supp. 1993) (repealed 1989); Iowa Code Ann. ss 709.2–.4 (West 1993); Me. Rev. Stat. Ann. tit. 17A, s 251 (1983 & Supp. 1989); *id.* s 252 (repealed 1989); Miss. Code Ann. 97-3-65 (3) (Supp. 1993); Mo. Ann. Stat. s 566.010.2 (Vernon Supp. 1993); Mont. Code Ann. ss 45-5-502 to -503 (1993); N.C. Gen. Stat. s 14-27-8 (1993); N.D. Cent. Code s 12.1-20-01 to -03 (1985 & Supp. 1989); Neb. Rev. Stat. ss 28-319 to -320 (1985); N.J. Stat. Ann. s 2C:14-5(b) (West 1982); N.M. Stat. Ann. ss 30-9-10 to -12 (Michie Supp. 1993) (repealed 1991); Or. Rev. Stat. ss 163.355–.375 (1987); Utah Code Ann. s 76-5-407 (Michie 1990 & Supp. 1993); Vt. Stat. Ann. tit. 13, s 3252 (Supp. 1989); Wis. Stat. Ann. s 940.225(6) (West Supp. 1989).

5. See, e.g., Ala. Code Ann. s 13A-6-60 to -65 (1982 & Supp. 1993) (stating that spouse can be charged with rape or forcible sodomy, but cannot be charged with sodomy in the second degree, sexual misconduct or sexual abuse); Ariz. Rev. Stat. Ann. s 13-1406.01 (1993) (criminalizing sexual assault of a spouse); Ark. Code Ann. s 5-14-103 (Michie 1987 & Advance Code Service 1992–93) (stating that rape not a crime if spouse is less than sixteen years of age and is mentally defective or mentally incapacitated; carnal abuse in the second degree and sexual abuse in the second degree not crimes if

the spouse is mentally defective or mentally incapable); Cal. Penal Code s 262 (West Supp. 1994) (stating that no arrest or prosecution unless violation is reported within one year); Conn. Gen. Stat. Ann. s 53a-70(b) (West Supp. 1993) (stating that sentence for spousal rape suspendable, non-spousal rape sentence not suspendable); Idaho Code s 18-6107 (Michie Supp. 1993) (stating that crime only if force or threat of immediate bodily harm); Kan. Stat. Ann. ss 21-3501.02, .17, .18 (Supp. 1993) (stating that husband can be charged with rape and aggravated sexual battery, but not sexual battery); La. Rev. Stat. Ann. s 14.41 (West Supp. 1993) (stating that no crime if spouse is mentally incapable of resisting or of understanding the nature of the act); Md. Crim. Law Code Ann. s 27-464D (Repl. vol. 1987 & Supp. 1989) (stating that husband can be charged with rape only if force used); Mich. Comp. Laws Ann. s 750.5201 (West 1991) (stating that no crime if spouse is mentally incapable or mentally incapacitated); Minn. Stat. Ann. s 609.349 (West 1987) (stating that no crime for lesser degrees); Nev. Rev. Stat. Ann. s 200.373 (Michie 1992) (stating that crime of "sexual assault of spouse" available only if force or threat present); N.H. Rev. Stat. Ann. s 632-A:2 (1986 & Supp. 1993) (stating that no crime if spouse is mentally defective); N.Y. Penal Law s 130.00 to -.70 (McKinney 1987 & Supp. 1993) (stating that marital exemption unconstitutional only with respect to forcible rape, forcible sodomy and forcible sexual abuse); Ohio Rev. Code Ann. s 2907.02 (Anderson 1993) (stating that spouse can be charged with rape only if force or threat of force; spouse cannot be charged with sexual battery); Okla. Stat. Ann. tit. 21 s 1111 (Supp. 1994) (stating that spouse cannot be charged unless force or violence used or threatened); 18 Pa. Cons. Stat. Ann. s 3103 (Purdon Supp. 1992) (stating that no crime for lesser degrees); *id.* s 3126–28 (Purdon Supp. 1992); R.I. Gen. Laws s 11-37-1-6 (1993) (stating that no crime if spouse is mentally incapable); S.D. Codified Laws Ann. s 22-22-1.1 (1993) (stating that spouse cannot be charged with rape unless the defendant is armed, the victim suffers serious bodily injury, or if the spouses are no longer cohabitating or are legally separated); Tenn. Code Ann. s 39-13-507(b) (Supp. 1993) (stating that spouse cannot be charged unless couple living apart and one spouse has filed for separation or divorce or if spouse armed with weapon or similar article or victim suffers serious bodily injury); Tex. Penal Code Ann. ss 21-02(a), to -12 (Vernon 1984 & Supp. 1994) (stating that husbands can be charged with only "aggravated sexual assault"); Va. Code Ann. s 18.2-61 (1993) (establishing a ten-day reporting requirement; stating that spouse can be charged only with first and second degree rape); Wash. Rev. Code Ann. s 9A.44.060 (West Supp. 1994) (stating that no crime for rape in the third degree); W. Va. Code s 61-8B-6 (Michie 1992) (stating that first degree rape only; lesser penalty than nonmarital rape); Wyo. Stat. s 6-2-307 (1993) (stating that no crime if spouse is mentally incapable).

6. *Cf.* S.D. Codified Laws Ann. s 22-22-1.1 (1988) (recognizing spousal rape).

7. *See* "Note, To Have and to Hold," *supra* note 2, at 1270–72.

8. See, e.g., Ky. Rev. Stat. Ann. s 510.010(3) (Baldwin 1993) (recognizing action only if petition filed for separation or divorce and parties living apart); S.C. Code Ann. s 16-3-658 (Law. Co-op. Supp. 1993) (stating that spouse cannot be charged unless couple living apart and must be reported within thirty days; first and second degree only); S.D. Codified Laws Ann. s 22-22-1.1 (1993) (stating that spouse cannot be charged with rape unless defendant is armed, the victim suffers serious bodily injury, or unless the

couple is living apart); Tenn. Code Ann. s 39-13-507(b) (Supp. 1993) (stating that spouse cannot be charged unless couple living apart and one spouse has filed for separation or divorce or if spouse armed with weapon or similar article or victim suffers serious bodily injury).

9. Many states include cohabitants within the scope of the marital rape exemption. *See* Conn. Gen. Stat. Ann. s 53a–70(b) (West 1985); Ky. Rev. Stat. Ann. s 510.010(3) (Baldwin 1993); Mont. Code Ann. s 45-5-511 (1989); 18 Pa. Cons. Stat. Ann. s 3103 (Purdon 1983).

10. See *supra* notes 1–4 and accompanying text.

11. *But see* Michael Hilf, "Marital Privacy and Spousal Rape," 16 *New Eng. L. Rev.* 31, 43–44 (1980) (recognizing that limited spousal immunity supports marital privacy rights and encourages reconciliations); "Comment, Forcible and Statutory Rape: An Exploration of the Operation and Objectives of the Consent Standard," 62 *Yale L. J.* 55, 74 (1952) (recognizing a policy of protecting reliance on behavior of others should prevail over the demand for protection of the woman's right to withhold consent).

12. 347 U.S. 483 (1954).

13. *See, e.g.,* "Note, To Have and to Hold," *supra* note 2, at 1270.

14. See *infra* text accompanying notes 95–101.

15. For the argument in detail, see "Note, To Have and to Hold," *supra* note 2, at 1267–72.

16. *Cf.* Eisenstadt v. Baird, 405 U.S. 438, 446–54 (1972) (recognizing that by providing dissimilar treatment for married and unmarried persons who are similarly situated, the contraception statute violated the equal protection clause of the Fourteenth Amendment).

17. See *infra* text accompanying notes 69–93.

18. *See,* e.g., Catharine A. MacKinnon, *Toward a Feminist Theory of the State* 215–37 (1989); Mary E. Becker, "Prince Charming: Abstract Equality, 1989 *Sup. Ct. Rev.* 201.

19. See *infra* text accompanying notes 27–67.

20. See *infra* text accompanying notes 69–93.

21. See *infra* text accompanying notes 95–101.

22. Examples include the Civil Rights Act of 1875, partially struck in the Civil Rights Cases, 109 U.S. 3 (1883), and the Civil Rights Act of 1964, 42 U.S.C.A. ss 2000a to 2000h-5 (West 1982), upheld in Katzenbach v. McClung, 379 U.S. 294 (1964).

23. See *infra* text accompanying note 105.

24. For a general discussion, see Laurence H. Tribe, *American Constitutional Law* ss 16-13 to -17, at 1465–88 (1988).

25. For general discussions of the rationality approach to equal protection, see John Hart Ely, *Democracy and Distrust* 145–48 (1980); Gerald Gunther, "Foreword: In Search of Evolving Doctrine on a Changing Court: A Model for a Newer Equal Protection," 86 *Harv. L. Rev.* 1, 20–24 (1972); Frank I. Michelman, "Politics and Values or What's Really Wrong with Rationality Review?," 13 *Creighton L. Rev.* 487 (1979); Cass R. Sunstein, "Naked Preferences and the Constitution," 84 *Colum. L. Rev.* 1689, 1697–98, 1713–14 (1984); Peter Westen, "The Empty Idea of Equality," 95 *Harv. L. Rev.* 537, 569–77 (1982).

26. For a detailed discussion of these constraints, see Tribe, *supra* note 24, ss 16-1 to -6, at 1438–54.

27. Craig v. Boren, 429 U.S. 190, 197 (1976) ("classifications by gender must serve important governmental objectives and must be substantially related to achievement of those objectives").

28. Washington v. Davis, 426 U.S. 229, 239–41 (1976) (advising that a statute must have a racially discriminatory purpose to violate the equal protection clause).

29. *See, e.g.,* Williamson v. Lee Optical Co., 348 U.S. 483 (1955) (recognizing that several provisions of a state statute governing opticians were rationally related to legitimate governmental ends and did not violate the equal protection clause of the Fourteenth Amendment).

30. *See* City of Richmond v. J. A. Croson Co., 488 U.S. 469, 490–97 (1989) (plurality opinion) (advising that a searching judicial inquiry is required to determine whether racial classifications are suspect or benign); Regents of University of California v. Bakke, 438 U.S. 265, 291 (1978) (stating that racial and ethnic distinctions are inherently suspect and require "exacting judicial examination"); Brown v. Board of Education, 347 U.S. 483, 495 (1954) ("Separate educational facilities are inherently unequal.").

31. *See* Loving v. Virginia, 388 U.S. 1, 9–11 (1967) (applying strict scrutiny to determine that an interracial marriage proscription statute constituted invidious racial discrimination). *But see* Korematsu v. United States, 323 U.S. 214, 216, 223 (1944) (recognizing that strict scrutiny applied, but the act was upheld as not constituting invidious racial discrimination).

32. *See Loving,* 388 U.S. at 9–11 (stating that classifications based solely on race have no legitimate purpose).

33. *See* Rostker v. Goldberg, 453 U.S. 57, 79 (1981) (advising a gender classification requiring only men to register for draft was not invidious and not unconstitutional); Michael M. v. Superior Court, 450 U.S. 464, 468–69 (1981) (plurality opinion) (accepting a California statute that punishes only males for raping females does not unconstitutionally discriminate on the basis of gender).

34. This insight explains the Court's uncertainty over whether gender-based discriminations hurt or help women, or discriminate against men rather than women. *See, e.g.,* Califano v. Webster, 430 U.S. 313 (1977) (*per curiam*) (accepting a more lenient formula to calculate social security benefits for women than for men); Califano v. Goldfarb, 430 U.S. 199, 207–08 (1977) (plurality opinion); *id.* at 217–18 (Stevens, J., concurring in the judgment) (recognizing a gender-based difference between widows and widowers for social security benefits).

35. *See, e.g.,* Craig v. Boren, 429 U.S. 190 (1976); Stanton v. Stanton, 421 U.S. 7 (1975); Weinberger v. Wiesenfeld, 420 U.S. 636 (1975); Frontiero v. Richardson, 411 U.S. 677 (1973); Reed v. Reed, 404 U.S. 71 (1971).

36. *See, e.g.,* Califano v. Webster, 430 U.S. 313 (1977); Schlesinger v. Ballard, 419 U.S. 498 (1975); Kahn v. Shevin, 416 U.S. 351 (1974).

37. 426 U.S. 229 (1976).

38. *See id.* at 239, 242.

39. *See id.* at 239–41.

40. The vision is also, in some of its forms, unquestionably feminist. For a strong defense and explication of the virtues of the model from a feminist point of view, *see* Wendy Williams, "Notes from a First Generation," 1989 *Chi. Legal F.* 99.

41. In an article capturing both the spirit and the content of this critique, Mary Becker provocatively dubbed the promise of formal equality inherent in the rationality model "Prince Charming." *See* Mary E. Becker, "Prince Charming: Abstract Equality," 1989 *Sup. Ct. Rev.* 201 (arguing that formal equality would not help and often would hurt women's actual well-being).

42. *See* Martha Fineman, "Challenging Law," 42 *Fla. L. Rev.* 25 (1990); *and* Robin L. West, "The Difference in Women's Hedonic Lives," 3 *Wis. Women's L. J.* 81 (1987).

43. C. Gilligan, *In a Different Voice: Psychological Theory and Women's Development* (1982).

44. S. Firestone, *The Dialectic of Sex: The Case for Feminist Revolution* (1970).

45. M. Belenky, *Women's Ways of Knowing: The Development of Self, Voice, and Mind* (1986).

46. Arlie Hochschild, *The Second Shift: Working Parents and the Revolution at Home* (1989).

47. West, *supra* note 42.

48. T. Olsen, *Silences* (1978).

49. *Id.*

50. *See generally* Christine Littleton, "Women's Experience," 1989 *Chi. Legal F.* 23; "Note, Toward a Redefinition of Sexual Equality," 95 *Harv. L. Rev.* 487, 499 (1981).

51. *See generally* MacKinnon, *supra* note 18, at 215–34 (critiquing formal equality).

52. *See generally* Becker, *supra* note 41 (critiquing formal equality).

53. *See generally id.*

54. *See* Christine Littleton, "Reconstructing Sexual Equality," 75 *Cal. L. Rev.* 1279 (1987).

55. *Id.* at 1296–97.

56. *Id.*

57. MacKinnon *supra* note 18; Becker, *supra* note 41; Ruth Colker, "Antisubordination above All Sex, Race, and Equal Protection," 61 *N.Y.U. L. Rev.* 1003 (1986).

58. *See* Colker, *supra* note 57, at 1007–16.

59. *Id.*

60. Becker, *supra* note 43, at 247.

61. *See generally* MacKinnon, *supra* note 18, at 215–37 (developing an antisubordination theory of equality).

62. Catharine A. MacKinnon, *Sexual Harassment of Working Women* 117 (1979).

63. *See generally* MacKinnon, *supra* note 18, at 215–37 (developing an antisubordination theory of equality).

64. The antisubordination model has much to commend it, not only to women's progress, but also as a constitutional rule. It is the essence of simplicity. Any doctrine developed under this model would not bear the burdens of two-tiered review, suspect class analysis, the real difference doctrine, and the intent requirement. As MacKinnon noted, "the only question for litigation" is whether the statute subordinates women or challenges that subordination. MacKinnon, *supra* note 62, at 117; *see also supra* text accompanying note 62. The antisubordination model of equal protection, however, also is riddled with problems, many of them pragmatic. Most important, because of its simplicity, the antisubordination model could be extremely difficult to apply to particular cases:

it is much easier to state the standard than to ascertain whether a particular piece of legislation has met the standard. Feminist scholar and lawyer Sylvia Law explains:

> Professor MacKinnon's approach is ambitious, but it adds unnecessary complexity to the application of sex equality doctrine in a large number of cases. The determination of what reinforces or undermines a sex-based underclass is exceedingly difficult. Professor MacKinnon may overestimate judges' capacities to identify and avoid socially imposed constraints on equality. She disregards our history in which laws justified as protecting women have been a central means of oppressing them. Most fundamentally, her proposed standard may incorporate and perpetuate a false belief that a judicially enforced constitutional standard can, by itself, dismantle the deep structures that "integrally contribute" to sex-based deprivation.

Sylvia Law, "Rethinking Sex and the Constitution," 132 *U. Pa. L. Rev.* 955, 1005 (1984). Even accepting Law's criticism, the major problem with the model is somewhat simpler: for whatever reasons, antisubordination approaches to equal protection, regarding sex or race, have not met with judicial acceptance.

65. Civil Rights Cases, 109 U.S. 3 (1883).
66. *Id.* at 25.
67. See *supra* note 25 and accompanying text.
68. *See generally* "Note, To Have and to Hold," *supra* note 2, at 1259–60, 1267–70 (discussing gender-based marital rape exemption statutes and citing states that currently have such statutes in force).
69. *See* Craig v. Boren, 429 U.S. 190, 197 (1976).
70. *See supra* note 35.
71. *See* Reed v. Reed, 404 U.S. 71, 75–76 (1971).
72. *See* "Note, To Have and to Hold," *supra* note 2, at 1256–58.
73. *See Craig,* 429 U.S. at 197.
74. *See supra* note 13 and accompanying text.
75. *See* People v. Liberta, 64 N.Y.2d 152, 474 N.E.2d 567, 573, 485 N.Y.S.2d 207, 213 (1984).
76. *Cf.* Washington v. Davis, 426 U.S. 229, 239–42 (1976) (discussing neutral classifications and adverse impacts in a Title VII racial discrimination context).
77. M. Hale, *Historia Plactorum Coronae: The History of the Pleas of the Crown* 636 (1736).
78. For a good discussion of the history of the exemption, see "Note, To Have and to Hold," *supra* note 2, at 1255–58.
79. *Id.* at 1259–60.
80. See *supra* text accompanying notes 30–32.
81. *See* Craig v. Boren, 429 U.S. 190, 197 (1976).
82. Indeed, the "privacy" cases under the substantive due-process doctrine, including Roe v. Wade, 410 U.S. 113 (1973), itself, seems to bolster such an argument. *See generally* Griswold v. Connecticut, 381 U.S. 479 (1965); Pierce v. Society of Sisters, 268 U.S. 510 (1925); Meyer v. Nebraska, 262 U.S. 390 (1923).
83. See *supra* notes 76–79 and accompanying text.
84. *See* "Note, To Have and to Hold," *supra* note 2, at 1267.
85. *Model Penal Code* ss 213.0, .6 (1989).

86. See *supra* notes 41–62 and accompanying text.

87. See *supra* note 11.

88. *See generally* D. Russell, *Rape in Marriage* (1983) (describing the effects of marital rape exemptions); West, *supra* note 42.

89. *See generally* West, *supra* note 42.

90. See *supra* notes 62–64 and accompanying text.

91. See *supra* note 65 and accompanying text.

92. For the Supreme Court's most recent affirmation of its adherence to a rationality model, and rejection of an antisubordination model, see City of Richmond v. J. A. Croson Co., 488 U.S. 469 (1989).

93. *See* Civil Rights Cases, 109 U.S. 25 (1883).

94. *See, e.g.,* Brown v. Board of Education, 347 U.S. 489 (1954). For a general argument to the effect that *Brown* and its progeny should best be understood as within an antisubordination framework, see David A. Strauss, "Discriminatory Intent and the Taming of Brown," 56 *U. Chi. L. Rev.* 935 (1989).

95. 426 U.S. 229, 244–48 (1976).

96. See *supra* notes 25–34 and accompanying text.

97. See *supra* notes 53–60 and accompanying text.

98. The subsidiary rules the Court has developed under the rationality model likewise can be understood as ensuring that the equal protection law is rendered susceptible to the most traditional, legalistic, and even classical understandings of the requirements of justice. The intent requirement for race-neutral and gender-neutral classifications adversely impacting on the suspect class most notably has the effect not only of severely restraining the reach of the equal protection clause but also of limiting the court to traditional forms of analysis. Intent requirements run throughout the law, including tort, contract, and criminal law. The intent requirement in adverse impact cases under the Fourteenth Amendment has the effect of transforming constitutional questions into the most traditional, as well as narrowest, legal inquiry imaginable: Who is guilty of wrongdoing, with what *mens rea,* who was thereby hurt, and by how much?

99. There is no doubt, of course, that the Court is the ultimate interpreter of constitutional meaning. *See* Cooper v. Aaron, 358 U.S. 1, 18–20 (1958) (reaffirming that the judiciary is the ultimate interpreter of the Constitution).

100. Robert Kennedy's decision to send in the National Guard during the desegregation campaigns in the south, for example, appears to be a paradigm instance of protection-type executive enforcement of the equal protection guarantee.

101. *See* U.S. Const., amend. XIV, s 5; *see also* Katzenbach v. Morgan, 384 U.S. 641, 650 (1966) (stating that section 5 of the Fourteenth Amendment is a positive grant of legislative power authorizing Congress to exercise its discretion in determining the need for and nature of legislation to secure Fourteenth Amendment guarantees).

102. See *supra* note 1.

103. The New York Court of Appeals, to its credit, has struck the marital rape exemption on this ground. *See* People v. Liberta, 64 N.Y.2d 152, 474 N.E.2d 567, 485 N.Y.S.2d 207, 219–20 (1984).

3. *The Meaning of Equality and the Interpretive Turn*

1. For a general introduction to these claims, see Stanley Fish, *Is There a Text in This Class?* (1980). For an introduction to the legal literature, see *Interpreting Law and Literature: A Hermeneutic Reader* (S. Levinson and S. Mailloux ed., 1988).

2. For the angst, see Owen M. Fiss, "Objectivity and Interpretation," 34 *Stan. L. Rev.* 739 (1982). For the excitement, see Mark V. Tushnet, *Red, White, and Blue: A Critical Analysis of Constitutional Law* (1988).

3. *See* Fiss, *supra* note 2. *See also* Paul Carrington, "Of Law and the River," 34 *J. Legal Educ.* 222 (1984).

4. For a lengthy argument to this effect, see Stanley Fish, "Fiss v. Fish," 36 *Stan. L. Rev.* 1325 (1984).

5. See *infra* notes 19–26 and accompanying text.

6. An eloquent "citizen's interpretation" of the second amendment was provided by Elaine Scarry, "War and the Social Contract: The Right to Bear Arms," 2 *Yale J. L. & Humanities,* 119 (1990).

7. For a general introduction to critical legal theory, see the Harvard Law Review Association, *Critical Legal Studies: Articles, Notes, and Book Reviews Selected from the Pages of the Harvard Law Review* (1986).

8. *See generally* Fish, *supra* note 1, and Stanley Fish, *Doing What Comes Naturally: Change, Rhetoric, and The Practice of Theory in Literary and Legal Studies* (1989). *But see* Sanford Levinson, "Law as Literature," in *Interpreting Law and Literature: A Hermeneutic Reader, supra* note 1, at 155, for a very different, and more political, understanding of the hermeneutic tradition and its consequences for legal interpretation.

9. Fish, *supra* note 1, at 303–71.

10. Fish, *supra* note 4, at 1339.

11. *Id.* at 1346.

12. In one passage Kennedy describes that freedom in this way:

    > The judge, cannot, any more than the angst, avoid the moment of truth in which one simply shifts modes. In place of the apparatus of rule making and rule application, with its attendant premises and attitudes, we come suddenly on a gap, a balancing test, a good faith standard, a fake or incoherent rule, or the enthusiastic adoption of a train of reasoning all know will be ignored in the next case. In terms of individualism, the judge has suddenly begun to act in bad faith. In terms of altruism, she has found herself. The only thing that counts is this change in attitude, but it is hard to imagine anything more elusive of analysis.

    Duncan Kennedy, "Form and Substance in Private Law Adjudication," 89 *Harv. L. Rev.* 1685, 1776 (1976). *See also* Duncan Kennedy, "Freedom and Constraint in Adjudication: A Critical Phenomenology," 36 *J. Legal Educ.* 518 (1986).

13. *See* Duncan Kennedy, "Distributive and Paternalist Motives in Contract and Tort Law with Special Reference to Compulsory Terms and Unequal Bargaining Power," 41 *Md. L. Rev.* 563, 564–65 (1982).

14. *See* Tushnet, *supra* note 2.

15. Mark Kelman, "Interpretive Construction in the Substantive Criminal Law," 33 *Stan. L. Rev.* 591, 592–93 (1981).

16. Stanley Fish, "Introduction, or How I Stopped Worrying and Learned to Love Interpretation," in *Is There a Text in This Class?* 14 (1980).

17. Kelman, *supra* note 15, at 670–71.

18. Kennedy speaks of Judge Wright's decision in *Williams v. Walker-Thomas Furniture Co.*, 350 F.2d 445 (D.C. Cir. 1965) in this way. *See* Kennedy, "Form and Substance," *supra* note 12.

19. See, e.g., Barbara H. Smith, *Contingencies of Value: Alternative Perspectives for Critical Theory* (1988) for a complete argument to this effect.

20. Ronald Dworkin introduced the Christie example into the legal literature in Ronald A. Dworkin, "How Law Is Like Literature," in *A Matter of Principle* 150–51 (1985). Stanley Fish offers a rejoinder in "Working on the Chain Gang: Interpretation in Law and Literature," 60 *Tex. L. Rev.* 551, 559–62 (1982).

21. *But see* Thomas C. Grey, "The Constitution as Scripture," 37 *Stan. L. Rev.* 1 (1984).

22. McCulloch v. Maryland, 17 U.S. (4 Wheat) 316 (1819).

23. For a striking example of constitutional interpretation that focuses almost exclusively on the specialness and uniqueness of the document, see Michael Perry, "The Authority of Text, Tradition, and Reason: A Theory of Constitutional 'Interpretation'," 58 *S. Cal. L. Rev.* 551 (1985), and Michael Perry, "Moral Knowledge. Moral Reasoning, Moral Relativism: A 'Naturalist' Perspective," 22 *Ga. L. Rev.* 955 (1986).

24. It is often assumed, at least in casual conversation about the consequences of critical legal theory, that the lack of a distinction between law and politics follows from the indeterminacy claim alone. It is part of the purpose of this chapter to show that it does not. From the premise that the text or original intent of a law lacks a determinate meaning, and hence cannot bind interpretation, it does not follow that nothing binds interpretation. Nor does it follow that legal and political discourses are not distinguishable on grounds other than the determinacy of the former.

25. This aspect of judicially created law is explored in Cass R. Sunstein, 33 *The Partial Constitution* 319–347 (Harv., 1993).

26. Robin L. West, "Progressive and Conservative Constitutionalism," Chapter 9, this volume.

27. The classical treatment of the formal equality model is Tussman & Jacobus tenBroek, "The Equal Protection of the Laws, 37 *Cal. L. Rev.* 341 (1949). For an argument to the effect that the classical definition is empty of content, see Peter Westen, "The Empty Idea of Equality," 95 *Harv. L. Rev.* 537, 542, 560–77 (1982).

28. Perhaps the best short account of this view can be found in Catherine A. MacKinnon, "Sex Equality: On Difference and Dominance," in *Toward a Feminist Theory of the State* 215 (1989). *See also* Sunstein, *supra* note 25.

29. See, e.g., Kenneth Casebeer, "Running on Empty: Justice Brennan's Plea, the Empty State, the City of Richmond, and the Profession," 43 *U. Miami L. Rev.* 989 (1989); Richard Delgado, "On Taking Back Our Civil Rights Promises: When Equality Doesn't Compute," 1989 *Wis. L. Rev.* 579; Michel Rosenfeld, "Decoding Richmond: Affirmative Action and the Elusive Meaning of Constitutional Equality," 87 *Mich. L. Rev.* 1729 (1989); David A. Strauss, "Discriminatory Intent and the Taming of Brown," 56 *U. Chi. L. Rev.* 935 (1989) [hereinafter "Taming of Brown"]; David A. Strauss, "The Myth of Colorblindness," 1986 *Sup. Ct. Rev.* 99, 104–5.

30. I discuss this contrast in greater detail in West, *supra* note 26.
31. 438 U.S. 265 (1978).
32. 488 U.S. 469 (1989).
33. *Id.* at 492–93 (opinion of O'Connor, J.).
34. *See* Strauss, "Taming of Brown," *supra* note 29.
35. See *supra* note 29.
36. 347 U.S. 483 (1954).
37. *See* Strauss, "Taming of Brown," *supra* note 29.
38. Regents of the University of California v. Bakke, 438 U.S. 315–20 (1978).
39. City of Richmond v. J. A. Croson Co., 488 U.S. 493 (1989).
40. For a similar argument to this effect from an intentionalist perspective, *see* Knapp & Michaels, "Intention, Identity and the Constitution: A Response to David Hoy" (unpublished manuscript on file with author) (arguing that from an intentionalist perspective, *Brown* was correctly decided).
41. Mark Tushnet remains the best critical constitutional scholar from this theoretical perspective. *See* Tushnet, *supra* note 2, at 70–107.
42. A good short treatment of both the history of the amendments and their judicial interpretation as supportive of an antisubordination or antisubjugation principle can be found in Laurence H. Tribe, *American Constitutional Law* s 16–21 (2d ed. 1988).
43. *See, e.g.,* Loving v. Virginia, 388 U.S. 1 (1967); Brown v. Board of Education, 347 U.S. 483 (1954); Plessy v. Ferguson, 163 U.S. 537 (1896) (Harlan, J., dissenting); Strauder v. West Virginia, 100 U.S. 303 (1879).
44. *See generally* Robert Bork, *The Tempting of America: The Political Seduction of the Law* 74–84 (1990).
45. City of Richmond v. J. A. Croson Co., 488 U.S. 520–21 (1989) (Scalia, J., concurring) (citations omitted) (emphasis added).
46. *Id.* at 490–91 (O'Connor, J., concurring) (emphasis added).
47. *See, e.g.,* Alan D. Freeman, "Antidiscrimination Law: A Critical Review," in *The Politics of Law: A Progressive Critique* 96 (D. Kairys ed., 1982).
48. *Id.*
49. See *supra* note 29.
50. 426 U.S. 229, 247–48 (1976) (advising that prudential constraints on the Court's powers of enforcement make implausible an expansive reading of an equal protection clause that would invalidate state action with adverse impact on a suspect class).
51. Act of March 1, 1875, ch. 114, 18 Stat. 336.
52. *See generally* J. tenBroek, *The Anti-Slavery Origins of the Fourteenth Amendment* 192–95 (1951).
53. *See* Civil Rights Act Cases, 109 U.S. 3 (1883).
54. *See* West, *supra* note 26.
55. 448 U.S. 448 (1980).
56. Katzenbach v. Morgan, 384 U.S. 641 (1966) suggests that it should.

4. Reconstructing Liberty

1. *See* Collin v. Smith, 578 F.2d 1197 (7th Cir.) (finding ordinances in Skokie, Illinois, designed to block march by Ku Klux Klan, unconstitutional), *cert. denied,* 439 U.S. 916 (1978).

2. *See* United States v. Eichman, 496 U.S. 310 (1990) (finding federal statute criminalizing flag desecration unconstitutional); Texas v. Johnson, 491 U.S. 397 (1989) (finding same).

3. *See* R.A.V. v. City of St. Paul, Minnesota, 505 U.S.——, (1992). For arguments to the effect that hate speech should not be constitutionally protected, see Richard Delgado, "Words That Wound: A Tort Action for Racial Insults, Epithets, and Name-Calling," 17 *Harv. C.R.-C.L. L. Rev.* 133 (1982); Charles R. Lawrence, III, "If He Hollers Let Him Go: Regulating Racist Speech on Campus," 1990 *Duke L. J.* 431; Mari J. Matsuda, "Public Response to Racist Speech: Considering the Victim's Story," 87 *Mich. L. Rev.* 2320 (1989). *But see* Nadine Strossen, "Regulating Racist Speech on Campus: A Modest Proposal?" 1990 *Duke L. J.* 484.

4. *See* Wisconsin v. Yoder, 406 U.S. 205 (1972). In *Yoder,* after balancing the state's interest in education against impingement on the fundamental right of the Amish to raise children in a manner consistent with religious precepts, the Court held unconstitutional a parent's conviction for refusing to send his child to a public school past the eighth grade. *Id.* at 234.

   The Rehnquist Court, however, may be moving away from the general principle cited in the text. *See* Employment Division, Department of Human Resources of Oregon v. Smith, 494 U.S. 872 (1990) (holding that an Oregon statute criminalizing nonrecreational drug use does not infringe the First Amendment rights of Native American Church members absent showing specific intent to burden the minority religion).

5. The phrase apparently originated in Justice Cardozo's majority opinion in Palko v. Connecticut, 302 U.S. 319 (1937). In *Palko,* the Court held that the kind of double jeopardy risked by a state statute permitting the state to appeal criminal cases (1) did not "violate those 'fundamental principles of liberty and justice which lie at the base of all our civil and political institutions'" *Id.* at 328 [citing Hebert v. Louisiana, 272 U.S. 312, 316 (1926)]; (2) was not "of the very essence of a scheme of ordered liberty" *Id.* at 325; and (3) was not unconstitutional. *Id.*

6. 367 U.S. 497 (1961).

7. *Id.* at 541–43 (Harlan, J., dissenting) (citations omitted).

8. *See* Pacific Mutual Life Insurance Company v. Haslip, 499 U.S. 1 (1991) (Scalia, J., concurring); Michael H. v. Gerald D., 491 U.S. 110 (1989). In both cases, Justice Scalia argues that the liberty protected by substantive due process should be limited to those liberties historically and traditionally protected against precipitous majoritarian abridgment.

9. *See, e.g.,* Rust v. Sullivan, 500 U.S. 173 (1991) (finding that a regulation forbidding federally funded clinics to counsel regarding abortion does not violate the constitutional right of privacy or free speech); Hodgson v. Minnesota, 497 U.S. 417 (1990) (holding constitutional a state statute requiring notice to both parents regarding an abortion request by minors if accompanied by judicial bypass); Smith, 494 U.S. 872 (1990) (deciding that a state statute criminalizing nonrecreational drug use does not violate the

First Amendment rights of Native American Church members); Webster v. Reproductive Health Services, 492 U.S. 490 (1989) (holding state statutes regulating abortion constitutional; Roe v. Wade (deciding the trimester scheme is explicitly questioned and arguably overruled); Bowers v. Hardwick, 478 U.S. 186 (1986) (finding a statute criminalizing homosexual or heterosexual sodomy does not violate constitutional norms of privacy).

10. According to Justice Scalia, the most important things the Court should protect in the name of the liberty protected by the due process clause of the Fourteenth Amendment are not the private decisions that occur in the spheres of life necessary to the preservation of true individual autonomy, but, rather, the decisions or spheres of life that historically and traditionally have been understood as insulated against state encroachment. *See Haslip,* 499 U.S. at 1; *Michael H.,* 491 U.S. at 110. It should be apparent at once that this is a far narrower concept of ordered liberty than that articulated by Justice Harlan in Griswold v. Connecticut, 381 U.S. 479, 501–2. Instead, it implies a very different and much more limited conception of what, concretely, must be protected against state encroachment. Stating the idea in the negative, under Justice Scalia's analysis, unless a sphere of decisionmaking has been historically and traditionally protected, it is not a part of the liberty protected against state encroachment. For example, according to this approach, neither the so-called liberty to engage in extramarital sex, premarital sex, same-sex relations, or nonreproductive sex (*cf. Bowers,* 478 U.S. at 192–95), nor the liberty to procure a legal abortion (*see Rust,* 500 U.S. at 173 (1991); *Hodgson,* 497 U.S. at 480–501; *Webster,* 492 U.S. at 532–37), nor the liberty of a father to pursue a relationship with a child born to a woman married to another man [*see Michael H.,* 491 U.S. at 118–30 (Justice Scalia writing for the Court)], nor the liberty of worshipers in the Native American Church to ingest peyote as part of religious rituals (*see Smith,* 494 U.S. at 876–90) are a part of the liberty constitutionally protected against state encroachment, although all such liberties would be protected under Justice Harlan's account of liberty. This is because historically and traditionally we have not protected these decisions, regardless of whether or not sexual life, parental responsibility, or spiritual practices are spheres of decision making central to individual autonomy. That we have not historically and traditionally protected these liberties, of course, is evidenced by the existence of the sodomy laws, fornication laws, prohibitions against homosexuality, and criminalization of abortion and nonrecreational drug use challenged in these and similar cases. The decisions from the Rehnquist Court over the last five years, partially embracing Justice Scalia's approach and truncating or abolishing a wide range of individual liberties, substitute tradition for the liberal understanding of autonomy as the criterion for determining whether an individual liberty must be protected. This marks a profound turning point in the development of our conceptual understanding of what ordered liberty requires.

I discuss the difference between Justice Scalia's approach to liberty and that of Justice Brennan and the Warren Court generally in chapter 5. *See also* Michael H., 491 U.S. at 136–56 (Brennan, J., dissenting) (defending the more liberal Warren Court approach).

11. *See* Sir Isaiah Berlin, "Two Concepts of Liberty," in *Four Essays on Liberty* 118 (1969).

12. *Id.* at 121–22.

13. Thus, so-called welfare rights are not protected constitutionally. *See, e.g.,* Harris v.

McRae, 448 U.S. 297 (1980) (upholding the Hyde Amendment prohibiting federal funding of abortions for the poor as constitutional); San Antonio Independent School District v. Rodriguez, 411 U.S. 1 (1973) (finding no constitutional right to an education). *See generally* Frank I. Michelman, "Welfare Rights in a Constitutional Democracy," 1979 *Wash. U. L. Q.* 659 (1979) [hereinafter "Welfare Rights"]; Frank I. Michelman, "Foreword: On Protecting the Poor through the Fourteenth Amendment," 83 *Harv. L. Rev.* 7 (1969).

14. Samuel Warren & Louis Brandeis, "The Right to Privacy," 4 *Harv. L. Rev.* 193 (1890).

15. Berlin, *supra* note 11, at 126–27. Although it is a common belief that negative liberty and positive liberty are two sides of the same coin, or in some way are correlated with each other, this need not be the case, as Berlin tried to show in his famous essay. *Id.* at 131. A society can be rich in one kind of liberty but poor in the other. For example, as individual citizens, we might enjoy a great deal of negative freedom such as the right to speak, worship, or be free of arbitrary arrest even though we live in a virtual dictatorship. A dictator may decide in the interest of stability or for relatively more benign reasons to grant citizens a broad sphere of inviolable freedom within which they may do as they please, even though they have no say in the governance of the society, no vote, and no right to political representation or participation. In such a society, the individual would enjoy extensive negative liberty but no positive liberty.

   On the other hand, a society might be a perfectly functioning democracy, in fact as well as theory, yet it may grant absolutely no negative freedom to the individual citizen. This was the possibility that major classical liberal thinkers from Mill to Berlin both saw and feared in Western democracies. A governing majority, perfectly representative of the public's will, might decide to strip individuals of all negative freedom and dictate on ideological grounds what individuals should think and believe, what they should read, and how and whom they should worship. Such a society might be rich in positive freedom but poor in negative freedom. As Mill insisted, ensuring to each and every individual an equal power to oppress others is no guarantee of liberty. A majority, no less than a tyrant, can squelch the negative freedom necessary for individuality, genius, creativity, spontaneity, and life itself to flourish. *See generally* John Stuart Mill, *On Liberty* (1859).

16. *See, e.g.,* DeShaney v. Winnebago County Department of Social Services, 489 U.S. 189 (1989) (stating the constitutional guarantee to liberty is triggered by state action, not by mere inaction); Flagg Bros. v. Brooks, 436 U.S. 149 (1978) (stating same).

17. *Rodriguez,* 411 U.S. at 35.

18. On the need to create constitutional entitlements to these so-called welfare rights and arguments to the effect that the Constitution should guarantee them, *see* Patricia J. Williams, *The Alchemy of Race and Rights: The Diary of a Law Professor* (1991); Michelman, "Welfare Rights," *supra* note 13.

19. *See generally* Michelman, "Welfare Rights," *supra* note 13, at 659–60.

20. *See* Pierce v. Society of Sisters, 268 U.S. 510, 535 (1925) (finding the statute requiring public rather than private education of children an unconstitutional infringement of the "liberty of parents and guardians to direct the upbringing and education of children under their control").

21. *See* Meyer v. Nebraska, 262 U.S. 390 (1923) (holding that a state law prohibiting

the teaching of any modern language other than English unconstitutionally infringes freedom of parents to oversee children's upbringing and education).

22. *See* San Antonio Independent School District v. Rodriguez, 411 U.S. 1, 22–24 (1973).

23. *See* Roe v. Wade, 410 U.S. 113 (1973).

24. *See* Harris v. McRae, 448 U.S. 297 (1980) (upholding a federal law withholding funds for even medically necessary abortions and finding no general constitutional right to an abortion, only the right to contract for abortion free of state interference); Maher v. Roe, 432 U.S. 464 (1977) (deciding that the equal protection clause does not compel a state to pay for medically necessary abortions, although it may pay for indigent women's childbirth expenses).

25. Rust v. Sullivan, 500 U.S. 173 (1991).

26. *See* Hudnut v. American Booksellers Association, 771 F.2d 323 (7th Cir. 1985), aff'd, 475 U.S. 1001 (1986). For a discussion of the injurious consequences of private-market censorship of unpopular ideas, see Louise Armstrong, "Dissent for the Duration . . . : Louise Armstrong Talks to Andrea Dworkin," *Women's Review of Books,* May 1986, at 5.

27. CBS v. Democratic National Committee, 412 U.S. 94 (1973) (stating that the refusal of CBS to accept DNC's editorial advertisements did not violate the latter's constitutional rights). According to the Court in *CBS,* to limit journalistic discretion in the name of First Amendment rights would be "anomalous" and a "contradiction." *Id.* at 120, 121.

28. The Court upheld the fairness doctrine, a complex set of regulations imposing obligations on broadcasters to provide balanced treatment of opposing points of view, in Red Lion Broadcasting Co. v. FCC, 395 U.S. 367 (1969), but the case has generated a vast array of criticism. *See, e.g.,* Kenneth Karst, "Equality as a Central Principle in the First Amendment," 43 *U. Chi. L. Rev.* 20 (1975); L. A. Powe, Jr., "Or of the [Broadcast] Press," 55 *Tex. L. Rev.* 39 (1976).

29. *See Hudnut,* 771 F.2d at 328–34. See generally Catharine A. MacKinnon, "Pornography: On Morality and Politics," in *Toward a Feminist Theory of the State* 195–214 (1989) [hereinafter *Feminist Theory*].

30. R.A.V. v. City of St. Paul, Minnesota, 505 U.S. —— (1992).

31. Williams, *supra* note 18, at 73. Williams is perhaps our only eloquent contemporary poet-lawyer.

32. *See* DeShaney v. Winnebago County Department of Social Services, 489 U.S. 189, 196–97 (1989).

33. Mill specifically defended the polygamous practices of the Mormons on just these grounds, but he did so without considering, and perhaps not noticing, that those practices endanger the very individual liberties specifically defended in near absolute terms in earlier sections of his famous essay. *See* Mill, *On Liberty, supra* note 15, at 73.

34. *See generally* Arlie Hochschild, *The Second Shift: Working Parents and the Revolution at Home* (1989); Susan Moller Okin, *Justice, Gender and the Family* (1989); Richard Delgado & Helen Leskovac, "Review Essay—The Politics of Workplace Reforms: Recent Works on Parental Leave and a Father-Daughter Dialogue," 40 *Rutgers L. Rev.* 1031 (1988); Nancy E. Dowd, "Work and Family: Restructuring the Workplace," 32 *Ariz. L. Rev.* 431 (1990); Jana Singer, "Women's Work," *Rep. from the Inst. for Phil. and Pub. Pol'y* no. 1, 11 (Winter 1991).

35. *See* Hochschild, *supra* note 36.
36. For an eloquent treatment of the conflict between mothering and the production of culture, *see* Tillie Olsen, *Silences* 203–12 (1978).
37. *See* John Stuart Mill, *Utilitarianism* (1863); John Stuart Mill, *On Liberty, supra* note 15.
38. Frank I. Michelman, "Law's Republic," 97 *Yale L. J.* 1493 (1988); Cass R. Sunstein, "Beyond the Republican Revival," 97 *Yale L. J.* 1539 (1988).
39. *See, e.g.,* Betty Friedan, *The Feminine Mystique* (1983); Simone de Beauvoir, *The Second Sex* (1952).
40. *See* MacKinnon, *Feminist Theory, supra* note 29, at 195–214; Catharine A. MacKinnon, "A Rally against Rape and Sex and Violence: A Perspective," in *Feminism Unmodified: Discourses on Life and Law* 81–93 (1987) [hereinafter *Feminism Unmodified*]; Diane E. H. Russell, *Rape in Marriage* (1982).
41. Margaret T. Gordon & Stephanie Riger, *The Female Fear* (1989).
42. Adrienne Rich, "Compulsory Heterosexuality and Lesbian Existence," in 5 *Signs: Journal of Women in Culture and Society* 631–60 (Summer 1980).
43. I have explored this in more detail in Robin L. West, "The Difference in Women's Hedonic Lives: A Phenomenological Critique of Feminist Legal Theory," 3 *Wisc. Women's L. J.* 81 (1987).
44. In the example of unequal distribution in the private nuclear family of childraising responsibility, there may well be no state action.
45. *See, e.g.,* Griswold v. Connecticut, 381 U.S. 479 (1965); Pierce v. Society of Sisters, 268 U.S. 510 (1925); Meyer v. Nebraska, 262 U.S. 390 (1923). These privacy cases protect traditional, patriarchal, and familial arrangements (both nuclear and otherwise), and, with the exception of the abortion decision, all protect private and social practices that have a pronounced negative impact on women's self-esteem, self-definition, and self-worth. See MacKinnon, *Feminist Theory, supra* note 29, at 184–95 (holding a similar critique of the Court's privacy doctrine as insulating patriarchy).
46. *See Griswold,* 381 U.S. at 485–86.
47. *See* Roe v. Wade, 410 U.S. 113, 152–53 (1973).
48. *See Pierce,* 268 U.S. at 534–35.
49. *See* Wisconsin v. Yoder, 406 U.S. 205, 230–34 (1972).
50. This is what is meant by the phrase "the personal is political." *See generally* MacKinnon, *Feminist Theory, supra* note 29, at 41, 94–95, 119–20.
51. A dramatic example is the so-called marital rape exemption, which exempts wives from the protection of rape law and exempts husbands from its reach. *See* Chapter 2, this volume.
52. Letter from Abigail Adams to John Adams (March 31, 1776), in *The Adams Papers: Adams Family Correspondence, Dec. 1761–May 1776* 369–70 (L. H. Butterfield et al. eds., 1963). *See also* Alice S. Rossi, *The Feminist Papers: From Adams to Beauvoir* 7–15 (1973).
53. Eleanor Flexner, *Century of Struggle: The Woman's Rights Movement in the United States* 145–50 (1975).
54. *See* Mary E. Becker, "The Politics of Women's Wrongs and the Bill of 'Rights': A Bicentennial Perspective" 59 *U. Chi. L. R.* 453 (1992).
55. See *supra* note 3 and accompanying text; *see also* West, "Ideal of Liberty," *supra* note 10.

56. See *supra* note 3 and accompanying text.
57. *See* MacKinnon, *Feminist Theory, supra* note 29, at 195–214; MacKinnon, *Feminism Unmodified, supra* note 42, at 184–94.
58. *See* Chapter 2. See also "Note, To Have and To Hold: The Marital Rape Exemption and the Fourteenth Amendment," 99 *Harv. L. Rev.* 1255 (1986).
59. This was reflected in the since-discarded self-appellation of feminism during the 1960s and early 1970s as a movement of "Women's Liberation."
60. Jacobus tenBroek, *Equal under Law* (originally *The Antislavery Origins of the Fourteenth Amendment*) (1965).
61. *Id.* at 234–39.
62. *See* Ku Klux Klan Act of Feb. 28, 1971, ch. 99, 16 Stat. 433, ch. 22, 17 Stat. 13; Public Accommodations Act of March 1, 1875, ch. 114, 18 Stat. 335.
63. Such liberties would include the negative liberties to move freely about or simply to live; to contract to sell or buy property; and to earn a wage for one's labor, along with the positive liberties to vote, run for office, and assume the rights and responsibilities of full political citizenship.

5. The Ideal of Liberty

1. 491 U.S. 110 (1989).
2. *See id.* at 121–30 (Scalia, J.); *id.* at 136–57 (Brennan, J., dissenting).
3. *See id.* at 127 n.6 (joined by Rehnquist, C. J.).
4. *See id.* at 121–30.
5. *See id.* at 127 n.6 (referring to "the most specific level at which a relevant tradition . . . can be identified").
6. *See id.* at 121–30.
7. *See id.* at 126–27.
8. *See id.* at 139–41 (Brennan, J., dissenting).
9. On this ground, Justice O'Connor objected to Scalia's formulation of due process clause analysis. She thus refused to concur in the footnote in which he made the argument. *See id.* at 132 (O'Connor, J., concurring).
10. Under Scalia's test, the following cases all seem incorrectly decided: Cruzan v. Director, Missouri Department of Health, 497 U.S. 261 (1990) (upholding the right to die); Roe v. Wade, 410 U.S. 113 (1973) (upholding the right to an abortion); Griswold v. Connecticut, 381 U.S. 479 (1965) (upholding the right of married persons to use contraception); and Eisenstadt v. Baird, 405 U.S. 438 (1972) (upholding the right of unmarried individuals to use contraception). On the other hand, his test seems consistent with the decision in Bowers v. Hardwick, 478 U.S. 186 (1986) (denying the right to engage in consensual sodomy).
11. *Michael H.*, 491 U.S. at 136–57 (Brennan, J., dissenting).
12. 410 U.S. 113 (1973).
13. 478 U.S. 186 (1986).
14. 497 U.S. 261 (1990).
15. *See id.* at 302 (Brennan, J., dissenting).
16. 381 U.S. 479 (1965).

17. 405 U.S. 438 (1972).

18. *Cruzan,* 497 U.S. at 261.

19. *See* Roe v. Wade, 410 U.S. 152–56 (1973); *Eisenstadt,* 405 U.S. at 453–55; *Griswold,* 381 U.S. at 485–86; *Cruzan,* 497 U.S. at 278–80.

20. 478 U.S. 186, 199–214 (1986) (Blackmun, J., dissenting).

21. *See* John Locke, *Two Treatises of Government* 132 (T. Cook ed., 1947) ("The natural liberty of man is to be free from any superior power on earth, and not to be under the will or legislative authority of man. . . . The liberty of man in society is to be under no other legislative power but that established by consent in the commonwealth."); John Rawls, *A Theory of Justice* 202 (1971).

22. *See* John Dewey, *Liberalism and Social Action* 31 (Capricorn ed., 1963). *See also* John Dewey, *Individualism Old and New* 89 (1930).

23. *See* Rawls, *supra* note 27, at 204–5 (arguing that worth of liberty is adversely affected by poverty, ignorance, or "lack of means generally").

24. *Cf.* Thomas C. Grey, "Eros, Civilization, and the Burger Court," 43 *Law & Contemp. Probs.* 83 (1980) (arguing that need for social order, not respect for liberty, lies behind the liberal justices' willingness to grant constitutional protection to sexual freedom).

25. *See* Cass R. Sunstein, *The Partial Constitution* 40–68 (Harv., 1993); Cass R. Sunstein, "Sexual Orientation and the Constitution: A Note on the Relationship between Due Process and Equal Protection," 55 *U. Chi. L. Rev.* 1161, 1170–78 (1988) [hereinafter "Sexual Orientation"].

26. *See* Sunstein, *The Partial Constitution, supra* note 31, at 884–86; Sunstein, "Sexual Orientation," *supra* note 31, at 1170–78.

27. 198 U.S. 45 (1905).

28. Sunstein does not make this argument in any one place, but I would reconstruct it from his suggestions in "Sexual Orientation," *supra* note 32, and *The Partial Constitution, supra* note 32, as follows. The "liberty" that the individual possesses, and which is protected by the Fourteenth Amendment, tends to be understood as incorporating a "baseline" of common law origins. This, in turn, has the effect of constitutionally protecting the given distribution of wealth and privilege against legislative change. Generally, this reliance on unexamined baselines is misplaced. Overreliance on improper baselines for constitutional decision making, Sunstein would argue, haunts not just due process interpretation, but several areas of constitutional law. Because of this recurrent reliance on common law baselines, a legislature that upsets the entitlements provided by the common law is viewed as having "acted," acted "affirmatively," and acted affirmatively in a way that upsets pre-legal individual liberties. On the other hand, a legislature that leaves those entitlements intact has not acted, but it has respected liberty. Similarly, a law that redistributes such entitlements is regarded as "redistributive," and hence a violation of liberty, of the takings clause, and possibly of the contracts clause. For these reasons, such a law is acting outside the scope of police power, whereas a law that leaves those entitlements intact is regarded as having respected liberty. A law that upsets these "natural" entitlements is regarded as impermissibly biased, and a law that leaves them intact is regarded as "neutral." This was also the underlying rationale of the major substantive due process cases from the Lochner era.

The repudiation of *Lochner,* Sunstein argues, should be understood as a repudiation of precisely this understanding of the exalted constitutional status of common law entitlements, rather than a repudiation of judicial activism or an affirmation of legislative supremacy. Common law entitlements may or may not be entitled to constitutional protection; whether they are depends on the clause and the context. In some spheres of constitutional decision making, this reliance on the common law as the baseline of constitutionally protected interests is entirely proper—the contracts clause and the takings clause are two examples. But in a large number of other contexts it is entirely inappropriate. It is inappropriate, for example, for us to judge whether or not the state action requirement has been met by appeals to hidden baselines of common law entitlements, such that if those baselines have been violated, the state has acted, but if they have been maintained, there is no state action. The repudiation of *Lochner* is a repudiation of this view that the existing distribution of entitlements and wealth is a function of "nature" and hence an aspect of our natural liberty. That distribution is a function, generally, of the common law—very much a state, and governmental, creation.

Although Sunstein is not tremendously clear on the point, his understanding of the repudiation of *Lochner* seems to teach this lesson regarding substantive due process. To the considerable degree that the substantive due process doctrine depends on this conception of the common law as the baseline for determining infringements on personal liberty, the doctrine in its entirety—rather than just one possible interpretation of it, and certainly rather than judicial activism per se—should be understood as undermined by the repudiation of *Lochner.* Like the takings clause and the contracts clause, liberty under the due process clause during the *Lochner* era was understood by reference to hidden common law baselines establishing entitlements. But unlike the contracts or takings clause, the "substantive due process" doctrine is, in its entirety, a mistake; furthermore, it is a clearly "repudiated" one. If substantive due process must mean what it meant to the Lochner Court—that state redistribution of existing entitlements violates liberty—then it should be abandoned, for that was the central message of *Lochner*'s repudiation.

29. *See* Cass R. Sunstein, *The Partial Constitution* (1993).

30. *Id.* at 272.

31. *See* Catharine A. MacKinnon, *Feminism Unmodified* 164–66 (1987) [hereinafter *Feminism Unmodified*], Catharine A. MacKinnon, *Toward a Feminist Theory of the State* 159–70 (1989) [hereinafter *Toward a Feminist Theory*].

32. *See* MacKinnon, *Feminism Unmodified, supra* note 37, at 164–66; MacKinnon, *Toward a Feminist Theory, supra* note 37, at 163–70.

33. *See The Federalist* No. 10 (J. Madison).

34. *See* Sunstein, "Sexual Orientation," *supra* note 31, at 1171.

35. The most notable exception, of course, is Brown v. Board of Education, 349 U.S. 294 (1954).

36. *See, e.g.,* City of Richmond v. J. A. Croson Co., 488 U.S. 469 (1989) (increasing the evidentiary burden on minorities to show violation of the Fourteenth Amendment's equal protection clause by requiring specific proof of past discrimination); University of California v. Bakke, 438 U.S. 265 (1978) (restricting affirmative action by limiting consideration of race in admissions decisions); Washington v. Davis, 426 U.S. 229

(1976) (reducing evidence available to minorities sufficient to prove discrimination by finding that disproportionate effects alone do not warrant conclusion of purposeful discrimination).

37. See *supra* notes 26–29 and accompanying text.

6. Toward a First Amendment Jurisprudence of Respect

1. George P. Fletcher, "Constitutional Identity," 14 *Cardozo L. Rev.* 737, 741 (1993).
2. R.A.V. v. City of St. Paul, Minn., 112 S. Ct. 2538 (1992) (striking down St. Paul's hate speech regulation as content-based and thus violative of the First Amendment).
3. *See* Fletcher, *supra* note 1, at 740–46.
4. *Id.* at 744–45.
5. Patricia J. Williams, *The Alchemy of Race and Rights* 73 (1991).
6. *See, e.g.*, Richard Delgado, "Words That Wound: A Tort Action for Racial Insults, Epithets, and Name-Calling," *Harv. C.R.-C.L. L. Rev.* 133 (1982); Charles R. Lawrence III, "If He Hollers Let Him Go: Regulating Racist Speech on Campus," 1990 *Duke L. J.* 431; Mari J. Matsuda, "Public Response to Racist Speech: Considering the Victim's Story," 87 *Mich. L. Rev.* 2320 (1990).
7. *See, e.g.*, Ronald Dworkin, "The Coming Battles over Free Speech," *N.Y. Rev. Books,* June 11, 1992, at 56–58, 61.
8. *See* Stanley Fish, *Is There a Text in This Class?* (1980); Stanley Fish, *Doing What Comes Naturally* (1989).
9. 112 S. Ct. 2538 (1992).
10. *See* Fletcher, *supra* note 1, at 741, 745–46.
11. *See* Dworkin, *supra* note 8, at 56.
12. "Riots in Los Angeles: A Plea for Calm," *N.Y. Times,* May 2, 1992, at 6.

7. Constitutional Skepticism

1. *See, e.g.*, Planned Parenthood v. Casey, 112 S. Ct. 2791, 2874 (1992) (Scalia, J., joined by Rehnquist, C. J., White & Thomas, JJ., concurring in the judgment in part and dissenting in part): "The issue is whether [abortion] is a liberty protected by the Constitution of the United States. I am sure it is not. I reach that conclusion . . . because of two simple facts: (1) the Constitution says absolutely nothing about it, and (2) the longstanding traditions of American society have permitted it to be legally proscribed."
2. For examples of originalist interpretation and defenses of originalism, see Raoul Berger, *Federalism: The Founder's Design* (1987) (advocating the doctrine of original intent for constitutional interpretation); Raoul Berger, "Against an Activist Court," 31 *Cath. U. L. Rev.* 173 (1982) (rejecting an activist theory that the judiciary was given unlimited, unaccountable power, checked only by judicial "self-restraint"); Raoul Berger, "New Theories of 'Interpretation': The Activist Flight from the Constitution," 47 *Ohio St. L. J.* 1 (1986) (rejecting activist theories and defending original intent); Robert H. Bork, "Original Intent: The Only Legitimate Basis for Constitutional Decision Making," 26 *Judges' J.* 12 (Summer 1987) (arguing that judges must follow the intention of the framers); Robert H. Bork, "The Constitution, Original Intent, and Economic Rights,"

23 *San Diego L. Rev.* 823 (1986) (arguing that the framers' intent is the only legitimate basis for constitutional decision making and binds judges); Antonin Scalia, "Originalism: The Lesser Evil," 57 *U. Cin. L. Rev.* 849 (1989) (asserting that framers' intent is the necessary method by which to interpret the Constitution).

3. For an example of "consensualist" interpretation, see Penry v. Lynaugh, 492 U.S. 302 (1989) (holding that interpretation of the Cruel and Unusual Punishment Clause depends on community consensus).

4. Those adopting this view include Bruce Ackerman, Ronald M. Dworkin, and John Hart Ely. *See generally* Bruce Ackerman, *Reconstructing American Law* (1984); Bruce Ackerman, *Social Justice and the Liberal State* (1980); Bruce Ackerman, *We The People* (1991); Ronald M. Dworkin, *Taking Rights Seriously* (1977); John Hart Ely, *Democracy and Distrust: A Theory of Judicial Review* (1980).

5. *See, e.g.,* Mark V. Tushnet, *Red, White, and Blue: A Critical Analysis of Constitutional Law* 6–11 (1988) (contrasting some of the main elements of the liberal and republican traditions); Paul Brest, "The Misconceived Quest for the Original Understanding," 60 *B.U. L. Rev.* 204, 224–37 (1980) (rejecting originalism and defending nonoriginalist adjudication, which accords presumptive weight to the text and original history, but does not treat them as authoritative or binding). For an impassioned argument against the "indeterminacy thesis" on this ground, see Owen M. Fiss, "Objectivity and Interpretation," 34 *Stan. L. Rev.* 739, 742–62 (1982) (arguing against a new nihilism that insists that objectivity is impossible and that interpretation is based on the judge's own values).

6. *See, e.g.,* George P. Fletcher, "Constitutional Identity," 14 *Cardozo L. Rev.* 1, 26–27 (1992) (stating that college speech codes are undesirable, unconstitutional, and at odds with our constitutional identity); Suzanna Sherry, "Speaking of Virtue: A Republican Approach to University Regulation of Hate Speech," 75 *Minn. L. Rev.* 933 (1991) (arguing against the use of university hate speech regulations); Nadine Strossen, "Regulating Racist Speech on Campus: A Modest Proposal," 1990 *Duke L. J.* 484 (arguing that unless words are covered by "fighting words," an exception to First Amendment ordinances suppressing them is unconstitutional).

7. J. Peter Byrne, "Racial Insults and Free Speech within the University," 79 *Geo. L. J.* 399 (1991) (arguing that the Constitution can and should be read to afford universities the authority to prohibit racial insults by member of the academic community); Richard Delgado, "Campus Antiracism Rules: Constitutional Narratives in Collision," 85 *NW. U. L. Rev.* 343 (1991) (analyzing antiracism rules in terms of both a First Amendment and a Fourteenth Amendment problem); Charles R. Lawrence, III, "If He Hollers, Let Him Go: Regulating Racist Speech on Campus," 1990 *Duke L. J.* 431 [hereinafter "Regulating Racist Speech"] (stating that regulations are both desirable and constitutional); and Mari J. Matsuda, "Public Response to Racist Speech: Considering the Victim's Story," 87 *Mich. L. Rev.* 2320 (1989) (proposing legal sanctions for hate speech and thus rejecting an absolutist First Amendment position).

8. *See* Ronald Dworkin, "Liberty and Pornography," 38 *N.Y. Rev. Books,* Aug. 15, 1991, 12; Barry W. Lynn, " 'Civil Rights' Ordinances and the Attorney General's Commission: New Developments in Pornography Regulation," 21 *Harv. C.R.-C.L. L. Rev.* 27, 48–56 (1986) (concluding that supporters of sex discrimination ordinances do not ad-

vance principles acceptable to society that truly support free expression and personal privacy).

9. Catharine A. MacKinnon, "Pornography: On Morality and Politics," in *Toward a Feminist Theory of the State* 195–214 (1989) (condemning pornography as that which exploits sexual and economic inequality for gain); Catharine A. MacKinnon, "Not a Moral Issue," 2 *Yale L. & Pol'y Rev.* 321, 336–40 (1984) (arguing that the First Amendment should not protect pornography because pornography suppresses women); Catharine A. MacKinnon, "Pornography, Civil Rights and Speech," 20 *Harv. C.R.-C.L. L. Rev.* 1, 22–32 (1985) (defining pornography as a civil rights violation and arguing for the constitutionality of an antipornography ordinance); Catharine A. MacKinnon, "Pornography: Social Science, Legal and Clinical Perspectives," 4 *Law & Ineq. J.* 17, 38–49 (1986) (part of a panel including Edward Donnerstein, Cheryl A. Champion, and Cass R. Sunstein).

10. Indeed, constitutional scholars may be more reluctant to take a critical stance toward the Constitution than does the general public. This might explain why constitutional scholars tend to be more skeptical of the wisdom of constitutional amendments than the latter. For example, a number of liberal constitutional scholars testified to both the constitutionality and desirability of a federal law to ban flag-burning, apparently in part because they feared that the alternative was a far more egregious constitutional amendment. *See* "Statutory and Constitutional Responses to the Supreme Court Decision in *Texas v. Johnson:* Hearings before the Subcommittee on Civil and Constitutional Rights of the Committee on the Judiciary, House of Representatives," 101st Cong., 1st Sess. 55–64, 107–24, 222–26, 444–47 (1989) (statements of Walter Dellinger, Laurence Tribe, Charles Fried, and Cass Sunstein).

11. Derrick A. Bell, *And We Are Not Saved: The Exclusive Quest for Racial Justice* (1987) (examining the intricacies of the barriers to racial equality established in law).

12. Alan D. Freeman, "Antidiscrimination Law: The View from 1989," 64 *Tul. L. Rev.* 1407 (1990) [hereinafter "Antidiscrimination Law"] (examining antidiscrimination laws as evolved in Supreme Court opinions since 1954); Alan D. Freeman, "Race and Class: The Dilemma of Liberal Reform," 90 *Yale L. J.* 1880 (1981) (book review of Derrick Bell's *Race, Racism, and American Law* examining to what extent anything can significantly be done about the unique problem of racism without focusing on class structure and the forces that maintain it); Alan D. Freeman, "Race, Class and the Contradictions of Affirmative Action," 7 *Black L. J.* 270, 270–74 (1982) (discussing racism, not as just another form of oppression, but in terms of problems of interdependence, remedial programs, and class struggle); Alan D. Freeman, "Race, Rights and the Quest for Equality of Opportunity: A Critical Legal Essay," 23 *Harv. C.R.-C.L. L. Rev.* 295, 316–25 (1988) (responding to the symposium entitled "Minority Critiques of the Critical Legal Studies Movement" and discussing two arguments, the "indeterminacy critique" and the "contradiction critique" of the movement); Alan D. Freeman, Monroe Fordham, and Sidney Willhelm, "A Hurdle Too High: Class-Based Roadblocks to Racial Remediation: A Panel," 33 *Buff. L. Rev.* 1, 4–10, 15–17 (1984) (analyzing the barriers to ending racial discrimination).

13. Mark V. Tushnet, "An Essay on Rights," 62 *Tex. L. Rev.* 1363 (1984) (developing a version of the critique of rights and exploring the epistemological basis of that critique).

14. Mary E. Becker, "The Politics of Women's Wrongs and the Bill of 'Rights': A Bicentennial Perspective," 59 *U. Chi. L. Rev.* 453 (1992).

15. Mari J. Matsuda, "When the First Quail Calls: Multiple Consciousness as Jurisprudential Method," 11 *Women's Rts. L. Rep.* 7, 8–10 (1989) (arguing for multiple consciousness, a deliberate choice to see the world from the standpoint of the oppressed, as a jurisprudential method).

16. Akhil R. Amar, "Our Forgotten Constitution: A Bicentennial Comment," 97 *Yale L. J.* 28 (1987) (analyzing how history is used to interpret our supreme law and how we can make history by changing it); Akhil R. Amar, "Philadelphia Revisited: Amending the Constitution outside Article V," 55 *U. Chi. L. Rev.* 1043 (1988) (asserting that constitutional amendments need not be limited by the Article V amending process or judicial review and that, instead, amendment should be by direct appeal to, and ratification by, the people); Akhil R. Amar, "The Bill of Rights as a Constitution," 100 *Yale L. J.* 1131 (1991) (proposing an integrated overview of the Bill of Rights, illustrating the interaction between that document and the Constitution as originally drafted and refuting the notion that they represent two very different types of regulatory strategies); Akhil R. Amar & Widawsky, "Child Abuse as Slavery: A Thirteenth Amendment Response to DeShaney," 105 *Harv. L. Rev.* 1359 (1992) (arguing that child abuse is analogous to slavery and that the Thirteenth Amendment therefore imposes an affirmative obligation on the state to prevent it); Ruth Colker, "Antisubordination above All: Sex, Race and Equal Protection," 61 *N.Y.U. L. Rev.* 1003, 1058–66 (1986) (proposing a new model for equal protection analysis, antisubordination, which finds it inappropriate for certain groups in society to have subordinated status because of their lack of power in society as a whole and would eliminate power disparities between groups).

17. Catharine A. MacKinnon, "Reflections on Sex Equality under Law," 100 *Yale L. J.* 1281, 1282–97 (1991) (interpreting the Constitution's general equality mandate to combat the problem of sex inequality).

18. See *supra* note 6.

19. 163 U.S. 537, 552 (1896) (Harlan, J., dissenting) (stating that the Fourteenth Amendment targets discrimination by law, rather than societal discrimination).

20. 488 U.S. 469, 528 (1989) (Marshall, J., joined by Brennan & Blackmun, JJ., dissenting) (arguing that the program setting aside a percentage of contracts for minorities is constitutional).

21. Sir Isaiah Berlin, "Two Concepts of Liberty," in *Four Essays on Liberty* 118 (1969) (distinguishing the "negative" liberty to do as one pleases within a designated sphere from the "positive" liberty to live a particular kind of life).

22. Martin Luther King, Jr., *Why We Can't Wait* 83 (1963) (describing the impact of racism on the self-image of African-American children).

23. See *supra* text accompanying notes 1–4.

24. Frank I. Michelman, "Law's Republic," 97 *Yale L. J.* 1493 (1988) (contending that only through a modern reconsideration of constitutional thought can we hope to make sense of the American belief that political liberty calls for a government "of the people, by the people"); Frank I. Michelman, "Foreword: Traces of Self-Government," 100 *Harv. L. Rev.* 4, 66–73 (1986) (exploring migration of self-government from the people to the Court); *see also* Cass R. Sunstein, "Beyond the Republican Revival," 97 *Yale L. J.* 1539

(1988) (asserting that the common opposition between liberalism and republicanism is a false one).

25. Michelman, "Law's Republic," *supra* note 25; Michelman, "Foreword: Traces of Self-Government," *supra* note 25.

26. Owen M. Fiss, "A Life Lived Twice," 100 *Yale L. J.* 1117 (1991) (focusing on Justice William J. Brennan and his achievements as a liberal justice on the Supreme Court); Owen M. Fiss, "Reason in All Its Splendor," 56 *Brook. L. Rev.* 789 (1990) (examining the importance of procedural fairness before the deprivation of life, liberty, or property); Owen M. Fiss, "State Activism and State Censorship," 100 *Yale L. J.* 2087 (1991) (stating that the principle of freedom that the First Amendment embodies is derived from the democratic nature of our society and is essential for collective self-determination).

27. Sunstein, *supra* note 25.

28. Paul Brest, "Congress as Constitutional Decisionmaker and Its Power to Counter Judicial Doctrine," 21 *Ga. L. Rev.* 57 (1986) (exploring whether Congress has the ability to engage in constitutional interpretation); Paul Brest, "Constitutional Citizenship," 34 *Clev. St. L. Rev.* 175 (1986) (arguing that the Supreme Court is not authorized to decide issues of public morality); Paul Brest, "Further Beyond the Republican Revival: Toward Radical Republicanism," 97 *Yale L. J.* 1623 (1988) (stating that we must abandon our obsession with courts and work toward decentralization and democratization).

29. See *supra* text accompanying note 5.

30. John Stuart Mill, *On Liberty* (1859).

31. *See, e.g.*, Civil Rights Cases, 109 U.S. 3 (1883) (holding that Fourteenth Amendment claims require a show of state action).

32. DeShaney v. Winnebago County Department of Social Services, 489 U.S. 189, 195–97 (1989) (holding that the due process clause does not impose on the states an affirmative obligation to protect a son from an abusive father).

33. Jacobus tenBroek, *The Antislavery Origins of the Fourteenth Amendment* (1951), reprinted as Jacobus tenBroek, *Equal under Law* (1969) ("[T]he national protection of men in their natural rights or of citizens in their privileges and immunities . . . extended to individuals without regard to the private or governmental character of the violator . . . .").

34. Day-Brite Lighting, Inc. v. Missouri, 342 U.S. 421, 429 (1952) (sustaining a law requiring employers to give employees four hours off from work with pay for them to vote); Lincoln Fed. Labor Union v. Northwest Iron & Metal Co., 335 U.S. 525, 537 (1949) (upholding state "right to work" laws requiring that employment decisions not be based on union membership); Olsen v. Nebraska, 313 U.S. 236, 246–47 (1941) (upholding a law fixing maximum employment agency fees as constitutional); United States v. Darby, 312 U.S. 100, 125–26 (1941) (upholding federal wage and hour requirements); United States v. Carolene Prods. Co., 304 U.S. 144, 154 (1938) (rejecting due process challenge to federal prohibition of interstate shipment of skimmed milk mixed with nonmilk fats); West Coast Hotel Co. v. Parrish, 300 U.S. 379, 400 (1937) (sustaining state minimum wage law for women); Nebbia v. New York, 291 U.S. 502, 593 (1934) (upholding New York's Milk Control Board's minimum and maximum price fixing).

35. 347 U.S. 483, 495 (1954) (holding that racial segregation of public schools violates the Fourteenth Amendment).

36. Charles R. Lawrence III, "Education for Black Power in the Eighties: Present Day Implications of the Bakke Decision," 10 *Nat'l Black L. J.* 58, 59–60 (1987) (arguing that *Brown* implies that all segregation in American public life is invalid); *see also* Lawrence, "Regulating Racist Speech," *supra* note 7, at 431, 438–444 (arguing that *Brown* supports the regulation of hate speech in the educational setting).

37. Matsuda, *supra* note 15, at 9 (asserting that "the multiple consciousness I urge lawyers to attain is not a random ability to see all points of view, but a deliberate choice to see the world from the standpoint of the oppressed").

38. Matsuda, *supra* note 7, at 2321 (arguing in favor of criminal and administrative sanctions as an appropriate response to racist speech).

39. Lawrence, "Regulating Racist Speech," *supra* note 7, at 439 (arguing that segregation was racist speech).

40. Patricia J. Williams, "Alchemical Notes: Reconstructing Ideals from Deconstructed Rights," 22 *Harv. C.R.-C.L. L. Rev.* 401, 404 (1987) (arguing against the part of critical legal studies that rejects rights-based theory).

41. Kimberle W. Crenshaw, "Race, Reform and Retrenchment: Transformation and Legitimation in Antidiscrimination Law," 101 *Harv. L. Rev.* 1331, 1336 (1988) (arguing that, because racism is a central ideological underpinning of American society, critical legal studies should focus on it, as well as on legal consciousness).

42. Bell, *supra* note 11 (using the mode of a fairy tale to explain why racial equality has not been achieved in the more than thirty years since Brown v. Board of Education).

43. Freeman, "Antidiscrimination Law," *supra* note 12, at 1408–9 (arguing that recent Supreme Court cases ruling against affirmative action programs are not the result of recent historical whimsy, but are "firmly rooted in the contradictory character of anti-discrimination law, the agenda of which was constrained at the outset by abstract principles of formal equality that would surely reassert themselves in time").

44. Richard Delgado, "Norms and Normal Science: Toward a Critique of Normativity in Legal Thought," 139 *U. Pa. L. Rev.* 933, 937 (1991) (arguing that critiques of normativity in legal studies "place[] the reformer in no worse position than he or she occupied before, and [are] no more threatening to the cause of social transformation than earlier critiques of law-as-logic or law-as-empirical-science").

45. MacKinnon, *supra* note 17, at 1297 (arguing that because the "similarly situated" requirement controls equality claims, the laws of sexual assault and reproductive control have not been subject to constitutional attack).

8. The Authoritarian Impulse in Constitutional Law

1. Paul Brest, "Constitutional Citizenship," 34 *Cleveland St. L. Rev.* 1, 6 (1986).

2. *Id.* at 1.

3. *Id.*

4. *See, e.g.,* Bowers v. Hardwick, 478 U.S. 140, 145 (1986); Roe v. Wade, 410 U.S. 113, 116, 148, 159 (1973).

5. *See* Herbert Wechsler, "Toward Neutral Principles of Constitutional Law," 73 *Harv. L. Rev.* 1 (1959).

6. *Bowers,* 478 U.S. at 140.

7. *Id.* at 145.
8. *Roe,* 410 U.S. at 113.
9. *Id.* at 116, 148, 159.
10. For a strong endorsement of this position, *see* Frank Easterbrook, "The Supreme Court, 1983 Term—Foreword: The Court and the Economic System," 98 *Harv. L. Rev.* 4 (1984).
11. *But see* Brown v. Board of Education, 347 U.S. 483 (1954).
12. *Mill on Bentham and Coleridge* 39 (F. Leavis ed. 1950); John Stuart Mill, "On Liberty," in *The Utilitarians* 473 (Dolphin ed. 1961); John Stuart Mill, "Utilitarianism," in *The Utilitarians* 399 (Dolphin ed. 1961). For a discussion of Mill's pragmatism, see Robin L. West, "In the Interest of the Governed: A Utilitarian Justification for Substantive Judicial Review," 18 *Ga. L. Rev.* 469 (1984); Robin L. West, "Liberalism Rediscovered: A Pragmatic Definition of the Liberal Vision," 46 *U. Pitt. L. Rev.* 673 (1985).
13. John Dewey, *Liberalism and Social Action* (1935).
14. *Aristotle's Politics* (H. Apostle & L. Gerson eds., 1986); *Nicomachean Ethics: Aristotle* (M. Ostwald ed., 1962).
15. Roberto Unger, *The Critical Legal Studies Movement* (1986); Roberto Unger, *Knowledge and Politics* (1975).
16. Alisdair MacIntyre, *After Virtue* (1981).
17. *See, e.g.,* Roberto Unger, "The Critical Legal Studies Movement," 96 *Harv. L. Rev.* 563 (1983) (defending superliberalism).
18. *See, e.g.,* Paul Brest, "Who Decides?," 58 *S. Cal. L. Rev.* 661 (1985).

9. Progressive and Conservative Constitutionalism

1. Among the classic articulations of the "liberal-legalist" regime, *see, e.g.,* Herbert Wechsler, "Toward Neutral Principles of Constitutional Law," in *Principles, Politics, and Fundamental Law* (1961); John Hart Ely, *Democracy and Distrust: A Theory of Judicial Review* (1980).
2. *See, e.g.,* Robert Bork, *The Tempting of America* (1989); Richard Posner, *The Economics of Justice* (1981); Raoul Berger, "Federalism: The Founders' Design—A Response to Michael McConnell," 57 *Geo. Wash. L. Rev.* 51 (1988); Raoul Berger, "Originalist Theories of Constitutional Interpretation," 73 *Cornell L. Rev.* 350 (1988); Raoul Berger, "New Theories of 'Interpretation': The Activist Flight from the Constitution," 47 *Ohio St. L. J.* 1 (1986); Raoul Berger, " 'Original Intention' in Historical Perspective," 54 *Geo. Wash. L. Rev.* 296 (1986); Raoul Berger, "Some Reflections on Interpretivism," 55 *Geo. Wash. L. Rev.* 1 (1986); Raoul Berger, "The Activist Legacy of the New Deal Court," 59 *Wash. L. Rev.* 751 (1984); Raoul Berger, "G. Edward White's Apology for Judicial Activism," 63 *Texas L. Rev.* 367 (1984); Raoul Berger, "Against an Activist Court," 31 *Cath. U. L. Rev.* 173 (1982); Robert Bork, "Neutral Principles and Some First Amendment Problems," 47 *Ind. L. J.* 1 (1971) [hereinafter "Neutral Principles"]; Frank Easterbrook, "Method, Result, and Authority: A Reply," 98 *Harv. L. Rev.* 622 (1985) [hereinafter "A Reply"]; Frank Easterbrook, "The Supreme Court, 1983 Term—Foreword: The Court and the Economic System," 98 *Harv. L. Rev.* 4 (1984); Frank Easterbrook, "Legal Interpretation and the Power of the Judiciary," 7 *Harv. J. L. & Pub. Poly.* 87 (1984); Frank Easterbrook, "Substance and Due Process," 1982 *Sup. Ct. Rev.*

85; Frank Easterbrook, "Statutes' Domains," 50 *U. Chi. L. Rev.* 533 (1983); Michael McConnell, "The Role of Democratic Politics in Transforming Moral Convictions into Law" (Book Review), 98 *Yale L. J.* 1501 (1989); *see also* Richard Epstein, *Takings: Private Property and the Power of Eminent Domain* (1985); *and* James Wilson, "Justice Diffused: A Comparison of Edmund Burke's Conservatism with the Views of Five Conservative, Academic Judges," 40 *U. Miami L. Rev.* 913 (1986).

3. Mark V. Tushnet has produced the most consistent and incisive critical constitutional scholarship in *Red, White and Blue: A Critical Analysis of Constitutional Law* (1988). For a general introduction to the thinking of the Critical Legal Studies movement, see Mark Kelman, *A Guide to Critical Legal Studies* (1987).

4. *See*, e.g., Catharine A. MacKinnon, *Toward a Feminist Theory of the State* (1989); Catharine A. MacKinnon, *Feminism Unmodified* (1987); Laurence H. Tribe, *American Constitutional Law* (2d ed. 1988); Laurence H. Tribe, *Constitutional Choices* (1985); Frank I. Michelman, "Law's Republic," 97 *Yale L. J.* 1493 (1988); Frank I. Michelman, "The Supreme Court, 1985 Term—Foreword: Traces of Self-Government," 100 *Harv. L. Rev.* 4 (1986) [hereinafter "Traces of Self-Government"]; Frank I. Michelman, "Welfare Rights in a Constitutional Democracy," 1979 *Wash. U. L. Q.* 659, 677 [hereinafter "Welfare Rights"]; Suzanna Sherry, "Outlaw Blues" (Book Review), 87 *Mich. L. Rev.* 1418 (1989); Suzanna Sherry, "Republican Citizenship in a Democratic Society" (Book Review), 66 *Texas L. Rev.* 1229 (1988); Suzanna Sherry, "The Ninth Amendment: Righting an Unwritten Constitution," 64 *Chi.-Kent L. Rev.* 1001 (1988) [hereinafter "The Ninth Amendment"]; David A. Strauss, "Discriminatory Intent and the Taming of Brown," 56 *U. Chi. L. Rev.* 935 (1989) [hereinafter "The Taming of Brown"]; David A. Strauss, "The Myth of Colorblindness," 1986 *Sup. Ct. Rev.* 99; Cass R. Sunstein, *The Partial Constitution* (Harv., 1983); Roberto Unger, "The Critical Legal Studies Movement," 96 *Harv. L. Rev.* 563 (1983).

5. *See generally* Tushnet, *supra* note 3.

6. *See* Epstein, *supra* note 2.

7. *See*, e.g., Michelman, "Law's Republic," *supra* note 4. This basis for distrust of majority power is a central theme in liberal as well as progressive thought. *See* John Stuart Mill, *On Liberty* (1859).

8. 410 U.S. 113 (1973).

9. 478 U.S. 186 (1986).

10. 492 U.S. 490 (1989).

11. For liberal arguments against *Roe*, see Ely, *supra* note 1, at 11–41, and M. Perry, *Morality, Politics and Law* 572–78 (1988).

12. For progressive arguments in support of *Roe*, see Webster, 109 S.Ct. 3067 (Blackmun, J., dissenting); "Brief for the National Coalition against Domestic Violence as Amicus Curiae Supporting Appellees," *Webster*, 492 U.S., at 490; Olsen, "Unraveling Compromise," 103 *Harv. L. Rev.* 105 (1989); Suzanna Sherry, "Women's Virtue," 63 *Tul. L. Rev.* 1591 (1989).

13. 488 U.S. 469 (1989).

14. *See*, e.g., Strauss, "The Myth of Colorblindness," *supra* note 4.

15. See *infra* notes 55–60 & 106–108 and accompanying text.

16. See *infra* notes 64–69 and accompanying text.

17. See *infra* note 136 and accompanying text.

18. See *infra* notes 23–32 and accompanying text.

19. See *infra* notes 75–83 and accompanying text.

20. Bruce Ackerman, "The Storrs Lectures: Discovering the Constitution," 93 *Yale L. J.* 1013, 1022 (1984).

21. Owen M. Fiss, "Objectivity and Interpretation," 34 *Stan. L. Rev.* 739, 753–54 (1983).

22. *Id.* at 754.

23. *See, e.g.,* P. Devlin, *The Enforcement of Morals* (1965); Ronald Dworkin, " 'Natural' Law Revisited," 34 *U. Fla. L. Rev.* 165 (1982); *cf.* H.L.A. Hart, *Law, Liberty and Morality* (1963).

24. McConnell, *supra* note 2, at 1504 (citation omitted).

25. The most striking example in the legal literature is Epstein's demonstration in *Takings* of the unconstitutionality, as well as irrationality, of the "New Deal" legislative reforms of the first half of the century. Epstein, *supra* note 2. Bork criticizes Epstein on precisely this ground in *The Tempting of America*. Bork, *supra* note 2, at 229–230. Bork's adamant originalism, however, is more similar than dissimilar to Epstein's constitutional critique of redistributive politics. For Bork, as for Epstein, it is law, the original Constitution, and the reasoned, judicious mindset its interpretation requires, that must take precedence over the political desires of presently constituted majorities. Only where the Constitution dictates majoritarian rule does Bork allow the majority unfettered say.

    For a general critique of the modern conservatives' hostility toward politics, see Mark Kelman, "On Democracy-Bashing: A Skeptical Look at the Theoretical and 'Empirical' Practice of the Public Choice Movement," 74 *Va. L. Rev.* 199 (1988).

26. For critiques of this strand of conservative thought, see Henderson, "Authoritarianism and the Rule of Law" (unpublished manuscript, on file with author); Sherry, "The Ninth Amendment," *supra* note 4, at 1010–11; Wilson, *supra* note 2, at 913; James Wilson, "Constraints of Power: The Constitutional Opinions of Judges Scalia, Bork, Posner, Easterbrook and Winter," 40 *U. Miami L. Rev.* 1171 (1986).

27. *See* Robin L. West, "The Celebration of Authority" (Book Review), 83 *NW. U. L. Rev.* 977 (1989).

28. Richard Posner calls this moral outlook a "morality of obedience" and identifies it with "mature values." *See* Richard Posner, *Law and Literature: A Misunderstood Relation* (1988). For a critical account of the morality of obedience as defended in Posner's work, see West, "The Celebration of Authority," *supra* note 27.

29. *See, e.g.,* Michael McConnell, "A Moral Realist Defense of Constitutional Democracy," 64 *Chi.-Kent L. Rev.* 89 (1988); Edwin Meese, "The Law of the Constitution," 61 *Tul. L. Rev.* 979 (1987).

30. The longevity of the Constitution, for example, plays a major role in justifying the various forms of conservative legalism endorsed by Richard Posner. *See, e.g.,* Posner, *supra* note 28; *see also* McConnell, *supra* note 29; Meese, *supra* note 29.

31. For a critical account, *see* Sherry, "The Ninth Amendment," *supra* note 4.

32. *See, e.g.,* Epstein, *supra* note 2.

33. Some version of moral Darwinism pervades the writings of the normative wing of the law and economics school, as well as modern public choice writings. *See, e.g.,* Epstein, *supra* note 2; Posner, *supra* note 2.

34. *See* Lon Fuller, *The Morality of Law* 33–91 (1964).

35. *See, e.g.,* Devlin, *supra* note 23; McConnell, *supra* note 2. I do not mean to imply that any of these individual theorists support these outcomes in particular.

36. H.L.A. Hart, *The Concept of Law* (1961); H.L.A. Hart, "Positivism and the Separation of Law and Morals," 71 *Harv. L. Rev.* 593, 620–21 (1958).

37. *See* Bork, "Neutral Principles," *supra* note 2; Easterbrook, "A Reply," *supra* note 2, at 627–29. Lon Fuller seemed to assume, in his debates with Hart, that a duty to obey the law followed naturally from positivist premises. *See* Fuller, *supra* note 34, at 106–18. Some forms of legal positivism lend themselves to this interpretation, legitimating the natural lawyer's complaint that legal positivism carries with it conservative and even authoritarian implications. *See* Henderson, *supra* note 26.

38. *See* Richard Posner, *The Problems of Jurisprudence* (1991); *and* Posner, *supra* note 2.

39. 492 U.S. 490 (1989).

40. 478 U.S. 186 (1986).

41. *Id.,* at 196–97 (Burger, C.J., concurring).

42. Devlin, *supra* note 23, ch. 1.

43. *Bowers,* 478 U.S. at 190–91, 194–95.

44. Lochner v. New York, 198 U.S. 45 (1905).

45. 347 U.S. 483 (1954).

46. 492 U.S. 490 (1989).

47. 489 U.S. 189 (1989).

48. 492 U.S. 302 (1989).

49. 492 U.S. 361 (1989).

50. 491 U.S. 110 (1989).

51. 492 U.S. at 490.

52. 489 U.S. at 189.

53. 492 U.S. at 361; 492 U.S. at 305.

54. 491 U.S. at 123–32.

55. 488 U.S. 469 (1989).

56. Kenneth Casebeer, "Running on Empty: Justice Brennan's Plea, The Empty State, the City of Richmond, and the Profession," 43 *U. Miami L. Rev.* 989, 1007 (1989); Richard Delgado, "On Taking Back Our Civil Rights Promises: When Equality Doesn't Compute," 1989 *Wis. L. Rev.* 579; Michel Rosenfeld, "Decoding Richmond: Affirmative Action and the Elusive Meaning of Constitutional Equality," 87 *Mich. L. Rev.* 1729 (1989); Patricia J. Williams, "The Obliging Shell: An Informal Essay on Formal Equal Opportunity," 87 *Mich. L. Rev.* 2128 (1989).

57. *Croson,* 488 U.S. at 493–94 (citation omitted).

58. *Id.,* at 518–28 (Scalia, J., and Kennedy, J., concurring).

59. *Id.,* at 520–21 (Scalia, J., concurring) (quoting A. Bickel, *The Morality of Consent* 133 (1975)).

60. *Id.,* at 490–91.

61. *See, e.g.,* the work of Berger, cited *supra* note 2; *and* Bork, cited *supra* note 2.

62. *See* Bork, *supra* note 2; Bork, "Neutral Principles," *supra* note 2.

63. Id.

64. Easterbrook, "A Reply," *supra* note 2, at 627–29.

65. McConnell, *supra* note 2, at 1536–37.

66. Lochner v. New York, 198 U.S. 45, 74 (1905) (Holmes, J., dissenting).

67. In this regard, see the discussion of *Lochner* in Posner, *supra* note 28, at 281–88, and Posner, *supra* note 2, at 383–86.

68. That communal authority is premised on social power is an organizing tenet of critical theory. *See, e.g.,* M. Foucault, *Discipline and Punish: The Birth of the Prison* (1977) [hereinafter *Discipline*]; M. Foucault, *The History of Sexuality* (1978) [hereinafter *Sexuality*]. For parallel arguments in the legal literature, see Kelman, *supra* note 3, at 213–33, and Robert Gordon, "Critical Legal Histories," 36 *Stan. L. Rev.* 57, 71–116 (1984).

69. *See, e.g.,* Foucault, *Discipline, supra* note 70; Foucault, *Sexuality, supra* note 70.

70. *See* Kelman, *supra* note 3, at 151–85.

71. This is, of course, the central insight of the Critical Legal Studies movement. *See, e.g., Essays on Critical Legal Studies* (Harvard Law Review Association ed., 1986); David Kairys, "Introduction," *The Politics of Law* 5 (D. Kairys ed., 1982); "Critical Legal Studies Symposium," 36 *Stan. L. Rev.* 1 (1984).

72. *See generally* Barbara Hernstein-Smith, *Contingencies of Value: Alternative Perspectives for Critical Theory* (1988).

73. *See generally* Mill, *supra* note 7. For an argument that modern liberals fail to read Mill correctly, that his theory is progressive and requires the state to engage in discrimination between conceptions of the good life, see Robin L. West, "Liberalism Rediscovered: A Pragmatic Definition of the Liberal Vision," 46 *U. Pitt. L. Rev.* 673, 688–93 (1985).

74. See *supra* note 24 and accompanying text.

75. Adrienne Rich, *On Lies, Secrets and Silence: Selected Prose, 1966–1978* (1979); *see also* Andrea Dworkin, *Intercourse* (1987); Andrea Dworkin, *Woman-Hating* (1974); Catharine MacKinnon, *Feminism Unmodified, supra* note 4.

76. Adrienne Rich, "Compulsory Heterosexuality and the Lesbian Continuum," in *Blood, Bread, and Poetry* 51–52 (1986).

77. Martin Luther King, Jr., "I Have a Dream," in *Words of Martin Luther King* 95–97 (C. S. King ed., 1983).

78. Duncan Kennedy, "Form and Substance in Private Law Adjudication," 89 *Harv. L. Rev.* 1685, 1776 (1976).

79. Roberto Unger, *False Necessity: Anti-Necessitarian Social Theory in the Service of Radical Democracy* (1987); Unger, *supra* note 4.

80. Unger, *supra* note 81, at 9, 164.

81. Storytelling, particularly the telling of stories relating experiences of subordination, plays a major role in antisubordination progressive legal thought, as well as in progressive political thought. *See, e.g.,* Richard Delgado, "Storytelling for Oppositionists and Others: A Plea for Narrative," 87 *Mich. L. Rev.* 2411 (1989); Lynne Henderson, "Legality and Empathy," 85 *Mich. L. Rev.* 1574 (1987); Mari J. Matsuda, "Public Response to Racist Speech: Considering the Victim's Story," 87 *Mich. L. Rev.* 2320 (1989).

82. Martin Luther King, Jr., "Letter from Birmingham City Jail," in *Why We Can't Wait* 84–86 (1963). For a critical commentary, *see* David Luban, "Difference Made Legal: The Court and Dr. King," 87 *Mich. L. Rev.* 2152 (1989).

83. Sherry, "The Ninth Amendment," *supra* note 4, at 1013.

84. Easterbrook, "A Reply," *supra* note 2, at 627.
85. Duncan Kennedy, "Freedom and Constraint in Adjudication: A Critical Phenomenology," 36 *J. Legal Educ.* 518, 562 (1986).
86. 488 U.S. 469 (1989).
87. 426 U.S. 229 (1976).
88. Sherry, "The Ninth Amendment," *supra* note 4, at 1010–11 (citations omitted).
89. Strauss, "The Myth of Colorblindness," *supra* note 4.
90. MacKinnon, *Feminism Unmodified, supra* note 4, ch. 13.
91. *See* "Brief for the National Coalition Against Domestic Violence as Amicus Curiae Supporting Appellees," Webster v. Reproductive Health Services, 109 S.Ct. 3040 (1989); Robert Goldstein, *Mother Love and Abortion* (1988); MacKinnon, *Feminism Unmodified, supra* note 4, ch. 8; Tribe, *American Constitutional Law, supra* note 4, at 1353–56; Tribe, *Constitutional Choices, supra* note 4, at 243–45; Ginsburg, "Some Thoughts on Autonomy and Equality in Relation to Roe v. Wade," 63 *N.C. L. Rev.* 375 (1985); Kenneth Karst, "The Supreme Court, 1976 Term—Foreword: Equal Citizenship under the Fourteenth Amendment," 91 *Harv. L. Rev.* 1, 53–59 (1977); Sylvia Law, "Rethinking Sex and the Constitution," 132 *U. Pa. L. Rev.* 955 (1984).
92. See Chapter 2, and "Note, To Have and to Hold: The Marital Rape Exemption and the Fourteenth Amendment," 99 *Harv. L. Rev.* 1255 (1986).
93. Sylvia Law, "Homosexuality and the Social Meaning of Gender," 1988 *Wis. L. Rev.* 187; Cass R. Sunstein, "Sexual Orientation and the Constitution: A Note on the Relationship between Due Process and Equal Protection," 55 *U. Chi. L. Rev.* 1161 (1988).
94. Michelman, "Welfare Rights," *supra* note 4.
95. MacKinnon, *Feminism Unmodified, supra* note 4, at 40.
96. 347 U.S. 483 (1954).
97. Strauss, "The Myth of Colorblindness," *supra* note 4, at 100.
98. Unger, *supra* note 4.
99. *Id.* at 612–13.
100. Patricia J. Williams, "Spirit-Murdering the Messenger: The Discourse of Finger-Pointing as the Law's Response to Racism," 42 *Miami L. Rev.* 127 (1987).
101. *See, e.g.,* Michelman, "Welfare Rights," *supra* note 4.
102. *Id.* at 677 (citations omitted).
103. See *supra* note 106 and accompanying text.
104. Frank I. Michelman, "The Supreme Court, 1968 Term—Foreword: On Protecting the Poor through the Fourteenth Amendment," 83 *Harv. L. Rev.* 7, 9 (1969) (citations omitted).
105. Sherry, *supra* note 12, at 1597 (citation omitted).
106 262 U.S. 390 (1923).
107. *Id.,* at 399.
108. 367 U.S. 497, 522–55 (1961) (Harlan J., dissenting).
109. 381 U.S. 479, 499–502 (1965) (Harlan, J., concurring).
110. *Poe,* 367 U.S. at 542–48 (Harlan, J., dissenting); *see also Griswold,* 381 U.S. at 499–502 (Harlan, J., concurring).
111. *Id.* at 153.

112. MacKinnon, *Feminism Unmodified, supra* note 4, at 98.
113. *See, e.g.,* Olsen, *supra* note 12; *see also supra* note 102.
114. Webster v. Reproductive Health Services, 492 U.S. 490, 537 (1989) (Blackmun, J., dissenting).
115. *Id.* at 557 (Blackmun, J., dissenting) (citation omitted).
116. Law, *supra* note 104, at 222–28.
117. *See* "Brief for Respondent," Bowers v. Hardwick, 478 U.S. 186 (1986); Henderson, *supra* note 83, at 1638–49; Law, *supra* note 104, at 224, 234–35; Law, *supra* note 102, at 955.
118. *See* Sunstein, *supra* note 104, at 1163–64, 1170–78; Henderson, *supra* note 83, at 1645–49; *see also Bowers,* 478 U.S. at 216, 218–20 (Stevens, J., dissenting).
119. Tribe, *American Constitutional Law, supra* note 4, at vii–viii.
120. *See* Strauss, "The Taming of Brown," *supra* note 4; *see also* Harris v. McRae, 448 U.S. 297 (1980); Beal v. Doe, 432 U.S. 438 (1977); Poelker v. Doe, 432 U.S. 519 (1977); Maher v. Roe, 432 U.S. 464 (1977).
121. For a full discussion of this point, see Cass R. Sunstein, 33 *The Partial Constitution* 319–347 (Harv., 1993).
122. *See* Fiss, *supra* note 21, at 753; *cf.* Robin L. West, "Adjudication Is Not Interpretation: Some Reservations about the Law-as-Literature Movement," 54 *Tenn. L. Rev.* 203, 210–19 (1987).
123. The notable exception, of course, is *Brown v. Board of Education,* 347 U.S. 483 (1954).
124. Perhaps the clearest example of this attempt to square a circle, and to accommodate antimajoritarian judicial review with participatory theories of republicanism and democracy, is Michelman, "Traces of Self-Government," *supra* note 4. For a full discussion of this point, see Paul Brest, "Constitutional Citizenship," 34 *Clev. St. L. Rev.* 175 (1986).
125. Lochner v. New York, 198 U.S. 45 (1905).
126. Epstein, *supra* note 2.
127. Fiss, *supra* note 21, at 754.

10. The Aspirational Constitution

1. James B. Thayer, "The Origin and Scope of the American Doctrine of Constitutional Law," 7 *Harv. L. Rev.* 129 (1893).
2. *Id.* at 151, 155.
3. *Id.* at 156.
4. *Id.* at 155–56.
5. *Id.*
6. *Id.*
7. *See* Paul Brest, "Constitutional Citizenship," 34 *Clev. St. L. Rev.* 175 (1986); Dorothy E. Roberts, "Punishing Drug Addicts Who Have Babies: Women of Color, Equality, and the Right of Privacy," 104 *Harv. L. Rev.* 1419 (1991); Cass R. Sunstein, "Beyond the Republican Revival," 97 *Yale L. J.* 1539 (1988), in addition to Chapter 9, this volume.
8. *See* Mary E. Becker, "Judicial Review and Women's Rights" (unpublished manuscript,

on file with author); Louis M. Seidman, "*Brown* and *Miranda*," 80 *Cal. L. Rev.* 673, 680 (1992) (arguing that two seemingly aggressive decisions were actually "tactical retreats").

9. I discuss this ambivalence in some detail in Chapter 7.

10. On the property-protecting intent of the drafters, see Richard A. Epstein, *Takings* (1985); Jennifer Nedelsky, *Private Property and the Limits of American Constitutionalism* (1990); Bernard H. Siegan, *Economic Liberties and the Constitution* 30–31 (1980). On the Constitution's complicity in preserving racial hierarchy, see Derrick Bell, *And We Are Not Saved: The Elusive Quest for Racial Justice* (1987). On its role in preserving sexual hierarchy, see Catharine A. MacKinnon, "Reflections on Sex Equality under Law," 100 *Yale L. J.* 1281 (1991). And for a striking example of the use of the Constitution to preserve cultural and linguistic hierarchies, see Justice Harlan's dissent in Plessy v. Ferguson, 163 U.S. 537, 552–64 (1896) (Harlan, J., dissenting).

11. Lochner v. New York, 198 U.S. 45 (1905). *See generally* Adkins v. Children's Hospital, 261 U.S. 525 (1923) (invalidating law establishing minimum wage for women); Adair v. United States, 208 U.S. 161 (1908) (invalidating federal and state legislation forbidding employers to require that employees agree not to join a union); Chicago, M. & St. P. Ry. v. Minnesota, 134 U.S. 418 (1890) (invalidating state statute authorizing a commission to set final and unreviewable rates); *see also* Allgeyer v. Louisiana, 165 U.S. 578 (1897) (articulating the concept of liberty of contract).

12. *See* City of Richmond v. J. A. Croson Co., 488 U.S. 469 (1989) (invalidating city's affirmative action plan under the Equal Protection Clause). *But see* Metro Broadcasting, Inc. v. FCC, 497 U.S. 547 (1990) (upholding federal broadcasting policies that favored minority-owned enterprises).

13. *See* R.A.V. v. City of St. Paul, 112 S. Ct. 2538 (1992) (invalidating hate speech statute on First Amendment grounds).

14. *See* Seidman, *supra* note 8; Becker, *supra* note 8.

15. Thayer, *supra* note 1, at 149.

16. *Id.*

17. *See* Mary E. Becker, "The Politics of Women's Wrongs and the Bill of 'Rights': A Bicentennial Perspective," 59 *U. Chi. L. Rev.* 453 (1992); Sunstein, *supra* note 7.

18. Becker, *supra* note 8.

19. Bruce A. Ackerman, "Beyond Carolene Products," 98 *Harv. L. Rev.* 713 (1985); Derrick A. Bell & Preeta Bansal, "The Republican Revival and Racial Politics," 97 *Yale L. J.* 1609 (1988) (expressing skepticism that blacks would even be included in Sunstein's new vision of republicanism).

20. I am indebted to Mary Becker for helping me see that this really is a separate argument. Becker, *supra* note 8.

21. *See, e.g.,* Cass R. Sunstein, *The Partial Constitution* 9–10 (1993); Paul Brest, "Constitutional Citizenship," 34 *Clev. St. L. Rev.* 175 (1986); Lawrence G. Sager, "Fair Measure: The Legal Status of Underenforced Constitutional Norms," 91 *Harv. L. Rev.* 1212 (1978); Robin L. West, "Progressive and Conservative Constitutionalism, Chapter 9, this volume.

22. See authorities cited *supra* note 25.

23. I argue this in more detail in Chapter 1.

24. H.R. 1133, 103d Cong., 1st Sess. (1993); S. 11, 103d Cong., 1st Sess. (1993).

25. H.R. 423, 103d Cong., 1st Sess. (1993); H.R. 431, 103d Cong., 1st Sess. (1993).

26. *See* Akhil R. Amar, "Forty Acres and a Mule: A Republican Theory of Minimal Entitlements," 13 *Harv. J. L. & Pub. Pol'y* 37 (1990).

27. I argue this in Chapter 4.

28. H.R. 1133, 103d Cong., 1st Sess. (1993); S. 11, 103d Cong., 1st Sess. (1993).

29. H.R. 25, 103d Cong., 1st Sess. (1993); S. 25, 103d Cong., 1st Sess. (1993).

30. 42 U.S.C. SS 12101–12213 (1990).

31. George P. Fletcher, "Law as Discourse," 13 *Cardozo L. Rev.* 1631 (1992).

32. Thayer, *supra* note 1, at 144.

33. Stanley Fish, *Doing What Comes Naturally* (1989); Stanley Fish, "Fish v. Fiss," 36 *Stan. L. Rev.* 1325 (1984).

34. Owen M. Fiss, "Objectivity and Interpretation," 34 *Stan. L. Rev.* 739 (1982).

35. Fish uses the Christie example in his response to Dworkin in Stanley Fish, "Working on the Chain Gang: Interpretation in Law and Literature," 60 *Tex. L. Rev.* 551 (1982).

36. For an argument to the effect that this is the underlying justification for the rule of precedent, see Anthony T. Kronman, "Precedent and Tradition," 99 *Yale L. J.* 1029 (1990).

37. *See* Bruce Ackerman, *We the People* (1991).

38. Robin L. West, "The Meaning of Equality and the Interpretive Turn," Chapter 3, this volume.

39. *See* City of Richmond v. J. A. Croson Co., 488 U.S. 469 (1989); Regents of the University of California v. Bakke, 438 U.S. 265, 289–90 (1978) (Powell, J.); Antonin Scalia, "The Rule of Law as a Law of Rules," 56 *U. Chi. L. Rev.* 1175 (1989). *See generally* Richard Posner, "The *DeFunis* Case and the Constitutionality of Preferential Treatment of Racial Minorities," 1974 *Sup. Ct. Rev.* 1; William Van Alstyne, "Rites of Passage: Race, The Supreme Court and the Constitution," 46 *U. Chi. L. Rev.* 775 (1979). *But see* John Hart Ely, "The Constitutionality of Reverse Discrimination," 41 *U. Chi. L. Rev.* 723 (1974); Gary Peller, "Race Consciousness," 1990 *Duke L. J.* 759.

Index

Robin West is Professor of Law at Georgetown University
Law Center, where she teaches and writes in the fields of
Constitutional Law, Feminist Legal Theory, and Law and
Literature. She is the author of *Narrative, Authority,
and Law.*

Library of Congress Cataloging-in-Publication Data
West, Robin,
Progressive constitutionalism: reconstructing the
Fourteenth Amendment / Robin West.
p.   cm. — (Constitutional conflicts)
Includes index.
ISBN 0-8223-1525-4 (cl)
1. Equality before the law—United States.   2. United
States—Constitution—Amendments—14th.   I. Title.
II. Series.
KF4764.W47   1994
342.73'085—dc20
[347.30285]   94-17146 CIP